QUEST

A SEARCH FOR SELF

Sarah Cirese

College of Marin

QUEST
A SEARCH FOR SELF

Holt, Rinehart and Winston   New York Chicago San Francisco Atlanta
Dallas Montreal Toronto London Sydney

Library of Congress Cataloging in Publication Data

Cirese, Sarah.
    Quest: a search for self.

    Bibliography: p. 409
    Includes index.
    1. Self-actualization (Psychology) 2. Self-
perception. I. Title.
BF637.S4C57   158′.1   76-46346

ISBN 0-03-012996-6

Associate Publisher	Deborah Doty
Managing Editor	Jeanette Ninas Johnson
Project Editor and Photo Research	Peggy Middendorf
Production Manager	Annette Wentz
Art and Design	Robert Kopelman

Acknowledgements   cover photo courtesy of N. W. Ayer ABH International.
p. 5   Poem from "Little Gidding" in *Four Quartets* by T. S. Elliot, copyright 1943, by T. S. Elliot; copyright 1971, by Esme Valerie Eliot. Reprinted by permission of Harcourt Brace Jovanovich, Inc. and Faber and Faber Ltd.
pp. 6–7   Relaxation exercise adapted from Samuels and Bennet, *The Well Body Book* (1973), pp. 8–9, with the permission of Random House, Inc.
p. 12   Poem from *Experiences In Being,* by B. Marshall. Copyright © 1971 by Wadsworth Publishing Company, Inc. Reprinted by permission of the publisher, Brooks/Cole Publishing Company, Monterey, California.
pp. 17, 314   Excerpts from *Philosophy: An Introduction to the Art of Wondering* by James L. Christian. Copyright © 1973 by Rinehart Press, A Division of Holt, Rinehart and Winston. Reprinted by permission of Holt, Rinehart and Winston.
pp. 41, 327   Figures of human brain from *Understanding Human Behavior* by James V. McConnell. Copyright © 1974 by Holt, Rinehart and Winston. Reprinted by permission of Holt, Rinehart and Winston.
p. 48   Box 3.1 reprinted with permission of Macmillan Publishing Co., Inc. from *Three Roads to Awareness* by Don Fabun. Copyright © 1970 by Kaiser Aluminum & Chemical Corporation.
p. 60   Poem from *The Poetry of Robert Frost* edited by Edward Connery Lathem. Copyright 1916, © 1969 by Holt, Rinehart and Winston. Copyright 1944 by Robert Frost. Reprinted by permission of Holt, Rinehart and Winston, Publishers.
pp. 81–2, 83, 88   Excerpts from *The Magic Years* by Selma Fraiberg (1959), pp. 121, 124, 135. Reprinted by permission of Charles Scribner's Sons.
p. 95   Poem from *Yevtushenko: Selected Poems,* translated by Robin Milner-Gulland and

Dedicated to the memory of my father,
      to my mother
      and my children
      and to Asharla, the goddess of work and love.

PREFACE

For the past two years my life and energy have been divided among three jobs — being a mother, teaching college courses in psychology and behavioral science, and becoming an author. I had been doing the first two for some time, but writing was new to me. I found it difficult, exciting, frustrating, and deeply rewarding. Through my work on *Quest* I have discovered much about myself and have unexpectedly enriched my knowledge of, and respect for, the field of psychology. It is my hope that this book will benefit readers as it has me.

Although several ideas, dozens of pages, and thousands of words did not survive the many rewritings of the text, my original goal, purposes, and general organization have remained essentially unchanged. The goal of *Quest* is an increased understanding of the human adventure — the searching and growing we experience as we journey between birth and death. By intent, this theme ignores distinctions between healthy and sick psychological processes and the concept of psychological adjustment to "normal" patterns of behavior.

One purpose is that common to all psychology textbooks: the presentation of contemporary thinking, research, and findings from psychology and the behavioral sciences. A second purpose is that of encouraging readers to become actively involved in their own self-discovery and self-realization. To this end, *Quest* contains many explorations and suggestions for both individual and classroom exercises. I have also included information on widely used techniques of maximizing growth.

Quest is divided into four sections. In the first I introduce the process of self-discovery, major viewpoints on the nature of human growth and personality, and concepts of human potential and its actualization. Chapter 1 considers psychological growth as the process of exploration. Chapter 2 is a discussion of the ways our understanding is influenced by psychological theory and our attitudes toward self and others. Chapter 3 describes human possibility, interaction with our physical and social environments, and development through a lifetime.

In the remaining sections I develop the theme that questing is a lifelong process. THEN . . . , NOW . . . , and BEYOND . . . consider growth and self-discovery in the past, present, and future, respectively. THEN . . . consists of Chapters 4 and 5, the quests of early childhood and those of later childhood and adolescence. NOW . . . contains seven chapters. Chapter 6 presents the quest for identity and self-actualization as processes of self-awareness and self-knowledge. Chapter 7 considers the quest for intimate relationships through the development of honesty and trust. Chapter 8 deals with the quest for sexual fulfillment through acceptance and understanding of human sexual potentials. Chapters 9 and 10 present the quest for personhood undiminished by sex-role stereotypes. Chapter 11 discusses the quest for competence based on feelings of self-worth and a belief in the worth of life. Chapter 12 traces the quest for unboundedness through expanded conscious. BEYOND . . . consists of Chapter 13, the quests in the later years of life, and Chapter 14, a consideration of death and dying as the final stages of human growth. Chapter 15 is a brief retrospect.

I am mindful, as I finish the book, of the major role so many have had in making it possible. With help I have survived the very heavy work load and have been able to find personal growth and achievement in the process. It is impossible to individually acknowledge many of those who contributed. I am deeply indebted to three groups of people: other authors, my own instructors over the years, and my students. Thank you all for providing many questions, intellectual stimulation, and some answers—the stuff of which books are made.

My gratitude to those who have helped in improving, criticizing, and sharing in the work is boundless. One person, Albert Brewster, has earned more thanks than I can express in a brief acknowledgement. Part of Al's work was writing, rewriting, editing, questioning, challenging, proofreading, and preparing the glossary. Every paragraph in *Quest* bears the mark of his skill with words, his talent for turning awkward sentences into smooth prose, and reflects his fine ability to recognize sloppy thinking behind unclear passages. My gratitude to Al extends beyond appreciation and admiration of his work. Through weeks and months of struggle, working and reworking, frustration and accomplishment, he was there. He was there when I needed to talk, to laugh, to relax, even when I needed to be alone. There were times when no one could live with me, but he did. There were times when it seemed even our relationship would not survive the strains imposed by deadlines, lack of sleep, and the daily grind. Without his faith, support, good humor, and love I could not have done it.

Many colleagues and friends have also supported and helped me. My special thanks go to Diane Wickstrom of the Behavioral Sciences Department at the College of Marin. Her assistance included providing me with a table to work on, access to her large library, tasty meals, last-minute typing, and encouragement. Another College of Marin colleague, Don Homlund, was not only instrumental in getting the book off to a good start; he cheered me on thereafter. Diane and Don both read much of the manuscript and offered many helpful suggestions for improving it. Among the others who deserve special recognition for assorted last-minute services are Susan Harrow, Gertrude Brewster, Thea Jobse, and Don Palmer.

I received invaluable help from several people who, though I have never met them, consented to read, review, and comment on the early drafts of the manuscript. I was fortunate indeed to receive support and criticism from Dr. Frank McMahon of Southern Illinois University, Dr. Valda Robinson of Hillsborough Community College in Tampa, Florida, Dr. Wayne Hren of Los Angeles Pierce College, Dr. Thomas K. Saville of Metropolitan State College in Denver, Colorado, and Dr. E. R. Hertweck of Mira Costa College in Oceanside, California. My deepest thanks to each of you, especially Drs. Robinson and McMahon, who were keenly sensitive to my efforts and who offered so many excellent suggestions.

I received much assistance from those associated with Holt, Rinehart and Winston, in particular Emmett Dingley, Deborah Doty, and Peggy Middendorf, all of whom had faith in and lent direction and much-needed patience to an unpublished writer. And to Jean Howard and Dianne McMaine, who typed and retyped the several drafts, my appreciation not only for a job well done, but also for the encouraging comments along the way.

My final and warmest gratitude goes to my children, who so easily came to accept a mother who typed from dawn to late evening, who gave up so many week-end outings because of "the book," and who organized the bibliography. Both of you, Lesley and Jeffrey, are sources of inspiration, joy, and daily delight. My thanks and love for being and growing with me all the while.

Larkspur, California   S. C.
November 1976

CONTENTS

The longest journey
is the journey inwards
Of him who has chosen his destiny,
who has started upon his quest
for the source of his being.

Dag Hammarskjöld
(Markings)

QUEST
A SEARCH FOR SELF

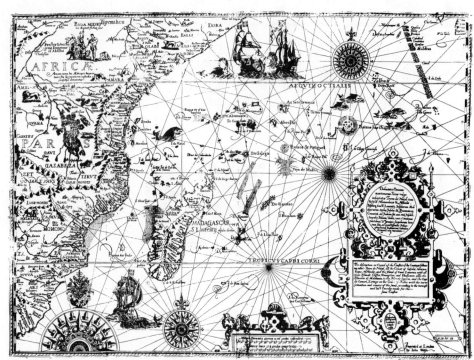

1

THERE
IS
NO MAP

Planned Parenthood — World Population.

The day I saw my first rainbow, arching through the afternoon sky after a thundershower, I was with my next door neighbor. He was a fine old man I always called Grandpa Strange. Grandpa told me that there was a pot of gold at the end of that rainbow. Surely, I thought, the most wonderful thing would be to find that big pot of riches. "How can I get to it? Show me where it is, please, Grandpa Strange," I begged.

"No," the old man said softly. "Be happy with the rainbow. I used to spend my time looking for that gold, but I never found it. Can't rightly say where it is. Guess I never had the right map." He was silent for a long time, then smiled down at me, his eyes twinkling. "Let's just look for a while from here. Anyway, I've heard tell the rainbow disappears when you get close."

I no longer dream of finding a pot of gold. I have seen many rainbows over the years, and know that they all disappear in time. But I've often wished I had a map, directions that I could rely on. A map for living would alert me to dead-end paths, and keep me from making mistakes. It would show me the way to happiness and let me skirt the deserts of loneliness and the jungles of self-doubt. I don't have a map. The best I can do is guide myself by remembering the turns I have taken before and where they have led. The best I can do is learn what I can from others who have journeyed before and who are journeying beside me. The best I can do is try to recognize the guideposts and milestones left by artists, writers, psychologists, and other students of human behavior. The best I can do is be aware of where I am now and what I am discovering along the way. There is no map for self-discovery.

If not maps, what can you expect from this book? It may serve as a searchlight, showing some of the many paths which can be taken. It may give you guideposts, clues about which paths are likely to lead to wastelands and which will lead to further paths. It may show you milestones, signs of progress on the journey. But you will not find yourself in any one paragraph or page between these covers. You will find yourself only in your responses to the contents, and in the living out of your life.

We each make our own quests. We each live our own lives, and the living takes a lifetime. Life is not so much given as it is made. It is a string of todays, this one and the next and the next. Each today leads to a new today, but each day is for its own living. Life is being and becoming. When it is all over, we aren't anywhere or anything we haven't been or done along the way to the end.

For this is the journey that men make: to find themselves. If they fail in this, it doesn't matter much else what they find (Michener, 1949, p. 488).

EXPLORATIONS

We shall not cease from exploration
And the end of all our exploring
Will be to arrive where we started
And know the place for the first time.

T. S. Eliot
("Little Gidding")

The explorations in this book are offered as aids to discovering your self. Some may take you to unexplored frontiers of self-knowledge, others to territory you only rarely visit; still others will take you into familiar neighborhoods. All of the explorations can help in changing the

Michael Weisbrot

abstractions and generalizations of the text into personal experience. Much of the education you have had in the past consisted of sponging up and retaining the knowledge presented to you until you had to squeeze it out at examination time. That approach will not be appropriate to this book. A quest is self-initiated and self-perpetuated. It does not come from a book; it begins and progresses with activity—your activity. If you try to have a passive relationship with this book you may find it confusing, difficult, and frustrating. I caution you not to look for answers here, but for questions. I encourage you to build a personal relationship with the discoveries you make in doing the explorations.

If you are attentive to yourself as you do the explorations, they will yield their greatest value. Approach them in a spirit of adventure and openness, as though you were a child discovering the world. Imagine that you have lost your wallet and are making a frantic search for it, retracing the steps you took earlier today. Your attention is focused on a single objective: finding that wallet; everything else is pushed out of mind. You may or may not find the wallet, but you certainly are missing many potential experiences while looking. Instead of looking for something in particular, be open to as much experience as you can with the explorations.

A final point: these particular explorations are only suggestions. Your instructor and the members of your class should modify them to suit your needs. If you want others there are excellent explorations for individuals and groups in the books listed at the end of this chapter.

Starting

Anyone who has ever written a book hopes that readers will give it full attention. I have this hope, and I have another as well. I hope that the quest you are on is important enough to you that you will make for yourself quiet, nondistracting conditions in which to work on the explorations. This may mean telling those people who make demands on your energy that you are going to be busy for a while and cannot be interrupted. It may mean setting aside that time of the day when you know you are most alert and ready to work. It will often mean letting go of routine preoccupations, such as worrying about what happened earlier in the day or what might happen later. For those of you who spend most of your time doing for or with others, or who are used to attending to outer rather than inner experiences, pursuing these explorations may feel selfish and unproductive at first. I can only hope that you are important enough to yourself to make the effort.

I suggest that you use a short relaxation exercise before each exploration. This following one can free a great deal of your psychological and physical energy, making it available for discoveries.

Sit in a comfortable chair, both feet on the floor, your hands relaxed in your lap (see drawing). Close your eyes. Take a deep breath, hold it briefly, then exhale slowly. Do this three times, allowing your body to become relaxed. Now inhale

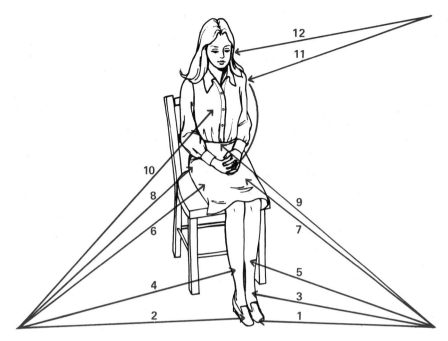

again, and as you exhale this time imagine you are sending your breath down to your toes to relax them (1). With the next breath, relax the soles of your feet (2). Then relax your ankles in the same way (3). Continue, with each breath, to relax: the muscles of your lower legs, first the right (4), then

the left (5).

thighs, right (6) and left (7).

buttocks (8); the muscles in and around your genitals.

stomach (9); lower back.

chest (10); upper back.

down through your shoulders to the tips of your fingers (11).

Now your head (12); first your forehead, then

cheeks,

eyelids,

and jaw muscles.

Let your jaw drop. Let go with all the muscles in your face, jaw, neck, throat,

and tongue.

You are now relaxed and have freed yourself from the world of telephones, assignments, and deadlines. Count to three before you open your eyes. (Adapted from Samuels and Bennett, 1973, pp. 8–9.)

KEEPING A JOURNAL

One of the best techniques I know for self-discovery is keeping a journal. Writing lets you catch and hold elusive thoughts, images, and concerns. From the many approaches to journal keeping, here are the suggestions I give to my classes.

Your Things: Get a notebook. Get a pen.

The kind of book you use often affects the way you use it. You can carry a small book with you wherever you go, to catch stray thoughts on the wing, in the field, before the bus, after class. A large book gives you room to wander as you write, to pick out the meaning of your day's activities, and provides a stage for those experiences dancing on the edge of forgetfulness. Lined paper keeps you straight and tidy, giving form to experiences that otherwise might seem formless. Unlined paper turns you free, breaks down the confines of parallel lines, lets you write large. Consider dividing the book into sections: school, friends, dreams, for example. In any event, use it to collect your scattered notes and your scattered thoughts in one place. Choose a durable, relatively permanent book; it will become a part of you. Use pen. Pencil fades, is hard to read, smudges, and will tempt you to erase. You want to discover yourself here, not to correct yourself.

Your Time: Find a good time for writing. Write regularly.

You can make entries any time you are free to dip down into your busy buzzing stream of consciousness. You might want to set aside a specific time of day for writing (early morning, late at night). Or you may feel that you can get in the best mood between other activities, using these still moments of solitude as a respite before stepping out into the world again.

    If you write something every day, you will be weaving many seemingly unimportant, easily forgotten threads of experience into a pattern that will give richness to the fabric of your life. Letting your book gather dust for a week may leave you with too much detail to enter comfortably, or without anything to write at all. A short reach of time between you and an experience can sometimes help you grasp its meaning in what has

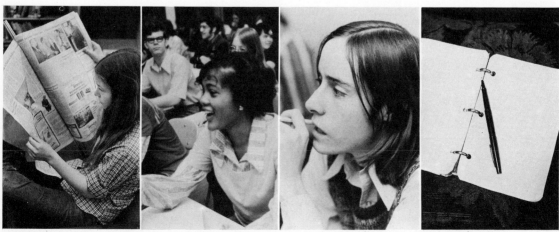

National Education Association Publishing, Joe Di Dio.   Michael Weisbrot

followed. But if you let weeks go by without writing, you will find yourself writing stories, inventing experiences, and losing the value of the journal as a record of day-to-day life.

Your Purpose: See what you can do.

There are many possibilities in keeping a journal. You can explore yourself in various moods, while doing various things. You can examine those parts of you that writing will bring to the surface of your awareness. You can visit areas of yourself that are not open to others, areas even you don't know all that well, having missed them in the rush of living. A journal can be your mirror, reflecting against one another your inner and outer worlds, stopping in time those timeless qualities that make up your sense of self. A journal is someone to talk to—or something: an experience, feeling, situation. A journal gives you an instant, slow-motion replay of things as they were, or it can give you a speculative view of how they might have been. Your notes are a laboratory of the self in which to experiment, a toy with which to play, a studio in which to create. Here you can put to use all the techniques you used as a child in learning about your world—examining, pushing, pulling, expanding, opening, closing, tasting, smelling. You can use these if you break the habits of judging, blocking, censoring, and trying to be practical. Your book can be a collection of those varicolored bits and pieces that make your individual mosaic, or it can be a tunnel into your previously unexplored depths.

Your Style: Use whatever works for you.

Below are some journal themes that have worked for others. Among them you may find roadsigns that will speed you in your search for a direction. Whether you begin with these or not, your personal style and content will quickly impress itself on your journal.

> Above all, keep in mind that you are writing for yourself,
> and for yourself alone.
> Don't try to write for anyone else.
> *Anyone.*

Dreams   Best collected right after waking, before you get up or talk with anyone. The smallest detail can be revealing.

Fantasies   Daydreams, recurring or startling thoughts, scenes of the future and the past, the absurd and the ultimate. What triggered your flight? Why did you go where you went?

Time and energy   In the course of a day, where does it all go? Are your resources going into things which are important to you? In the right proportions? What are your priorities? Keep track for a while.

Feelings   The subjective: emotions, anxieties, delights, fears, highs. When? Where? How? With whom?

Relationships   Dialoguing with others. Redoing conversations. Look for distortions. What do you blame on others? What do they blame on you? How many "if onlys" do you have? "Yes, buts"?

Classes/work   What are you learning? How? What do you know now that you
    didn't earlier? Are you procrastinating? Turned on? Are you doing as well as
    you know you can? Any gripes? What is missing?

Decisions   List the pros and cons. What are all the alternatives? Follow up the
    choices you didn't make. What would have happened if? What might happen
    if?

Nonsense   Start with something weird, garbled. Follow it around. Where does it
    take you? What are you feeling?

Ideas/thoughts   Put a bunch together, mix them up and find some new ones.
    Take one and make it a dozen. Use your own, or one from your reading. Paste
    in a newspaper clipping and react to it.

Drawing/poetry   Use any form that allows you to feel you are expressing your-
    self.

Explorations   Keep an account of the *Quest* explorations in your journal.

Your Picture: Write a summary of your journal.

Give yourself an objective review. What have you done? What haven't
you done? What does your journal say to you *about* you? What are your
themes? Your patterns? You will be able to answer these and other questions after a few months.

Pay close attention to what you have not included; are your friends,
family, children, classes in there? Have you kept a record of your outer
experiences only? Well, what were you thinking or feeling all that time?
Were there reasons why you didn't include some things? Does the answer say something about who and what you value in your life? Has anything changed since you began writing: your view of your life, of others?
Have you resolved anything? What are you still working on?

After you have reflected on what you have written over several
months, write a summary. Write it as an objective description of a unique
person.

EXPLORING ON YOUR OWN

Each life contains a wealth of material to be discovered by self-exploration. But many of us pass up opportunities for discovery because we
"don't have the time," or because we suspect we won't like what we
find.

A common clue that something is available for discovery is a feeling
that is not quite right for the situation you are in. The feeling may persist
for some time, as do depression and anxiety. Or it can be a momentary
outburst of emotion, such as a tearful rage over a slight incident. A clue
can also be a physical symptom: a tension headache, a fluttery stomach,
or great fatigue after a full night's sleep. If you want to take one of these
clues and use it for self-exploration, I suggest the following steps developed by Muriel Schiffman (*Self Therapy: Techniques for Personal
Growth*, 1967, and *Gestalt Self Therapy*, 1971, both by Self Therapy
Press). Do not think of this as a therapeutic tool (for curing an illness) but

Michael Weisbrot

as a way to discover a bit more about why you do the things you do and who you are.

Step 1.   *Recognize an inappropriate reaction.* Ask yourself: "Is my feeling the right feeling for this situation?"

Step 2.   *Feel the apparent emotion.* Don't dismiss your feeling because it seems inappropriate, childish, or irrational. It will probably disappear sooner or later if you avoid it, but then you will have lost the opportunity to use it for self-exploration. So, *feel* the feeling. You don't have to *do* anything, just be aware of your sensations and the phrases that cross your mind ("I would like to kill him!"). It is sometimes helpful to talk to someone about your feelings. Pick a friend you trust, one who is a good listener, not someone who will use you as a mirror for his or her problems or who will try analyzing you. You simply need to express yourself.

Step 3.   *What else did I feel?* Inappropriate feelings are cover-ups for other, hidden emotions. They shield us from pain or diffuse underlying emotions stronger than those we are aware of. It may take some courage and detective work to find the deeper emotion. Look back at the situation. Was there, for the briefest moment before the apparent emotion, another feeling? Was another feeling drowned out, unattended?

A hidden emotion must also be felt as part of discovery. Be aware of what is happening in your body: heart beat, stomach, the palms of your hands, breathing, perspiration, and so on. These are some of the reactions which accompany an emotion. When the hidden emotion is discovered, the apparent feeling will disappear. It will be unimportant.

For me, anger is sometimes an apparent emotion that hides some deeper feeling such as fear. For instance, my daughter comes home an hour later than I expected her. I immediately begin scolding her angrily. Later I find that anger was a mask for the unbearable fear that she wasn't going to come home at all.

Once you have felt the hidden emotion, continue exploring.

Step 4. *What does this remind me of?* What does this situation make you think of? When have you reacted this way before? Have you ever shown peculiar attitudes toward this kind of problem before? Step back and take an objective view, as though you were an outsider observing your behavior. What does it look like you are doing? Keep asking until you find a strong feeling.

Step 5. *Look for the pattern.* Have I ever covered up this emotion before? When? In what circumstances am I apt to use this apparent emotion to cover up what I am really feeling? This is not an attempt to come up with intellectual insights into your personality. Rather it is a technique for recognizing patterns of self-deception which may be keeping you from self-knowledge. If you look diligently enough you may find patterns which go back to your childhood. Many of us are still living out situations which took place ten or fifteen years ago.

Much of the confusion we have in our relationships with others is due to our expressing apparent but not real emotions. You may have seen this in your friends ("Why is she so upset? I didn't say anything."), but it will be harder to see in yourself until you set about exploring. Keep feeling and keep asking: "What else?"

EXPLORING IN GROUPS

> I say words
> You say words
> And I walk alone.
>
> You say words
> I say words
> Words words words
> And I walk alone.
>
> There's a place where I go
> It's a place no one knows
> That's the place where I found
> The me that is I
> Not the me that you know.
>
>   . . .
>
> In this place where I go
> In this place no one knows
> I look at you, you look at me
> I hear you, you hear me
> I touch you, you touch me

And I know the me that is I
Not the me that you know.

. . .

B. Marshall
("Beginning")

Many of the explorations in this book include a suggestion that you share your discoveries or experiences with your class. Other explorations are designed to be done only with a group or partner; you cannot do them alone.

There are benefits in sharing self-discovery with others. One is that we learn how we are similar to others and how we differ from them. Knowing who we are relative to others is knowing something about ourselves. When we work with others we find that the snags we hit are often the same snags they hit. Another benefit is that in communicating with others we are also communicating with ourselves. We know better what we mean when we can say it to someone. I have often found that my thoughts about myself are clarified when I think out loud.

Being in a group does not guarantee self-discovery. We can be with others for years and still never learn anything of them or of ourselves. To make group explorations successful, it is vital that each member believe the others are people of goodwill. Trust, honesty, respect for oneself and for others create a climate of goodwill. When I disclose something about myself to others and they accept what I have given without rejecting, ridiculing, or pushing me to go further, we have all added to a feeling of trust. As trust and goodwill build in a group, fear and apprehension decrease. There is less and less fear that others in the group will disregard, disapprove of, or broadcast what a member says.

Self-knowledge *is* increased through communication. But it is the individual who must decide for himself or herself how to participate in group explorations. Each person should have the option of not participating at any time, without making excuses or giving reasons. One psychologist, Joseph Luft, has aptly used the expression "psychological rape" in referring to the cruel and potentially dangerous pressuring of someone into unwilling self-disclosure. It is necessary to know that others will not attempt psychological rape and that participants in a group will not allow themselves to be victims.

Your class might well discuss your feelings about self-disclosure at the beginning of the term and occasionally thereafter. Perhaps you can each accept that:

I am in charge of myself.
I choose when and how to participate.
I respect others' decisions to participate or not.
I will not interfere in that decision.

Awareness is most likely to be enhanced in a group that encourages clear communication. Communication is the sending and receiving of messages. In sending messages, try to be as genuine, to the point, and open as you can be. Get into the habit of making your statements about yourself in the first person: "I." When you don't use "I" to introduce personal feelings and thoughts you are not clearly telling others how you feel. You are losing an opportunity for learning and others can only *assume* you are talking about yourself and not someone else. It is almost second nature to make "You" instead of "I" statements, and so it may take conscious, deliberate work to develop the habit of staying with "I."

Using "I" statements will help to keep you focused on present feelings and thoughts. Undue attention to events remote in time and place can lead us far off the track. The explorations in Chapters 4 and 5 ask you to reflect on your past. The past as you see it now is well worth exploring, but it is not helpful to allow the past to eclipse the present. Ask, before you launch into a conversational history of your life:

What does this have to do with who I am now?
Am I trying to create an image?
Am I showing off?
Am I looking for sympathy, praise, or some other desired response?
Am I exploring myself?

These are also good questions to ask when you find yourself, at the end of a statement, far from where you began. If you habitually get off the point, it may be helpful to imagine you are sending a telegram: make every word count.

Receiving messages from others means listening to them. It is *hearing* what others are saying. Effective listening requires that we give our undivided attention to the person talking. This, as we all know, is not always easy, but it can be done if we make an effort to avoid daydreaming and distractions.

Active Listening

active listening

The technique called active listening is the best way to promote self-awareness in others (Adler and Towne, 1975). Active listening includes two parts: the first is paying attention; the second is letting speakers know that you have heard what they say. This sounds simple enough, but it differs widely from the usual manner of making conversation. In an everyday conversation, one person, A, says something. Another person, B, responds. Then A says something else, and B takes his turn, and so on. Conversations can, and usually do, get far away from what A originally said. Active listening, however, permits A to stay with her original message until she has made of it all that she can. This is not suitable for all communication, but it is very appropriate for increasing A's self-awareness.

Several types of responses are incompatible with active listening, tending to interfere with the self-awareness of a speaker. First, notice how active listening can work:

Michael Weisbrot

A is describing an argument she had with her father. She concludes by saying to B, "And then I felt so angry I just turned and walked away."

B listens and says, "You were really mad at your dad, weren't you? You had to get away from him."

A then knows that B has heard her and has understood. A is free to continue exploring and may discover more feelings, the reasons for her anger, and perhaps why she walked away.

Suppose, on the other hand, that B responded in any of the following ways. Put yourself in A's position: How would you feel if B said:

"Oh, you shouldn't have walked out!"

"What did you do that for?"

"That wasn't a very wise thing to do."

"You did just the right thing."

"I think you should tell him you're sorry."

"You poor thing."

"I think this shows your basic insecurity."

"Of course you did because he was being totally unreasonable."

"I know just how you felt. When I had an argument with my dad last week, I . . ."

"What happened then?"

"Don't worry. It'll all work out."

"Yes, and then you really felt guilty, didn't you?"

"Yeah. It's about time for lunch, isn't it?"

Active listening works because it prevents the judging, helping, questioning, analyzing, and avoiding illustrated above. Not one response of this sort will be of much benefit to A.

Judging Whether the judgement is positive or negative, it takes away the speaker's opportunity for self-judgement and implies that the listener is in some way qualified to pass judgement on the speaker's thoughts or actions. Negative judgement routinely makes us defensive rather than aware.

Helping   Trying to support or encourage someone can sometimes backfire. It can be confusing, for instance, to have someone assure you that "Everything is all right" or "It will all work out; just wait and see." Worse than confusing, it can be incorrect: sometimes things don't work out. Helping often amounts to depriving others of the responsibility and opportunity for taking care of themselves.

Questioning   Questions can be helpful in clarifying, but they are often used to direct another person's thoughts. They may lead to feelings of entrapment and defensiveness. The question "Why . . .?" demands a "Because . . .," and *becauses* are likely to be excuses, justifications, or automatic hand-me-down explanations.

Analyzing   Imposing one's theories or explanations on a speaker is apt to put him or her in an inferior position. You may think you understand something that the speaker doesn't, but in saying so you run the risk of being resented, in which case the content of your analysis will fall on deaf ears. It can also happen that your explanation is incorrect, which will certainly lead to confusion.

Avoiding   Joking, changing the subject, or withdrawing can make the speaker feel uncomfortable and unworthy. It may arouse anger as well.

The major goal in active listening is to allow the speaker to *own* what he or she feels, thinks, and believes without any interference. Many of the explorations in this book can give you practice in active listening.

BEGINNING THE QUESTS

A search for self is aided by purpose, by journal keeping, by exploring on your own, and by exploring with others. *Quest* will guide you through several areas of human concern, encouraging you to seek and discover who you are. The next two chapters are about perspectives and human potentials. The remaining chapters focus on these quests:

- The quest for *separateness and wholeness:* the search for self-knowledge and completeness.
- The quest for *intimacy:* the search for satisfying, close relationships and for the ability to make intimate connections.
- The quest for a *sexual perspective:* the search for an understanding of sexual potentials and human sexual expression, and the integration of sexuality into our lives.
- The quest for *personhood: female and male:* the search for human potentials beyond the limits imposed by feminine and masculine stereotypes.

- The quest for a *sense of competence:* the search for the knowledge that we are able to do what we want to do; the discovery of our physical, emotional, and intellectual potentials.
- The quest for *unboundedness:* the search for positive ways to free ourselves from routine and habitual modes of awareness.

The time is now. The place is here. The journey has begun. A fruitful quest is not a matter of chance, so I won't wish you luck. It is a matter of courage, awareness, and perseverance. These are the qualities which make our visions become realities. They keep us going and ensure discovery even when there is no map. Take courage. Be aware. Live.

The Mahayanas tell the story of a sage who once stood on a river-bank looking across at the opposite shore. Although the far side was but dimly visible through the river mists, he could see that it was unspeakably beautiful. The hills were green and the trees were all in blossom.

So he said to himself, "I want to go there." There was a raft tied at the river's edge. He untied the raft and began to paddle toward the distant shore.

The journey was long and hazardous for the currents in midstream were swift. The raging rapids tossed and turned the raft, and he had to work with all his strength to maintain his balance. From the center of the river both shores were lost from view, and there were times when he was not sure which way he was drifting. But he continued paddling, and in due time he reached the far shore.

He got out of the raft and said, "Ah, at last I am here. It was a perilous journey, but now I have reached nirvana." He looked about him. The hills were green and the trees were all in blossom.

Then he turned around and looked back. He could not see the opposite shore whence he came. Nor was there any river to be seen. And there was no raft (Christian, 1973, p. 491).

Suggested Readings

Andersen, Marianne S. and Savary, Louis M. *Passages: A guide for pilgrims of the mind.* New York: Harper & Row, 1973. Self-suggestion exercises for improving access to inner being, interpersonal relationships, and awareness of the infinite, accompanied by selections of poetry, prose, and photography.

Assagioli, Roberto. *Psychosynthesis.* New York: Viking, 1965. Part Two is a collection of techniques for releasing pent-up psychological energies.

Gunther, Bernard. *Sense relaxation.* New York: Macmillan, 1968; *What to do till the messiah comes.* New York: Macmillan, 1971. Two volumes of experiments in sensory awareness and relaxation.

Huxley, Laura A. *You are not the target.* North Hollywood, Ca: Wilshire, 1974. Recipes for transforming negative emotional energy into healthy, constructive living.

Schutz, William C. *Joy: Expanding human awareness.* New York: Grove, 1967. Techniques for groups, aimed at fulfilling our potentials—experiencing joy!

Stevens, John O. *Awareness: Exploring, experimenting, experiencing.* New York: Bantam, 1973. A wealth of methods for exploring awareness, inner self, communication, fantasy, and creativity; for use by individuals, couples, and groups.

M. C. Escher, "Relativity," Collection Haags Gemeentemuseum—The Hague.

SEEING AND BELIEVING: PSYCHOLOGICAL VIEWPOINTS

I am a human being, whatever that may be. I speak for all of us who move and think and feel and whom time consumes. I speak as an individual unique in a universe beyond my understanding, and I speak for man. I am hemmed in by limitations of sense and mind and body, of place and time and circumstances, some of which I know but most of which I do not. I am like a man journeying through a forest, aware of occasional glints of light overhead with recollections of the long trail I have already traveled, and conscious of wider spaces ahead. I want to see more clearly where I have been and where I am going, and above all I want to know why I am where I am and why I am traveling at all.

John Berrill
(Man's Emerging Mind)

Every age, every individual, asks the question: Who are we humans? The answer comes from the viewpoint or perspective that is characteristic of the time and the person.

In this chapter we look at our species according to certain psychological viewpoints, and we begin as well to understand our individual perspectives on humans in general and on ourselves in particular.

I have forgotten thousands of details from Social Sciences I. But I do remember the theme of the course, which my professor repeated over and over (so often that it became a catch phrase among his students). He ended many lectures with a restatement of it: "So you see, it isn't what *is* that counts; it's what man *thinks is*!" He never tired of showing us how, in Western history, viewpoints were decisive factors in social and scientific progress, and how they influenced the life of an age. When humans believed the earth was flat, ships did not venture out to sea lest they fall off the edge of the world. I later read how bewitching this kind of belief can be: "There were those who, venturing far out to sea, had heard the hissing roar as the fiery ball of the sun plunged beneath the water." (Brown, 1949, pp. 22–23) When Satan was thought to be an active agent on earth, eyewitnesses told of his entering women's souls and turning them into witches. Before the germ theory of disease was widely accepted, doctors had no inclination to wash their hands in preparation for surgery. Today we can see how these and other views of our ancestors were mistaken. But the human principle that shaped their world is as active today as it was then; for many it remains true that: what you see is what you get.

By believing in what they can't see, and by ignoring what they see but can't believe, humans have always tried to put the world into some kind of order. The need to make things make sense was strong in the past and continues to be strong today. We cannot live with too much uncertainty or too much chaos. To reduce our fears of the unknown, to control change, and to make the future predictable, we adopt viewpoints that explain what seems to be true as well as that which we do not understand. A viewpoint lets us experience the diversity of life, all its real and imagined parts, as an orderly pattern.

We rely heavily on those viewpoints that work well; that is, those that connect the pieces of an otherwise fragmented world or that make us more certain about the present and the future. And by depending on viewpoints we often give them an authority that resists our later attempts to change them. A picture of the world as a battlefield for good and evil, or democracy and communism, can, as recent history shows, lead to the deaths of thousands of people. You have only to read your daily newspaper or tune in on a TV news show to be convinced that people lose their lives daily, throughout the world, while challenging or defending viewpoints stamped with the official label TRUTH. When a viewpoint ceases to work, or is fought often enough by new and conflicting truths, it weakens and is eventually discarded.

While making the world understandable to us, viewpoints distort reality to some extent. This distortion comes from the guesswork inherent in explaining the unknown. What we *know* to be true often turns out to be an article of faith, true only because we believed it to be so. It would seem, for instance, that if the sun rises in the east and sets in the west, it *must* revolve around the earth.

PSYCHOLOGICAL VIEWPOINTS

Psychological viewpoints are those perspectives on human nature which we use to understand ourselves, our friends, and people in general. When we try to explain why we do the things we do, or how people relate, think, and feel, we are being psychological and are using a psychological perspective.

It is useful to distinguish two kinds of psychological viewpoint, which will be called *public* and *private*. Public psychological viewpoints are those we share, professionally or with the world at large. Private, or individual, perspectives are our subjective views about who we are, why people behave in certain ways, and so forth. Actually, no perspective is purely public (that is, none are totally *objective*), and many individuals include large portions of professional psychology in their private perspectives. Before exploring the nature of individual viewpoints, let's concentrate on the more general and abstract nature of public views.

Public Viewpoints

Public viewpoints about human nature originate in academic psychology. This young field, now barely one hundred years old, has as one of its major concerns the building and testing of theories about human behavior. Because public viewpoints are shared by large numbers of people, they must be definite; their concepts and terms must be clear. This is especially necessary to discussion, teaching, and experimenting—all academic activities.

There are several public psychological viewpoints. Each tries to understand and explain people in general, to apply to all or most human beings rather than to the individual. Each has its own language, makes its own assumptions, has a preferred method for testing these assumptions, and has developed its own methods for solving human problems. And, each emphasizes somewhat different aspects of humanness. Among the several public psychological viewpoints, there are three major ones: the psychoanalytic (or Freudian), the behavioristic, and the humanistic.

To get a feeling for the manner in which humans can be represented in psychological views, think of a viewpoint or perspective as a pair of spectacles. Just as lenses bring our vision into focus, so do viewpoints. Just as lenses distort somewhat, so do viewpoints. As an example, suppose that there is a set of lenses for each of the major psychological perspectives. Looking through each pair of spectacles, in turn, the similarities and contrasts of the three viewpoints are apparent. Using this metaphor, I will "try on" first a pair of psychoanalytic lenses, then a behavioristic set, and last a humanistic pair. Each gives a distinctive view, according to the assumptions that went into the prescription for the lenses.

psychoanalysis

A Psychoanalytic View

I can see that people are driven, driven by an innate, instinctual force. This force or energy, at work from birth to death, is sexual. Watching this energy at work, I am reminded that Dr. Freud called it libido.

libido

I see this libido at work in the three components of human personality. The primary component is selfish, uncompromising, willful, and demanding. Its concern is with the immediate gratification of needs; it operates on the principle "I want what I want when I want it." Dr. Freud called this component, or system, the id.

id

Another system, battling with the id's primitive urges, is delivering harsh commands: "You should; You shouldn't; You must; You mustn't." With these stern orders it is supporting ideals and creating guilt. It is the conscience. It is conceived by culture and nursed by parents. Parents' commands are internalized; rules and regulations that once controlled a person from the outside have become a built-in system of control. This

Michael Weisbrot   The Bettmann Archive

subtler system punishes individuals not with a spanking but by pinching their consciences whenever basic urges make them go against orders. Dr. Freud called this component of the personality the superego.

superego

I notice that as the id and the superego are struggling within a person, a third system is trying to mediate the battle. It weighs the consequences of incompatible acts, it reasons, and then suggests delay, or alternative action, to the other systems. As it strengthens with age, this third component becomes able, in most cases, to soften the demands of the id and the strictness of the superego. Its name is ego.

ego

The tug-of-war among these systems is often dramatic, so dramatic that people in whom such inner conflicts persist are quite anxious and, according to Dr. Freud, neurotic. I can see why the ego is considered the most important component in a balanced and healthy person. Because it is vital that the ego continue to function properly, to remain intact despite its dangerous position between the id and the superego, the ego devises ways to defend itself—and the person—against anxiety. This work is called ego defense.

ego defense

I can see some ego defenses at work:

repression

Here is a person who has been spared conflict by repression. His memories of a childhood trauma are blocked from his awareness; he cannot remember that he was beaten by his father and continues to believe that his father, like all good fathers, loves him.

There is a child who is jealous of her baby sister. Her hatred would create anxiety for her, so by the mechanism of denial she can believe that she is not jealous and by using reaction formation (the turning of a feeling into its opposite) she believes she loves the new baby.

denial
reaction formation

A man is displacing his anger onto a dog. He kicks the dog instead of confronting the real object of his anger, his father.

displacing

There is a young woman away from home for the first time. She has been very dependent on her parents and is homesick. She resorts to regression, that is, acting in childish ways and developing physical symptoms of illness that were useful for getting attention when she was a child.

regression

Here is a student whose id wishes to have fun watching TV but whose superego is saying "you shouldn't; you should study." His ego smooths over the conflict by allowing this rationalization: "This is an important TV show and I am just too tired to study. It'll do me more good to watch TV than to study."

rationalization

Armed with these defenses, some individuals turn aside feelings of anxiety, guilt, or conflict. But in others I see that the ego-mediator sometimes fails, for all its usual negotiating tricks. The clash of id and superego in these people often leads to their physical or mental breakdown.

Through these psychoanalytic lenses I see clearly the importance of childhood in life. As people grow from infancy to adulthood, their libidos are invested successively in different areas of the body—oral, anal, genital. This process is analogous to banking, for a person must withdraw energy from one area and reinvest it in another as he or she is maturing. These energy transactions often cause conflicts. The classic example of childhood conflict occurs around the age of five, when the child must transfer intense (sexual) love of the opposite-sex parent into a relationship of identity with the same-sex parent. During this process boys develop strong fears that they will be castrated, and girls become envious because they lack a penis. Dr. Freud calls this conflict the Oedipal situation.

Oedipus complex

Dr. Freud took pains to point out that the high drama of id-superego-ego conflict, the exercise of ego defense mechanisms, and the development of conflicts are all played on the stage of the unconscious. The people I see through my psychoanalytic lenses are unaware of what is going on inside themselves. The action unfolding there reaches their consciousness only in the shadowy disguises of dreams, slips of the tongue, fantasies, and symbols. Unaware of unresolved conflicts, some of which have been smouldering since childhood, people are nevertheless motivated by them. Their unfinished problems are obstacles to mature functioning.

unconscious

The view I have through these glasses is essentially negative. Humans, at the mercy of their irrational drives, appear self-serving. The sexual nature of their libidos is not necessarily loving sexuality. People's actions are determined by biological, instinctual forces from which they can never be free.

I am impressed, as I remove the psychoanalytic lenses, with the scope and detail of the view I have experienced. Who was Dr. Freud? And why is this view called psychoanalytic?

To begin with, Sigmund Freud (1856–1939) was a brilliant medical doctor (not a psychologist) whose views made a profound impact on the field of psychology and indeed on the entire Western world. Freud lived during one of the most sexually repressed periods of all time. His contemporaries considered all sexual behavior except that necessary to continue the species unhealthy and morally wrong.

Sigmund Freud. *Courtesy Sigmund Freud Copyrights Ltd.*

free association

As a doctor, Freud took a medical approach to problems; he saw an illness and developed a cure. His patients, mostly upper-class residents of Vienna, came to him because he was a neurologist. It was in the course of treating their nervous disorders that Freud developed a revolutionary cure: psychoanalysis. He encouraged his patients to talk, to free associate as he called it, until they overcame their resistances and could gain access to their unconscious. This procedure culminated when patients gained insight into the conflicts between id, ego, and superego and were thereby able to release their anxieties, to free their egos from the burden of over-defense, and to cast off their physical and neurotic symptoms.

The psychoanalytic lenses of today are not exactly those originally prescribed by Freud. Post-Freudians have refined his view, using their greater knowledge of the differences among cultures to help them understand differences in personality. They are aware, for example, that not all societies are as sexually repressed as Freud's was. Post-Freudians also pay attention to the many social demands on an individual, not just the biological demands. More of this trend, in the theory of Erik Erikson, will be seen in the next chapter. Today, the emphasis on primitive urges (id) has given way to concern with the ego and with normal, healthy, rational functioning. Still, the Freudian lenses remain gray, the view pessimistic; the theory continues to assume that people are not free but forever controlled by inner forces; the treatment is still medical. In this perspective, human growth is determined by the development of the genitals and culminates in mature sexual functioning.

Psychoanalytic theory is the dominant intellectual perspective on human nature.

behaviorism

A Behavioristic View

Human beings, through behavioristic lenses, appear to be animals in motion. All around me I see them acting and reacting—reacting to each other, to objects, to their situations. Trying to make sense of this jungle-like scene, I suddenly become aware that this human behavior is far from random. Some people are doing the same things over and over; certain situations seem to elicit similar behavior from different individuals. The regularity is comforting. Then it dawns on me that humans behave according to laws, much like those of physics which explain the behavior of matter and energy. This suggests that the behavior of other species is subject to the same kind of laws. If only enough were known about the behavior of lower animals, we might then know the whys and wherefores of human behavior.

Michael Weisbrot

stimulus-response

My behavioristic glasses focus most sharply on the link between situation and behavior, the stimulus-response link. Behavior is not random; it is related to the stimulus situation. Let me share a scene from the past with you:

We are in the laboratory of Dr. Watson. Recently, he has been doing some reading about a Russian physiologist, Dr. Pavlov. who works with dogs. Dr. Watson believes that he can apply the principles which Dr. Pavlov found in dog behavior to the behavior of a little boy. The toddler to become famous in this American laboratory is Albert. Today Albert is gurgling in delighted play with a furry, white bunny rabbit that Dr. Watson has provided. Suddenly Albert hears a loud report behind him. Now, as a normal baby he is terrified and bursts into tears. Dr. Watson repeatedly subjects Albert to the noise and the rabbit at the same time. A few days later Albert is again brought into the room and, when he sees the rabbit, he immediately begins to cry, without the help of the shocking

learn

noise. Albert has learned to fear something he previously liked. Furthermore, Albert's mother reports that he is afraid of anything that is white and furry—a ball of white yarn, a white beard, a white Teddy Bear. Al-

generalize

bert has generalized his learning to similar stimuli. Dr. Watson has proven that irrational fears, called phobias, are the result of associations made in childhood. Fears become generalized and, by the way, are rather persistent. Dr. Watson will have to take some time to help Albert unlearn his newly acquired fear (by forming a new association: rabbits and chocolate cake, for example). Dr. Watson is convinced, and has con-

classical conditioning

vinced many other American psychologists, that humans are the product of this kind of learning, called classical conditioning.

In this view I see classically conditioned human beings as completely passive. They are victims of intentional as well as unintentional associations. Not only do they stop at red lights and hesitate before littering, they also shrink from talking back to their bosses (in remembrance of Dad) and are nauseated at the sight of prunes (thanks to Mom). Creatures of habit, they keep responding to the same old stimuli in the same old ways, jerked through life like puppets on heavy chains of stimulus-response links. They get into difficulty when they are in situations that present them with conflicting stimuli. A red light and a green light signalling at the same time put the conditioned human into a hopeless fix.

discriminate

Then humans suffer when they can't tell the difference, can't discriminate, between stimuli: Infant Johnny receives warmth and unfailing tenderness from his mother; he gets cold, harsh punishment from Aunt Nora, Mother's twin. Until he learns to tell the women apart, he will know painful confusion in the presence of either.

This passivity of humans makes them morally neutral creatures. They naturally gravitate neither toward evil nor good behavior, but move and change direction only in response to the environment. Now humans are not as still as rocks; when they want something (we see) they can go after it. True, but humans in the behavioristic view cannot meet their needs in a random, capricious way. They learn many of their needs and learn what to do to gratify them. They learn these things according to principles of active learning called operant conditioning, a term applied to situations in which humans (and other animals) *operate* on the environment in some way. This operation will become clearer if we look in on some of the discoveries made by the contemporary dean of behavioristic psychology, B. F. Skinner.

operant conditioning

Dr. Skinner has a rat in a specially constructed box, a Skinner box. This rat is hungry, and, as is the way with hungry rats, he begins to poke around. After a poke here and a poke there, he accidentally hits a special lever in the box. Dr. Skinner has connected the lever to a food-pellet dispenser in such a way that each time the lever is tripped, a bit of food drops into the box. The rat eats his pellet and continues to poke, being a very hungry rat. He hits the lever again, and again is rewarded. Very quickly the rat is purposively banging away at the lever—rather strange and remarkable behavior for a rat. He bangs until he is full. If this rat is placed in this box every day when hungry, his behavior is completely predictable. Dr. Skinner tells us the rat has been conditioned.

I am reminded of a scene in Las Vegas: rows of bright-eyed people pulling levers with the same predictability as conditioned rats. The slot-machine owner is well aware of the principle which Dr. Skinner has carefully demonstrated in the laboratory. When a reward (called the *positive* reinforcement) is delivered on a random schedule (that is, every so often, but not regularly) a conditioned animal will push or pull his lever to the point of exhaustion, or perhaps bankruptcy.

reinforcement

random schedule

B. F. Skinner *(Harvard News Office Photo)*.

I can now see that much behavior is understandable and predictable according to conditioning principles. People are positively reinforced not only by food and money, but by approval, attention, grades, status, possessions—the list of positive reinforcements could be endless. People behave in those ways which increase the likelihood of obtaining positive reinforcement and in those ways which, conversely, decrease the likelihood of *negative* reinforcement (disapproval, pain, punishment, or going hungry). Behavior can be explained if enough is known about the situation—the kind and number of reinforcers which have operated in the past and which continue to operate in the present. Not only can it be explained, but (1) if the probability of reinforcement in the future can be discovered, future behavior can be predicted, and (2) if the availability of reinforcements can be controlled, behavior can be controlled.

In summary, I see that individuals are a composite of the reinforcing situations in their environments, past and present; they are products, rather than producers. They are shaped by the millions of associated events, objects, and reinforcers with which they come in contact. They are not free to will themselves above or beyond conditions and conditioning. The principles governing their behavior and behavior change are relatively simple and discoverable. The apparent complexity of human beings is merely a reflection of the countless symbolic and social events that serve as positive or negative reinforcements.

As I remove the lenses of behaviorism I am aware of the important contributions this viewpoint makes to an understanding of humanity. I am also aware that the world seems to resume a certain zest, a richness that I could not appreciate with the glasses on. Valuable as it is, the view of humans through these lenses is limited. Freud's determinism was internal, that of the behaviorists is external. People are bound just the same, unfree and machinelike. At the same time, I recognize that this deterministic viewpoint has proved very useful for the science of psychology. American psychology in particular has been devoted to it. Behaviorists have learned a great deal from their research and have been able to explain much of human behavior according to principles of conditioning derived from laboratory work.

Recently, some psychologists (Albert Bandura and others, for example) have deemphasized the role of reinforcement in their study of social learning. In their perspective, humans are not merely passive responders. Our learning and behavior are influenced by what we observe, our interpretations of the social situation, and our expectations of probable reinforcements. We learn by watching others' behavior. The role of language, rules, and verbal instructions in particular are viewed as properly determining what and how we learn. There is increased interest in how we select a particular behavior from many possible behaviors and in the fact that we learn many things we don't always do. (In other words, there is a difference between our learning and our performance.) Nevertheless, these social-learning viewpoints still emphasize what an individual *does,* and avoid suggesting that we act according to our internal states or unconscious conflicts.

Although the bulk of behavioristic effort has been thrown into research, behavioristic principles have also been used in the solution of practical problems. Improved techniques in teaching have included programmed instruction based on Skinner's principles. Several effective therapies modify behavior by changing its reinforcements. These approaches are extremely helpful for correcting maladaptive behaviors and allowing individuals to lead productive lives.

humanism

A Humanistic View

Putting on this pair of lenses, which comfortably mold to my eyes, I am immediately struck by the diversity of human beings. Every person I see is unique; no two are alike. Each man, each woman, each child is a whole, unified person. These whole people are busy, active; they are playing, working, crying, laughing, suffering, thinking, feeling, caring, worrying, grieving, growing—some are dying. Each is living his or her own personal existence, his or her own personal adventure. Each is free to make decisions, to make commitments, to take risks within the bounds of his or her own value system. Each makes an individual meaning of the problems, joys, events, and circumstances, of life-as-it-is-experienced. Each has a sense of Self created out of the private world of experience. Each discovers and develops his or her own potentials.

I see many people on their ways. Each has chosen a path which promises not only enrichment, but the development of unrealized potential.

One is exploring her body and her senses, the oneness of these with her intellect and emotions. She says, "I choose to resolve the mind-body tyranny with which I have lived for so long."

Another is a group member attempting to integrate his emotions and their expression into the rest of his experience, and in so doing to create

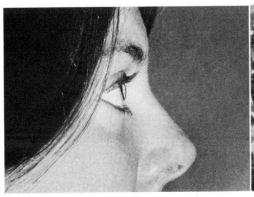

Michael Weisbrot

"*Le Moulin de la Galette,*" Renoir. *Photographie Bulloz.*

better personal relationships. He says, "I choose to express my whole being instead of my rational being alone."

Here is another, working to exercise her individual freedom, to give direction to her will, to make a difference in her life. She says, "I choose to take responsibility for myself."

Several are exploring philosophical, religious, and therapeutic approaches to nonordinary states of consciousness. They say, "We choose to unbind ourselves from linear, analytic views of reality."

Another is attempting to come to terms with his sexuality, to adopt those attitudes that free him to grow in his roles and behaviors. He says, "I choose to make available to myself a source of pleasure and self-esteem that has traditionally been denied me."

Several are bringing into their lives the quietistic traditions of meditative spiritualism. They say, "We choose to search for meaning beyond the action-oriented traditions of the Christian West."

One is improving the quality of her environment, creating growth-oriented, supportive surroundings for herself and others in which to work, play, and learn. She says, "I choose to abandon the desire to conquer and control my environment, whether it be human, animal, plant, or inanimate."

Yet, even as I watch these people on their individual quests, I do not feel in the separateness of their activities a sense of anarchy or chaos. There are indeed confusions, fears, and doubts, but I can see a purpose in each person and I am aware that their connectedness is vitally important. A harmony of care and concern for others smooths their transactions.

This rosy view of human beings through humanistic lenses is a refreshing contrast to the essentially steely picture I get from psychoanalytic or bevavioristic glasses. For one thing, the people I see here look very like the people I see every day on the street. They are whole people. I have found a statement that explains, in part, why this is so.

Humanistic psychology is primarily an orientation toward the whole of psychology rather than a distinct area or school. It stands for respect for the worth of persons, respect for differences of approach, open-mindedness as to acceptable methods and interest in exploration of new aspects of human behavior. As a "third force" in contemporary psychology it is concerned with topics having little place in existing theories and systems: e.g. love, creativity, self, growth, organism, basic need-gratification, self-actualization, higher values, being, becoming, spontaneity, play, humor, affection, naturalness, warmth, ego-transcendence, objectivity, autonomy, responsibility, meaning, fair-play, transcendental experience, peak experience, courage, and related concepts (*Articles of Association*, American Association for Humanistic Psychology).

There is no single master of the viewpoint; the voice of humanistic psychology is not solo, but choral. Abraham Maslow, Carl Rogers, Gor-

Carl Rogers (Photo by John T. Wood, courtesy of Carl Rogers).

don Allport, and others formulate theories; Fritz Perls leads the groups, Rollo May the philosophers; and dozens of others, past and present, all encourage psychology along the paths of growth. I do not see any patients on couches nor do I see many research laboratories. I do see shelves of books from every field of human inquiry. The humanistic chorus repeats the enduring questions about human existence over and over. It searches the realms of art, religion, and philosophy—both Eastern and Western—for answers. The view of humankind which they present is positive, thoughtful, unsystematic, and rather romantic.

I hesitate to remove these rose-colored lenses. They feel comfortable, and I find that I am happier with the view they give than I was with either the spectacles of the psychoanalyst of those of the behaviorist. As I remove them some questions occur to me: Why were these lenses fashioned? Why are they so comfortable?

Humanistic psychology, drawing from many sources which are neither psychological nor American, has developed in the last twenty years into an influential "Third Force" in American psychology. Humanistic psychology is a perspective whose time has come. By the 1960s most American psychologists had built lives of material affluence. By that time, too, many felt the poverty of empty personal relationships and the aridity of psychological thought divorced from the process of life. Abraham Maslow tells of his searching through the psychological literature for a discussion of *love*, and finding nothing. American psys/chology had, it seems, forgotten love.

holistic

Humanistic and holistic (whole person) approaches to human behavior go against the traditional currents of research psychology. Although the humanistic viewpoint has revitalized psychology, it is still widely criticized for not becoming respectably scientific. It is true that thinking about the enduring issues of humankind contributes little toward perfecting logical theories and research methodology. In fact, there is an inverse relationship between the two: as a topic becomes more relevant to life, the rigor with which it can be studied decreases; if relevance is low, rigor is high (Gardiner, 1970). On the other hand, humanistic psychology has broken down many of the pretenses within which psychology has barricaded and isolated itself. Psychology can now accept, or at least recognize, many formerly ignored nonscientific friends, coworkers, ancestors, and neighbors.

There are many psychological perspectives and theories about human behavior. No one is comprehensive enough to account for all that needs to be understood about humanness. Each viewpoint differs not only in the vocabulary it uses to describe concepts and processes, but also in its basic assumptions about why we do what we do. Psychoanalysts are most apt to try to understand a person's problems by analyzing internal conflicts and finding those that remain from early childhood. Behaviorists tend to look for the influence of past conditions, the nature of past reinforcements, and to solve problems by manipulating conditions and reinforcements. Humanists are most likely to seek understanding in the person's own interpretation of situations and to emphasize human potentials for growth.

Although public psychological viewpoints often disagree, they are valuable aids to understanding human behavior. Their value lies particularly in the fact that they are public, that we can share, examine, test, and attempt to verify or discount them. Each makes an order of human experience in a relatively objective way.

Private Psychological Viewpoints

"Live by the foma* that make you brave
and kind and healthy and happy."
—The Books of Bokonon. 1:5

Kurt Vonnegut, Jr.
(Cat's Cradle)

*Harmless untruths

Although private psychological viewpoints can resemble public psychological viewpoints, they differ in several important ways. Public perspectives, you remember, were likened to lenses through which everyone can look. I used the lenses of psychology, but I could have used economic or political lenses just as well. The viewer using a public perspective stands outside himself looking through a borrowed eyepiece. A private viewpoint, on the other hand, is not available to others unless the owner makes it so, for it is *always* a viewpoint taken from within the viewer.

Take the viewpoint of a nutritionist. Looking at two children both rubbing their stomachs and whining just before bedtime, her public (professional) perspective might lead her to say that "Many children in the United States go to bed hungry at night." The personal viewpoints of these children would tell a different story. Indeed, both children are going to bed hungry, but one would tell you she wishes she had eaten her dinner, and the other would have to confess that he really wants another dish of ice cream. Individual viewpoints do not always yield the same conclusions as those seen in public perspectives.

Private viewpoints differ from public ones in that we often use them without troubling to see whether they give a true picture of reality, and we sometimes cling to a private viewpoint even when we have evidence that it greatly distorts the world. For instance, we often stereotype people. We form opinions about individuals solely from their age, race, sex, profession, or political or religious preferences rather than taking account of their individual qualities. We may jump to the conclusion that an eighty-year-old man is a useless person if we stereotype old people as senile. Another type of viewpoint, similar to the stereotype, is prejudice. Prejudices are negative viewpoints held about groups of people and all members of those groups. Prejudice often figures in the way racial

stereotype

prejudice

groups are characterized. Stereotyping and prejudging simplify the world, but they also distort the ways in which we see individuals and events.

EXPLORATION 2.1

Believing and Seeing

Two men hear a woman cry, "Thief!" and turn to see a man dash into an alley carrying a purse. The victim's screams have brought a policeman to the scene, but the culprit is gone. Neither of the witnesses, John or Sam, is really sure what happened, but they both saw something. The suspect was black. John has been convinced all his life that blacks are lazy, no-good, robbing bums. Sam feels that blacks are his brothers.

Give an account of the crime that John reports to the policeman.

Now, give the one that Sam recounts.

Our experiences depend on who we are; that is, what our needs are, and what viewpoint we bring to a situation. A botanist, a florist, a poet, a writer, a man with an allergy, and a woman in love—each will view a rose from a different personal perspective. Each will bring a private understanding to bear on the same object. They would all agree that they see a rose, but all would not agree on the qualities or purpose of it, nor on their individual relationships to the flower. Our perspectives are a mixture of common knowledge ("A rose is a rose is a rose is a rose. . .") and our unique reactions. A rose is to study, to sell, to rhyme, to render, to avoid, or to buy, depending on who is viewing it.

EXPLORATION 2.2

Role Playing

One of the best ways to grasp the perspectives of others (and, in the process, to see our own more clearly) is to exchange places with them through role playing. In this exploration class members first think of some situation, a current problem or conflict, involving family or friends. The class then picks from among those suggested one or more of these situations to role play. You play the other person(s) in the situation and the other students play you. As an example: Your parents want you to stay in school but you want to quit. This is causing conflict in your family. You play your mother or father (or both) and others can take turns playing your role. After playing a scene, discover and make clear all viewpoints in the situation. Discuss these questions:

How does your perspective differ when you take another's role?

When you see someone else in your role?

What are effective and ineffective ways of conveying our viewpoints to others?

How can viewpoints be changed? strengthened? communicated?

How do our viewpoints function to stabilize the world?

That is, how do they prevent change?

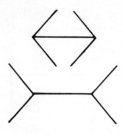

Not only do our viewpoints determine our experience, but experience is the stuff of which viewpoints themseleves are made. Private viewpoints are built on the experiences of each individual alone. From a very early age people, places, pains and joys, impressions—all contribute to our perspectives. And as each experience becomes part of our perspective, it then acts as a magnet to all future experiences. Some new ones it attracts; others it repels. A frightening encounter with a vicious dog, for example, can make us avoid all dogs in the future.

Even experiences of which we are not aware can affect our perspectives. R. L. Gregory has suggested that visual illusions such as this one (the Muller-Lyer arrow illusion, left) are powerful because we live in a world of rectangular shapes. Our experiences with distance and corners account for the illusory effect. The Zulus, who live in round huts and in a culture without many angles and lines, are not affected to the same degree by linear illusions. (For an explanation of why this is so, consult Gregory, 1966, Chapter 9.)

Sometimes we can be made to see something in a particular way by a mere suggestion. If I tell you that the picture on the left is an old woman with a big nose you will probably see an old woman. If I suggest instead that she is a young woman you may see the profile of a young woman looking off to the left.

Roger Lubin/Jeroboam, Inc.

EXPLORATION 2.3

Experience and Viewpoints

In a small group share your impressions about the photograph at the bottom of page 34. What are the different ways in which you describe the situation? How does your viewpoint relate to your experiences? (Adler and Towne, 1975, p. 133)

cognitive dissonance

We can and do hold contradictory viewpoints. We can handle these contradictions as long as they are not directly competing. When they are opposed, the cognitive dissonance (Festinger, 1957) can become unbearable, as happened with an acquaintance of mine. This middle-aged white woman was strongly prejudiced against blacks. She was a bigot. She got along quite well with her prejudice until a few years ago when she realized that it was no longer considered fashionable or intelligent to have bigoted views. Since she considered herself both fashionable and intelligent, there was a conflict: either her views of herself or her view of blacks would have to change. She made neither change. Instead, she formed a new viewpoint. She announced to me one day that she really held nothing at all against blacks. "All the blacks I've known have been fine people," she said. "It's the ones I don't know that I don't like."

Modifications in our viewpoints seldom occur suddenly. Once we have formed our basic notions about people and things (and groups of people and things), good and bad, like and dislike, we only gradually make minor adjustments. The process is like stuffing a shopping bag that is nearly full: you fill the corners with small stuff but the shape of the bag remains nearly the same. Our viewpoints change more slowly as we age. Generally speaking, it becomes ever more difficult with time to accept information or experiences that might upset the world we have created. The threat of change is a threat to our very selves. We become our opinions and beliefs as they become ours. If our viewpoints become fossilized, only powerful new experiences will alter them. Certain occasions can bring about completely changed viewpoints, as can, for instance, religious conversion or a flash of creative insight. Psychological therapy can transform viewpoints about one's self and about the difficulties that brought one to counseling. Ordinarily, the *evolution* of perspective is a lifelong process that includes very few complete revolutions in viewpoint.

personal constructs

The psychologist George Kelly (1955) has called private viewpoints personal constructs, which he defines as the ways in which we categorize our experiences. By using personal constructs we can abstract, interpret, judge, assess, anticipate, and label our world and ourselves. We can understand. The constructs "I am not successful enough," "I am unworthy," "I am in love," or "I am sincere," for example, influence our reactions to others. Kelly points out that while we may not be able to change events in our lives, we *can* come to view them differently.

A theory is a theory, not a reality. All a theory can do is remind me of certain thoughts that were part of my reality *then*. A statement or a "fact" is an emphasis — one way of looking at something. At worst it is a kind of myopia. A name is also just one way of seeing something. I can't make a statement about a reality without omitting many other things which are also true about it. Even if it were possible to say everything that is true about a reality, I still would not have the reality; I would only have the words. In fact, the reality changes even as I talk about it.

When I outgrow my names and facts and theories, or when reality leaves them behind, I become dead if I don't go on to new ways of seeing things (Prather, 1970, p. 30).

Forming viewpoints, using them, modifying, and refining them are lifelong processes. To the growing personality they are processes necessary to life, continuing until death, taking place faster or slower as we feel the need to understand the world around us and ourselves.

In summary, our private viewpoints are the perspectives by which the world is made understandable. Our private viewpoints are not borrowed lenses; they are our eyes. The ways we see the world are derived from our unique, individual, and very personal experiences. Although we assume others are perceiving the way we are, the same situation may have very different meanings to different people. No one has exactly the same private viewpoints as anyone else. Sometimes our viewpoints are inconsistent; they are not always logical. Our basic viewpoints are stable but we can modify them. Often our perspectives keep us from seeing all there is to see; this is especially true of our stereotyped and prejudiced points of view. This can also be true of our viewpoints about ourselves. Sometimes we stop growing by viewing ourselves as unchangeable or by being certain that we are only one way, that we cannot be any other. Private viewpoints are what we *think is*. And that, as the professor at the beginning of this chapter said, is what counts.

**EXPLORATIONS
2.4**

**Viewpoints
on This
Course**

(These are good explorations to write in your journal.)

1. Why are you taking this course? Clarify by responding to the following:
   These are my reasons for taking this class:
   These are my feelings about it so far:
   These are my objectives; this is what I would like to happen:
   This is how I will know that my objectives have been met:

2. Impressions of others. Write out short descriptions of how you *see* at least five people in your class. This is particularly good if you pick out people you don't know, that you've never met before. What are your first impressions of them? Put your descriptions aside. In a few weeks come back to them and *see* if your viewpoints have changed as you have had further experience. Are your first impressions lasting ones? Do your viewpoints of others change as you get more information?

In the following chapters you will have an opportunity to review many of your viewpoints, first as they developed through your childhood, and then as they function in your current life. Perhaps some of your perspectives will change.

SUMMARY

1. A viewpoint is a construction of the world that makes it understandable.
2. Public perspectives are those we share.
3. They consist of assumptions that are relatively objective and testable. Among the most widely accepted public psychological viewpoints are the psychoanalytic, which focuses on the internal dynamics of human behavior; the behavioristic, which sees what we do in response to our environment; and the humanistic, a holistic viewpoint concerned with all that is peculiarly human.
4. Private viewpoints are built from life experience. They become part of everything we are and do, thus influencing our experience. Private viewpoints include our stereotypes, prejudices, and personal constructs. They are relatively stable but evolve through a lifetime.

Suggested Readings

Allport, Gordon W. (Ed.) *Letters from Jenny.* New York: Harcourt, 1965. The story of a mother-son relationship, and Jenny's personality, as revealed in her correspondence; interpreted from three different psychological perspectives.

Castaneda, Carlos. *Teachings of Don Juan: A Yaqui way of knowledge.* New York: Ballantine, 1968; *A separate reality: Further conversations with Don Juan.* New York: Simon and Schuster, 1971; *Journey to Ixtlan.* New York: Simon and Schuster, 1972; *Tales of power.* New York: Simon and Schuster, 1974. Castaneda's experiences with nontraditional points of view, those of Don Juan as well as his own; provides a fascinating introduction to the difference between "looking at" the world and "seeing" it.

Freud, Sigmund. *The basic writings of Sigmund Freud.* New York: The Modern Library, 1938. Essays on topics such as forgetting, slips of the tongue, dream interpretation, infantile sexuality, wit, and taboo. From the more than 20 volumes Freud wrote, this is a good selection to begin with.

Maslow, Abraham H. *Toward a psychology of being.* (Rev. ed.) Princeton, N.J.: D. Van Nostrand Co., 1968. A now classic statement of a foremost "Third Force" psychologist; on humanistic psychology, growth, creativity, values, and the future of psychology.

May, Rollo. (Ed.) *Existential Psychology.* (2d. ed.) New York: Random House, Inc., 1969. A collection of essays by May, Maslow, Rogers, and others on the influence of existential philosophies in psychology.

Rogers, Carl R. *On becoming a person.* Boston: Houghton Mifflin, 1961. A widely acclaimed statement of Rogers' belief that personal growth is possible for all of us.

Skinner, B. F. *Walden Two.* New York: MacMillan, 1948. A utopian description of society organized on Skinner's behavioristic principles; *Beyond freedom and dignity.* New York: Knopf, 1971. Skinner argues for a technology of behavior to replace prescientific notions of freedom and dignity, which he considers self-destructive.

Courtesy of Daniel & Charles Associates, Ltd. and Bristol-Myers.

3

HUMAN POTENTIALS AND THE QUESTS WE SHARE

The purpose of this chapter is to present a viewpoint on human development. This viewpoint will be very broad and consist of a number of subviews that have been woven together to give the reader a perspective on the human life cycle. The chapter stands back, as it were, and points out the several routes along which the human quest is traveled.

The topics to be discussed here are:

po-ten-tial n. 1. The inherent ability or capacity for growth, development, or coming into being. (see *latent*).

American Heritage Dictionary

- Potentials, in the species and the individual
- Environmental influences on the individual
- The effect of time

The human quest is a search for a way of living that will make actual one's potentials. It is the process by which we discover and fulfill our possibilities for growth. I find that the easiest approach to understanding this process is by way of a model. My model ignores many details of the world it represents, but it will serve to give you a general picture of human potentials as I see them.

(a)

The model begins with a single dot (a). This represents a newly conceived human being, a human egg just fused with a human sperm.

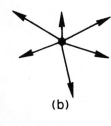

(b)

The next drawing (b) shows the same being after it has grown and developed a bit, say at birth. The arrows emanating from the dot represent the few potentials that this human being has actualized. At birth these would include the ability to live outside its mother's body, the ability to take nourishment through its mouth, to urinate, and so forth. I am using arrows here to suggest that this is a dynamic process, in operation continuously, and never fixed or static. Look at (b) again and try to imagine that from the dot at its center new arrows are breaking out now and then and starting to lengthen; arrows already emerged are growing longer at different rates; and any one arrow will grow now quickly, now more slowly. This dynamic growth goes on night and day, day after day.

(c)

In (c) the same individual is shown much later in life, perhaps at the beginning of college. Some arrows have lengthened, new arrows have emerged, and a couple of arrows are not moving. These last, the flat-headed ones, are dormant for the time being; they are unattended potentials.

If I could show (a), (b), and (c) in a time-lapse photograph, you would see that some of these arrows stopped lengthening a long time ago. Others would appear to have stretched a good distance in the last few years. Perhaps next year there will be more new ones, and those which are now dormant may be revived. At the end of a lifetime, this person will have many arrows of many varying lengths.

In the model's terms, this chapter will be looking at the kinds of arrows (that is, human growth potentials) we share and the extent to which we lengthen (or actualize) them. We will be looking at what the arrows stand for and how far they can be extended in certain circumstances.

SPECIES POTENTIAL

How far can humans stretch? What are the upper limits of growth? To what extent can we develop our capabilities? Any answer to these questions must take account of our inherent characteristics, those determined by our genes.

Every part in the human body (with the possible exception of the appendix) and every function those parts perform, singly or together, helps define human capacity. We have evolved as a unified, though immensely complicated, living system. All of our adaptations, from the two feet on which we stand to the thumb which opposes our forefinger, from our smooth and relatively hairless skin to the shape of our teeth, have given us *human* potential. The foundation of human potential is our basic human anatomy and physiology, the structures and functions which determine the range of what is physically possible. Human strength and endurance, size, and shape are human limits.

Our brains, more than any other structure, set us apart as a species. **cortex** The size and the complexity of the cortex (the outer covering of the

Michael Weisbrot

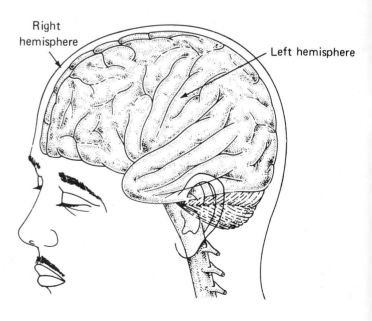

Right hemisphere

Left hemisphere

brain) and the central nervous system (the brain and the spinal cord together) are our most distinctively human characteristics. And these structures influence the operations of all other body systems. Everything we do is either directed by the brain or, at the very least, observed and recorded by it.

instincts

It is the brain which frees us of the instincts by which most other animals live. The complex structures within our skulls give us a great deal of flexibility in our behavior, letting us modify our actions according to experience to a far greater degree than any other species. We are not bound by rigid programs of behavior established by our genetic inheritance. We are not tied to fixed stimulus-response patterns of thought and action. We are capable of an awesome array of symbolic activities.

As far as can be seen at the present time, symbolic capacity is the key to man's uniqueness. . . . Symbolic ability allows man not only to know, as all animals do in variable measure, but to know that he knows, to reflect and to conclude. Man is the animal who not only measures time, or what he thinks is time, but creates it. . . . His symbolic capacity accounts for his capacity to free himself conceptually from the here and now of the stimulus situation, allowing him to conceive of new modes and models, to conjure new dimensions, new worlds (Kinget, 1975, p. 8).

We are a species which can learn, remember, and relearn if necessary. We can communicate our thoughts, plans, and feelings in words. We can experience joy and fear, sadness and delight. We are the only species which laughs and cries intentionally. These capabilities are found at the base of every human potential.

As a species, human beings have both limits and potentials. We are not physically equipped to swing through the trees, bring down prey with our bare hands, or fly away from our enemies. But we can, thanks to our brains, invent strategies of behavior and technologies to aid us in achieving our goals.

genetic

As individuals of our species, our potentials will vary within a range of what is possible for human beings as a whole. The specific traits that each one of us shows will depend on the particular combination of genetic material laid down by our parents. A human baby could have long legs or short legs, thanks to inheritance, but it would not have fins or hooves. A person who inherits potentials for long, muscular legs and physical coordination has the possibilities of becoming a dancer or a sprinter. Some of us inherit the potential to understand higher mathematics or to create symphonies. Just as we inherit different physical and intellectual potentials, we also seem to be born with tendencies to be emotionally expressive, irritable, active, or calm (Korner, 1971). Every opera singer, basketball player, scientist, poet, artist, musician—indeed every human being—has his or her talents in part because of genetic heritage. But our genes determine only a part of our destinies.

National Education Association Publishing, Joe Di Dio.

EXPLORATION 3.1

Inherent Potentials

Make this exploration in groups of five or six. Use a brainstorming technique (throwing out ideas as fast as they come to you, without stopping to evaluate or judge them) to answer this question:

What would we be able to do if we had three hands? What in our lives would change?

After a few minutes stop and review your discussion.

Would life be better or worse than it is with two hands?

PERSON/ENVIRONMENT

Environmental influences also play a vital part in shaping human potential. People do not exist except in relationship to the surroundings with which they are in constant interaction. In operation at all times is a system of exchange between humans and, for example, the atmosphere, as we exchange carbon dioxide for oxygen. We exchange our energy for money, which we trade for things. We exchange smiles and letters with other people; we sometimes trade gunshots with them as well. Physical, chemical, or social connections between people and the world in which they live are necessary and inescapable influences on potential.

The nature of these influences can be seen in a scheme by the psychologist Abraham Maslow, designed to show the organization of human needs. It is in fulfilling these needs that we interact with our environment.

In Maslow's arrangement, human needs form a pyramid or hierarchy.

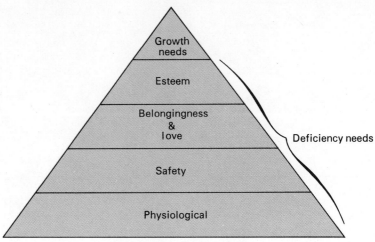

Maslow's hierarchy of needs.

The lower part of the pyramid is built of deficiency needs: physiological, safety, belongingness and love, and esteem. The more fundamental a need—the lower it sits in the hierarchy—the more vital is the necessity to fulfill it. Each higher need can be attended to only when the one beneath it is met. After we have turned to a higher-order need, we must continue to fulfill our more basic needs.

Our most basic needs are *physiological*. Without sufficient and continuous supplies of food, air, water, shelter, and opportunities for sleep, we perish. We interact with our environments to meet these needs for bodily maintenance. When we run low of something or are in danger of not receiving supplies (such as food), we are highly motivated to remove the deficiency. When we are satisfied and assured that the environment can provide for us, we are then able to attend to higher-order needs.

The next order of needs are *safety* needs. We want to be physically safe and psychologically secure, and to count on a friendly and supportive environment. We want to feel that we will not be destroyed by physical or human forces. Security and safety are gained in a stable world, one which is ordered, consistent, and routine to some degree. It feels safe to know that the morning will bring light, that we are adequately sheltered from harsh weather, that our dams will hold back the flood waters.

At the next level upwards, *belongingness and love* needs must be satisfied through our interactions with other people. Only in interpersonal relationships can we satisfy our hungers for affection, appreciation, and a sense of having a rightful place in society. We all work hard to achieve the feeling that we belong and that our relationships with others are based on their love for us. Lack of love and the inability to feel loved are deficiencies. Without the satisfaction of love needs, humans cannot develop further. Babies who don't get loving care are retarded in their physical and mental development, even though their physiological needs are met (Bowlby, 1952). Belongingness and love needs exist throughout our lives.

The next level of needs met by interacting with our environment are *esteem* needs. One aspect of esteem is self-esteem, which is positive when we meet our standards for achievement. We feel good about ourselves when we are confident that we can master our chosen tasks in life. We also feel good when we gain the respect of others for what we do. We rely on others for prestige, status, recognition, and reputation. When we cannot fulfill our esteem needs, we feel a sense of inferiority, helplessness, and discouragement.

We also have needs which are *not* the result of deficiencies. These are referred to by Maslow as *growth* needs. The need for self-actualization is a growth need arising from our natural tendency to act in ways which express our potentials and capabilities, whatever they may be (see Chapter 6). The need for understanding is another growth need, expressing our desire for awareness, meaning, and consciousness of ourselves and the external world. Our esthetic needs express the desire for beauty in our lives. Growth needs are ultimate. They form the apex of a triangle of needs.

EXPLORATION 3.2

Needs

Complete the following phrase with as many short, spontaneous responses as you can think of:

I need _____.

When you have completed a list, share it with a partner. How are your lists similar, different?

Classify your needs as physiological, safety, belongingness, esteem, growth needs. Which category is largest? Is it the most important one in your life?

If you were given a million dollars (tax-free) tomorrow, which of your needs would you still be striving to meet? (In other words, how much human satisfaction do you think money can buy? Which of the things you need do not have a price tag? Which satisfiers could you get with money alone?)

Human interaction with the environment is necessary for the satisfaction of our physical needs as well as those which Maslow called our higher needs. The characteristically human patterns of our relationship with the world, those which impress themselves so strikingly on our environment, are the result of the flexibility and symbolic capabilities of our brains. As a species, we do much more than simply draw sustenance from the world around us; we change our world to suit us, making it a dynamic counterpart of ourselves. We create and modify our environment to a greater degree than does any other species, adapting our physical surroundings to our needs rather than abandoning them when they no longer suit us.

Man is a singular creature. He has a set of gifts which make him unique among the animals: so that, unlike them, he is not a figure in the landscape—he is a shaper of the landscape. In body and in mind he is the explorer of nature, the ubiquitous animal, who did not find but has made his home in every continent (Bronowski, 1973, p.19).

In modifying our environments, that is, in creating culture, we influence our potentials and limitations. It is with the products of social living, more than with "raw" environment, that we interact to meet our needs. Our families and other organizations, our technology, our forms of government and law, and our educational institutions—these are cultural intermediaries between humans and the natural world.

Culture influences the ways in which the needs of people are met. It sets the rhythm of daily and yearly living by which many physiological needs, such as eating and sleeping, are regulated. One culture might push us to meet the demands of a "nine-to-five" business schedule; another would allow us a break for tea or an afternoon siesta. Culture determines how we meet our safety needs. It gives us a general understanding of what to fear and when to feel safe. It eliminates certain dangers in our lives (the threat of polio, for example) but can produce others (the automobile and the possibility of destruction by nuclear weapons). Culture

Courtesy of The Amencan Museum of Natural History.

teaches us both how to control aggressions and how to kill each other. All cultures provide means for meeting belongingness and love needs, primarily through family groups. Social, political, and athletic organizations are cultural ways to belong. Esteem is culturally defined. Some cultures grant status and esteem according to family membership (who you are), others to individual achievement (what you do). Some use a mixture of both.

Cultural *differences* account for the great variety of ways in which human potentials are realized. Consider, for example, the ways culture directs us, how institutions shape our behavior. They reward us for developing in certain ways and punish us for not doing so. Don Fabun has summarized the types of reward and punishment used in our cultural institutions (see Box 3.1, p. 48). With every reward and every punishment we are nudged into particular ways of actualizing our potentials. The potentials we strive to actualize will be those which we have been led to believe in, to value, and to feel we should develop.

The opportunities and limits presented by a culture will depend on the technology, political system, state of science, arts, and values — in other words, on the spirit of the age — that characterize it. The age into which one is born will set the broad stage on which the play of life is cast. Whether one's age is that of Reason, Enlightenment, Anxiety, or Aquarius will influence the potentials an individual chooses to actualize or ignore. A particularly strong influence in recent times has been the level of technology, which has affected both the quality of our lives and the development of human potential.

. . . mass-production of automobiles has made it necessary for millions of men and women to learn the art of driving at high speed. In the process a number of hitherto latent potentialities were actualized in the trainees. Who, a bare sixty years ago, seeing Queen Victoria in her pony-drawn bathchair, could possibly have imagined that within a single lifetime ladies of comparable age and dignity would be stepping on the gas along the Pennsylvania Turnpike or cornering at fifty miles an hour on the Corniche? (Aldous Huxley, 1965, p. 37)

EXPLORATION 3.3 **Culture and Potentials**	As a class, make a list of all the things you each did yesterday which you couldn't have done in 1900. (Did you talk on the phone, drive sixty miles an hour, flush the toilet, etc.?) Discuss the impact of cultural developments, technological and other kinds, on our lives. What beliefs do we have which might limit potentials? (I grew up sharing the "knowledge" that no one could run a mile in less than four minutes, for example.)

So far we have seen that human potentials depend partly on our genetic inheritance. Some things are possible because we are human, and,

BOX 3.1

REWARD AND PUNISHMENT SYSTEMS IN OUR SOCIETY

Reward	Punishment
If you expend your energy the way we want you to,	
you'll get . . .	if you don't you'll get . . .

Business

A job	Fired
Advancement	No promotion
Salary increases	No raises
Prestige	Nonrecognition
Security	Insecurity

Religious Order

Acceptance	Nonacceptance
Participation	Excommunication
Salvation	Damnation
Heaven	Hell

Educational Institutions

Acceptance	Nonacceptance
Advancement	Nonadvancement
Graduation	Expelled
Higher degrees	No degrees
Chance for a better job	Poorer job

Political Institutions

Participation	Ineligibility
Appointment	Passed over
Elected	Defeated
Deification	Obscurity

Military

Accepted	Not accepted
Promotion	Passed over
Permanent rank	Temporary rank
Medals and honors	Court martialed
Retirement at rank	Dishon. discharge

Social and Fraternal

Acceptance	Blackballed
Exposure to others	Excluded
Committee work	Not appointed
Officer position	Not elected
Retirement banquet	Expulsion

(Fabun, 1970, p. 25)

by the same token, others are impossible. Each human inherits particular potentials, all within the range of human potentials, which will bear upon what he or she can and cannot do. Our physical and, especially, our social and cultural environments contribute both possibilities and limitations to the actualization of inherent potential. Environment may either help or hinder the development of genetic capacity. Two individuals with the same genetic inheritance (that is, identical twins), if raised in different environments, will likely show different traits, interests, and abilities:

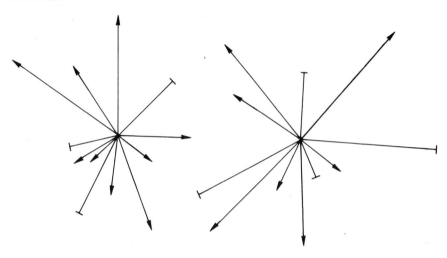

**EXPLORATION
3.4**

**Your
Potentials**

Although we can never be sure of the upper limits of our potentials, this exploration will help you know a bit more of yourself and your possibilities. We can know something of our potentials by surveying our interests, skills and talents, achievements, and activities on which we spend our resources (energy, time, and money). Think about your potentials in the following areas:

Physical (physical activities, fitness, health, sports, etc.)

Emotional expression (laughing, crying, yelling, etc.) and emotional feelings (sadness, elation, depression, anger, anxiety, worry, etc.)

Intellectual (learning abilities, thinking, decision-making, planning ahead, knowledge of the world in general, special knowledge of your personal world, etc.)

Interpersonal/social (living and working with others, social interactions, social skills, family life, friendships, etc.)

Special and creative abilities (mechanical, artistic, musical, foreign languages, particular job skills, etc.)

Other (spiritual, extrasensory perception, meditation, etc.)

Jot down things which are important to you in each area. Many activities will overlap as you think about all the potentials involved. (For example, your abilities in expressing anger toward a friend are both emotional and interpersonal.) These areas are just suggestions to get you started thinking about the variety of your potentials, so it isn't important to stick closely to the list.

When you have done a pretty thorough inventory, use the following figure to make a Model of You. Suppose the center dot is where you began life and the outer ring is at the end of your life. Draw in an arrow for each potential you wish represented, indicating, by the length of the line, how far you feel you have realized or actualized the potential in your life so far. Use an arrowhead on those potentials you are still developing, a flat tip on dormant potentials.

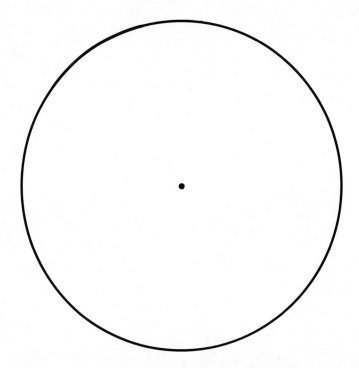

Play around with this model, adding things as they come to mind. Remember, each arrow is independent of every other; the length is relative to your own life, not to someone else's or to what someone else has told you about yourself.

PERSON/ENVIRONMENT/TIME

In the arrow model on page 40, you saw that potentials change considerably between birth and college age. From this we should expect further changes by middle age. Time is important in determining the number and kind of human potentials.

Changes in potentials result from changes over time in both people and their environment. An individual's physical maturation follows a schedule set by human genetics. The environment—the society in which a person lives—influences development by making demands and providing possibilities. These demands and possibilities differ at successive stages of human development, though people living in the same culture tend to develop according to similar patterns.

A scheme for looking more closely at the timing or stages of human development is that of Erik Erikson (1963, 1968). The groundplan of life, Erikson believes, unfolds in eight stages. Each stage is characterized by a developmental problem (a psychosocial crisis) that is the focus of the most important interactions between the individual and his or her environment. The outcome of these interactions is a balance between the positive and negative experiences we have while meeting our problems. Given a reasonable environment, our potential for positive development enables us to maintain a positive balance in the long run. No problem will ever be solved once and for all, but each stage does prepare us for the next.

Each of the eight stages, outlined below, is defined by a positive outcome versus a negative outcome, and by the age range within which it occurs.

psychosocial crisis

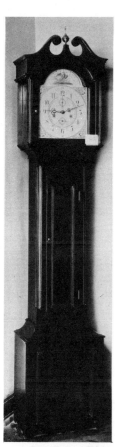

Seth Thomas Clocks.

Trust vs. Mistrust	First year
Autonomy vs. Doubt and Shame	Second and third years
Initiative vs. Guilt	Preschool age
Industry vs. Inferiority	Early school age
Identity vs. Role Confusion	Adolescence
Intimacy vs. Isolation	Young Adulthood
Generativity vs. Self-absorption or Stagnation	Middle Age
Integrity vs. Despair	Old Age

Trust vs. Mistrust

At birth the trustworthy protection of the womb is gone. Since a baby is not able to meet its own demands and has few communication skills, satisfaction must be supplied by others. The degree to which an infant can trust those who care for it depends on the quality and consistency of love from its caretakers. If they are inconsistent, inadequate, or rejecting, mistrust will be the outcome. Erikson feels that the ratio of trust to mistrust during this stage will characterize all later relationships.

Autonomy vs. Doubt and Shame

Although still relatively dependent, a child of two and three is able to walk, climb, hold onto things, let go of things, pull and tug—all skills which contribute to the sense of being able to "do it myself." Toilet and

Courtesy of The Farm.

bowel training is the area in which the child learns to regulate his body according to social conventions. If the child lacks self-control, he will develop a sense of shame and a sense of doubt.

A sense of autonomy comes from the ability to control oneself and to approve of oneself. Compliance or, sometimes, stubbornness accompany feelings of doubt and shame. Lifelong tendencies toward either self-assurance or self-doubt emerge as the resolution of this stage.

Initiative vs. Guilt

Preschool children are capable of devising their own ways of playing, their own rules, their own sentences and ideas. They can initiate their own behavior. Self-initiated behavior calls for judgements and entails risks. A child must make some decisions: Is this behavior correct or incorrect? Will I be praised for my accomplishments or scolded for my mistakes? Being incorrect, making mistakes, and being punished bring about guilt—the feeling that one shouldn't have done what one did. An overwhelming sense of guilt can inhibit activity. The balance at this stage is between acting in spite of risks versus inhibition or guilt.

Industry vs. Inferiority

The school-age child is concerned with how things work, what the rules are, and with making things. Activities now take on more clearly defined objectives. School provides the technical materials and knowledge that allow the child to be industrious, to build. Teachers, as well as parents, now encourage work, reward a task well done, and downgrade a job poorly done. The child can develop a sense of being able to work—of mastery and accomplishment—or a sense of being inferior. The critical ratio at this state is between a sense of accomplishment and a sense of inadequacy.

Identity vs. Role Confusion

This is the period during which an individual attempts to integrate self-images with the images others have of him or her. Who he or she is, has been, and will be are pulled together into a self-picture that makes sense. Identity, according to Erikson, includes at least three areas of self-concept. One is sexual. The adolescent must cope with a new, adult body and adult sexual urges, and must meet adult sex-role requirements. Another is vocational. By adolescence one begins to ask "What am I going to be when I grow up?" A third area is a search for social values by which to guide one's life. Failure to form an identity results in a sense of confusion about who one is. The outcome of this stage is a balance between a sense of identity and a confusion of roles.

Intimacy vs. Isolation

Erikson defines intimacy as "the capacity to commit [oneself] to concrete affiliations and partnerships and to develop the ethical strength to abide by such commitments, even though they may call for significant sacrifices and compromises." (1963, p. 263) Intimacy may develop between both opposite-sex and same-sex partners. It presumes the ability to share with and care for another person without losing one's identity in

National Education Association Publishing, Joe Di Dio.

the process. When intimacy is not achieved, a person is subject to a sense of isolation. The outcome is a balance between commitment and the sense of being alone, without anyone to care or to care for.

Generativity vs. Self-absorption or Stagnation

Generativity, which continues through middle age, is the concern for creation and with making this a better world for the next generation. A person is now able to be concerned with conditions beyond his or her own development and immediate family. Generativity is an aspect of parenthood, but is also a problem for nonparent adults who are active in improving the world. Failure to give one's energy toward creating better conditions results in a state of stagnant self-concern. The outcome of this adult stage rests between a sense of contribution (or creation) and stagnation.

Integrity vs. Despair

Old age is the time for reflection. It is a time to survey the past and to integrate all that has passed in a lifetime. Integrity is "... the acceptance of one's one and only life cycle as something that had to be and that, by necessity, permitted of no substitutions . . . " (Erikson, 1963, p. 268). A lack of integration in old age is signified by a fear of death. "Despair expresses the feeling that the time is now short, too short for the attempt to start another life, and to try out alternate roads to integrity." (1963, p. 269)

A ground plan of human development underlies the actualization of our potentials. Our biological maturation takes place in a culture—which makes demands on us and permits us certain ways of developing—according to our level of maturity. Our inherent potential for reading, for example, must mature before we are physically and psychologically able to read. Our culture must then provide us with books, instruction, and an expectation that we will develop this potential.

Erik Erikson sees the interactions between maturity and culture as stages of growth, each defined by a problem. We never solve these once and for all, but at each stage in our lives we add to our personal histories the outcome of our encounter with a previous problem. This history is unbroken throughout our lives, making it possible to continuously actualize our potentials.

**EXPLORATION
3.5
Crises**

On each of the lines below, place an "X" where you feel you are right now in your life. Remember that each line represents a crisis we meet time and again in our lives. Autonomy, for instance, is a quality which we achieve over and over, though it is a dominant concern in our preschool years.

Mistrust _____ Trust

Doubt and Shame _____ Autonomy

Guilt _____ Initiative

Inferiority _____ Industry

Role Confusion _____ Identity

Isolation _____ Intimacy

Stagnation _____ Generativity

Despair _____ Integrity

Which of these crises is (are) most important in your life right now? How do you know? How do the problems you are currently working with in your life relate to these stages?

SUMMARY

1. Potentials are our capacities for growth and development. Certain potentials are ours because we are human; each human will actualize his or her unique potentials.
2. The environments within which we live influence the actualization of our potentials. We interact with environments to fulfill our needs: physiological, safety, belongingness and love, esteem. According to Abraham Maslow our highest needs are growth needs.
3. Humans have the capacity to create and modify environments, to build culture. Culture in turn presents us with opportunities and limits for the actualization of potentials.
4. Human potentials are shaped and actualized throughout life. Our development through time is represented in Erik Erikson's eight stages of man.

Suggested Readings

Ardrey, Robert. *The territorial imperative.* New York: Antheneum, 1966. The author argues, persuasively if not rigorously, that much of human social behavior is similar to that of lower animals.

Erikson, Erik. *Childhood and society* (1950). (2d ed.) New York: Norton, 1963. A classic presentation of Erikson's psychosocial theory of development, including interesting case studies and cross-cultural material.

Kinget, G. Marian. *On being human: A systematic view.* New York: Harcourt, 1975. A comprehensive answer to the question: What is human about human beings?

Maslow, Abraham. *Motivation and personality.* (2d ed.) New York: Harper & Row, 1970. Maslow's theory of human motivation and his study of self-actualizing people; *The further reaches of human nature.* New York: Viking, 1971. A synthesis of Maslow's ideas on biology, creativity, thinking, needs, and the role of science in the study of human nature.

Montagu, Ashley. *Man and aggression.* (2d ed.) New York: Oxford, 1973. A collection of arguments against the concept of innate human aggressiveness.

Murphy, Gardner. *Human potentialities.* New York: Basic Books, 1958. An optimistic exploration of human possibilities: human nature is not determined solely by biological makeup nor bound by cultural inheritance.

White, Robert W. *Lives in progress.* (3d ed.) New York: Holt, Rinehart and Winston, 1975. An intensive and illuminating psychological study of the lives of three individuals from childhood to their fifties.

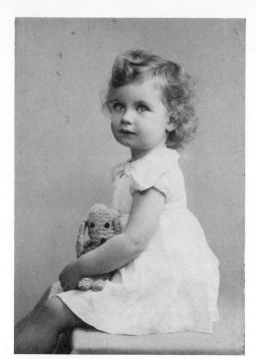

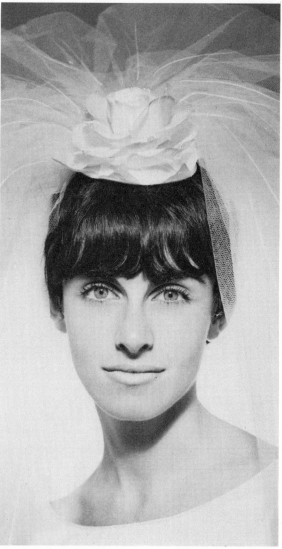

Courtesy of C. Hamilton.

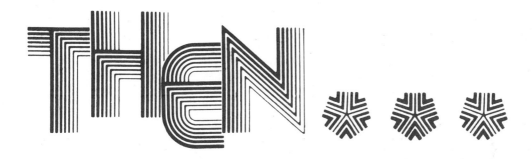

THEN · · ·

I was a baby and I was a child. Now I'm grown up. My babyhood and my childhood were important: they contributed to who I am today. What I am now includes what I was. I wouldn't be exactly as I am now without exactly the past I had.

The conditions and situations of my past are gone. I cannot live my life over again. But the past is not entirely gone. Much of it exists in the present as memories. Even those experiences that I can't remember are stored in me. No doubt some memories have been distorted in my brain's storehouse, squeezed or stretched to fit in alongside others. Some are beyond my reach, stored so far back that I'll never get to them. Some are hidden purposely because it would pain me to see them. Many are deep enough that recovering them will take a lot of work. But all of my past is a part of my present.

How can we profit from looking over a past that cannot be changed and that is sometimes inaccurately remembered?

We can examine the choices we have made, and the paths we have traveled as a result of those choices, learning better where we are now by discovering what has led us here. Such an examination was made by the poet Robert Frost in "The Road Not Taken":

Two roads diverged in a yellow wood,
And sorry I could not travel both
And be one traveler, long I stood
And looked down one as far as I could
To where it bent in the undergrowth;

Then took the other, as just as fair,
And having perhaps the better claim,
And because it was grassy and wanted wear;
Though as for that, the passing there
Had worn them really about the same,

And both that morning equally lay
In leaves no step had trodden black.
Oh, I kept the first for another day!
Yet knowing how way leads on to way,
I doubted if I should ever come back.

I shall be telling this with a sigh
Somewhere ages and ages hence:
Two roads diverged in a wood, and I—
I took the one less traveled by,
And that has made all the difference.

We can better know present habits and patterns of behavior by looking for them in our past. We can discover where we have acted automatically and missed a chance to actualize our potentials. We can also appreciate how we have contributed to our growth.

We can look for undeveloped potentials. Which have we left partly done or barely begun as we concentrated on others? Are there potentials that we wish to develop further? The answers are best discovered by an examination of the past.

We can sometimes come to an understanding of why we remember the past as we do. We can learn its meaning and importance to us, how it stands in our thoughts.

It is possible to hang onto the past so desperately that we cannot grasp the present. We can dwell on our "If only's": If only I could return to those carefree days of childhood. If only my parents had done a better job. If only I had done this instead of that. If only. . . . We are hanging onto the past when we resent and regret it. We can also avoid the past. When we do, for whatever reason, it is not useful for making changes today.

Looking back over our early years allows us to know that we are adults. We can find the business we have left undone and take the opportunity to finish it. Most unfinished business remains as persistent bad feelings, unsettled scores, and unspoken words—relationships we have not changed. For many of us it is our relationships with our parents that must be changed before we can really grow up. The founder of Gestalt Therapy, Fritz Perls, said it this way: "You can always blame the parents . . . and make parents responsible for all your problems. Until you are willing to let go of your parents, you continue to conceive of yourself as a child." (1969, p. 42)

It is often fun to recall old times, the times of childhood and youth and happiness. And it is sometimes unpleasant to look back; life was not always what we would have wanted it to be. But only when we see it can we know and accept: that's the way it was.

Courtesy of Sarah Cirese.

4

BEGINNING THE QUESTS

This chapter is a guide to our earliest years, those before we start school at about age six. During this period our parents and family are primary influences at a time when we are most susceptible to influence. Every theory of human development emphasizes the importance of infancy and early childhood for later development. Freudian theory, especially, pays attention to early conflicts and their resolution, holding as it does that our later life is determined by events occurring in these first years. Later events also contribute to our growth, but there is never again such a short time during which we will learn so much.

This period of life is the most inaccessible to most of us, the hardest to recall accurately. Some of it occurred before we could speak, much of it while we had only an imperfect grasp of symbols. But because psychological knowledge of the first six years is great, by trying to piece them together we can learn much. Humans show great similarity, and vary within a narrower range of differences, at this time than at any other in their life cycle. It is therefore easier to make accurate generalizations about childhood, our own and others', than it is about later periods. Even if our own memories fail us, a search through these years turns up milestones for our understanding of how quests are begun. Milestones in the first six years are:

- separation from the womb at birth, dependency on our caretakers, fears of becoming too separate
- the importance of close human contact during early life, the effects of losing contact or fearing that we will
- gender identity and learning to act according to it
- sex education at home through seeing, hearing, and assuming
- development from helpless beginnings to the rapid mastery of many tasks
- starting from our naive experience of life; the changes we go through in learning to grow up

SEPARATENESS AND WHOLENESS

Each of us begins to live separately at the moment of birth, from the instant the umbilical cord is severed. Never, from this moment onward, will we regain the closeness to another human being that we enjoyed in the womb. In there we were cared for perfectly, without reservation. Unless our mothers introduced poisons into our shared systems, we were safe. As long as she didn't take a severe fall, we would not be hurt. Nothing to worry about, nothing to do, except to give a kick now and then when we became restless or uncomfortable. From this point of view, it is not surprising that some doctors and psychiatrists think of birth as a shock to infants.

Shock or not, we become *psychologically aware* of our separateness only gradually. In the beginning we are not able to distinguish the boundaries between Me and Not-me. The sounds, sights, odors, and tastes of our earliest days *are* ourselves; they are variations on the general delight and distress that constitute our infant universe. But slowly we begin to separate ourselves from the blur of sensations in which we have been swirling.

It takes months—some would say years—for us to understand that other people, our caretakers in particular, are separate from us. For although we are physically separate, we are still dependent on others to provide for our physical needs. In order to stay alive long enough to become functionally separate, human infants must be kept warm, fed, and given attention. They are not equipped for solitary survival from the start, as many lower animals are. This prolonged dependence, together with a developing sense of separateness, leads to a phase of development, around the age of one, known as "separation anxiety."

Jimmy's mother started back to work when he was six months old. At first there was no problem at all; the sitter reported that Jimmy was a good and contented baby. Within a few months however, Jimmy began to protest loudly when Mama left for work. He began crying the minute she left and no amount of reassurance could placate him. He acted as though he was afraid that he would never see her again. After a couple of months of daily anguish for Jimmy (and much guilt for his mother) he ceased becoming so upset. He was now old enough to realize that Mama did, indeed, come back every evening.

Defenses

The emotional ties between us and those on whom we depend seem as vulnerable as our umbilical cords proved to be. Our earliest fears are that these psychological attachments will be severed. To escape these fears about being abandoned or rejected, we devise *coping* or *defense mechanisms* (see Chapter 2). Our defense mechanisms distort reality to suit us, and that distortion sometimes includes ourselves. As children we use the same devices that adults use, although we are less sophisticated in their application. Those defenses that work well for us will likely be the ones we carry into adulthood; patterns of coping are laid down very early. Here are some examples of preschool defense mechanisms:

Denial   This is the process of denying or trying to deny a reality. It is often called a primitive defense mechanism because, although it may seem to work for a child, it is a weak defense for adults.

"I did not spill the milk," says Suzy, looking down into the puddle on the floor as if it had spilled itself.

"The glass just broke all by itself, Mommy."

"I stayed dry all night," says Tommy, hoping that his words will blind his mother to the wet bed.

"You aren't my *real* mommy," Joan rages. "My real mommy would always love me and never spank me!" Somewhere out in the wide world there is an ever-patient, always-loving *real* mother to whom Joan can turn in fantasy.

projection

Projection This is attributing our actions or thoughts to someone else. In projecting we stop keeping our selves separate when it is more to our advantage to create another the culprit:

"But, Daddy, *he* started the fight," says Danny, while his brother Tim insists "He was fighting with me," each arguing that all the fault belongs to the other child.

A favorite projection of my children was, "You *made* me lose it!"

Projection is a means to avoid blame:
  "You did it."
  "She did it."
  "They did it."
  but never "I did it."

Some children make up imaginary playmates who, in addition to acting as companions, are available to take the blame for misdoings and mischief. Debby, for example, was an only child. Her "friend" Katy often joined the family for lunch. It was Katy who always left the crumbs, sneaked an extra cookie, spilled the juice. Katy also wrote on the walls, misplaced Debby's things, and, one day, was naughty enough to pull all the stuffing out of Debby's Raggedy Ann.

withdrawal

Withdrawal Psychologically or physically removing oneself from a threatening or demanding situation is a mechanism which underlines our separateness.

Three-year-old Kevin's parents began to worry that he might be partially deaf,

Courtesy of the National Park Service.

until they realized that what he couldn't hear were messages such as "Time for bed now," "Clean up your toys before lunch," "Turn off the TV." He chose to tune out what he didn't *want* to hear.

When a child has experienced anxiety or pain in a situation he may refuse to repeat any part of the situation. No amount of coaxing could entice Laurie into the swimming pool after some older children had splashed water into her face.

Some children withdraw into fantasies, finding the world they create less hostile than their real worlds.

Regression   This is a common form of defense against the anxieties of growing up. A child may revert to baby talk, thumb sucking, and bed wetting if the demands of being a big boy or a big girl seem too heavy, or if a new baby in the home seems to be getting all the attention. Regression is a form of rebellion against the pressures of being autonomous, an unconscious wish, perhaps, to return to the safe, warm environment of the womb.

Separateness and Culture

By the age of six, children have taken enormous strides toward autonomy. They are still in the care of parents and in need of their support, but they have already gained a fundamental sense of separateness. The following passage suggests how the influence of parental attitudes affects this process and how parental attitudes themselves differ across cultures.

. . . differences in maternal behavior seem to derive from different philosophies, or attitudes, about the infant. The American mother believes that her child is basically passive, and it is her job to mold him—to make him into an active, independent child. As a result, she feels she must stimulate him. The Japanese mother believes her infant is basically independent and active and it is her job to soothe him and make him dependent upon her and the family. . . . One could not ask for a clearer example of the importance of cultural attitudes on the rearing practices of the mother, and subsequently, on the behavior of the infant and older child (Mussen, Conger, and Kagan, 1974, p. 226).

In general, parents in the United States set out early to prepare the child for an independent existence. Mothers and fathers who don't do so, who are overly protective, are criticized for "spoiling" their children.

Becoming separate from our parents or caretakers is the first step toward achieving the inner integration toward which we will move for the rest of our lives. This separation begins as we undertake our own activities, develop tastes and preferences of our own, display "our own minds," and give up at least a portion of the tight emotional dependency of babyhood. In order to keep growing from this stage we must learn to deal with our fears of being alone, abandoned, rejected. To be human is to be alone, and to know that we are. Fears of that aloneness, and tolerance for it, will, in a balance unique to each of us, influence the ways in which we grow as individuals.

EXPLORATION
4.1

Aloneness

Can you recall *ever* being alone as a very young child (in a car, lost in a crowded store, with a new baby sitter)? Try to recreate this experience in your mind, summoning up the feelings that accompanied it. When you have imagined yourself alone or lost, next try to relax, telling yourself not to panic, that you are safe, that you *can* wait without crying until your parents return.

What was your family's attitude toward independence?
  Did you eat all your meals together?
  Work on individual projects?
  Take your vacations and play together?

Do you recall being lonely as a child?
  What were the circumstances?

If you were an only child, how did you feel about it?
  Special? Neglected? Lonely? Bored?

If you had a large family, did you have privacy?
  Were there opportunities for quiet and solitude amidst your brothers and sisters?

Did you ever think you were adopted?
  What were your make-believe parents like?
  If you were indeed adopted, what were your thoughts or fantasies about your real parents?

Do you use any of the defense mechanisms mentioned in this chapter?

Do you ever deny something in order to get off the hook?

How often do you blame others for your failures?

Do you ever expect or want others to do something for you and then become angry or depressed because they aren't what you expect them to be?

Is one of your responses to frustration to withdraw? How easily can you give up or retreat in the face of a threatening situation?

Do you fall back on childlike responses (crying, tantrums, name-calling) when you feel threatened?

Are any of these patterns habitual for you, that is, do you feel you have always been like this?

INTIMACY

Both Erikson and Maslow recognize the importance of the human love-bond. According to Erikson our very first task in life is to develop a trusting relationship with our caretakers. Maslow considers our needs for security and belongingness as second only to biological survival. An ex-contact comfort

perimental psychologist (Harlow, 1959, 1966) has found that monkeys, in order to develop normally, require the security of physical contact with a soft, furry mother monkey, or at least a fuzzy mother-substitute. This same contact comfort is important for human babies as well. An infant craves touching, holding, cuddling—contact with another warm, human body.

During our first two years of life we become attached to those who care for us. We are comfortable, secure, and happy in the presence of these special people, and easily distinguish them from others. Even by the second six months of life we are highly discriminating.

The child at 8 months is sitting in his high chair, playing with his cereal. A strange woman enters the kitchen and stands facing the baby. The infant studies the stranger for 10 seconds; his face tightens, and suddenly he begins to cry. It is clear that the stranger has elicited the cry, for if the stranger leaves the child becomes happy again. If the stranger reappears, it is likely that the child will cry again (Mussen, Conger, and Kagan, 1974, p. 208).

stranger anxiety

Stranger anxiety, as this fear is called, is well known by pediatricians, who seem to evoke terror in their infant patients. It can happen even to fathers. My father traveled a great deal during my brother's first half year and was greeted with shrieks of fright whenever he returned. This normal expression of anxiety gradually disappears during the second year, much to the relief of doctors, fathers, and children themselves. The ability to form strong attachments to familiar, reliable caretakers is the first stage of human love relationships.

Love and Children

symbiotic

Human relationships are symbiotic, that is, mutual and interdependent, each party giving and each taking. Parent/child relationships are no exception, although parents hold the burden of responsibility. Parents must care for and nourish their dependents, both physically and psychologically. Parents are nourished in return by a caring relationship with a child. They are rewarded by the knowledge of being important to the child and in the pleasure of receiving love from him or her. The baby's quiet gurgle and instant smile help sustain the relationship. But the larger stream in this two-way flow of love is unquestionably toward the child, whose needs for love require satisfaction regardless of the parent's ability to give it.

Infants are like sponges, soaking up affection. It is hard to imagine their becoming saturated. On the other hand, it is possible for a child to receive too little attention and human affection. Infants placed in foundling homes where they are physically cared for but not given parental affection can become socially and physically retarded.

The institutionalized babies vocalized very little; they showed no cooing, no babbling, and little crying. Moreover, they did not adapt their postures to the

Michael Weisbrot

arms of an adult, "they felt something like sawdust dolls; they moved, they bent easily at the proper joints, but they felt stiff or wooden." (Quote from Provence, *Infants in Institutions.*) (Mussen, Conger, and Kagan, 1974, p. 219).

It is a testimony to the human potential for growth-through-love that these deprived infants recover when their environment is changed to one in which they can secure adequate tender, loving care. We have a re-markable ability to recover from early lack of love, as long as it is not prolonged or severe.

Occasionally we read of parents who, unable to cope with parenting, batter or otherwise abuse their children. These parents, it turns out, are in many cases past victims of child abuse themselves. They come to take their rage and frustration out on their children.

. . . a young mother, pregnant with her second child, remembers lying in bed around 2:00 a.m. listening to the baby cry in the next room. She recalls a feeling of hate at that moment for the child, who woke her out of a sound sleep. It had been a long day of frustrations. She felt negative feelings begin to build up. She went to the kitchen and heated a bottle of milk in a pan of boiling water. She then set the bottle aside, took the pan of scalding hot water, stood over the crib, and poured the water over the baby. The father got out of bed and found the baby writhing in the crib and the mother standing by, pan in hand, expressionless, eyes blank (Wheeler, 1972).

Love and Punishment

We all have many things to learn as children — how to be responsible, how to do the right things, how not to do wrong things. A technique used by some parents is to threaten to withhold their love unless their

Michael Weisbrot

children act in the correct ways. Love is used in a kind of barter: "I will love you as long as you behave; I won't love you if you misbehave."

"Mommy loves you when you close the door."

"Daddy won't love you if you poke that dog."

"If you loved Mommy, you wouldn't have lost your shoe."

"How could you do that when you know how much I love you?"

"You just don't care about me at all."

Threatening to withdraw love is an effective tool in molding a child's behavior. It is also as likely to make a child dependent as it is to make him compliant. Suppose this kind of parent/child relationship becomes the model for a child's later relationships. He may grow into the adult who is ever fearful of losing a friend's or partner's love unless he acts in accordance with the friend's wishes.

Brothers and Sisters

Many of us have intimate relationships with others in our families besides our parents: our siblings. The nature of sibling relationships depends somewhat on the number of children in the family and the rank one holds in the birth order. When siblings are born close together they have opportunities to spend a great deal of time together, to share experiences, and to share the love of their parents. It is this last which can be a trying experience for the first-born, who is used to undivided attention.

I can recall clearly the day my parents brought home my infant brother in a basket. He was wonderful, lying there sound asleep. I wanted to wake him and give him some of my favorite food, spinach. The next memory I have is of scurrying around the house, grabbing everything I could which belonged to him — rattles, clothes, diapers, bottles — and stuffing it all into a paper bag. I took the bag to my mother and said, "OK. It's time to take him back!" It hadn't taken me long to realize that sisterhood was not all bliss.

Jealousy, rivalry, envy, and hostility in interpersonal relationships

are experienced very early in life. The relationship patterns we develop
with other children in the family can teach us ways of handling hostility
which will be helpful, or harmful, in later relationships. One psychologist (Toman, 1970) theorizes that adult relationships may duplicate the
ones we have had with brothers and sisters.

Suppose that the *older brother of a sister* marries the *younger sister of a brother*.
They are getting in marriage precisely the peer relation that they had at home.
He is used to a girl his junior, and she to a boy her senior. Hence there should be
no conflict over their dominance rights. And both of them are used to the other
sex, so they should have no great sex conflicts either. If this fellow had married
an oldest sister of sisters, however, he could have expected some problems. Both
partners would expect to have seniority rights and each one would try to rule the
other. In addition, the wife would have had little experience in getting along
with men (Toman, 1970, p. 45).

**EXPLORATION
4.2

Family
Relationships**

Were you an important person in your mother's and father's lives?

Did you have a special friendship with either or both of them?

Were you too close, required to make up for the lack of adult affection in your
parents' lives?

Did your parents tell you that they loved you?
   That they didn't love you? Hated you?

Do you feel that you were abused as a child? How?

Did your parents accept you unconditionally or did you have to be good to
win approval?

Were you jealous of your brothers or sisters?
   Very much so?
   Did you feel that they were loved more than you?

Did you learn to fear and avoid strangers?
   How? Why?

Do you feel critical about nurturing and taking care of others?
   When?
   Do you do it anyway? Why or why not?

Do you ever feel protective, responsible, parental in a relationship?
   Under what conditions?

What messages did you get about marriage?
   What was the content of those which showed reservations?
   Did your parents assume that you would marry?

Were your parents good friends?

What did you get from them (or other adult models) about how intimate
partners should behave toward each other?

What do you think of Toman's hypothesis?
   Does it agree with your experience or that of people you know?

SEXUAL PERSPECTIVE

We come into the world equipped to experience pleasure. From the beginning we can distinguish between those sensations and situations that are pleasant and those which are distressing or uncomfortable. This ability is the cornerstone of our sexual lives; on it we build our potentials for sensual pleasure.

By accident, at first, a baby discovers the physical delights of sucking its thumb or fondling its genitals. With experience, the infant learns to deliberately seek these pleasures and to find the means to others: being cuddled, stroked, and touched; tasting the warm smoothness of milk; sucking, biting, and licking. It learns to take an active part in its own sensual satisfaction.

But an infant's sexuality is not an adult's. A baby rubs its genitals without the mature self-awareness that will accompany masturbation at fifteen. Sensual pleasure does not yet carry for the infant a full charge of sexual significance, in either physical or emotional terms.

Starting To Learn

This sexual significance begins to take shape as soon as we are able to listen, to watch, and to relate with others. Parents' attitudes about nudity, how they touch and treat each other, and their unspoken feelings are perceived by children long before they hear anything about "the birds and the bees." Observing the behavior of our parents and others around us, we gradually put together a picture of the world in which sex occupies a just and delightful place or in which it is considered an evil intruder to be looked on with distaste if not denied altogether.

The greatest form of sex education is Pop walking past Mom in the kitchen and patting her on the fanny and Mom obviously liking it. The kids take a good look at this action and think, "Boy, that's for me." (William Masters, in M. H. Hall, *Psychology Today*, July 1969, p. 57)

Language overlays a child's natural capacity for sensual pleasure. Words can clarify a child's understanding of his sexuality or they can cloud it. Out of ignorance, embarrassment, or a felt desire to protect their daughter, parents may deny her the correct (scientific) names for her anatomy—vagina, clitoris, breasts. Their son may learn his attitudes in words that carry degrading connotations: dick, pussy, screwing, knocking up. It is not always easy for a parent or a child to find the right words, and often we just avoid the effort, as is illustrated in the women's health book *Our Bodies Our Selves:*

When I was six years old I climbed up on the bathroom sink and looked at myself naked in the mirror. All of a sudden I realized I had three different holes. I was

very excited about my discovery and ran down to the dinner table and announced it to everyone. "I have three holes!" Silence. "What are they for?" I
asked. Silence, even heavier than before. I sensed how uncomfortable everyone
was and answered for myself. "I guess one is for pee-pee, the other for doo-doo
and the third for ca-ca." A sigh of relief; no one had to answer my question. But I
got the message—I wasn't supposed to ask "such" questions, though I didn't
fully realize what "such" was about at that time (The Boston Women's Health
Book Collective, 1973, pp. 31–32).

Some Things Get Mixed Up, Others Become Clear

During toilet training the messages we receive about elimination become involved with our sexual learning. The organs "down there," between our legs, are a source of pleasurable sensation when we urinate
and have bowel movements. These pleasures are subject to increasing
demands for control. We must learn to postpone bodily urges until we
are in the right circumstances (on the potty, not in bed or on the carpet).
In learning to control ourselves we come easily to think of the genital
area as "messy," "dirty," and "nasty." We may even confuse our products with the parts that produce them:

Jay, aged two years nine months, had for several days suffered from fecal reten-
tion, and accepted the toilet only with much coaxing. Once seated he peered between his legs, pointed to his testicles, and told his mother, earnestly, "Those are
mine; I *need* them." His mother, sensing he was telling her something about his
reluctance to use the toilet, assured him that only his bowel movements dropped
in the toilet—not his testicles. Appearing relieved, he passed a bowel movement
(Rothchild, 1973, p. 7).

About the time we are learning to control elimination, we begin to
learn that we are not entirely free to touch our own genitals whenever
we wish to. We learn that it is unacceptable in this culture to masturbate,
at least publicly. One parent might slap her child's hand with a sharp
"Don't ever do that again!" Another parent will try to teach her child that
he can play with his penis at home, in his bedroom, but not when
Grandma is visiting, and definitely not when they are out shopping. Still
another will try to distract the child with another activity whenever she
puts her hands between her legs. Before we enter school we have all
learned, either directly or indirectly, that the exploration of our own bodies must be done discreetly, if we still have the courage to do it at all.

Where Do Babies Come From?

Among the thousands of questions children ask, there are always many
about how babies get started, where they come from, and how they get
out. Although parents sometimes try to hide their embarrassment or lack
of knowledge in stories about the stork, finding babies at the hospital,

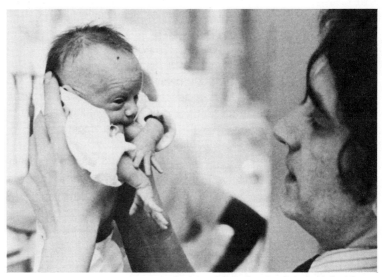

Courtesy of Columbia—Presbyterian Medical Center.

the supermarket, in the doctor's bag, under a giant toadstool, or in mail-order catalogues, such fables are not easy for children to swallow.

Most children make many guesses about their mothers' and fathers' roles in reproduction, trying to make sense of what they have been told and what they know of life. "One bright child explained, 'Good babies start from good food. They grow in mommy's stomach and pop out from her belly button. Bad babies start from bad food. They come out from the B.M. place.' " (Ginott, 1965, pp. 185–186) Another writer tells of a boy who was taken to a farm when his mother was due to give birth to another child. Upon his return he said, "Look, Daddy, I know everything, but just tell me, did Mommy go to the bull, or did the bull come to Mommy?" (Balint, 1954, p. 97)

EXPLORATION
4.3
Sexuality

Recall your family's words for sexual anatomy.
    Were expressions such as "dee-dee," "thing," "down there" used?
    What were the words used for elimination?

Were you encouraged to ask questions about sex?
    Discouraged?
    Do you remember any specific responses?

Can you recall your parents explaining reproduction to you?
    Did your mother tell you about pregnancy or nursing?
    What did you learn from your father about "the birds and the bees?"

What messages did you get about touching your genitals?

What about sex play with other children?
    Were the messages specific or general?

Can you remember any time when, in trying to figure things out for yourself, you came up with wrong answers about reproduction or other aspects of sexuality?

Your parents' sexuality:

Did they ever display physical affection in front of you?

Were you aware that they made love?

Did they seem confortable with their bodies, appear in the nude easily?

Did you ever see them making love? What was your reaction?

If you were the child of a single parent, what do you remember of her (or his) sex life?

Was it open, hidden, a source of conflict?

Are you aware of judging areas of sexuality (masturbation, nudity, intercourse, etc.) according to parental messages that you have made your own?

Can you be specific?

MALE/FEMALE

"It's a Girl!!" . . .	"It's a Boy!!" . . .
her, she, hers	him, he, his
pink	blue

Sugar and spice, and every-
    thing nice
	Frogs and snails and puppy-
	    dog tails

dainty, cute, sweet	athletic, muscular, rough
dresses, blouses, bonnets	overalls, shirts, caps
dolls, doll houses	tinker toys, guns
clean	dirty
lace and ruffles	T-shirts and jeans
Little Miss Muffet	Little Jack Horner
Sat on a tuffet,	Sat in a corner,
Eating her curds and whey;	Eating a Christmas pie;
Along came a spider,	He put in his thumb,
And sat down beside her,	And pulled out a plum
And frightened Miss Muffet	And said, "What a good boy
away.	am I!"
tomboy	sissy
Barbie	Ken
weak, dumb, passive	strong, smart, active
quiet, demure	noisy, courageous
sit to pee	stand to pee
cross your legs and sit still	adventure and discover the world
Snow White, Sleeping Beauty	Prince, Knight in Shining Armor
cry	fight
cling, whine	bully, brave
stay home	roam
Cinderella, Cinderella	Goosey, Goosey Gander
Dressed in yella	Whither shall I wander?
Went upstairs	Upstairs and downstairs,
To find a fella	And in my lady's chamber
dependent	independent
Olive Oyl, Blondie, Betty	Popeye, Dagwood, Fred
"Daddy's little girl"	"Mommy's big boy"

Each of us must have received many messages, every day of our childhood, reminding us that we were female or male. Researchers in the area of gender identity (Money and Ehrhardt, 1973) feel that by the age of *eighteen months* we already have a solid, well-established, and unchangeable notion of which sex we are. By this time our brains have been indelibly stamped, as it were, "I-am-girl-not-boy" or "I-am-boy-not-girl." From this age onward, at the core of our personality, we retain a female or male code.

As soon as parents see their baby's genitals, they may begin to think of, and to treat, their child in a sex-stereotyped manner. Activities, names, pronouns, toys, expectations, dreams — all are often chosen by a single criterion: external genitalia. Although cultures differ somewhat in the content of female/male distinctions, every culture includes a set of male expectations for boys and a set of female expectations for girls.

Since the core of our gender identity is set so very early — even before we are able to utter a complete sentence — and since there are obvious physical differences between girls and boys, and many differing expectations, we should find female and male children behaving very differently. But we don't. Two psychologists (Maccoby and Jacklin, 1974a) have recently reviewed virtually all published research on psychological differences between girls and boys. They reviewed studies of many variables, including social responsiveness, suggestibility, self-esteem, motivation to achieve, styles of learning, analytical, verbal, visual-spatial, and mathematical abilities, and aggressiveness. Of all these qualities, only one has been systematically found to differentiate preschool boys from girls: aggression.

Boys are more aggressive physically and verbally. They engage in mock-fighting and aggressive fantasies as well as direct forms of aggression more frequently than girls. The sex difference manifests itself as soon as social play begins, at age two or two and a half. From an early age, the primary victims of male aggression are other males, not females (Maccoby and Jacklin, 1974b, p. 110)

Boys and girls are more alike than they are different in early childhood. The differences parents notice between their female and male children are usually the result of the parents' expectations and beliefs about differences. We tend to believe that little girls are more sensitive, fearful, timid, anxious, compliant, maternal, and passive than little boys, and that boys are more competitive and dominant than girls. Yet none of these traits has been objectively established as an inherent girl/boy difference.

We must conclude from our survey of all the data that many popular beliefs about the psychological characteristics of the two sexes have little or no basis in fact. Yet people continue to believe, for example, that girls are more "social" than boys, or are more suggestible than boys, ignoring the fact that careful observation and measurement show no sex differences. . . . As a result, myths live on that would otherwise rightfully die out under the impact of negative evidence (Maccoby and Jacklin, 1974b, p. 112).

We Are Carefully Taught

So far we have seen that at a very young age we already know our girlness or boyness, that little boys and little girls don't *act* differently except in aggressive behaviors, and that the beliefs of our culture lead to expectations of sex differences. These beliefs are molds which themselves help create the differences between men and women which appear later in life (see Chapters 5, 9, and 10). A key process in the perpetuation of this cycle is that even as children we learn the myths ourselves.

Here are some of the ways children described boys and men, girls and women for one researcher (Hartley, 1959, pp. 457–468):

Boys: ". . . have to be able to fight in case a bully comes along . . . need to be smart; they need to be able to take care of themselves; they should have more ability than girls . . . they are expected to get dirty; to mess up the house . . . and to get into trouble . . . ."

Men are: ". . . strong, ready to make decisions, protect women and children in emergencies. . . . They must be able to fix things, they must get money to support their families . . . men are the boss . . . they get the most comfortable chair in the house . . . fathers are more fun to be with . . . and they have the best ideas."

Girls: ". . . have to stay close to home; . . . to play quiet and more gently than boys, they are often afraid; . . . like playing with fussing over babies, and sitting and talking about dresses . . . spelling and arithmetic are not as important for them as for boys."

Women: ". . . are indecisive and they are afraid of many things; they make a fuss over things; they get tired a lot . . . they are not very intelligent. . . . Women do things like cooking and washing and sewing because that's all they can do."

Even though a child's mother has a career, is not afraid or indecisive, and even though his or her father is not the boss of the family, the child will have learned the traditional sex-stereotyped functions of women and men before school age. These stereotypes help simplify the world for a young child.

But There Is a Difference

By the age of five or six it is clear to all children that their genitals are a permanent part of their bodies and that in structure they share a basic similarity with all other members of their sex. In this culture, children know that little boys have a penis, that they always will, and that they have this feature in common with their fathers and with other men. Some know that little girls have clitorises, that they always will, and that they have this feature in common with their mothers and with all women. It is the basic difference in sex organs which clearly differentiates little girls from little boys, women from men.

Provided that a child grows up to know that sex differences are primarily defined by the reproductive capacity of the sex organs and to have a positive feeling of pride in his or her own genitalia and their ultimate reproductive use, then it does not much matter whether various child-care, domestic, and vocational activities are or are not interchangeable between mother and father. It does not even matter if mother is a bus driver and daddy a cook (Money and Ehrhardt, 1972, p. 14).

EXPLORATION 4.4

Sex Roles

How did your parents act out their roles?

Who in your family was responsible for:

paying the bills	planning weekends, vacations
cooking dinner	taking care of sick children
cleaning out closets	deciding on major purchases
mending, washing clothes	deciding which brand to buy
deciding where to live, when to move	entertaining
	taking care of the yard
household repairs	making money
emptying the trash	discipline

In what ways was your father masculine? Feminine?

In what ways was your mother feminine? Masculine?

If you grew up in a one-parent household:

How was the missing parent represented?

What was your single mother's (father's) attitude toward men (women)?

Did you have early contact with father or mother substitutes?

Did you see your missing parent regularly, occasionally, never?

What were your parents' expectations of you as a boy or girl?

Can you remember being discouraged away from certain toys, games, clothes, or expressions because they were not right for you as a girl, or as a boy?

Were you ever encouraged in cross-sexual preferences for these things?

What were the messages you got about what you'd "be" when you grew up?

Were you influenced one way or the other about your future reproductive role?

Did either your mother or father resent having children?

Are you aware of critical or judgmental attitudes toward men or women that you inherited from your parents? Such as,

"Men should . . ."

"Women are . . ."

SENSE OF COMPETENCE

> But what am I?
> An infant crying in the night?
> An infant crying for the light?
> And with no language but a cry!
>
> Alfred Lord Tennyson
> ("In Memorium")

Nothing seems more helpless, or less competent, than a baby lying in its crib wailing about who knows what. It can do nothing for itself; it must rely on others for its every need; it is utterly passive in its relationship to the world in which it was born. Many adults, like Tennyson in his poem, admit to feeling like an infant when they are powerless to make themselves heard or, if heard, to make their needs clear. They, as the infant, have no language but a cry.

But is a newborn baby so helpless? Parents will tell you that an infant's cry is usually impossible to ignore. It must be attended to. Unlike the drip of a faucet, or the cry of a child next door, the cry of one's own infant cannot be shut out of one's awareness. Mothers say, as do fathers sometimes, that the urge to respond to the distress of one's own child seems overwhelming, irresistible, built-in like a genetic "sense of responsibility." Be that as it may, the ability to cry, if you notice how efficiently it mobilizes attention, appears to be the foundation on which all future competence is built.

There is no question about the speed with which a baby develops competence. During the first two years of life a child increases its rate of activity and ability to an astonishing degree. It learns to sit up, crawl, hobble, and walk; coo, gurgle, and talk. It pushes things, pursues them, puts them in its mouth, and holds them up triumphantly. Although encouraged, few of these activities are taught; nevertheless, some inherent curiosity about the world motivates the baby to explore, to exercise its senses and newly acquired abilities in unreflective interaction with its surroundings.

Me Do

The "terrible twos" refers to a period of struggle that starts when a child, with a couple of years experience in the world, decides to "do it myself." The child can become stubborn, negative, bossy, contradictory—all in an attempt to gain a degree of self-reliance and control over his or her world. A little girl rages because she wants to wear her favorite dress day after day, however soiled it has become; a boy nags and thrashes as he begs to be picked up one minute and screams to be set down the next. An exasperated parent finds it difficult to keep in mind that the children's insistence on active participation in things that con-

National Education Association Publishing, Joe Di Dio.

cern (and do not concern) them is a stage in their developing motivation to master the skills of living. As children learn to feed themselves, and to do the many other things learned in the first couple of years, they will work on these new skills over and over again as if in fear that the ability will disappear if not practiced.

Doubt

The period under discussion here, in Erikson's terms, overlaps the stage of self-functioning (Autonomy) between ages two and three and the period of self-starting (Initiative) between ages three and five. You will recall that these stages resulted in a balance, or proportion, between a positive and a negative outcome. So far in this section we have been looking at the positive side of the competence balance sheet. The negative outcome is also important to the development of competence and a sense of competence.

Shame and doubt, the negative possibilities in the Autonomy stage, are the results of failing at what we ought to be able to do, either by our own or by others' standards. As early as two years of age, children can be inhibited from taking risks by a *fear of failure*. If they think they might fail, or if they doubt their ability to succeed, the children are likely to avoid trying rather than take a chance at experiencing feelings of shame. They withdraw, do nothing, and therefore, avoid failing.

Doubts about one's competence can come from an imperfect understanding of the world:

When my friend David was two and a half years old, he was being prepared for a trip to Europe with his parents. He was a very bright child, talked well for his age and seemed to take in everything his parents had to say with interest and enthusiasm. The whole family would fly to Europe (David knew what an airplane

National Education Association Publishing, Joe Di Dio.

was), they would see many unusual things, they would go swimming, go on trains, meet some of David's friends there. The preparation story was carried on with just the right amount of emphasis for a couple of weeks before the trip. But after a while David's parents noticed that he stopped asking questions about "Yurp" and even seemed depressed when he heard his parents talk about it. The parents tried to find out what was troubling him. He was most reluctant to talk about it. Then one day, David came out with his secret in an agonizing confession. "I can't go to Yurp!" he said, and the tears came very fast. "I don't know how to fly, yet!" (Fraiberg, 1959, p. 121)

The degree to which we develop a fear of failure affects the standards we set for ourselves and the amount of risk we are willing to take, sometimes for the rest of our lives. In our first few years we may set patterns that govern our behavior to the end by:

Setting our standards so low that there is no possibility of failing, no accepting challenges to harder and harder tasks, remaining fixated on the easy ones.
Setting our standards so high that there is no possibility of meeting them, not because there is something wrong with us but because the task itself is too difficult.

By following either of these patterns we can protect our self-image, whether it is good or bad, on the one hand by not risking a failure and on the other by not giving ourselves a chance at success. Neither situation allows a realistic evaluation of competence.

Guilt

Guilt is the negative possibility in the stage of Initiative. The knowledge that "I can do it" competes with the injunction "you may not." Completing a task you have set yourself, in spite of the continuing notion that you should not have done it, leaves you with the feeling of guilt.

Thirty-month-old Julia finds herself alone in the kitchen while her mother is on the telephone. A bowl of eggs is on the table. An urge is experienced by Julia to make scrambled eggs. She reaches for the eggs, but now the claims of reality are experienced with equal strength. Her mother would not approve. The resulting conflict within the ego is experienced as "I want" and "No, you mustn't" and the case for both sides is presented and a decision arrived at within the moment. When Julia's mother returns to the kitchen, she finds her daughter cheerfully plopping eggs on the linoleum and scolding herself sharply for each plop, "NoNoNo. Mustn't dood it. NoNoNo. *Mustn't* dood it!" (Fraiberg, 1959, p. 135)

Guilt can arise in response to our doing what we should not have done, or to our *not* doing what we should have done. The *shoulds* and *musts* and *ought tos* that are the kindling for a burning sense of guilt are an important part of what we learn as children. They stoke our conscience, which then moves us on our first steps toward being civilized. Conscience acts as a personal censor who lets us know *before* we act whether our actions are right or wrong. We used to wait for judgement and direction from our parents, but when we have developed even the rudiments of a conscience we are freer to guide ourselves.

Such freedom can be a mixed blessing. There are problems we meet in deciding the right thing to do. We have heard conflicting messages from our parents and others about right and wrong, thus making conscience a two-edged sword.

In the beginning was I, and I was good. Then came in other I. Outside authority. This was confusing. And then other I became *very* confused because there were so many different outside authorities. Sit nicely. Leave the room to blow your nose. Don't do that, that's silly. Why, the poor child doesn't even know how to pick a bone! Flush the toilet at night because if you don't it makes it harder to clean. DON'T FLUSH THE TOILET AT NIGHT—you wake people up! Always be nice to people. Even if you don't like them, you mustn't hurt their feelings. Be frank and honest. If you don't tell people what you think of them, that's cowardly. Butter knives. It is important to use butter knives. What foolishness! Speak nicely. Sissy! Kipling is wonderful! Ugh! Kipling (turning away) (Rogers and Stevens, 1971, p. 1).

Our *shoulds* and *musts* may become tyrannical, overbearing, imprisoning, suffocating—leaving us barely room to live.

Michael Weisbrot

I should love my mother, always, no matter what.
I must always be considerate.
I shouldn't be selfish.
I shouldn't be this way.
I mustn't cry.
I shouldn't feel hurt.
I must be quiet.
I should always be happy.
I shouldn't be tired.
I mustn't talk back.

I mustn't touch anything.
I should clean up my plate, even if I'm not hungry.
I must like Aunt Emmy.
I shouldn't hit little girls.
I should be better.
I should be what I am not.

EXPLORATION
4.5

Childhood
Competence

Think back to the messages you received from your parents about your competence. Imagine you are a child again.

What can you hear them saying about
your abilities   your looks
your intelligence   your future
your worth

Which of the messages you recall are part of your own self-evaluation?

Were your parents right? Have you lived up to their expectations?

Do you still feel guilty about something you did as a child?
    What?

Do you feel especially good about some childhood achievement?
    What was it?

How much of a risk-taker were you as a child?

Were you shy?

Physically active? Do you remember lots of scrapes and scratches and bruises?

Did you adventure out into the neighborhood, or were you happiest in the safety of your home?

Do you recall failing at something as a child? What?
    Can you call up the feelings you had at the time?
    Were you angry, hurt, guilty, disappointed?

What are your attitudes toward failing now?
    Do you willingly risk it? Do you always fail?

Whether we feel guilt about them or not, the "mistakes" of early childhood make an important contribution to a sense of competence. By learning to avoid mistakes we also learn to deal with the material obstacles we meet in life. We must fall often in perfecting our ability to walk. We have to record many bumps, scrapes, and bruises in order to learn what is "too fast" for us, "too far," and "too hard." On our own we find out that stoves are hot, that milk spills from an overturned glass, that popsicles melt in the sun, that five blocks will stand and six fall, that clocks do not work with their insides removed.

In addition to the gains they make from learning on their own, children benefit also from praise and expectations of self-reliance from their parents. Messages that seem to further children's competence are those which make large of their successes and minimize their "failures."

"Good boy, you've put that shirt on all by yourself. The tag? That means this is the back. Do you want to turn it around?"
"It was very thoughtful of you to bring a tissue for Baby's nose. Here, help Daddy pick up these we don't need on the floor."
"What a big boy to keep the bed dry all night!"
"Good for you, pouring your own milk. I'll help you clean up the spills."
"That's right. Good. Now, what comes after *N*?"

On the other hand, messages that the child is wrong—can never do anything right—can become thorns in the child's self-evaluation.

"You dummy! Can't you ever do anything right?"
"You can't do that. Here, let me do it for you."
"You're a born loser."
"Stupid kid! When are you going to learn?"
"You'll never amount to anything!"
"Grow up and act right."
"You're so slow, you won't be finished with that until doomsday."
"When they give out booby prizes, you'll get the biggest one for sure."
"What'd you have to make such a mess for?"
"You'd be rich if I gave you a nickle for every time you've spilled the milk."
"You are unquestionably the clumsiest kid I have *ever* seen."
"Watch what you are doing or you'll goof up again!"

UNBOUNDEDNESS

There was a time when meadow, grove and
   stream,
The earth, and every common sight,
   To me did seem
Appareled in celestial light,
The glory and the freshness of a dream.
It is not now as it hath been of yore;
   Turn wheresoe'er I may,
      By night or day,
The things which I have seen I now can see no
   more.

                              William Wordsworth
                              ("Intimations of Immortality")

Many of us, with the speaker in Wordsworth's poem, are surprised to find that we have lost something since childhood, or at least misplaced it. A delightful way of seeing the world and of being in it, a sense of freedom and joy, a life somehow less complicated, more spontaneous—these seem to have been smothered beneath the weight of being grown up, to have been bound by the fetters of adulthood. How was it that we were less bound in childhood and what is it that we, as adults, seem to have lost?

As children, we are unbound in the ways we experience the world. Children deal with the world *honestly*. They are not yet entangled in the politics of grown-up experience. Children are trusting, unprejudiced, open-minded, and unskilled in psychological games. Treachery, deceit, and willfull maliciousness have to be learned, as does sarcasm. Children experience the world *creatively*. Children are not born with adult conventions of orderliness; they are free to tap their own inner sense of order. Designs do not have to be symmetrical, drawings do not have to represent things "out there." Gravity and other "laws" of the universe, which adults take for granted, are worth a childish challenge. Logic is not inherent in anything. A process can be delightfully absorbing without a thought of a finished product. Children experience the world *absolutely:* pleasure and pain; good and bad; yes and no; forever and never; right and wrong; good guys and bad guys. To the young child shades of gray between black and white are incomprehensible. If something is bigger, it is more; if it is taller, it is simply bigger. What happens, happens, without necessary causes.

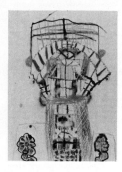

To children still poised between the worlds of inner and outer realities, dreams are more than events of the daylight world. Two sisters, five and three-and-a-half years old, used to wake early and tell their dreams. One morning the three-and-a-half-year-old said: "I don't need to tell you my dream, for you were in it, so you already know." "But it was *your* dream, I was in my own. I don't know anything about yours until you tell me." "But you were *there*. I saw you with my own eyes." As the argument continued, the small child burst into tears. "Stop teasing me. You were *there*. I saw you plain as I see you this minute. You are making fun of me." (Wickes, 1968, p. 258)

Children's experience is a mix of their inherent potentials and the freedom granted by their social roles. It is a vast meadow, lush with potentials, bounded by a few widely scattered social restrictions.

A Child's Potentials

Young human beings have potentials for being:

Impulsive and spontaneous   Young children's responses are immediate and lacking in inner restraint. Children live very much in the present, rather than in the past or the future. Their inner direction, which would be their only direction without adult intervention, is inevitably geared toward satisfaction, the attainment of pleasure and the avoidance of pain. As children we try to snatch what we want, indulge our moods, and we are impatient with — if not downright opposed to — postponing our needs. Our perceptions of the world are centered in "now" and "me."

Expressive   Children have the capacity to show their feelings and inner states easily, whether joy or distress, anger or fatigue. Even without words, they can use their faces, bodies, a wide range of babbles, coos, sputters, whines, cries, and farts to express where they are, what they like and dislike, their needs for attention. Children don't wear masks of false feelings to impress others or to hide their true emotions. The expressions are direct, open, and authentic.

Curious and intuitive   Children are naturally curious. Their desire to explore has no goal other than the satisfaction of discovering whatever turns up in their path. Making sense of what one finds as a child is an intuitive process, primitive and unsophisticated by adult standards. The understanding that follows is often apt to be "wrong." But wrong answers (unless they introduce fears), are not of great import to a child.

One evening I was reading a favorite bed-time story to my three-year-old son. We came to a page with a drawing of the mama bird pulling a worm out of the ground, a picture he had seen many times. I casually asked him about the picture. "What is the mama pulling on?" I asked. "A pipe," was his swift and assured response. It didn't matter to him at all that it didn't "make sense" for mother birds to pull up the plumbing for their hungry babies. If the picture looked like a pipe to him, it was a pipe.

Intuition, imagination, and childish magic rule over reason during the earliest years. Fantasy is given its full reign and the "facts" by which adults live do not discourage it.

Sensuous and affectionate   The world of infants does not extend very far from their bodies. It is a world of things close to them—tastes, smells, temperatures, and textures are the stuff it is made of. There is no panoramic vision in infancy; babies can only focus a few feet beyond themselves. Thus, the sensations we first develop are those giving us information of proximity, closeness to our own bodies.

The infant is not disgusted by his feces; he quite likes their smell. . . . [L]ong before he knows and remembers how his mother looks, [he] knows how she smells and tastes. Very likely, angry or frightened mother tastes and smells rather different from good or comfortable mother to the infant, just as she will look very different to him as he grows older. . . . He tastes and sniffs and touches earlier and better than he perceives with eye and ear. . . . Only very gradually and slowly does the emphasis shift from the proximity to the distance senses (Schachtel, 1949, pp. 24-25).

The exclusive importance of those things close to the baby's own body gradually dwindles as he or she develops the senses of vision and hearing. But being close to and in contact with objects which give pleasure is vital throughout childhood. Being a child is to unself-consciously want physical contact with others, to delight in cuddling, hugging, and all forms of touching.

The self-indulgent, self-centered world of childhood is not a bed of thornless roses. Impulsive actions can lead to disasters. Uncensored expressions can result in disapproval. Intuition and magical thinking can create frightful anxieties. Inadequate and incomplete perceptions can be quite confusing.

I recall the story of a two-year-old girl who developed a morbid fear of ants. She cried out in terror when she saw one because, she said, the ants would eat her up. Her parents were completely baffled because the same little girl would cheerfully put her fist in the mouth of any big dog who came up to greet her and never accused even the most ferocious animal in the zoo of a wish to eat her up. The child's grandmother remembered that one day when she opened the kitchen cupboard she discovered some ants. Mimi, the two-year-old, was in the kitchen when grandmother threw up her hands in alarm and said to the cook, "Those ants are here again. They will eat everything up!"

In the marvellous world of the two-year old, if there are ants that will eat *everything* up, they will eat up a little girl, too (Fraiberg, 1959, p. 124).

Being a child is being frightened by strange and unknown situations, by nightmares, and by one's own imagination. It is also being frustrated, angry, hurt, bored, uncomfortable, and subject to the whims of a world beyond control or understanding.

A Child's Role

Compared to the roles falling to adults, the roles of children in this culture are unbound. From the beginning of life we are being socialized in preparation for adult life and must live in a household governed by adults, but we only gradually and unconsciously accept adult limitations. Restrictions which are less binding upon children than adults include:

Clocktime. Children are freer to respond to their personal biological rhythms than adults. The time to sleep is when fatigued, the time to urinate is when the bladder is full, the time to cry is when the stomach is empty. Infants have no lunch hours, timeclocks to punch, appointments to keep, or birthdays to remember.

Responsibilities are few, needs cared for, bills paid, decisions made, deadlines, headaches, and ulcers not yet discovered. Our only concerns are for ourselves, and many of the responsibilities for our care are someone else's duties.

Perfection and *high performance* are not demanded of us. There is little need to be consistent or always right. Our mistakes, accidents, transgressions are expected, if not forgiven. As children we are free to engage in trial and error over and over again.

Feelings and *reactions* don't have to be carefully disguised. Anger, pleasure, impatience, sadness, glee—all emotional expressions—may be displayed with less restraint than allowed in adulthood.

Becoming Bound

These freedoms are apparent only in comparison with the demands, responsibilities, and pace of adult life. Children do not lead completely unrestricted or independent lives. From birth onward we begin to be bound more and more every year by the rules, roles, and ways of thinking and perceiving that will one day qualify us for adult status.

We take on the ways of the world and become bound and socialized, both willingly and, sometimes, eagerly whenever we are praised for acting "grown up." Without too much awareness we assimilate the viewpoints of our culture as interpreted and conveyed to us by our parents. The language we speak will be the language(s) of our parents. Although we are born with the potential for making the sounds of all languages, we develop only those of our native tongue. (For instance, American children lose the potential for swallowing an "r" in a precisely French manner.) Acquiring language is an important step in acquiring a way to think, for language shapes and molds the way we perceive and understand. With language come clichés, stereotypes, and the ability to generalize and make artificial distinctions. Language is vital in organizing the world. It also limits our experience. If we feel a certain emotion and our language doesn't provide us with adequate words to express it, we are apt to lose not only the ability to describe and share our feeling but the ability to feel it as well. It has been suggested by one psychologist (Schachtel, 1949) that because the English vocabulary is relatively poor in words to describe smells and tastes, our experiences for smell and taste sensations remain undeveloped. Language frees us to participate in the adult world, but it also binds us.

Early childhood is a training ground in the values of our family's socioeconomic class and ethnic group. As children we learn to be comfortable with those things which our families provide. Traditions and conventions with which we are in daily contact become habitual, unquestioned ways of doing and seeing things and stay with us even though we forget the reasons behind them.

A bride served baked ham, and her husband asked why she cut the ends off. "Well, that's the way mother always did it," she replied.

The next time his mother-in-law stopped by, he asked her why she cut the ends off the ham. "That's the way *my* mother did it," she replied.

And when grandma visited, she too was asked why she sliced the ends off. She said, "That's the only way I could get it into the pan." (James and Jongeward, 1971, p. 97)

Today early family influences are tempered by the conventions of the television screen. Children spend hours sitting in front of a device which teaches them, among other things, that they should buy anything that is new and that it is acceptable to adopt violent solutions to problems.

We have no choice about being bound into society. It is in the nature of being human and social that we become socialized, civilized, and acculturated in some way; we must trade in our self-structured and self-centered world for a shared social reality. We must learn those conventional perceptual habits and automatic ways of thinking by which other humans organize the world. In the bargain we gain abilities and perceptions which make us fit to live with others, but we risk losing some of the freshness, clarity, intensity of experience, richness of detail, the sense of wholeness and oneness which enliven a child's unbound perceptions.

A Child's World

Adults can reach the unbound world of childhood through art, poetry, music, dreams, fantasies, and chiildren's literature. A wonderful example of this last is a beautiful book called *Tiger Flower* (by Robert Vavra, illustrated by Fleur Cowles, 1969, published by Reynal). This is a tale of a backwards world where "everything that should be small, is big." A bird accidentally flies into this world and taunts a tiny tiger, who replies:

You see, if you're born a jungle beast
You have to be big and fierce
the way jungle beasts are supposed to be
or life becomes unpleasant for you.
Here, where nothing is as it should be,
no one has to be anyway but the way he is (p. 28).

In the preface to this book, a renowned violinist describes the dimensions of a child's unbound world:

The child's world is a world of symbols, shapes and sizes until that dismal day when it is taught to put a label on each and every thing it has felt, touched and smelt, and forced to shrink it by a name.

The child's world is the poet's world where dimensions differ only according to feeling, not fact, that place of the fourth dimension that eludes all but painters, poets, lunatics and the players of musical instruments. And it even eludes those at times. That is why they remain children, eternally committed to chasing after it, clinging to the tatters of those clouds of glory with which we are all born and which only rationalization can rip off. . . .

But beautiful things are not fearful in the innocent world because there one has curiosity instead of terror and a suppleness of mind that adjusts itself to the wonder of the unexpected as easily as the pupil of the eye to the fluctuations of light and dark.

Here then is a little book that is the right way up. A glimpse of a world wherein there is so much time and limitless space that no one has to confine or categorise out of meanness of heart, for fear that there won't be enough beauty or enough truth to go around unless you frighten others away.

Yehudi Menuhin
(preface to *Tiger Flower*)

EXPLORATION
4.6

A Child's World

Imagine you are again two-and-a-half feet tall.

What do things look like?

Take an imaginary tour of your house. How do things look to you from down there? How many things are too high or too big for you?

Is there anything which might make you afraid?

Imagine you can't read, that letters are just funny looking designs with no meaning. (This is very difficult for most of us, by the way.)

What would be missing from your life if you could not understand the written word?

What would be harder or easier for you?

What can you think of that was peculiar to your family—a way of seeing things or doing things—which you adopted as perfectly natural until you found out that other people thought or acted differently?

Do you ever wish you were a child again?

When?

What are your present fantasies about your childhood?

Was it heaven or hell, or both, or what?

Here is an experiment for the classroom: Have someone prepare several small bottles with an aromatic substance in each (for example, garlic, cinnamon, vanilla, musky perfume, moth balls). Pass the bottles around the class so that everyone can get a good whiff. Close your eyes and let each smell trigger off any early childhood memory it will.

Do you find yourself back in situations you rarely think about any more? Tell the class about them.

Create something. Pretend you are a child drawing a picture.

Let yourself go and make whatever you want without worrying whether it's right or wrong.

How do you feel?

Do one thing each day this week that you used to enjoy doing as a young child but have given up now that you are grown up. Buy some bubble gum, fly a kite, roughhouse with the dog, eat ice cream with your fingers, deliberately make a mess. . . .

How do you feel?

SUMMARY

1. By school age we have begun to be independent and to have a good sense of ourselves as individuals. However, our lives are still family centered; our caretakers have been the most important people in our lives. Our needs for love, affection, and human contact have been met, sometimes imperfectly, within the family.

2. Most of us have observed how adults around us interact. We have asked some questions about sex and making babies. We know, without a doubt, that we

are either male or female, and we have made a good beginning toward knowing how to act as boys or girls.

3. In our first years we have received messages from our parents about our competence; we have also found that there are many things in the world to master.

4. We have experienced the world in the free, magical way of children, but we have also acquired language and, thus, have begun to be bound by conventions.

Suggested Readings

Farson, Richard. *Birthrights: A bill of rights for children.* New York: Macmillan, 1974. Provocative arguments for children's liberation.

Fraiberg, Selma H. *The magic years.* New York: Scribner, 1959. A delightfully written account of personality development during the first five years of life.

Kagan, Jerome. *Understanding children: Behavior, motives, and thought.* New York: Harcourt, 1971. Two essays on children's insatiable need "to know" and the development of thinking processes; valuable suggestions for those who live and work with children.

Satir, Virginia. *Peoplemaking.* Palo Alto, Ca.: Science and Behavior Books, 1972. A book for everyone who wants to understand self-worth, communication, family systems, and the family's link to society. Includes valuable exercises for changing destructive family patterns.

Wickes, Frances G. *The inner world of childhood.* (Rev. ed.) New York: New American Library, 1966. A classic of the Jungian tradition, on imagination, dreams, and fantasy in children.

Michael Weisbrot

5

SHAPING UP

So there stood youth and there childhood together,
trying to look into each other's eyes
and each offending, but not equally.
Childhood spoke first, "Hullo then.
It's your fault if I hardly recognized you.
I thought you'd be quite different from this.
I'll tell you honestly, you worry me.
You're still in very heavy debt to me."
So youth asked if childhood would help,
and childhood smiled and promised it would help.

Y. A. Yevtushenko
("Zima Junction")

We have begun our quests and passed many milestones during our first years at home. We have come to know the world as a child can know it. We have also come to know it as revealed to us by our parents. We have been challenged, as Erik Erikson would say, with the developmental tasks of achieving Trust, Autonomy, and Initiative.

At around six years of age our lives take a new turn. We start our formal education and an increasing involvement in the world beyond our childhood home. The quests we have begun are now subject to further shaping; we are more and more molded by the hands of other adults and of friends, less and less by our parents.

We are also developing our capacities to shape ourselves, to make our own plans and decisions. We learn how to pursue and sustain our own interests as we are challenged at the stage Erikson labels Industry. We come to new beginnings at puberty, when our bodies change dramatically and we approach adult status. We shape and reshape ourselves over and over again in the adolescent search for Identity.

No other species takes so many years to reach maturity. It takes us this long because we have much learning, shaping, and development to do.

The long human childhood is marked by increasing individuality. A group of six-year-olds is much more alike in behavior, ability, and interests than a group of eighteen-year-olds. We will have, in the dozen years between six and eighteen, developed many of our individual potentials. We will have built layer upon layer of continuous individual experiencing, each layer adding to our uniqueness. What we do in those dozen years is based on our first six years; we continue the development begun then. And we set the stage for our futures.

socialization

The major task of these years is to acquire a working knowledge of our culture, its values, and ways of doing things. We are preparing for adult life. It is a time of intense socialization, the process of learning how to live with others. Socialization continues throughout life, but this is the period during which we get heavy doses of the formal and institutional varieties. Socialization is a process which requires us to compromise: we learn to consider the wants and needs of others as well as our own; we learn to wait; we learn to be similar to others by sacrificing some of our individuality. The paradox with which we live throughout this period is that even while we are becoming more and more individual, we are also learning how to conform. The pull of these opposing demands is often fierce during adolescence.

In contrast to the first six years of life, the second dozen provide us with many accessible memories. Most of us can remember incidents from grade school; almost all of us those from our high school years.

The heart of this chapter will be your recollections. The explorations here are designed to provoke your memory and to bring out your individual personal histories. The milestones for the last years of childhood and the entrance into adulthood are:

- beginning school, conforming to peer groups, the struggles to define identity
- special same-sex friendships in grade school, the effects of adolescence on our social relationships and first loves
- further ways males learn masculinity, females femininity, and the impact of puberty
- learning about sex with other children and alone, dramatic changes in sexual learnings after puberty
- developing academic and social skills in school and with friends
- the finalization of boundedness to adult modes of experiencing

SEPARATENESS AND WHOLENESS

The first day of school marks the beginning of the long process of separating from one's parents and of becoming part of the larger world outside the family. The influence of parents weakens. Schools, teachers, and peers move us in new and sometimes conflicting ways as they mold our behavior and attitudes to conform to cultural standards. We may continue to sit at our family table for many years, as sons or daughters, but we are all the while building individual places for ourselves, setting ourselves apart from our parents and siblings (see Exploration 5.1).

In junior high and high school one can seek membership in any of numerous informal groups. There are fashion cliques, delinquent gangs, hobby clubs, and notable crowds (such as class officers, athletes, and popular girls). These informal groups are valuable as a source of approval and for the security and sense of belonging they give — to those who are in. They also encourage heterosexual mixing, giving young men and women the opportunity to socialize — if they belong.

Not all adolescents belong to such groups; some are excluded, some are shy. Not belonging can lead to a sense of isolation, to withdrawal, to a defensive aloofness, or to dependence on one's family for social ties.

Courtesy of the Ford Foundation.

Michael Weisbrot

Belonging, on the other hand, can lead to what Robert White calls *social enslavement,* a compulsive conformity to group expectations and painful loneliness when away from the group. "The person's preferences, tastes, and opinions are those that are sanctioned by the group, and he takes no chances of giving offense or incurring disapproval. Some adolescents show awareness of differing impulses in themselves but have no courage

**EXPLORATION
5.1

Early
Separateness**

In what way was your first day at school important?
     Was it frightening, or exciting?

Was your ethnic, social, or religious background special compared to those of other kids in your neighborhood or school?
     Did you feel different because your family was different?

How did you learn that not all families did things the way yours did?

Was your family close-knit, doing things together, or were the members separate in their activities and interests?

Did you ever feel like a loner as a child, withdrawing into your own world, believing that no one understood you?

How did you feel about being different from other children your age? Superior? Inferior?

Do you remember another child who was lonely, different, odd?
     How did you react to him or her?

Were you on a team, in Boy Scouts, Girl Scouts, or Camp Fire Girls, a neighborhood gang, or other group?
     How did your belonging influence your values and attitudes?

Make a list of the ways you conformed in junior and senior high school. Consider your tastes, preferences, activities, what you spent money on.

How important was it to be like everyone else, not to be out of step?

Were you part of a gang, clique, or in-group of some kind?

What were the qualifications for being in the group?

Was belonging important to you then?

What did you get from this group or groups?

What conflicts did you feel between the demands of your friends and those of your parents?

What were the circumstances?

Where did you usually place your loyalty?

Did you openly rebel against your parents and family? How?

What aspects of your parents' life-style or values did you question in high school?

Did you disagree with their religious, political, or social values?

Did you challenge any of the hopes or plans they had for you?

In what ways were you determined to make your life different from theirs?

How many times did your family move or did you change schools between ages 6 and 18?

How did this affect your friendships?

Did you, in childhood or adolescence, experience the loss of someone close to you?

Did a friend, sibling, or parent die? In what ways are you stronger, or not, for having experienced this separation?

As an adolescent, did you spend much or little of your time alone?

Happily or unhappily?

Did you remember feeling confused or anguished about who you were in adolescence?

Did you ever feel that you didn't know who you were, that you wanted to be somebody different from yourself, or that you were just waiting to grow up and be somebody or something?

When you finished high school, how well could you answer the question: Who am I?

to assert them; others truly lose contact with what is inside and define themselves in terms of what others want and expect. Compulsive conformity takes a heavy toll on individuality." (White, 1976, p. 321)

The difficulties of becoming independent from one's family, of being enslaved by or excluded from groups, and of forming a sense of individual identity come all at once for most high school students. Many are constantly troubled by some form of the question: Who Am I? The answer must account for the past and present; it also points to the future—

Who will I become? Vocational, religious, political, economic, and other values come up for questioning as we try to resolve our conflicts and discover which stand we will take as our own (see Exploration 5.2).

INTIMACY

We are capable of forming intimate friendships, according to the psychologist Harry Stack Sullivan, when we are able to be sensitive to another's needs and to care about them. Before we develop these capacities, our relationships are mostly within the family and they are mostly self-centered. Typically, children in their early years at school form close relationships with a same-sex "best" friend. These friendships are often intense, the friends spending every moment they can together. Quarrels among such pairs are stormy, reconciliations usually joyful.

Adolescence is difficult for many people largely because intimate relationships at this time become difficult to achieve. Parent-child relationships are often strained as children strive for independence. Same-sex friendships are threatened as friends become interested in the opposite sex. They can also be threatened by fears of homosexual attachment—parents' fears or our own. Teenagers are encouraged to form opposite-sex liaisons, on the one hand, but are also told they are too young to really be in love or seriously attached. Our society sees the early and mid-teen years as a time for exploring a number of interpersonal relationships, although this period is thought still too early in life to decide on a permanent mate, or to make long-lasting commitments.

While needing companionship, acceptance, and love, the teenager is often adrift and without close human contact. Old relationships from the

National Education Association Publishing, Joe Di Dio.

If you had a "best" friend in grade school, what made that friend special?
    What did you share?
    How did you fight?
        About what, and how did you make up?
    What did you give to your friend? What did he or she give to you?
    How did you make decisions about what to do?

Did any of the following figure in your elementary school relationships? If so, how?
    jealousy
    loyalty
    possessiveness
    dominance
    envy

Do you see patterns in your current relationships which you can trace back to childhood? What about:
    dominance
    possessiveness
    being the one who leans
    being the one who is supportive
    being loyal to a friend no matter what
    being left out

preteen years may have become competitive. Current opposite-sex relationships are unstable, or lacking complete involvement. In order to achieve some semblance of intimacy adolescents often engage in romantic fantasies, comfortable but not always deeply satisfying "steady" arrangements, or numerous impersonal sexual encounters.

Take yourself back to junior high school.

Photograph by T. O'Reilly.

**EXPLORATION
5.4**

**Adolescent
Friendships**

How did your friendships change during junior high school?
    When and how did you become aware of changes in your relationships with members of the opposite sex?
    Did you find yourself in competition with friends of the same sex?
    Did your relationships with brothers or sisters change? How?

Can you recall an intimate moment with your parent(s) when you were in junior high school?
    Were there any?
    If not, what do you think were the reasons?

Describe your dreams and fantasies of an ideal mate when you were 13.
    What was he or she like?
    What did the two of you do in your fantasies?

What were your major confusions about intimacy when you were 13 and 14?
    What to you were "puppy love," infatuation, crushes, "the real thing"?

During adolescence, what kind of teachers or other adults were you infatuated with?
    Were crushes on adults ever a source of pain for you?
    Did you keep crushes to yourself or did you share them with a friend, with the object of your longing?

Did you read teen literature or romance stories?
    What did you feel about it?
    What did it do for you?

Describe your relationships with movie or music stars of the same or opposite sex.
    Did you spend much time dreaming about them?

Describe in detail your very first love object.
    How old were you?
    How well did you know him or her?
    What qualities attracted you?
    What did this person look like?
    Was your relationship with this person firsthand or did you worship from afar in silence?
    Was your love returned?
    What happened to your feelings about this person?
    Do you still see him or her, dream about what was or what could have been?
    Is this person in any way like any of your subsequent love objects? (Edward Brecher, in *The Sex Researchers,* suggests that early adolescence may be the time of human attachment or imprinting. Those attributes of our first love will be the ones we look for in all later love relationships. Is this hypothesis true for you in any way?)

imprinting

Were romance and love more important to the girls than the boys in high school?

How was any difference shown?

In high school, if you had made plans to do something with a friend of the same sex and then, later, got a chance to go out with someone of the opposite sex, what did you do?

Did it make any difference to your status among your peers whether or not you had an opposite-sex friend?

Whether you had a date on the weekend? A steady?

What did you do about it?

Was it important to your parents?

During high school, when you didn't have a date on Saturday night, what were you most apt to be doing?

Were these activities enjoyable in themselves or did you often wish you were with someone special or feel bad because you weren't out having fun like everyone else?

Did you have a best friend in high school?

Are the two of you still good friends?

Was this relationship marked by jealousy, loyalty, possessiveness, dominance, envy?

What were the bases of your friendships with same-sex peers?

Did you really enjoy each other's company?

Did you share interests and activities?

Could you show your real feelings and get support?

Were your friends a source of status for you?

Did you hang around with them because they attracted members of the opposite sex?

Did you ever lie or boast about your sexual activities to gain their respect?

Can you think of an intimate moment you had with your parent(s) during your last year in high school?

SEXUAL PERSPECTIVE

We enter elementary school with a child's body and leave high school with the body of an adult. Puberty, the metamorphosis which usually takes place between the ages of 12 and 14, is the beginning of a new, adult sexuality. Not only do we undergo physical changes, we also experience dramatic changes in our sexual perspectives and potentials.

Many developmental theorists believe, as did Freud, that between the age of six and puberty a child's sexuality is "latent," that during this period we are sexually inactive, until our adult hormones switch us on. Although it is true that before puberty our physical growth has little sexual significance, during this time we are certainly not sexually dormant.

Take yourself back to your grade school years.

EXPLORATION
5.5

**Early
Sex Education**

Recall the kind of sex play you engaged in with other children.
> Did you play "doctor" and do physical exams on each other?
> What others kinds of sexual explorations did you share with your friends?
> Did you masturbate with other kids?
> Children come to know that they must keep their sex play secret. How did you learn this?
> Were you ever caught?
> How did you feel?

What sexual activities did you engage in alone?
> Did you masturbate? Often or seldom?
> What were your feelings: reproach, guilt, shame, fear?
> Were any of these feelings strong or were they mild?
> How did you feel about the sensations you experienced as you explored your body?

Playgrounds and streets are major sources of sexual vocabulary, sex information, and sex misinformation.
> Which sex words did you pick up from peers in grade school?
> Were they taboo or "dirty" words?
> Did you use them at home in front of your family?
>> If you did, what happened?
>> If you didn't, what did you expect to happen? Why?
> Did you exchange sex jokes with your friends?
>> Did you understand them?
>> Did you feel comfortable telling or hearing them?
> Was there any difference in the way you talked about sexual matters when you were with friends of the same sex and when you were with those of the opposite sex?

Did you exchange knowledge about reproduction or intercourse with your friends?
> If so, were these discussions accurate or did you pick up a lot of fallacies?
> If you and your friends had questions, where did you go for information: books, parents, older children?

Do you recall seeing animals copulating when you were a child?
> How did you react?

Did you receive formal instruction about sex or reproduction in grade school?
> Were any adults besides your parents (for instance, teachers or ministers) helpful sources of sex information?
> Did your parents approve of sex education in the schools or did they feel it was their job to teach you?
> If sex was discussed in school, was it a topic freely talked about in a mixed class or were the girls separated from the boys?
> Did your teachers handle sexual topics with ease or were they ever embarrassed?
> Were you always satisfied with the answers to your questions?
> Were they ever unable to answer?

Michael Weisbrot

What sex information did you get at home?

> What were your parents' reactions to your questions?
>
> Were your parents adequately informed?
>
> Were they at ease and easy to talk to?
>
> Did they ever take you aside for a private talk or a lecture about "the birds and the bees"?
>
>> How did you feel about these talks?
>>
>> How did they?

How and when did you become aware that your mother (and other women) menstruated?

> What was your mother's attitude about menstruation?
>
>> Was it a burden to her?
>>
>> Did she act "odd" at certain times of the month?
>
> Did she explain anything about menstruation to you?

Were you curious about your parents' sex life?

> Were they open or secret about it?
>
> Did you feel free to ask them about it?
>
> What were your feelings when you discovered that your parents made love?
>
> Did you get the impression that they enjoyed their sex lives?
>
> Did their attitudes ever puzzle, frighten, or disgust you?
>
> Did they ever ask to be left alone in their bedroom?

Were you ever aware that either of your parents was having an extramarital affair?

> That they were masturbating?
>
> Did your father visit prostitutes?
>
> How did you feel about these activities?

How did you first learn about prostitution, rape, VD, homosexuality, birth control, child molesters?

With these recollections in mind, design what you would consider an ideal program of sex education for school-age children today. If and when you are a parent, what would you want your children to know and feel about sexuality? What role should parents, schools, churches play? Discuss your thoughts with your class. Go to your school or public library to find books that explain sex to children. Evaluate the usefulness of these books. Can you find information for children which asserts that sex is pleasurable? Is intercourse always explained as having the goal of reproduction?

Puberty and Beyond

Around 12 to 14 years of age, we get a new body. It feels, looks, sounds, and smells unlike the one we have been living in so far. We don't have any choice about these changes or their timing. The unmistakable signal that girls are beginning womanhood is the first menstrual period; for boys the indicator is the first ejaculation, either by masturbation or as a nocturnal emission. Both these events are biological milestones in our sexual histories. However, the psychological significance of menstruation is of a quite different order than that of ejaculation. A monthly discharge of blood from your body is in no way erotic, sensuous, or "sexy." The onset of menstruation is an event of reproductive importance. It marks the start of a woman's potential fertility and will be a regular reminder of it for the next 30 to 40 years. Males, on the other hand, begin manhood with intense, erotic, *sexual* activities. Most young men are keenly aware of an increased erotic sensitivity; many also find it accompanied by guilt or anxiety. Differences in the meaning of sexual maturation for men and women contribute to a difference in their sexual attitudes. Men experience their own eroticism earlier and more intensely than do most women (Gagnon and Simon, 1973).

Recall the period of your puberty.

**EXPLORATION
5.6

Puberty**

What changes do you remember from this period?
　　What happened first (changes in body shape, hair, voice, etc.)?
　　How did you feel about these changes?
　　Did you share your feelings with friends? Parents?
What were you early to mature, late, or average for your crowd?
　　If you were not average, what were your feelings about being out of step?
　　Did you try to either hide or emphasize your body changes?
　　Did you feel comfortable in the locker or shower room at school?
WOMEN: What was your first menstrual period like?
　　Did you feel you were adequately prepared?
　　Were you glad, annoyed, frightened?
　　Were you embarrassed about hygiene?
　　How did you feel about the changes in your body shape, breasts, and hips?
　　Were you self-conscious?
　　Did you worry about being too small or too large?
　　Did you begin masturbating at puberty?
MEN: What was your reaction to wet dreams?
　　Were you concerned about your mother finding evidence on the sheets?
　　Did you begin masturbating or masturbate more at puberty?
　　　　How did you feel about it?
　　　　Were you ever caught, or fearful of being caught?
　　Do you recall erotic fantasies from this time?
　　　　Were they exciting? Disgusting?
　　　　Did you tell anyone about them?
　　Did you ever worry about getting an erection in public or at the "wrong" time?
　　　　What did you think others would think about it?

During adolescence we begin to change our attitudes about and behavior towards same-sex and opposite-sex friends. What kinds of messages did you get about being physically close to friends of your own sex?

Were you free to hug, touch, hold hands, roughhouse?

Were you ever aroused by contact with a same-sex friend?

How did you feel?

How early was heterosexual pairing off begun in your school?

Was there status in pairing?

Were you one of the first or last to have a boyfriend/girlfriend?

Did you go steady?

How did you first learn sexual technique, such as kissing, how to touch or arouse someone of the opposite sex, other skills in "making out"?

How did you learn what was right and wrong?

What were your early attitudes toward one-to-one sexual experiences:

experimental

taking things slow and easy

anxious or guilty

pushing to see how far your partner would go

trying to set and obey limits about touching, contact, acceptable behaviors

giving in to please a partner

fear of rejection

worry about your reputation

concern about getting caught

other?

Did you ever discuss your feelings with the person you were with? With anyone else—a friend, parent, or other adult?

Michael Weisbrot

How did any of these attitudes change with experience?

When you had set certain standards about sexual behaviors, how did you manage to maintain them?

What were your feelings if you did not stay within the bounds you had established?

If you exceeded the bounds of the person you were with?

Did you experience pressure to give up your virginity?

What kind of pressure? From whom?

If you remained a virgin through high school, how did you feel?

Did you find one set of expectations about your sexual behavior from your peers and another from your parents?

Was this a conflict for you?

How did you handle it?

Was birth control information available to you?

Were you careful about using contraceptives?

Before or after a pregnancy?

If you weren't always careful in using birth control, what were the reasons you did not choose protection?

Did you experience a double standard for sexual behavior during adolescence, one kind of behavior being expected of males and another of females?

Were women expected to hold back and men expected to get all they could? Were men expected to appear experienced and dominant? What were the local standards about having many partners? How did any double standard affect you?

MALE/FEMALE

Although our basic gender identity is established before we begin school, the many years of childhood and adolescence are important to our learning, through observation and practice, what it is to be *feminine* females and *masculine* males by our culture's standards.

Learning femininity is somewhat easier than learning masculinity. Girls get an early acquaintance with what women are and what they do. In the home, a girl continues to have opportunities to practice those skills she will need as a housewife. Girls are not under the same pressure as boys to give up childish behaviors in order to grow up. And even while being allowed to be passive and dependent, girls are also permitted to include tomboyish activities in their play. There are fewer restrictions on girls' than on boys' behavior, dress, and interests; that is to say, the lessons girls learn about being a girl are not as rigid as those given to boys.

Children of both sexes are reared chiefly by females (mothers and female elementary school teachers). Most fathers spend relatively little

Michael Weisbrot

time at home with their children, so young boys learn about masculinity from women. Boys learn less by watching and more by being told. If a boy sees his mother working at home, and learns that what she is doing is women's work, then it is not for him. He gets many notions of maleness from television and other indirect sources. Boys are pushed to give up childish, dependent behavior and to avoid feminine displays or "sissy" activities. Boys are expected to change more, to grow up faster than girls. What they are, and are not, to be and do is more clearly defined.

Masculine and *feminine* are opposites, to be one is to be not the other. In learning what we should do, we must learn what we should not do. This is especially true for boys: learning to be masculine is learning to be (or trying to be) competitive, active, dominant, aggressive, but most of all, to be *not feminine*.

While it is thought that we learn to conform to masculine and feminine images prescribed by society, the evidence is unclear about how well we actually do learn. Tendencies toward aggressive behavior, as in the earlier periods of life, are seen more in boys. By early adolescence only two other differences have been reliably distinguished: girls, on the average, begin to score higher on verbal tests; boys, on the average, are better at visual-spatial tasks (those requiring an ability to visualize objects in space). For many other supposedly sex-linked traits, no real differences have been established (Maccoby and Jacklin, 1974).

Review the ways in which you behaved as a male or female during middle childhood (Exploration 5.7).

At puberty we outgrow our childish bodies and take on those physical characteristics that are obvious signs of our femaleness and maleness. The preceding section explored the influence of this change on sexuality; here let's consider some of the effects puberty has on adolescent sex-role learning.

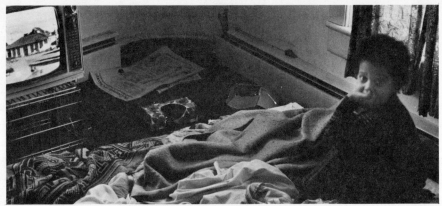

EXPLORATION 5.7

Sex Roles in Childhood

With your class, make a list of programs you watched on TV as a child. Also list the books, comics, and movies which were your favorites.

What were the sex-role models that these sources of entertainment presented?

What kinds of women appeared?

What were their traits and activities?

What about the men?

Which of these women and men conformed to a sex-role stereotype and which didn't?

Name five heroes you learned about in grade school. Name five heroines.

Could you extend each list to ten? More?

What was special about these people?

Check the activities in the following list which you engaged in even once, either in grade school or high school:

whined when you didn't get your way	played short stop
had your ears pierced	had a paper route
changed a diaper	rode your bike all over town
wore perfume	wore pants
baked cookies	went hunting or fishing
ironed a shirt	climbed to the top of a tree
did the grocery shopping	got in a fist fight
babysat for money	bashed in the fender of the family car
cried when you were angry	fired a gun
wore a skirt	repaired a flat tire
washed out a pair of socks	wore a white shirt and tie
giggled	bit your lip to avoid crying
flirted	built a motor that ran
embroidered, knit, or crocheted	spit on the sidewalk
served a meal to your family	swore at your father
went on a diet	lifted weights
chewed your cuticles	grew a moustache
dusted the living room	made an obscene gesture
shaved your legs	rode on a large motorcycle, alone

Compare the things you did with what the other females and males in your class did.

Did the women do more activities in the left-hand column?

Men more in the right?

(You will probably find both sexes engaged in many of these.)

When (if) you did things which were clearly appropriate for the other sex, how did you feel?

What were the reactions of your friends, parents, grandparents, teachers?

As a child or youth, did you ever have fantasies about becoming:

(MEN) the most beautiful, desirable man in the world?

(WOMEN) the most powerful, influential woman in the world?

In your experience was it easier for a girl to be a tomboy than it was for a boy to act like a girl? If so, why do you think there was a difference?

How did school program you for your sex roles?

Think about the kinds of classes you took, incidents on the playground, the teachers who were your models, extracurricular activities, etc.

Choose a partner in your class. Spend five minutes telling your partner about each of the following people:

Your same-sex parent

The same-sex adult whom you consider the most important in your life

Your opposite-sex parent

The most important opposite-sex adult in your life.

As you are talking, pay attention to the way you are describing these people, the traits you are choosing to relate. (If you were missing a parent, describe a parent-substitute, if you had one.)

Do you see ways you are very like any of these people?

The exact opposite?

You are likely to find some patterns of identification and imitation doing this exercise. You may discover that you have modeled yourself after certain aspects of each of these adults. I was surprised to find that I didn't have any important male adult model besides my father.

Switch places and listen to your partner.

Girls' bodies are usually transformed into an adult shape before comparable changes take place in boys. Thus girls get a head start (and much encouragement) in becoming concerned with their appearance. It is *being*—being attractive, popular, and sought-after—rather than doing, which is often stressed for young women. Evaluations of self are frequently based on comparisons with friends and with stereotyped ideals of femininity.

Looks are important for males too, but more as part of an overall image a young man must create for himself. This image rests largely on what he *does* (or can convince others he does). It covers any weakness, fear, timidity, or other perceived flaw (including virginity). Males are

Michael Weisbrot

under considerable pressure to perform, as in sports or academics. Some young men become caught up in proving their masculinity in antisocial or delinquent behavior.

**EXPLORATION
5.8**

**Adolescent
Images**

How important to you were your looks when you were an adolescent?
    What did you want to change in order to be more desirable or more like others?

What kind of an image did you create for yourself during high school? What did you do in order to be acceptable to your peers, teachers, and parents?

How did your relationships with your family change after puberty?
    Did your family treat you more as a grown-up than before?

How important were vocational goals to you during high school?
    Were these plans central to your self-concept?
    How influential were your parents' suggestions or demands when you considered various occupations? Other adults'?
    How much thought did you give to choosing either your father's or your mother's jobs?
    What pressure did you feel to follow in their footsteps?

Were marriage or parenthood prospects in your adolescent plans for the future? How important did they seem?
    Did you take it for granted that you would be a wife, husband, mother, father?
    Were these roles central or would they be incidental to your occupation?
    How much of your future hinged on finding a mate?

SENSE OF COMPETENCE

Before starting school, our basic sense of competence is shaped by the mastery of certain tasks on our own and by our parents' opinions of our abilities. In school we are confronted with new challenges almost daily, new demands that we perform in specific ways, and increasing pressure to demonstrate our proficiency at various tasks set for us. We may find that skills which were perfectly acceptable at home, even praised by our parents, are unimportant or inadequate at school. We must now measure up to the expectations of teachers and peers.

Many children have resources and flexibility enough to cope with school, to take the challenges in stride, to begin to actualize their intellectual and social potentials. Others do not, and may find themselves, quite early in their grade-school years, feeling hopelessly inadequate. Sometimes a teacher's expectations take no account of differences between potential and actual performance. These expectations may be based on a child's ethnic or socioeconomic status, on the performance of an older sibling in a previous class, or on another teacher's evaluation. Schools offer opportunities to develop a sense of incompetence as well as a sense of competence.

The major emphasis in school is on intellectual achievement, on the mastery of fundamental and then increasingly sophisticated language skills, and on cultivating mental work habits. School is also a framework in which our social and interpersonal competencies are shaped. We must learn how to participate effectively in organized groups, to assume leader and follower roles, to get along with our peers. These social skills

National Education Association Publishing, Joe Di Dio.

are not measured by examination but by our success in making and keeping friends, by our popularity, and by our ability to please and influence

---

**EXPLORATION
5.9**

**Early
Competence**

List the things you were good at in elementary school and in junior high school.

How did you know you were good?

Were these accomplishments achieved in the classroom? On the playground or athletic field? In social situations?

Were you good at any of your hobbies or interests pursued outside of school?

Were you best at things you did alone or were you best at things which required group participation, teamwork, or partnership?

List the things you were *not* good at. What was characteristic of these activities, and how did you know your performance was poor?

What were your favorite subjects in school?

Were you good at them?

What were your most disliked subjects in school?

Were you poor at them?

When and under what conditions were you turned off in school?

Did you ever come to feel that school was a drag, bad, or threatening?

Generally, how were you at the mechanics of learning?

For example, at following instructions

being prompt

neat

fast

attentive?

What were the consequences of being either good or poor at these things?

Did you ever feel that you were handicapped in school? How? (Physically, economically, socially, etc.?)

In grade school and then in high school, how competent were you at the following:

competing	trying harder
playing fair	showing off
taking turns	leading
sharing things	following
losing	controlling your temper
winning	taking responsibility
finishing things	being assertive
starting things	saying the right thing
cooperating	getting the right answers

How did you feel about grades and report cards?

Were they important?

Did they reflect your abilities and performance accurately?

our peers. Social failures can fracture an otherwise sound sense of competence.

The longer we are in school, the more often our academic skills are tested and graded. It becomes a fact of life that our competence will be judged by others and judged relative to the performance of our competitors. Those of us who do not compete well are subject to feelings of infe-

---

EXPLORATION 5.10

Adolescent Competence

Repeat Exploration 5.9 as it applies to your high school experiences. Did any of your high school experiences lead you to discover what you were good at?

During adolescence what, to you, was your greatest achievement?
Do you still value that area of activity?
If not, why?

How important were your good grades to your parents?
To your peers?

In high school, what things were you afraid of failing at?
What maneuvers did you use to avoid feeling like a failure?
Did you lower your standards, quit, blame someone or something else, etc.?

Did you drop out of high school?
What were your feelings then?
How do you feel about it now?

Did you learn how to be a procrastinator in high school?
If so, in what circumstances: schoolwork, interpersonal relations, under pressure?
How did you feel about yourself when you put things off until the last minute?
Do you continue procrastinating today?

During periods when there wasn't much to do, or when few demands were being made on you, did you have trouble getting started on those things which needed doing?

What did you learn about taking exams in high school?
Were they threatening?
Did you learn how to cheat?
How did you feel about yourself if you cheated, or when you failed an exam?

Was there a stigma on very bright, high-achieving students in your high school?
Were they popular?
Did the stigma (if any) apply more to one sex than the other?

Did you ever get the feeling that you ought not to be too good at something?
That others would ridicule you if they knew you were better than they?

National Education Association Publishing, Joe Di Dio.

riority and failure. These feelings all too often do not motivate us to try harder; they lead us instead to the conclusion that we are not competent and that school is unprofitable. Negative feelings about the value of school are characteristic of high school dropouts. Today, one in every four students drops out of school before finishing (White, 1976).

Even if we are capable, academic achievement may not fit the image we want to create with our peers. If our social group is not impressed by brains we can learn to hide our intellectual abilities. For instance, the bright high school girl does not conform to the feminine stereotype. Her conflict is expressed in the saying "Men never make passes at girls who wear glasses"—or who carry stacks of books, or who study hard, or get As in calculus. Many highly talented young women will settle for Bs rather than jeopardize their feminine image or their desirability in the eyes of men (Horner, 1969).

UNBOUNDEDNESS

It is primarily during the long learning period of our school years that we become bound to our culture's ways of thinking, perceiving, and acting. From the first to the twelfth grades we are yearly strengthening those potentials which will make us fit to live by conventional viewpoints. We learn to see things in the right perspective, to come up with the right answers, and to act in the right ways.

During the primary grades our mental capacities develop to where we gradually come to perceive order, logic, objective reality, and to undertake rational thinking (Piaget, 1952). The major purpose of formal instruction in school is to develop in us a certain kind of consciousness. We must learn the rules, symbols, and perspectives by which rational

EXPLORATION 5.11

Unboundedness and Culture

How many situations can you recall in which you learned there is *one right* answer?

In what ways did you learn about being on time?
>Was your family regular or irregular about meals and bedtimes?
>What were your parents' attitudes towards time?
>Did you learn by watching TV (where things change regularly on the hour and half-hour) that you missed things if you weren't "on time?"
>How often were you tardy for school or late for your social events? What happened?

Do you recall times when you had to cover up your emotions? To squelch spontaneous expressions?

In what ways were you discouraged from being sensuous—looking at, tasting, listening to, or touching things?

Recall a time when you were punished for daydreaming.
>Where were you?
>Why in this situation was it important that you pay attention?
>Who punished you?
>How? (Were you scolded, shamed, deprived, given extra work?)
>How did you feel?

In grade school can you remember being encouraged in the creative use of your imagination?
>Were you praised for fantastic stories, weird drawings, offbeat or original ideas?

Can you remember being criticized for, or having to redo, original work because you didn't follow rules, like spelling or punctuation rules, because the teacher couldn't tell what your drawing represented, or because your ideas were too novel (therefore wrong)?
>How did you feel?

Were creativity, originality, and fantasy encouraged in your family?
>How?

Did the members of your family share their dreams? Daydreams?
>Was there any regular interest in or attention paid to inner experiences?

Recall the kinds of daydreams you had in early adolescence. Which of the following functions do you think they had for you?
>fulfilling some wish or desire you had
>making you a hero
>rehearsing some future event
>redoing a past event, making it have a happy ending
>supplying some missing ingredient (like sex or romance) in your life
>escaping some unpleasant demand or task
>getting rid of someone or something you didn't like
>imagining violence, aggression
>creating beauty and harmony
>playing around with ideas, trying to make them make sense
>other functions

National Education Association Publishing, Joe Di Dio.

thought is governed and conducted. We must learn what a fact is and how to express and manipulate facts with words and numbers. We must learn to separate fantasies from facts and to keep them separate. These are the hallmarks of conventional mental activity in Western cultures.

The older we get the more we are encouraged to put aside our childish ways. We must come to experience less naively, less creatively, and in less than absolute terms. In this culture we become adjusted, scheduled, and socialized with programs that do not tolerate much playfulness, impulsiveness, expressiveness, or sensuousness. Methods of actualizing our potentials for intuitive modes of thought, for contact with our inner world and dreaming, are almost totally neglected by formal education. We are taught to cover up our feelings, to be responsible, to mind clocktime, and to perform in logical ways. Many of the lessons we get are subtle but nonetheless powerful. We are given enough practice during our youth that the majority of us are effectively bound to dominant modes of thinking, perceiving, and acting by the time we are grown up.

During the second decade of life we begin to experience the world as adults. We are no longer expected to play as we did when we were children. Playing is a luxury; we are to be more serious and sensible. There are pressures to be grown up and responsible; we need to become independent. In many people there is a reluctance to become bound too soon by the commitments of adult life and, at the same time, a desire to extend one's experience.

During the 1960s, a large number of young people tried to create a sense of adolescent unboundedness by becoming "flower children." Youths of the 1970s, although not as blatant in their expressiveness, have been influenced by the attitudes and experiments of their predecessors. Many, for instance, resist commitment by cultivating an attitude of "hanging loose." Hanging loose is being unbound by promises for the future (next year, tomorrow, anytime later than now) and being free of concern for anyone else. There is a feeling that only the most immediate experience is valid, whether the experience is music, physical adventure, or sex.

**EXPLORATION
5.12**

**Adolescent
Culture**

Did you experience pressures from your parents or teachers to be more responsible as a teenager?
  What were your reactions?
  Did you have a "hang-loose" attitude?
  Did you feel needs to be free?

How large a part of your adolescent life were drugs and the drug scene?
  How do you feel about the way you approached drugs now that you are out of high school?

What messages did you get about drugs from the following? (What was said? What did you observe these people doing?)
  family
  users
  abstainers
  teachers
  pushers in your school

What did you learn from other sources, like films, TV?

What did you learn about drugs as:
  an escape
  a means to get high
  a requirement of belonging to a group?

Did you use alcohol? With family? Peers? Alone?

How did you feel about alcoholics as a teenager?

Did you judge your parents' use of alcohol and pills?

What ways, if any, did you get high without drugs in high school? Describe your highest experience.
  Was it with or without drugs?

What was the most creative thing you did in high school?
  Were you rewarded? How?

Contemporary teen culture offers most adolescents the opportunity to experiment with drugs. While some teenagers never use drugs, or only use them occasionally, others find that drugs are the dominant focus of their lives. There are many reasons for the flourishing of the drug scene in high school culture, including our belief in the power of drugs. We may take drugs to satisfy our curiosity, to alter states of consciousness,

Michael Weisbrot

expand perception, escape reality, get stoned, or to do what others are doing. Although adults continue to make great efforts to prevent teen-agers' access to drugs, most adolescents do not find it difficult to get dope if they feel it is important. (The topic of drugs is discussed further in Chapter 12.)

SUMMARY
1. The purpose of this chapter has been to engage you in a review of your life between the ages of six and eighteen.
2. Your answers should have led you to recognize some of the potentials you have actualized in these areas:
    Expressing your individuality and conforming to your peer group
    Forming childhood friendships and opposite-sex relationships
    Learning about sexuality
    Becoming feminine or masculine
    Developing competence, both academic and social
    Thinking and perceiving as an adult

Suggested Readings
Erikson, Erik. *Identity: Youth and crisis.* New York: Norton, 1968. An extended inquiry into identity and identity confusion.
Friedenberg, Edgar Z. *The vanishing adolescent.* Boston: Beacon Press, 1959. Essay describing the plight of the American adolescent in a society with vanishing opportunities for self-definition; *The coming of age in America.* New York: Random House, 1965. A sociological study of adolescent values in the United States, particularly excellence and individuality versus conformity.

Goodman, Paul. *Growing up absurd.* New York: Vintage, 1960. A lively, eccentric discussion of the difficulties young people encounter in a "phony" culture.

Ralston, Nancy C. and Thomas, G. Patience. *The adolescent: Case studies for analysis.* San Francisco: Chandler Publishing Co., 1974. Eighteen case studies illustrating some typical behavior patterns and problems of adolescents.

Michael Weisbrot

As young adults we follow paths begun during our first two decades. During childhood and adolescence we have developed or actualized some of our potentials; others have remained dormant. Now we make more and more decisions that will direct the course of our lives through the present and into the future. We make decisions that separate us from our childhood families. Some of the ties keeping us firmly anchored as a son or daughter are severed. We may cling for a while, as though fearful of being set adrift, or we may be anxious to take a leap into independent, adult life. However we manage it, there is a separation between parent and child to be made. We are expected to assume adult responsibilities sooner or later.

By accident or steadfast pursuit we take steps to establish ourselves as adults. We may start by reducing the number of alternatives we have: we decide what and where we don't want to be, who we don't want to be with. Or we decide where we do want to be, what we do want to do, who we do want to be with.

The years between 20 and 30, for most of us, are years of decision and commitment. We make commitments we intend to keep for a long time — commitments about occupation, and about where and how to live. We make plans with others, many of us by marrying and beginning a family of our own. In Erikson's terms we are resolving the psychosocial stage of Intimacy and beginning that of Generativity.

Generally, the thirties are years of doing what we earlier set out to do. We devote out time and energy to getting ahead. We make money, accumulate debts and possessions, struggle, survive, work, relax, and worry. We become established, but not without making some changes. Sometimes we change jobs, communities, and life-styles several times. We move, rearrange, readjust, and come to be more settled.

By our forties and fifties we can see more clearly what we have been committed to and where our earlier decisions have led us. We also see what we have passed by. There seem to be fewer and fewer chances to make major changes. There are few beginnings (for instance, careers or families) for most. It is now that we begin knowing we are older; perhaps we are feeling wiser. But the indisputable fact is: we are not young any more.

Whatever our age, wherever we are in the life cycle, we still have the potential for growth. We are not destined to grow up and cease expanding our lives. Only if we limit our growth by refusing to allow for change, only if we live by plans alone and ignore our present, only if we do not quest will we stagnate. We do not quest for the future; the future comes in its own time. We quest to know ourselves in the present, to live immediately. Just as we are powerless to change the past, we waste potential by trying to "fix" the future. We actualize potentials by giving ourselves room to become what we are.

Chapters 6 through 12 consider several of the quests engaging us through the forty to fifty years of middle life. As earlier, there are milestones to guide us on the journeys we make as adults. In these chapters we see our growth as

- increasing self-awareness and self-knowledge
- developing honesty and trust with others
- acceptance of sexuality
- understanding sex role stereotypes and personhood
- knowing the worth of self and the worth of life
- believing that the power to expand consciousness lies within us

In each of our several quests we find ways of maximizing our potentials for further travel, useful techniques for changing, growing, and becoming.

———for this is my story; it is the story of a man, not of an invented, or possible, or idealized, or otherwise absent figure, but of a unique being of flesh and blood. Yet, what a real living human being is made of seems to be less understood today than at any time before, and men — each one of whom represents a unique and valuable experiment on the part of nature — are therefore shot wholesale nowadays. If we were not something more than unique human beings, if each one of us could really be done away with once and for all by a single bullet, storytelling would lose all purpose. But every man is more than just himself; he also represents the unique, the very special and always significant and remarkable point at which the world's phenomena intersect, only once in this way and never again. That is why every man's story is important, eternal, sacred; that is why every man, as long as he lives and fulfills the will of nature, is wondrous, and worthy of every consideration. In each individual the spirit has become flesh, in each man the creation suffers, within each one a redeemer is nailed to the cross.

Few people nowadays know what man is. Many sense this ignorance and die the more easily because of it, the same way that I will die more easily once I have completed this story.

I do not consider myself less ignorant than most people. I have been and still am a seeker, but I have ceased to question stars and books; I have begun to listen to the teachings my blood whispers to me. My story is not a pleasant one; it is neither sweet nor harmonious, as invented stories are; it has the taste of nonsense and chaos, of madness and dreams—like the lives of all men who stop deceiving themselves.

Each man's life represents a road toward himself, an attempt at such a road, the intimation of a path. No man has ever been entirely and completely himself. Yet each one strives to become that—one in an awkward, the other in a more intelligent way, each as best he can. Each man carries the vestiges of his birth—the slime and eggshells of his primeval past—with him to the end of his days. Some never become human, remaining frog, lizard, ant. Some are human above the waist, fish below. Each represents a gamble on the part of nature in creation of the human. We all share the same origin, our mothers; all of us come in at the same door. But each of us—experiments of the depths—strives toward his own destiny. We can understand one another; but each of us is able to interpret himself to himself alone (Hesse, 1965, pp. 3–4).

Michael Weisbrot

THE QUEST
FOR SEPARATENESS
AND WHOLENESS

These are the questions:

Who am I?
Am I the person I think I am, or the person I show to others? Am I the person I
    wish to be?
How can I know who I am when others seem to be a part of me, and I seem to
    exist in some way inside them?
Why do I cling to others too tightly, or run from them, or strike out at them?
How can I be a whole person, unfragmented and complete?
How can I be everything I have the potential of becoming?
How can I become self-actualizing?

Self-actualization is the process of becoming the person *I am,* a whole
person, separate from others and yet living among them. My potential is
to become myself. The major milestone in this process is self-awareness.
The chief obstacle is anxiety. Succumbing to anxiety can lead to self-
defeat and self-alienation.

I lagged behind on a hike until I was out of sight or sound of my companions and alone, the only human being in an expansive field. For a few
minutes I felt as though I must be the only person on earth.
    In the middle of a conversation, I suddenly realized that I had been a
great distance away, lost in my own world of thought, far from my friend.
"I'm sorry, what did you say?"
    I woke feeling puzzled. I wasn't quite sure where I was or where I
had returned from. Later, at breakfast with my family, I realized they had
been there too, in my dream. But, of course, they hadn't been there at all.
I had experienced my dream with them, yet I had been entirely alone in
my self-created experience. I knew that I could never share my experience of them with them.

Perhaps you have had similar experiences, fragments of solitary existence. These times always remind me that I exist apart from all other
people, other animals, plants, or things. I am individual, body and
thoughts and feelings collected in a being that is uniquely me. I am separate.

SEPARATENESS

My physical separateness is evident. From the moment my umbilical
cord was cut, I have been physically independent. Those parts of me I
consider vital, my "insides," are separated by skin from the air. I could
be a sausage, my casing of skin marking the boundary between the world
of "me" and that of "not-me." I don't lose my distinctiveness when I
touch other people or things. I don't melt like butter, become atomic
bound, or mixed until all my unique lumps have disappeared in the
blend. I remain physically intact, and separate.

But I am not so separate that I could survive in a vacuum for more than a few minutes. My physical existence (at least) is supported by a system of exhange between me and my environment. I take food and water, sound and light, and contact with other people. Without these I would lose both biological and psychological integrity. To stay alive and well, things that were once "not-me" become "me," and some of "me," in turn, is paid out. I give the products of my metabolism: urine, feces, carbon dioxide, perspiration, sluffed skin cells and falling hair. The eggs in my refrigerator are "not-me" just now. Tomorrow morning, by way of a cheese omelette, they will become me. My physical separateness can be defined only a moment at a time; strictly speaking, with each breath it is new.

My psychological separateness often seems even less definite than my physical separateness. But I can feel it. It is a sense I have of myself as different from all other people. It is my subjective distinction between "me" and "not-me." My psychological separateness is my personal identity. It is my experience of myself as the singular sum of my acts, perceptions, thoughts, and memories. I am separate because I am my experience, and my experience is me. Whether I am with others on a crowded beach, eating Christmas dinner with my family, playing volleyball, stroking my child's forehead at bedtime, or standing in front of the mirror brushing my teeth—no matter what the situation, I am separate and alone in my experience of myself. Each of us is separate and alone in experience:

Which of us has known his brother? Which of us has looked into his father's heart? Which of us has not remained forever prison-pent? Which of us is not forever a stranger and alone? (Thomas Wolfe 1929, p. 3)

My separateness is not always apparent to me. My memories of people and places, thoughts about where I must be before noon, my plans for hiking this summer with my friends—these connecting webs of relationship between my self and others tend to obscure the boundaries be-

Sarah Cirese (Photograph by Michael E. Bry).

tween what is "me" and what is not. I do not feel separate, a stranger and alone, when I share my time and possessions and thoughts with others. Sometimes I feel attached to things and people. When an old friend departs I feel that something of me has gone too. Even when I misplace a favorite book or break a coffee cup I've used for years it can be as though I have lost or broken a piece of my self. These feelings of attachment, connectedness, and relatedness with others and things can be strong. John Donne expressed this idea centuries ago:

No man is an island, entire of itself; every man is a piece of the Continent, a part of the main; if a clod be washed away by the sea, Europe is the less, as well as if a manor of thy friends or of thine own were; any man's death diminishes me, because I am involved in mankind; and therefore never send to know for whom the bell tolls; it tolls for thee.

John Donne
("Devotions XVII")

Real Self and Personality

Self-experience changes from moment to moment. It is a "stream of consciousness," in the words of William James, and its flow lends a sense of fluidity to my separateness. In unbroken succession I recall driving to school this morning, I hear and see and feel myself typing, I look up at

---

EXPLORATION 6.1

Real Self

Assume a comfortable, relaxed position. Close your eyes. Repeat each of the following statements slowly and distinctly:

I *have* a body but *I am not* my body. My body is my instrument of experience and action. It is only an instrument. I treat it well. I try to keep it in good health, but it is *not* myself. I *have* a body, but *I am not* my body.

I *have* emotions, but *I am not* my emotions. I *have* hopes, fears, joys, and sorrows. I *feel* calmness, irritation, and excitement. I observe, judge, understand and direct my emotions. I *control* and use my emotions but they are *not* myself. I *have* emotions, but *I am not* my emotions.

I *have* desires, but *I am not* my desires. My desires are changeable and contradictory. I can be aroused, but my desires do *not* control me. I *have* desires but *I am not* my desires.

I *have* an intellect, but *I am not* my intellect. I can develop and discipline my intellect. Through it I can know the outer world and the inner world. My intellect is active but it is *not* myself. I *have* an intellect but *I am not* my intellect.

I am myself. I have a body. I have emotions. I have desires. I have an intellect. I can master and direct all these. *I am myself.*

(This exploration is adapted from Assagioli, 1965.)

the sound of rain, race outside to check the car windows, try to collect my thoughts and catch my breath. I scratch my ear, reach out blindly at a signal from the telephone, and forget everything else as I pour my attention into the receiver. My experience of myself is composed of chains, layers, and webs of alternating memories, physical acts, perceptions of stimuli, imaginings of future events, attention to internal stimuli. Psychologically, I am in constant motion, going from here to there, inside and out, from past to present to future, feeling now separate and now connected. Yet throughout this ceaseless experience, the focus of my consciousness is always "me."

How can this be so? What is it that keeps the flow from becoming unmanageably chaotic? How is it possible to speak of a "me" in all this mental rushing about? The relative consistency of my experience of myself comes from my core identity, which holds my personality together as a magnet restrains a scatter of metal shavings. This core can

real self

be called my real self.

If my real self were all of my personality, I would easily achieve separateness and wholeness. But my personality is complex, and not fully explained even by those theories of personality discussed in Chapter 2. Although personality theories differ in many ways, most share a concern with aspects of the quest for separateness and wholeness.

public self
self-image
self-ideal
self-concept

Among the important concepts of some theories are public self, self-image, self-ideal, and self-concept.

My *public self* is that aspect of my personality which I show to others; it is the person I wish others to see. This public self is sometimes a mask which conceals my real self. Often I use it to present myself as I think I should be. Sometimes it masks aspects of my personality which I am not aware of, and at other times I use it to hide feelings I am fully aware of but do not wish to reveal. Actually, the public self is many selves; we don different masks according to which face we feel we should present in various situations. Each of our social roles has its particular mask, for each role consists of a specific set of expected behaviors.

**EXPLORATION
6.2**

**Public
Self**

One person will sit in the middle of a circle of classmates. Each person in the surrounding circle will, in turn, describe the one in the center by using the sentence "You are _____." When you have been in the center, ask yourself: Does everyone in the group see me in the same way? Do their views of me differ from mine? After everyone has had a turn in the center, compare your discoveries.

Self-image is a picture I have of myself to which I refer from time to time to know who I am. I hold this picture for ready reference, but it is not always accurate. Self-image does not always coincide with the real self. It can be a distortion: I can picture my self as better, bigger, brighter than I am, or I can think of my self as worse, smaller, and less capable than I am. No matter how distorted my self-image, it is a representation I know well and one I will try to preserve unless it crumbles under the weight of contradictory evidence.

EXPLORATION 6.3

Self-Image

Answer the question "Who am I?" by writing out the sentence "I am _____." Do this twenty times consecutively. Include whatever spontaneously comes to mind: physical characteristics, roles, emotions, behavior, and so on.

Draw a picture of yourself.

What do these explorations show you of your self-image?

My *self-concept* is a constellation of attitudes I hold about my worth as a person. It is the value I place on myself. Self-concept can be based on many, or on only a few, traits and abilities. For example, I can have a fairly high regard for myself even though I know I am a very poor ice skater. Or I may believe myself an unworthy person because I have tried to stop smoking and have failed. My self-concept develops from comparisons of my self-image with my self-ideal. My *self-ideal* is the person I feel I could or would like to be. It is that standard of perfection by which I examine what I am and what I do. Failing to measure up to a self-ideal (for instance, failing to stop smoking) is often experienced as guilt.

EXPLORATION 6.4

Self-Ideal

Bring an object to class which symbolizes your self-ideal, the way you would like to be. Describe the qualities of this object that you feel you should strive to own as part of your self. Then compare and contrast yourself to the object: "I am like it in this way, but not in that way." Do *not* explain your observations, or make excuses, or indicate guilt or sorrow. Simply describe the similarities and differences in a matter-of-fact way.

I am not aware of my total personality, or of all my needs or wants. Some aspects of my personality I keep hidden from myself and try to keep hidden from others. This underside of the personality is often referred to as the *unconscious*. My unconscious contains material that I do not recognize or acknowledge as a part of myself, material that has not floated up into my stream of consciousness. It includes repressed memories—events from my past which would make me feel uncomfortable were I to recall them. It also hold thoughts which I reject as undesirable and aspects of my personality which I do not want to own. It includes whatever of my real self I am not in touch with.

Separateness and Others

We do not live in psychological isolation any more than we live in physical aloofness from our environment. Life is a process of continuous social interaction, and, as stated earlier, presents us with many opportunities for confusing "me" and "not-me." Where "me" ends and others begin is often unclear, for much of personality consists in experiences that include the influence of others.

The groundwork for confusion is laid in childhood, when we learn how we must be in order to live with others. In fact, our socialization occurs precisely because we have the potential to internalize the values and attitudes of others, and to make them our own. This is how we build our self-ideal. Self-ideal is constructed from the many expectations of our culture (especially those transmitted by our parents) that tell us what and who we should be. We incorporate cultural ideals into our personalities and then try to live up to them.

Our public self also begins to form in childhood as we learn to present ourselves to our parents and others. The older we get the more sophisticated and diverse our masks become, for we gain more and different audiences. The public self is *never* separate from others; it functions in response to public demand rather than to inner demand. Self-image and self-concept are both influenced by what others tell me about myself and how they react to what I do. Many times and in many ways others tell me who and what I am and what my value is. It is very easy for me to accept appraisals which I hear frequently from people who are important to me. No one is wholly uncontaminated by the influence of others; no one can be altogether psychologically "clean." If we were we could never live together.

Not only are others made part of our personalities, we push ourselves out into the world of things and people around us. The world into which we extend ourselves becomes familiar; the world beyond these limits is unfamiliar. The familiar is marked by what is sometimes called our

ego boundary

ego boundary. As we grow from childhood into adulthood, as more of the world becomes familiar, our ego boundary enlarges to contain ever more of what was previously separate from or unknown to us. Two complementary processes enable us to extend our ego boundaries. The first is

identification

identification.

We are said to *identify* with those things and people by which we define ourselves. Identification may expand my ego boundary to include my family, my friends, my race, my nation, my house, my car, or my clothes. When I identify with people my sense of "I" is lost, if only temporarily, in my sense of "we." When I identify with things they become "mine," or "ours." My ego boundary ends at those points where I see

Michael Weisbrot

clearly the line between "me-mine/we-ours" and "thee-thine/them-theirs." Them and theirs are foreign and unfamiliar to me; they exist outside my ego boundary. Although my ego boundary is clear to me, I may have difficulty sorting out its contents, that is, keeping "I" separate from "we" or from "mine."

EXPLORATION
6.5

Identification

Name three or four people in your class with whom you feel you identify. What characteristics of these people make you feel that part of you is "in" them? Who else do you identify with?

Now, list a few things with which you identify, things which are a part of your ego boundary (such as clothes, plants, car, art objects). How do you feel about these things in contrast with things outside your ego boundary? Would you feel unhappy if they were destroyed?

The second process by which we extend ourselves is *projection*. That is, we see in others aspects of personality that in fact belong to us. Our view of others, therefore, becomes a compound of what *we* are and of what *they* are. They become mirrors of ourselves, or partial mirrors. We sometimes think we are acting toward other people as separate, independent individuals when in fact we are reacting to what we have made of them. Projection is a common process and can be quite helpful in our relationships, for it allows us to feel empathy and to understand others. But, because we often project without knowing we are doing so, it can seriously hamper our ability to keep ourselves separate from others. We unconsciously project our needs, wishes, ideals and expectations onto others and hope that they will be met. Without fully understanding why, we are often disappointed that others aren't what we want them to be. (Parents are prone to feel this way about their children, lovers about each other.)

EXPLORATION
6.6

Projecting Expectations

We often do things because we *expect* others would want us to do them. What are the expectations you *think* these people have of you:

mother
father
opposite-sex friend
same-sex friend
instructor

Ask them if they *really* expect you to be the way you assume they do. You may find they don't!

Communication

Although we are not often aware of it, the habits many of us develop in communicating indicate our lack of separateness from others. We unwittingly capture others within our ego boundaries. For instance, we ask questions instead of making statements. Suppose I am at a party which has become very dull for me. I want to go home. Instead of saying so, I turn to my companion and say, "Do you want to go home now?" or "Isn't it time to go home now?" These questions allow me to avoid acknowledging my boredom and, in doing so, they undermine my separateness. I draw my companion into the web of my feelings. Or, suppose I say "You make me mad," rather than "I am mad at you." "You" are on the spot instead of me and my anger.

Now, take a situation in which one person, Bob, is clear about what he wants and expresses this to a friend: "I feel like spending the evening here with you in front of the fire. I'd like to stay."

The friend, Sally, is at first ambivalent, but given some time to choose, become clear: "I need to go to the library to start my term paper. I could start it tomorrow, though. Let me think about it. No, I feel more

Michael Weisbrot

like getting my research started. Thanks for asking me, though." Each has been clear with his and her self and with the other about their wants, though they did not want the same thing.

But see how the communication might have gone, given the same

---

EXPLORATION 6.7

Communication

Do this exploration in pairs or in groups of four or five. As you follow the directions, notice how a particular manner of communication feels to you. Do you feel detached, separate, blended with others? Where are your ego boundaries?

First, warm up by talking about anything you wish for about three minutes. Stop and review your verbal and nonverbal communication. Did you talk about yourself, about your environment, about others, about the present, past, or future?

Now, limit your communication in the following ways for about three minutes each: Remain aware each time of how you feel.

1. "It" statements. Every sentence each of you speaks must begin with "It . . ." (The subject of an "It . . ." statement is externalized, "it" is neither the speaker nor the listener. Do you feel detached from yourself and from others when speaking this way?)

2. "You" statements. Each of you begins every sentence with "You . . ." ("You" is sometimes used to mean "anybody" or "everybody," as in the phrase, "You know." It is also used to refer to a specific person, the listener: "You look nice today." Either kind of "You . . ." statement can be a way of disowning real self-experience or of being unseparate.)

3. "We" statements. Begin each sentence with "We . . ." ("We . . ." can be an expression of identification, indicating what we have in common or what we agree on. Or "we" can refer to "everybody" in the same way "you" does; it is nebulous. How does it feel to say "we" instead of "I"?

4. "I" statements. Say the same things you said in the "We" statements, but state them as your own, free of any others. (How does this feel?)

5. "Why . . .?" "Because . . ." One member begins with the question "Why . . .?" or "How come . . .?" and another responds with a reason or justification: "Because . . ." (Did you notice how demanding a "Why?" is? Every "Why?" implies that there is a "Because." When asked, "Why?" we often give an explanation even if we hadn't needed or thought of one, simply because we have been asked.)

6. Finally, use statements beginning with "I" and referring to another— "you"; for example: "I think you look nice today" or "I feel uncomfortable with you." (Making a statement about the way in which "I" experience "you" is the best way to keep us separate. How does this type of communication feel to you?)

(This exploration is adapted from *Awareness: Exploring, Experimenting, Experiencing* by John O. Stevens, pp. 100–105, © 1971 Real People Press.)

two people, but neither of them stating their own preferences:

Bob: "What do you feel like doing tonight?"
Sally: "Well, it's Friday night and it won't be too crowded at the library. I don't know."
Bob: "It's so cozy here. Wouldn't a fire feel good? Let's curl up."
Sally: "You never think about me. You only think about yourself. My paper is due Monday."
Bob: "Couldn't you start it tomorrow morning?"
Sally: "But you don't understand."
Bob: "Why don't you want to spend a nice quiet evening here with me?"
Sally: "Because."

With that Sally storms off to the library but finds her work doesn't go well. She is still fuming about Bob's inconsiderateness and her own dissatisfaction. She takes Bob and the argument along to the library with her; she is not separate enough to get on with her work. And Bob is probably fretting at home, feeling lonely and rejected. Neither is emotionally separate from the other.

Self-Disclosure

Self-awareness and real-self experience are related to the quality of our interactions with others. The real self is expanded by self-disclosure. A simple model, called the Johari Awareness Model (Luft, 1969), shows how this is so. Suppose self-knowledge is depicted as in figure (a) and self-revelation as in figure (b).

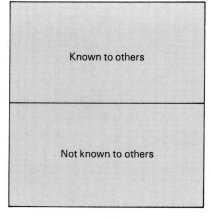

| Known to self | Unknown to self |

Known to others

Not known to others

(a)   (b)

The total person in relationship to others is represented by four quadrants:

	Known to self	Unknown to self
Known to others	1 Open	2 Blind
Not known to others	3 Hidden	4 Unknown

The Johari Awareness Model.

Quadrant 1 (Open) is a window to the self and the world; it is real-self experience

Quadrant 2 (Blind) is the presentation of self which others recognize but which we do not. It contains the material we disown or keep out of our awareness but which can be detected by others, often through nonverbal messages we send.

Quadrant 3 (Hidden) is what is known to self but not revealed to others.

Quadrant 4 (Unknown) contains motivations and feelings unavailable to either self or others; unconscious material.

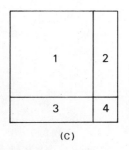

(c)

The size of any one quadrant is relative to the size of the other three. The more we acknowledge and reveal ourselves, the larger quadrant 1 will be, the more we can know ourselves. The virtue of this model is that it clearly shows the effect of being open with others. Self-knowledge increases as material is moved from quadrant 3 to quadrant 1. The less we keep hidden from others, the greater our real-self experience (c).

EXPLORATION 6.8

Self-Disclosure

Each member of a group transfers some piece of information about him or herself from quadrant 3 to quadrant 1 by writing it on a 3" x 5" card. Choose information which you know the others do not know about you (a feeling, thought, or motivation you have kept hidden). How did you feel about making something "private" available for others? Collect and shuffle the cards and have one group member read them without comment. Share your reactions.

WHOLENESS

Wholeness describes a personality whose several aspects fit together as though they were pieces of a jigsaw puzzle. In a *whole* personality, no parts are isolated, overlapping, or in the wrong place. Each is the "right" size for its slot. There are no gaping omissions. No substitute parts from another personality are used.

Separateness and wholeness work hand in hand. Separateness is achieved when we succeed in gathering all the correct "puzzle pieces' together, sorting those which belong from those which do not, making sure that each is the right size and shape.

Wholeness is a result of putting the pieces in place. It is achieved, to a large extent, by expanding consciousness, that is, by increasing self-awareness. As I become aware of neglected, rejected, and unfinished business in my life, I become more integrated or whole. Every piece of me that enters my awareness becomes part of my real self. The more material my real self encompasses, the more I understand my experiences and the less my life is cluttered with unaccountable events. When my thoughts, feelings, and actions are in a comprehensible relationship then I know that my experiences are an accurate reflection of my real self. My self-image becomes consistent with what I do.

People are not jigsaw puzzles, of course; they are never without the potential for a different arrangement of parts. There can be countless states of wholeness in the lifetime of an individual, countless times when one knows how aspects of one's personality fit one's experience. Wholeness is consistent with change and growth. We can change our minds, our friends, our style of living, our physical size and shape, even our names, and still remain whole. Personality is dynamic, not static. It is never a "finished" product.

The concept of wholeness refers also to the integration of other aspects of personality besides self-image. Public self, the presentation of ourselves to others, is sometimes a mask which covers our real self. As we become aware of our public self we do not present it automatically. It can be set aside when we choose to interact in ways which will disclose our real selves. There may still be occasions when we want to put up a front, but unless the public self can be shed it becomes a barrier between us and those with whom we wish to be close.

When self-ideal has been integrated in a whole personality, it becomes realistic. It is modified, if necessary, to give us standards which are personally and humanly possible. Our self-ideal is not necessarily abandoned, leaving us with no sense of how best to be, but it does become more congruent with our self-image. This allows our self-concept to be positive and self-affirming. I am able to become more of what I want to be and at the same time to feel good about myself as I am.

Unconscious Projection

In Chapter 4 we saw that children can use projection as a mechanism of
defense, for instance, as a way to avoid taking responsibility. Adults use
projection in exactly the same way. We have seen in this chapter how
projection serves to extend our ego boundaries, as when we project our
expectations. Projection is a process we are often unaware of. It can be
quite unconscious.

shadow

Carl Gustav Jung has given particular attention to unconscious projection in his theory of personality. Among the several personality components identified by Jung, three are often projected: the shadow, the

Carl Gustav Jung (*Na-
tional Library of Medi-
cine*).

animus
anima

animus, and the anima. The shadow is composed of those aspects of ourselves that we have rejected from our awareness or self-image. The animus is Jung's term for the masculine, assertive side of every personality; the anima is the feminine, passive component in everyone. The animus is expressed in a man's personality but usually the anima is silent, hidden in the unconscious. Women express their anima most fully, while their masculine side remains silent.

According to Jung, we project these three unconscious aspects of our personalities onto others. We project the shadow onto people of our same sex. A man will project his anima onto a woman; a woman, her animus onto a man. These people then complement us; they come to have those very qualities that are missing from our own self-image. When we are with them, we have the illusion of being more complete, more whole, than we feel when we are not with them. When we project we have given away, so to speak, part of our selves, and are less whole (and less separate) for having done so. And we do not relate to others as the people they really are; we relate to them as mirrors of ourselves (see Chapter 7).

**EXPLORATION
6.10
Projecting**

Unconscious projections are, by their nature, difficult to catch. But try this exercise anyway as an experiment in beginning to contact your shadow, animus, or anima.

Get into a comfortable position and close your eyes. Now, in your imagination "hear" the first name of a person of your sex. Let the name come to you, don't strain for it. Then let this name take shape as a physical being. Allow characteristics to attach themselves to it so that this person assumes a shape and becomes vocal and mobile. Let the picture become as sharp as it will.

Is this person like you in any way; different from you? Do you feel that you know him or her? Do you feel comfortable in his or her presence?

To attempt to find your animus or anima repeat the preceding exploration using the name of a person of the opposite sex. Ask yourself the questions you asked before. Does this person resemble any of your opposite-sex friends in any way?

Many psychologists have used ideas of separateness and wholeness in their work, though not always under these names. Jung, for example, speaks of *individuation*—the process by which a person becomes a psychological "in-dividual," a separate and indivisible unity or whole. Carl Rogers uses *self-consistency* and *congruence*. Thomas Harris, within the framework of transactional analysis, distills separateness and wholeness into the expression "I'm OK—You're OK." Fritz Perls has adopted the German term *Gestalt*, which translates roughly as "whole".

ANXIETY

Separateness and wholeness escape us when we allow anxiety to block the paths to them. Anxiety is usually characterized as a feeling of dread or apprehension. The feeling often has no readily apparent source; we are unable to say exactly what we feel apprehensive about. Nevertheless, anxiety makes itself felt throughout our bodies as well as our minds. We respond as though in an emergency, we prepare to fight or to escape something dangerous; heart rate increases, respiration speeds up, digestion stops and stomach muscles tighten, sweat breaks out. We are ready to act but don't, for the nature of the "emergency" is unknown. We may find that we can't think straight, we may begin to feel a sense of panic. This is a state one cannot tolerate for long.

There are many hypotheses about the sources of anxiety. In the following paragraphs are those consistent with the viewpoint of this text. Keep in mind that, with both anxiety in general and the anxiety of an individual at a particular time, the source lies outside our awareness—we are not immediately conscious of what makes us feel anxious, only of the feeling.

A primary source of anxiety is the fear of being abandoned. Karen Horney (1945) feels that anxiety is the result of this "basic anxiety" experienced in early childhood: the feeling that we might be or are being left alone and helpless in a hostile world. Earlier, in Chapter 4, we discussed "separation anxiety" in infants who realize their need for others who are not always available to them. Adults too have very basic needs for others and are threatened by the prospect of a solitary existence, of being left alone and left out. Clark Moustakas refers to this as "loneliness anxiety."

loneliness anxiety

**EXPLORATION
6.11

Loneliness**

Share with a group the loneliest experience you ever had. How did you feel? How do you feel about that experience now?

Fritz Perls believes that anxiety is simply the "gap between the now and the then." "Then" refers to any time, past or future, other than right now. It may be a past experience we wish to relive or undo; it can be a future plan or dream. Others have described anxiety as the consequence of comparing what is possible with what has been achieved. Still others (Moustakas, 1961) say it is the "fundamental breach between what one is and what one pretends to be." Anxiety has also been described as the outcome of a wish to make life permanent and stable. Anxiety often attends the making of choices, especially when the consequences of those

Michael Weisbrot

choices are not foreseeable. Since we make choices every day, there is ample opportunity for anxiety in our lives. It can immobilize us, even when we try to choose what to wear in the morning. It can cause great discomfort when we try to make decisions about what job to take, whom to marry, and where to live. The degree of anxiety is not always governed by the possible impact of the choice on our lives; it is more likely to rise and fall according to our perception of the amount of risk we must take.

A state of anxiety is uncomfortable, so uncomfortable that we will often use any means we have to reduce it to a manageable degree. Let's now look at how many of our attempts to cope with anxiety interfere with the achievement of separateness and wholeness in our personalities.

ANXIETY AND SEPARATENESS

Karen Horney (1945) has written that in attempting to reduce anxiety we adopt one of three major ways of relating to others. It is clear that if we choose one of these consistently and are unable to use other modes of relating we will never achieve true separateness.

Moving Toward Others

Our choices are designed to win us the affection and approval of others, especially those who are important to us. We act so as to please them and to live up to their expectations of us. We become sensitive to the possibility that others might reject us if we do not act in accordance with their wishes. We avoid actions which might result in losing love.

This behavior pattern can be adopted for use with large groups of others from whom we wish acceptance. For example, we direct our actions toward achieving popularity and the acceptance of our social peers. David Reisman (1950) refers to people who behave in this way as "other-directed."

We may decide to submerge ourselves in a relationship of dependence with another person who will take complete care of us. We cling to this "partner" with anxious devotion, counting on him or her to meet all of our needs.

security operations

Harry Stack Sullivan refers to our moving-toward-others behavior as "security operations." We maintain a feeling of safety in the esteem others have for us. Other people become instruments by which we reduce our loneliness anxiety. Simply stated, the less alone we are, the less loneliness we feel. These operations are successful in allowing us to feel loved, but they also put us in a position of dependence: we are bound to others, or to one other, for the sake of feeling safe. In order to sustain this sense of security, to reduce the possibility that others will deny us the affection we need, we try to present a desirable, even lovable public self. It becomes crucial that others not see our feelings of antagonism or distrust, or discover our imperfections and weaknesses, for they may think us less worth caring for.

Moving Away From Others

Behavior which leads us *away* from others can also be seen as an attempt to avoid the fear of being abandoned. The reasoning behind this view is: if I don't get close to others, then they can't hurt me, or leave me. I say "to hell with them," and reject others before they have the opportunity to reject me.

One kind of moving away is to take no interpersonal risks. We may restrict life within narrow confines, become modest, unassuming, and inconspicuous. In effect, we behave as though we believe that if others don't see us they can't reject us. A more active way of moving away from others is to assume an attitude of total self-sufficiency and independence. This is the highway of aloofness, along which there are no binding psychological ties with anyone or anything. Wilhelm Reich coined the term "psychic contactlessness" to refer to a state of being *among* but not really *with* others, which we achieve by avoiding any emotional contact with them.

psychic contactlessness

Moving Against Others

A step beyond moving away from others is moving against them: if I control or destroy others, then they can't control, destroy, or hurt me. Control is gained through power, power gained by glorifying strength and holding in contempt any weakness in others or in ourselves.

In order to move against others we must first depersonalize them.

Photograph by D. Doty.

They become objects or things to us as we discount their needs as human beings. We develop a self-ideal which does not include concern for the well-being of others. In this way we avoid the guilt which might arise from our manipulating them. Free of altruistic concerns, we are able to act on impulse to gratify our own needs. People who demand power are often seen as "self-centered" or "egocentric," terms which do not apply to the real self but to the inflated self-image of people in power.

EXPLORATION 6.12

Anxiety Reduction

In a group of 4 to 8 people take turns completing these sentences:
One way I move toward others is . . .
One way I move away from others is . . .
One way I move against others is . . .
Do you find yourself moving one way more than others?

ANXIETY AND WHOLENESS

Anxiety can be a product of internal conflicts between motives. We might want two incompatible things at the same time (for instance, wanting to stay in school full time in order to graduate, and also needing a job to survive.) Our desires are leading us in two directions. This type of **approach-approach** conflict is referred to as an approach-approach conflict. In other situations we may find that we want something that entails getting a negative outcome as well as a positive one. For example, breaking up a romance may get one out of a deteriorating relationship, but it may also mean **approach-avoidance** loneliness. This is an approach-avoidance conflict. A third kind of conflict arises when all choices seem to have negative consequences. For instance, a single woman gets pregnant and must choose between

avoidance-avoidance

getting an abortion, putting the baby up for adoption, or becoming an unwed mother. This is an avoidance-avoidance conflict.

EXPLORATION 6.13

Conflict and Defense

Do this exploration with a partner, each taking turns beginning. Start by describing to your partner some conflict you had or are in the midst of. Describe your own internal conflict: your conflicting motivations are the focus, not what others are doing to you. What is or was the struggle inside you? Was it an approach-approach, an approach-avoidance, or an avoidance-avoidance conflict?

Now, with your partner, examine your conflict objectively. Observe the situation as though you were not part of it, as though it belonged to someone else. See how defense mechanisms might prevent anxiety and block your real self by discussing these questions:

a. How would anxiety be reduced if some part of the situation were forgotten or ignored, that is, repressed?

b. Could you use rationalization to enhance self-image in this situation, by justifying your actions, providing excuses, or concluding that circumstances beyond your control were the cause of your conflict?

c. Would it be possible to reduce anxiety by denying realities, by denying certain possible options or solutions?

d. Would projection help you defend against the anxiety of making choices and accepting responsibility for those choices? Could you make someone else responsible or blame them in order to escape?

e. Is this a situation in which you might be able to displace your anger or hostility onto someone who did not deserve it in order to avoid confronting the person who did?

f. Is there a chance that you are using reaction-formation, that is, feeling the opposite of what you actually feel in order to enhance your self-concept?

g. Finally, how do you feel when you are being objective about a conflict? Does it seem less stressful to approach your conflict nonemotionally and rationally?

The process of analyzing a conflict can also be a defense, called intellectualization. Intellectualization can keep disturbing feelings out of awareness but it also requires repressing emotions. What would happen if you allowed yourself to feel some emotion—anger, sadness, guilt, or some other emotion? Relax and take a moment to be aware of your body, its tensions, your breathing, and heartbeat. What are you feeling?

In any conflict situation our anxiety is aroused. We must give up one thing to get another, or accept something we don't want to get what we do, or choose the lesser of two or more evils. Compounding our difficulties is the fact that we are not always clear about our priorities. (Which is more important, staying in school or getting a job?) We may also be unaware of our motives. We may not be fully aware, for instance, that we are hanging onto a relationship because we fear loneliness. Sometimes we deny motives or remain unaware of them precisely because we want to avoid conflict, and thus anxiety. We relegate feelings such as fear or anger to our unconscious. We often deny motivations that are not congruent with our self-image, public self, or self-concept. We then disown our real self.

The chief means by which we remain unaware of real self is repression. Repression is sometimes called motivated forgetting, the motivation being reduction of anxiety. We can forget the past, the present, and even the future. We repress the past by disowning or distorting memories. We are able to repress our present feelings (such as anger) by ignoring changes in heartbeat or breathing rates, or muscle tension, which accompany changes in emotional states. We repress the future by denying desires, forgetting plans, hopes, and appointments.

Repression results in a dis-integrated personality; the continual threat of potential anxiety keeps it fragmented. We must expend energy to keep disowned material out of our awareness. This cuts into energy we need for living and for wholeness. It is as though we build walls to keep our real self from contact with the other parts of our personality. We then must defend the walls.

Repressed material doesn't go away. We may be unaware of thoughts or memories because their contents are not available for inspection, but they can still exert influence on our physical being and motivate our behavior. Repressed anger, for example, becomes disguised as sick humor or malicious teasing. Much material worthy of repression carries with it emotion which gets trapped in our bodies as tension. Many of us store years of accumulated, but unattended, emotion in our muscles, particularly across our shoulders and in our stomachs.

We sometimes distort the meanings of events or people to prevent repressed material from leaking into awareness. These distortions (the defense mechanisms introduced in Chapters 2 and 4) reduce anxiety, but they also keep the real self from consciousness and distort realities. We adopt mechanisms in childhood and continue using them as long as they work to prevent anxiety.

OBSTACLES TO SEPARATENESS AND WHOLENESS

Struggling against anxiety cannot lead us to separateness or wholeness. Repressing our experiences cannot. Yet we persist in these behaviors. Why do we seem to need to defend out self-image, self-ideal, or public self at the expense of real-self experience? Why do we close down our awareness and become satisfied with partial experiencing?

One reason is that much of our behavior is unreflective routine. We spend many years developing habits of consistent living that stabilize self-image, self-ideal, and public self. Society, primarily through parents and teachers, rewards and punishes our behavior. Our habit patterns develop as we behave in compliance with these conditions. Once our patterns are fixed, we may spend most of our time and energy doing what we think is expected of us or rebelling, according to our disposition, but neither compliance nor rebellion strengthens the real self.

Another reason is that the real self can emerge only if we assume mature roles. When we are young we are allowed few experiences in making choices; others make them for us. Human childhood is long; we may find others making decisions for us for twenty years or more. Our real self cannot come into our awareness, nor can its full potential be realized until we make our own choices and take responsibility for them. Real self develops as we attempt to meet our own needs rather than trying to suit the needs and wishes of others. This takes time, a wide range of experiences, and the liberty to both choose and to make mistakes. Children and adults whose decisions are made by others cannot become separate or whole. For example, many people now feel that one of the greatest drawbacks of traditional women's roles (and other dependent-adult roles) is that they do not foster the actualization of the real self.

A third obstacle to separateness and wholeness is our attitude toward loneliness. Some cultures provide more occasions for loneliness anxiety than do others. America is one of these, according to Philip Slater. He points out, in *The Pursuit of Loneliness* (1970), that Americans share three social values which promote loneliness:

1. *Competition* is valued in preference to a sense of community. Americans from childhood are encouraged to compete, to try with all that we have to win out over others and to be better, rather than being guided to cooperate with others in the attainment of shared goals. We acknowledge that it is lonely at the top but this does not keep us from striving to be there or from trying to best our fellows.

2. We have become a society in which people are *uninvolved* in the social and interpersonal processes which govern our lives rather than being engaged in these processes. We are alienated from those who govern us politically. We have a technology and industry which removes us from producing our own need-satisfiers (food, clothing, shelter). Our society fails to confront social problems such as poverty and aging.

3. Our society prefers *independence* to dependence. In striving for individualism and independent living we neglect the fundamental human interdependence necessary for survival, the companionship necessary for nonanxious living.

Habitual patterns of behavior, being children and being treated as though we were children, and living in an idividualistic, competitive society which instills the fear of loneliness, all combine to lessen the opportunities we have to become self-actualizing.

Self-Defeat

neurotic

Self-defeating, or neurotic, behavior is persistent and inflexible behavior designed to avoid anxiety. Whether one moves toward others, away from or against them, or engages in defense—if any of these become one's exclusive response to anxiety, then one is working toward self-defeat. Limiting alternatives to only those which avoid anxiety renders one incapable of responding objectively to a situation. We all behave in this way at times. It is when we become unable to behave in any other way that we also block ourselves off from real-self experience. We pack our muscles with tension, nail our thoughts to familiar ground, and burn ourselves out creating smokescreens to prevent our real selves from perceiving or acting. Chronic sickness and fatigue with no apparent organic source, obsessive thoughts, and compulsive acts are characteristic of self-defeat. Another is a persistent sense of distress or discomfort that resists our efforts to allay it. Self-defeat allows few moments of joy, satisfaction, or creativity.

Self-defeating behaviors perpetuate themselves. People who have set self-defeating patterns tend to persist in them, even though their lives are never quite comfortable. They do so for the immediate relief the behavior gives them from the threats of anxiety. If I come to a fork in the road, go to the right and find my anxiety level goes down, I will continue to go right every time I come to a new fork. I will never know where the left path might take me. I will not be able to risk nor will I be able to recognize alternative routes.

Self-Alienation

When behavior exclusively serves self-image, self-ideal, or the public self, it cannot serve the real self, which becomes estranged from other aspects of personality, a process sometimes called self-alienation. A self-alienated person has feelings of being foreign to his or her self. There is little understanding of behavior, a sense of being split or not being true to self. Sometimes self-alienation is the feeling that "I'm not myself today," or "I don't know what possessed me to do that." Self-alienation has been described as a loss of contact with inner or body experiences. We become unable to discriminate accurately between experience that originates within us and that which takes place outside ourselves; the two become blended.

disembodiment

Ronald D. Laing (1965) describes the loss of contact with experience as disembodiment. According to Laing, the in-contact person is a whole of self and body; other persons and things remain separate: (Self/Body)–Other. Disembodiment is a split between the real self and the body so that one's body becomes otherness: Self–(Body/Other).

Disembodiment is a feeling that we can't control our experience.

Michael Weisbrot

Feelings, thoughts, and emotions seem to exist outside ourselves. There may be severe disorientations of time, place, and person as these modes are conventionally experienced. There is a lack of ability to discriminate between what is safe and what is dangerous, friendly and unfriendly. Emotional reactions will lack control and will be unrelated to the situation. We cannot then make decisions or choices. The most common label for persistent disembodied conditions is schizophrenia. In this state, according to Laing, the self exists in perpetual isolation, unable to relate to real people or real situations.

schizophrenia

Fritz Perls describes failure and success in becoming separate and whole in this way: "The crazy person says, 'I am Abraham Lincoln,' and the neurotic says, 'I wish I were Abraham Lincoln,' and the healthy person says, 'I am I, and you are you.'" (1969, p. 40)

SELF-ACTUALIZATION

Abraham Maslow and Carl Rogers have described self-actualizing people by the following characteristics (Christian, p. 72 ff.):

1. They experience life vividly "with full concentration and total absorption." Self-actualizing people are existential: they enjoy the present moments of life fully, not as a means to future ends, but as ends in themselves. Their lives are not perpetual preparation for the future; they enjoy living now.

2. They are aware of the real self. Self-actualizing people are unusually open to what is going on inside themselves. They experience fully their own thoughts, feelings, and states of being. Their self-images

are accurate reflections of their real selves; self-deception is minimal. They are realistic and resort to few myths about themselves or life. They can identify their defenses and give them up.

3. They take responsibility for themselves and their choices. Self-actualizing people don't conform to social norms but neither are they rebellious against society. They are able to choose to conform or not to conform, depending on the situation. Conforming or nonconforming is not important in itself, for they have a well-developed set of norms for themselves. They are ethical in the deepest sense. Their concern is expressed in a positive, constructive attitude toward all people and all things. They easily identify with the conditions of others. They care, and their caring is the wellspring of their ethical nature.

4. They make choices which are growth choices, making them without fear of the unknown. Self-actualizing people are comfortable with disorder, indefiniteness, doubt, and uncertainty. They don't have to know the answers. They can accept what is without trying to organize and label neatly all of life's contents.

5. They are distinctive and creative in living. Self-actualizing people are not necessarily creative in customary roles (artist, etc.) but in all they do. They have their own style which touches everything they do. They work to do well the things they choose to do.

Venturing

And to venture in the highest sense is precisely to be conscious of oneself. . . .

Soren Kierkegaard
(The Sickness unto Death)

Venturing is risking, seeking out experience. It is being authentic, related, and accepting of impermanence.

Authenticity   Authenticity is the result of living genuinely and honestly through our real self, having the courage to be, as Paul Tillich has said. In order to be authentic we must be aware, autonomous, and responsible for our choices. To be *autonomous* is to be separate and whole enough to choose what will satisfy the needs of our real self. We can choose among alternatives the "means-whereby" our needs will be met (Perls, 1969). We are able to say "yes" when we need to and we can say "no," without justification, excuse, or guilt. To take *personal responsibility* for our choices means to acknowledge that we have made all our own decisions, even if all we have decided is to let someone else choose for us.

Relatedness   Another venturing strategy is to experience the existential solitude of our lives. Moustakas refers to this as creative loneliness:

In creative loneliness there is an element of separation, of being utterly alone, but there is also a strange kind of relatedness—to nature and to other persons and through these experiences, a relatedness to life itself, to inspiration, wisdom, beauty, simplicity, value. A sense of isolation and solitude is experienced, but a relatedness to the universe is maintained. Only through fundamental relatedness can the individual develop his own identity. The individual's loneliness is an experience in growing which leads to differentiation of self. The person's identity comes into relief as he breathes his own spirit into everything he touches, as he relates significantly and openly with others and with the universe (1961, p. 50).

Acceptance of impermanence   Lives, things, relationships—all come into being and all end. In between there is change, and it is the change or transformation which accounts for our experience. My own understanding of the importance of change (and of the futility of striving to be permanently attached to things or others) has come through my work in ceramics and a book called *Centering* (1964) by Marion Richards.

When I began potting a few years ago, I spent many hours trying to learn to center a mound of clay on a wheel and to work it up into a sturdy pot. Many of the pots I started collapsed under my hands before I could pull them into shape. Of those I managed to shape, some cracked as they dried, others broke as they were being fired. I was frustrated and saddened at each failure. I wanted a lasting pot to represent my every effort. Then I read in *Centering*:

The fired pot . . . will disappear; it will be sold or given away. It will almost certainly be broken in time. . . . There is no freedom in attachment. The objects of our attachment depart from us, or we from them. Life's impermanence commonly creates pain and anxiety, conscious or unconscious, for people tend to equate life with permanence. (p. 34) [And] Is this not also the potter's chance: to live through, from dust to dust, the life of the pot? . . . The product is not what binds the artist to his craft. Nor the actor to the theatre. Nor the person to his being. It is the transformations. . . . (p. 143)

The reading of this book and my own experiences with potting had a profound impact on my acceptance of change and my understanding that it is the *process*, in both living and potting, that has value. The end will come to all pots, to all relationships, to all creations, and to all persons. Clark Moustakas says it too:

The exquisite nature of love, the unique quality or dimension in its highest peak, is threatened by change and termination. . . . To love is to be lonely. Every love eventually is broken by illness, separation, or death (1961, p. 101).

EXPLORATION
6.14

Self-awareness

Spend one hour or more totally alone—go off into the country, find an empty classroom, or shut yourself off from everyone in your house. Be entirely self-aware for this hour. Observe your self, your authenticity. Experience solitude and relatedness. Notice the changes around you and inside you as you experience self-awareness.

Repeat this exploration from time to time.

MAXIMIZING SEPARATENESS AND WHOLENESS

Self-discovery is not something we simply decide to do one day, like going on a picnic; it is a life-long process. It is the most important and challenging work we do in life, and sometimes the most painful. It can be pursued alone or with the help of others who facilitate, encourage, and support the struggle.

For many, psychotherapy is beneficial in gaining self-awareness. Professional therapists are usually trained as psychologists (in which case they have an advanced degree in psychology), psychiatrists (medical doctors who specialize in the treatment of mental and emotional disorders), or psychiatric social workers. These specialists in mental health refer to their procedures as therapy, counseling, or analysis; the term psychoanalysis is reserved for those using Freudian methods. In most states professional therapists and counselors must have passed qualifying examinations and be licensed to practice.

There are many therapeutic techniques, and most have self-knowledge as a goal. Some are based on a specific personality theory, while others are the result of borrowing ideas from many theories. Some therapies are individual, one-to-one interactions between two people; others are used in groups of from five or six to fifteen people. Some therapy uses a medical model, that of a medical expert healing a sick patient. Within the last fifteen to twenty years it has become increasingly apparent that therapy is also beneficial to normal, healthy people who desire to maximize separateness and wholeness.

There is nothing magic about any therapy. It is successful when one is committed to working and when the therapy situation fosters honesty and trust among all participants. Therapy is not the only route to achieving an integrated personality. At best however, it is a valuable short-cut to effective living.

Here are a few of the many types of therapy especially helpful in facilitating separateness and wholeness.

Gestalt therapy Gestalt techniques, developed by Frederick S. (Fritz) Perls, stress the wholeness of human experience. A major goal is experiencing in the "here and now." Gestalt techniques are used by many therapists in individual and group settings. Some of these techniques are:

Dream analysis. Perls felt that every aspect of our dreams represents an aspect of ourselves. Much of our disowned experience appears in dreams, so that by identifying with parts of a dream we can broaden our self-awareness.

Imaginary encounter. This technique places one in the "hot seat" with an empty chair opposite. The "hot seat" is where one works; the empty chair is where one puts projections. A dialogue, or conversation,

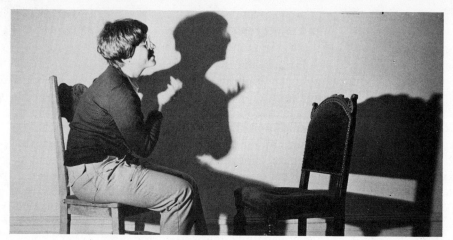

Michael Weisbrot

can take place with one's representations of others, bringing into focus difficulties in achieving separateness.

Body awareness. Nonverbal communication and awareness of body are improved and emphasized in Gestalt therapy.

A good resource for further information about Gestalt therapy is Frederick Perls, *Gestalt Therapy Verbatim* (Lafayette, Ca.: Real People Press, 1969).

Rogerian or client-centered therapy   This therapy is named for Carl Rogers, who pioneered the techniques and developed the idea that therapy is not for "sick" people alone. The goal of client-centered therapy is to make congruent all aspects of one's life and personality. The therapist's role, supportive and not analytic, is to help the client clarify thoughts, feelings, and motivations. Carl Rogers' book *Client-Centered Therapy* (Boston: Houghton Mifflin, 1951) provides an introduction to his method of therapy as a route to self-actualization.

Existential therapy   Taking its goals from existential philosophy, this therapy stresses the need for authenticity, confrontation with existence, personal responsibility, and the necessity for personal meaning in life. This therapy is neither tied to a specific personality theory (as is Rogerian therapy) nor noted for specific techniques (as is Gestalt therapy), but is founded on the view that we all choose to be what we are. A good introduction to an existential therapy is Victor Frankl, *Man's Search for Meaning* (New York: Simon & Schuster, 1970).

Jungian therapy   Carl Jung, who at one time studied with Freud, developed a complex and comprehensive personality theory. (Some of this theory has been presented briefly in this chapter.) Jung's theories and techniques, which include dream and symbol analysis, have become more widely studied and valued in the last ten years. The goal of Jungian analysis is the integration of personality. Like Freud, Jung was a prolific writer. No single work contains his entire theory, but a small paperback by Calvin S. Hall and Vernon J. Nordby, *A Primer of Jungian Psychology* (New York: New American Library, 1973), gives a good summary. For those wanting to sample Jung's original work, *The Portable Jung* (edited by Joseph Campbell, translated by R. F. C. Hull; New York: Viking, 1971) is handy. A Jungian approach, with special relevance to separateness and wholeness, is Esther M. Harding's *The "I" and the "Not-I": A Study in the Development of Consciousness* (Princeton, N.J.: Princeton University Press, 1965).

Psychosynthesis An Italian psychiatrist, Roberto Assagioli, has developed a personality theory similar in some ways to Jung's and has collected many diverse techniques by which one can attain "harmonious inner integration, true self-realization, and right relationships with others." Some techniques from psychosynthesis are included in this chapter. Assagioli has written about both the theory and method of psychosynthesis in *Psychosynthesis* (New York: Viking, 1971).

Primal therapy This involves an intensive process in which one reexperiences prior traumatic events that led to current neurotic behaviors. A "primal" is the experience of a key scene from the past; it involves the emotional realization of ultimate aloneness. Primal therapy is painful, but it can lead to an expanded range of emotions and a decreased need for defenses. The originator of Primal therapy, Arthur Janov, describes his techniques in *The Primal Scream: A Revolutionary Cure for Neurosis* (New York: Putnam, 1970).

Therapy and encounter groups Intensive group experience can be a profitable method for learning more about oneself, the impact one has on others, and for improving interpersonal communication. There are many kinds of groups with different goals and techniques. Some, often called sensitivity groups, focus on improving group dynamics and group functioning. Encounter groups encourage members to lower their defenses (to become more disclosing) while providing a psychologically safe climate for the expression of real-self feelings. Others, sometimes called awareness groups, help participants become more aware of sensory processes and self-expression. Group methods vary depending on the purpose of the group and the group leader or facilitator.

Suggested for those interested in encounter groups is *Carl Rogers on Encounter Groups* by Carl Rogers (New York: Harper & Row, 1970). A sampler that describes a dozen different kinds of groups, from encounter to Synanon to family and religious groups, is Jane Howard's *Please Touch: A Guided Tour of the Human Potential Movement* (New York: Dell, 1970).

SUMMARY

1. Although we are physically separate from our environment, we cannot exist without it. We are psychologically separate; we each experience in a unique and consistent way. But we do not always feel separate; we often feel attached to or part of others and they seem to be part of us.
2. Personality, as described in this chapter, consists of
    real self—the core of identity and experience
    public self—the masks we wear for others
    self-image—the picture we have of ourselves
    self-concept—the attitudes and values we have about self-image
    self-ideal—the self we strive to be
    We are not aware of our whole personality. The hidden aspects of personality are sometimes referred to as the unconscious.
3. We extend our ego boundaries by identifying with others and by projecting expectations or unconscious aspects of our personality onto others. The more open (or disclosing) we are with others, the more we know who we ourselves are.
4. Some forms of communication can blur the distinctions between "I," "you," and "we"—between self and others.
5. Wholeness is a state of personality integration. It is achieved by increasing self-awareness, by bringing the public self, self-image, and self-concept into accord with real-self experience.
6. Anxiety, a feeling of dread which is often not explained, places us in a state of physical tension, similar to a fear reaction. Anxiety is so unpleasant that we are prompted to remove it.
7. A primary source of anxiety is fear of loneliness. We move toward, away from, or against others in an attempt to reduce this anxiety.
8. Another source of anxiety is internal conflict. We often defend our self-image, public self, or self-concept at the expense of real-self experience to reduce anxiety.
9. We persist in rejecting the real self through habit, immaturity, and by taking on competitive, alienating, and individualistic values.
10. Self-defeat is a pattern of inflexible, persistent behaviors engaged in to reduce anxiety. Self-alienation occurs when the real self becomes dis-integrated from the rest of personality, or from the body.
11. Self-actualization, becoming the person we can potentially be, is the process of being authentic and of accepting impermanence. It is experiencing life as a process.
12. Many find the process of psychotherapy invaluable in becoming separate and whole. There are many forms of therapy which are helpful in achieving this goal.

Suggested Readings

Avila, Donald L., Combs, Arthur W., and Purkey, William W. *The helping relationship sourcebook.* Boston: Allyn and Bacon, 1971. A collection of writings by authorities in many of the helping professions, aimed at clarifying the nature of a helping relationship.

Green, Hannah. *I never promised you a rose garden.* New York: New American Library, 1964. An autobiographical novel about a young girl's retreat into an imaginary world of madness and her cautious return, with the help of her therapist, to reality.

Laing, Ronald D. *The politics of experience.* New York: Ballantine Books, 1967. A critical and challenging statement of Laing's view that social conditions perpetuate self-alienation as a "normal" state.

Moustakas, Clark E. *Loneliness.* Englewood Cliffs, N.J.: Prentice-Hall, 1961. A profound and absorbing essay on the reality of human aloneness, which encourages the reader to investigate his or her own solitude.

Warner, Samuel J. *Self-realization and self-defeat.* New York: Grove Press, 1966. A psychologist describes common patterns of self-defeating behavior as responses to anxiety and guilt, and how these patterns prevent the realization of potential.

Wheelis, Allen. *How people change.* New York: Harper Colophon Books, 1973. A noted psychologist and writer examines the freedom we have to make ourselves into something different and the processes, including therapy, by which we can change.

Michael Weisbrot

7

THE QUEST
FOR INTIMACY

Only connect!
Personal relations are the important thing for ever and ever, and not this outer
world of telegrams and anger.

E. M. Forster
(Howard's End)

159

Human potentials for intimacy are many. They reside in our ability to contact others by talking and listening, with physical touch, and through emotional expression. But not all of the ways in which we contact others are intimate. Intimacy is special; the quest for it is the search for genuine, authentic contacts with others. In this quest we ask

What is intimacy and why is it important?
How and when can I make intimate connections?
What does "love" mean?
How can I establish and maintain intimate relationships?

The milestones in our quest for intimacy are honesty and trust. Our quest is blocked when we are not open to intimate contacts, when our relationships are characterized by unequal giving and taking, and when we don't join another person in mutual commitment.

Two strangers on a crowded street make split-second eye contact as they pass. Each senses in the other's eyes the recognition of their shared humanity. At this moment each becomes more than an obstacle to the other's progress down the sidewalk.

Two students talk over their beer after class, intently discussing the lecture they've just heard. Each listens to the other and responds; both are oblivious to the chatter around them.

A father and his child watch their cat deliver kittens. Sharing this experience, they are equals in their human curiosity and wonder.

A wife has prepared a special dinner, now cold on the table. Her husband has just arrived home after being held up in traffic. Each is frustrated. She is disappointed and relieved that he is safe. He is tired and hungry. Their contact gains in intimacy as they make their feelings clear and express them without blame.

Two people, caring equally for each other, give and take pleasure in sexual intercourse.

These are examples of people making intimate connections.

THE INTIMATE CONNECTION

An intimate connection is between two people. The contact is such that each is "touched," either physically, emotionally, or intellectually. The situation is analogous to an electrical connection in that a circuit is opened, and "energy" flows from one person to the other. This flow is two-way; it allows communication to and from each, making possible a reciprocal exchange. The intimate connection can be viewed as a two-person feedback loop.

The physical, emotional, or intellectual contacts between two people can be intimate or not. Physical touch, to be intimate, must be purposeful, made with the intent of communicating. In our culture we are

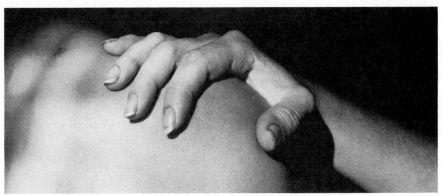

Michael Weisbrot

usually careful not to make accidental body contact with others. We avoid physical contact on a crowded street or in an elevator. We act as though our bodies extend a foot or so into the space around us and we often feel intruded upon if a stranger comes too close. We can make body contact without feeling violated only in certain structured situations, as when we play contact sports or take part in the ritual of shaking hands. Probing as it is, a doctor's physical examination is not intimate, for no communication is intended. Casual as it may seem, a light hand on a friend's shoulder can be intimate. So can a deep embrace or any kind of touch in between.

Intimate emotional contact is *nonverbal*. It is expressed through posture, facial expression, and eye contact, and often accompanies physical or verbal contact. We have a feeling that we have been touched—affected in an emotional way, and that we have touched the other person—affected them emotionally. Our vocabulary is poor in words that express emotional contact, so we have had to make do with references to *mood*, *chemistry*, and (lately) *vibes*.

Intellectual contact is *verbal*, most often spoken. (Written communication slows down the feedback process or, in the case of reading, often removes it.) Intellectual intimacy is a sharing of ideas in which partners understand each other and are understood exactly. Each gives and each receives what is said. Both attend to their need to communicate rather than, for example, to their need to make debater's points.

Intimate connections vary in intensity, duration, or circumstance. Our touch can be deep, penetrating, soft, or momentary. It can last for minutes or hours. We can make contact with strangers, lovers, or friends —whenever there are two of us.

Connecting and Growing

We cannot be in intimate contact with another person at all times. But a life without any intimate connections is stagnant. Both solitude and intimacy are vital to our growth. Touching and being touched (physically, emotionally, or intellectually) confirm our sense of being alive and allow us to make the exchange of ideas and feelings which gives value to life. We are renewed by human stimulation; we don't become stale· but can move out of our ruts and routines. We are spurred by acknowledged needs for contact. Without emotional stimulation our lives are dull, static, and bland. This holds for all emotional states brought about by intimate contact—love, anger, or sorrow. Intimacy acts for us as yeast does for bread dough: it lifts life, expands it, makes it lighter.

We can make many intimate connections in the course of our lives. But because they demand our full attention and awareness, each intimate connection usually lasts for only a short time. We move in and out of connectedness with others. Between connections we may be relating in nonintimate ways (as will be discussed in a later section) or not relating at all; that is, we may be alone.

At any one moment only one intimate connection is possible. The human capacity to receive, understand, and return messages is limited. We can focus our attention on only a few elements and in only one direction at a time. Attention is certainly one of the conditions of an intimate contact. Both persons must devote their full attention to the experience and to the union it establishes. Each is aware of self and other; neither allows external interference ("noise" or "static") to distract from this awareness. There are other conditions for intimate connection:

Intention has been mentioned as one. Both persons are open to or seeking contact with the other person. Both consider intimacy appropriate to the circumstances.

Reciprocity is another condition. The contact is, and remains for its duration, reciprocal. Each person is giving and each is receiving.

Equality is a vital condition. For the duration of the contact any status or social-role discrepancies between the pair are suspended. Both are equal in their relationship no matter what their age, sex, racial, or social differences. An intimate contact can only be made and maintained between psychologically equal people. If one person has more power, responsibility, or control in the relationship than the other, they will not be in intimate contact—although they may be relating in some other way.

EXPLORATION 7.1

Connect

Take some time in your next class meeting to make an intimate connection with the person next to you. After doing so, discuss the following questions:

Would you describe the connection as physical, emotional, intellectual, or some combination of these qualities?

Did you feel touched?

How would you descibe your attention while you were in contact?

How was the connection broken?

NONINTIMATE CONTACT

When intention, reciprocity, and equality are absent in a relationship it is unlikely that there will be intimate contact. By not intending to be intimate, by not being open to give and take, by not meeting others on the same level, we restrict intimate connections.

Lack of Intention

We often find ourselves with others in situations we feel are not appropriate for intimacy. Intimacy may even threaten the purpose for which we are together. We therefore engage in social manuevers to block or prevent intimate contact from occurring. Following are some conditions which diminish the chances of intimacy.

Sometimes we are *moving away* from or *against* others as a defense against loneliness. The paradox here is that the origin of our behavior is the wish for intimacy; however, the fear of rejection is stronger (see Chapter 6). Result: we are convinced that we don't want intimacy. Instead we "want" power, control, aloofness, or supremacy over others. The aim of preventing intimacy is almost always achieved in these circumstances.

The more we don't "want" or intend intimate connections with others the better we learn not to act from our real selves. We operate from our public selves and relate mask-to-mask. Preserving our own images and those of others is important. We guard against doing what we want to do in order to make sure we do what we should do, what is socially expected of us. An unintentional intimacy is startling.

I often think of the account of what *is* and *is not* intimacy told me by a middle-aged client. Once when he was traveling, he sat down next to a respectable, but lonely, woman in the lobby of his hotel. Within fifteen minutes, still unintroduced, he was having sexual relations with her in his room. Afterwards, as she got ready to go, she reached over and gently removed one of her hairs from his shoulder. Both of them were somewhat embarrassedly taken aback by the personal nature of the act. Later, he reflected that it was the only intimate act that had occurred between them (Coutts, 1973, p. 14).

Urban living isolates us. We do not attempt to make contact with our neighbors because they are strangers. In small or rural communities there is a sense of neighborhood that brings security. Outsiders are strangers, who might be dangerous. In large and impersonal cities, everyone who is not known to us personally, even people living next door, are strangers. We feel we must avoid truly personal exchanges for the sake of our own safety.

Much of our person-to-person contact is *trans*actional rather than *in-teractional. By this I mean that we meet and relate in order to achieve

Michael Weisbrot

some purpose other than intimate contact. There are three kinds of transactions prevalent in human relationships:

1. Transactions for production   We work with others in a means–end relationship established for the purpose of getting things done. We are often in an organization (such as a business firm) or an institution (like the family) whose structure requires that we preserve status differences, social roles, and public self-displays so that work will get done. Interactions between us, especially intimacy, would disrupt work. Person A does not make contact with person B because to do so would hinder their focus on product P:

(Note: The family based on the industrial model also relates this way. A and B are parents whose tasks are to "produce" the good child, P. Further note: Transactions of buying and selling follow the same model. A is selling P; B is buying P. Intimacy is inappropriate to money transactions.)

2. Transactions for profit   Today's social customs offer many "approved" ways of relating to others to enhance profit. Aristotle, in the third century, B.C., noted that some friendships are based on profit. For instance, we use social contacts to climb up the ladder of prestige. (Being seen with Smith will enhance my reputation because Smith has a higher status than I do.) We make contacts not to enrich our lives but to enrich our business. It is considered acceptable to want to be seen with and to "know" the right people. In these circumstances it becomes naive to trust or to be honest with others. We tacitly agree not to get too close. The more sophisticated our understanding of that agreement, the greater our chances for profit.

3. Transactions for "fun"   Aristotle also referred to friendships oriented toward pleasure and having a good time. A large part of our socializing is of this kind. We spend time with our friends and acquaintances having fun: partying, sailing, eating, playing cards, dancing, watching baseball games, chatting, and so forth — happy and secure in the knowledge that we are not "alone." These relationships can be very superficial. Conversation is light, the effort is to be amusing and amused, charming and hospitable. Serious intellectual or emotional contact among casual acquaintances might be very disturbing. Close physical contact is often carefully controlled because it might convey sexual or homosexual implications. It is also controlled because intimate contact during such social gatherings is inappropriate.

We may limit physical contact because it implies sex. There are situations in which intellectual, emotional, and limited physical contact are considered proper and are engaged in with intent, although any erotic contact is forbidden. For instance, in nearly all cultures, ours included, sexual intimacy between close blood relatives is prohibited. Brothers, sisters, mothers, fathers, sons, and daughters may make intimate contact of a physical nature but our prohibitions against incest draw the line at passionate physical connections.

Mores forbidding incestuous sexual relations are not the only sexual restrictions we learn in this culture. We learn to restrict much close physical exchange with others because we are not sure whether or not it will lead to or be interpreted as erotic exchange. We are particularly reserved with friends of the same sex. Physical restraint is necessary

Photograph by Michael Heron.

because it is traditional for us to express our wishes for sexual contact with body language rather than open verbal requests. Body language is more ambiguous than verbal language. When we mean to say "no" without doing so verbally or when we are not sure that we want sexual contact, we have to be very careful how we touch one another.

<table>
<tr>
<td>

**EXPLORATION
7.2**

**Personal
Space
and
Physical
Connection**

</td>
<td>

Find a partner, someone you do not know well.
Face each other and make physical contact.
Did you touch each other's hands?
Make contact using another part of your body (shoulder, foot, cheek).

   As you touch your partner and are touched, notice the effect on your sense of "personal space." How far beyond you does it seem to extend, and in what directions? When do you feel uncomfortable? How about your partner? How willing are you to allow someone to come into your "space"?

   Now, close your eyes and complete this sentence with the first words that come to mind: "If I let you get close to me, then . . ."

</td>
</tr>
</table>

Lack of Reciprocity

We sometimes make connections in the hope that intimacy will result. But even when we actively seek affection, caring, and sharing with others we do not always find it. Even when we intend to give, our affection is not accepted. When both people are not open or are not open to the same degree, to *both* giving and taking, intimate contacts between them are rare.

   Emotional incompetence is a barrier to intimate connections (see Chapter 11). If one or both people in a relationship have not developed a range of expressive emotions and an awareness of their own emotional states, there will be little emotional exchange. To be in touch with others we must be capable of being in touch with ourselves. We must be able to receive emotional messages ranging from anger to tenderness in order to make intimate connections. Without emotional competence, we have little to give and cannot adequately assimilate the emotional offerings of others.

   A relationship in which one person "needs" more than the other, or in which both people are taking and neither is giving, is apt to be poor in intimate contacts. We all need companionship and affection. But if we are not sufficiently separated from others and have not achieved wholeness in our own personalities, we will have unmet needs which we seek to meet through relationships with others. We "move toward others" (see Chapter 6) seeking in them what we are lacking in ourselves.

D-love   Abraham Maslow (1968) has called this seeking "D-love." D-love is deficiency love. It is sometimes prompted by anxiety about being left

Abraham Maslow
(*Courtesy of Bertha Maslow*).

alone or abandoned. Its chief characteristic is that one partner takes all that the other will give, but cannot make an equal and adequate return of care and affection. D-love is needing love; a person motivated by D-love will try to possess and control another because of need. The other is needed only for certain things (affection, for example) or only related to in certain ways (dependent or sexual ways, for example). The relationship becomes specialized and rigid when it works only in the service of filling deficits. True or spontaneous exchanges are threatening. Intimate contact with reciprocal giving and taking is incompatible with a D-love relationship.

EXPLORATION
7.3

**Giving
and
Taking**

(I think you'll find the value of this exploration less than the cost.)

1. Bring some change to class. With the class sitting in a circle, each of you place all the change you have in front of you. Know how much you have.

In turn, each person go over to someone else and take as much of that person's change as you wish. The money you take is yours to keep.

When each has had a turn at taking, use the money you have left, if any, to give to anyone in the group. The money you give is given for keeps.

Now that you've finished, how did you feel during the exchanges? Did you tense up when others were taking your money? Did you have any left to give? Did you give it away? Which was easier for you: giving or taking? Did you end up with more or less money than you started with?

2. If you are one of a couple (two people who know each other well and interact frequently) try this. Each of you take turns finishing these sentences, several times over, being as specific as you can:

I need . . .

I want . . .

Be as honest as possible. What did the exercise tell you about yourself? About your friend?

When one or both people are busy defending public self, self-image, or self-concept, they distort the messages they give and the messages they receive. This distortion may well act as an effective barrier against mutual giving and receiving. People who are defending do not hear, see, or feel what another is giving because they select only those messages which serve them—those which aid in their defense. They are sensitive to anything which might be threatening. Their ability to attend to the real self of another may be imprisoned by the narrow confines of their own public self or self-image.

Lack of Equality

Intimate connections do not occur while one person stands in a "superior" position to another. Intimacy can occur if a couple has the ability and the willingness to transcend or disregard differences or position. Intimate contact will be improbable in any circumstances in which people adhere rigidly to their social-role or psychological inequalities.

In our culture, it is the prerogative of a person of higher status to initiate physical touching with persons of lower status. For instance, in a hospital doctors will touch to express their support for each other, but nurses or others of lower ranks do not reach out to touch doctors, nor do they often reciprocate a doctor's touch (Rubin, 1973, p. 40). This is true of many status-different relationships and is both a result and a reinforcement of differences in power. Power relationships produce an overwhelmingly one-way flow of communication: downwards from the person holding power. It is not just physical touch, but all forms of intimacy which are restricted by power- or status-different relationships. Unless people put aside social standing and meet as equals, intimate contact is not going to occur.

Psychological power, too, is supported by nonreciprocal contact. A person who is trying to dominate another person will not succeed without the latter's cooperative submission. A dominant-submissive

---

EXPLORATION 7.4 Equality

Pair up and face your partner. For this exploration one member of the pair will be "A" and the other will be "B." Decide, before reading further, which of you is to be "A" and which is to be "B."

Now, *how* did you decide A and B? Did one of you simply say "I'll be A and you be B"? Did you discuss the matter? Did one of you defer to the other? Was your manner of deciding in this case typical of the way in which you decide things with others?

What do you think: can you be truly intimate with your "brother" if you are his keeper? Does responsibility for another's behavior or well-being interfere with intimacy? Discuss examples pointing either way in your life.

exchange is one of unequal power. So also are nurturing-receptive, giving-receiving, aggressive-passive exchanges. Both "bullying" and "taking care of" another are ways of asserting power; both will prevent intimate contact unless the more powerful is willing to let go of the power by, for instance, "submitting" or "receiving care."

So far we have discussed the many ways in which we can relate without intimacy. The ways we live — our routines and habits, our needs to get things done and to preserve status — are important, but they may give us few chances to connect. Problems in achieving separateness and wholeness, our emotional incompetence, and our needs to defend public self, self-image, or self-concept — these also interfere with intimacy. Before considering other types of relationships, take some time to observe nonintimacy in your own life. Just observe and be aware.

**EXPLORATION
7.5**

Nonintimacy

Set aside tomorrow for noticing. For at least one whole day keep track of the ways you see yourself or others:
> blocking intimacy by not intending it
> transacting rather than interacting
> limiting physical contact
> taking but not giving; giving but not taking
> needing but not connecting

Keep track of who you touch, who touches you, and how intimate the touches are.
> Who touches you where and how?
> Does anyone pat you on the head, or do you treat anyone in a condescending manner?

Notice also how others around your campus or elsewhere touch each other.
> Do you see anyone of "lower" status initiate touching with someone in a "higher" position?
> Do you think equal emotional or intellectual contact can be made between people of different status?

INTIMATE RELATIONSHIPS

Intimate relationships are those which provide the greatest opportunity for frequent intimate connections. We are not in continuous contact hour after hour with any single friend or partner. We all have other business in life which needs our attention, and we need to devote attention to ourselves. It is unrealistic to hope that every waking moment will be a contact moment. The more often we engage in intimate connection with another person, the more intimate our relationship with that person will be.

There is no limit to the number of intimate relationships we can have during our lifetimes. But at any one period in our lives we usually have time and energy for only a few. So we make selections, choosing those relationships which seem worthiest of our time and attention. Many of us choose to have only one intimate relationship at one time. Intimate relationships don't take care of themselves. They require attention and commitment.

Relationships which make connection possible are characterized by four qualities:

1. The firmest basis for an intimate relationship is *self-respect* and *self-knowledge*. The person who knows him or herself as a separate and integrated person can make many intimate connections. In order to achieve mutual interdependency we must maintain our own integrity. Shirley Luthman says, "I believe that the deepest kind of intimacy possible between human beings requires, as a base, that each person feel he is a separate whole person who wants to love and share, but who knows, without question, that he can survive emotionally alone." (1972, p. 117)

2. Another requirement for open communication, and thus for intimate relationships, is *mutual respect*. Each partner has unconditional positive regard (Rogers, 1959) for the other. A partner is accepted for who he or she *is*, as he or she is, without having to behave in any particular way. ("I care for you as you are," rather than "I would care for you if you were more tidy, less outspoken, and ____ or ____, etc.") The other person is esteemed for him- or herself, not for his or her performance.

Mutual respect, in turn, requires that the other be known as he or she "really" is. He or she is realistically appraised. It is possible for us to respect the images we have of others and for us to relate to those aspects of ourselves we have projected on to others. Respect for images or projections will *not* lead to open communication. We must keep our view of the other clear of our own expectations and wishes if we are to see others as they are.

Mutual respect includes caring for another. We have an active concern for the other's growth, happiness, and welfare. The happiness of the other is as essential to us as our own.

3. *Open communication* is required in intimate connections. When communication is open each partner is capable of self-disclosure. Each can interact from his or her real self without defending self-image or public self. There is trust in one's self and in another which generates a desire to be honest. An accompanying desire is to see the world from the other person's perspective. The limits of communication on any level — physical, emotional, or intellectual — are set by consent and not by fear.

4. An intimate relationship survives and prospers when each partner actively works toward open communication, respect for the other, and self-respect. The union is valuable, the other is valued, the self is valued.

Michael Weisbrot

Intimacy inevitably brings conflict. But *concern* for the welfare of one's self and the self of another allows conflict to enrich rather than destroy the relationship.

Active concern must also include the expectation that each partner in the relationship will grow and change over time, each in his or her own way and time. The relationship will also change. When relationships are set in concrete or cast in bronze, they die. All relationships eventually end in one way or another. Allowing them to change is allowing them to end when they are ready; it is not to kill them prematurely or to prolong them past the time they stop rewarding their participants.

B-love

Abraham Maslow (1968) has labeled the quality of concern in intimate relationships B-love. In contrast to D-love (deficiency love), B-love is love for the being of another and the growth of self and other through the relationship. B-love is not motivated by unmet needs; it is nonpossessive. It is characterized by a concern for the nurturance and growth of another. Each partner gives without regard for or the necessity of receiving in return. There is no need for emotional bookkeeping. B-lovers are separate and independent people on their own, but they can fully enjoy the pleasure of their relationships. B-love is experienced as pleasureable and holds a minimum of anxiety or hostility between lovers.

**EXPLORATION
7.6

Intimacy
and
Respect**

Answer these questions if you are now in or have been in a close relationship with another (of either the opposite or the same sex):
This is one way I show my self-respect in this relationship:
This is a way I show mutual respect:
This is a way consent is expressed in this relationship:
This is a way I show concern:

As in nonintimate relationships and D-love, intimate relationships and B-love can involve same-sex and opposite-sex pairs alike. It is most usual that we choose to have our closest relationships with members of the opposite sex.

LOVE

Intimacy, as I have been discussing it here, amounts to what some people call *love*. But *love* has many more shades of meaning, making it sometimes wider and sometimes narrower than intimacy.

Each of us has our own personal meaning of love, a meaning compounded of experiences, ideas, and associations collected throughout our lives. There are many sources for our knowledge of love. We have watched people in relationships and heard it said that "They act that way because they're in love." We see other people acting quite differently (our parents, for example), although they are "supposed" to be in love. We learn from movies and TV screens, from books, and from popular songs what love is. The notions conflict and we must pick out what we want love to mean for us. We learn to label particular feelings that we experience in particular situations. We feel warm and cuddly—we're in love. We feel sexually excited—we're in love. We feel mopey, lethargic, depressed—we're in love.

**EXPLORATION
7.7

Love**

Take a bit of time here to explore what love means to you. Complete the following sentences:

I feel loved when _____.
When I feel loved, I feel _____.
When I love someone I _____.
The finest love relationship I can think of is between _____ and _____.
This is a good relationship because _____.
When I use the word "love" I mean _____, and _____, and _____.

Love is not applied exclusively to adult heterosexual couples. We speak of love between parents and children, between the devout and God, between the patriot and his country.

The Greeks distinguished several kinds of love. Their definitions were based not on who was involved but on the motivation for, or quality of, the emotion. They used the word *eros* to mean passionate love, lust, or desire. They called brotherly love, or friendship, *philia*. The term *agape* referred to a spiritual love which is selfless and manifest in concern for one's fellow man with no expectation of receiving something in return (Katchadourian and Lunde, 1975). We currently stretch the one word "love" to refer to all three of these situations, as well as many others.

Romantic Love

One of the most common terms of love is "romantic love." This is the emotion which is *supposed to be* an essential ingredient in male-female love relationships. Romantic love today includes *eros, philia,* and *agape,* taking a large part of its flavor from *eros.* Romantic love in America is an import. Its ideals are those which were sung by twelfth-century troubadors in Western Europe. But the applications of romantic love ideals are uniquely American. Let's examine the conditions which spawned the romantic ideal and then look at how the ideal is at work today.

First of all, marriage and love were never popularly associated until they were joined in America. We are so used to the idea that love and marriage "go together like a horse and carriage" that it is a bit difficult to imagine marriage without love—as an ideal, of course. But then, horses and carriages don't always "go together" either, unless we put them together, and that is what Americans did with love and marriage.

European marriages, like those in most cultures of the world, were for centuries very much family affairs. Marriage was arranged by parents or even grandparents, with an eye toward social and economic advantage for the wife's and husband's families. As an institution, marriage served to build and hold together family empires by producing successors to inherit and pass on wealth. It was an instituion of the propertied classes, for the lower classes usually did not have enough wealth to make it worthwhile. Husbands and wives were not expected to love one another in an erotic way. They often lived in close companionship and with re-

Photograph courtesy of R. and C. Hamilton.

spect and some affection for one another, but these emotional ties were not necessary to the social and economic functions which marriage served.

Twelfth-century courts included a number of troubadors and courtiers who, between their knightly hunts and battles, occupied themselves by falling passionately in love with high-born ladies. The objects of their desires were other men's wives. The knights themselves were usually married, but their love was exclusively extramarital. When a courtier fell in love, it was not with an expectation that his love would be returned. He loved from afar, worshipping an image of his lady-love in song and suffering. His love was predestined. Fate caused him to fall in love, he was struck at first sight, and he was powerless to control his feelings. The romantic ideal of love is love unrequited. The reward of such love is not consummation but a mixture of agony and ecstasy achieved only through continuous yearning.

When romantic love was transplanted in America some four centuries later, its seedbed was the garden of marriage. For the first time in history love became not only appropriate to marriage, it became a requirement. Young men and women were more or less free to choose their own mates. Practical considerations, such as class, racial, and religious compatibility among the eligible were governed by restricted mobility (before the automobile) and a strong dash of parental indoctrination. Mate selection became wedded to the romantic ideal. Falling in love became very important as a condition which could determine the rest of one's life.

But to some historians of love, the romantic ideal has seemed less than ideal as a foundation for a life-long relationship. Denis de Rougemont believes romance provides no support at all. "We are [he says] in the act of trying out — and failing miserably at it, one of the most pathological experiments that a civilized society has ever imagined, namely, the basing of marriage, which is lasting, upon romance which is a passing fancy." (1949, p. 452) Courtly love involved people who lived apart. It was fired by the excitement of a strong emotional attraction that would not be cooled by consummation. And, at a distance, the object of one's love could be easily idealized. The conditions of marriage are quite the opposite: companionship of a quieter sort than any knight and his lady ever imagined, the routine of everyday life in the kitchen and the bedroom, and a clear view of one's partner as an imperfect though tolerable individual. "The logical and normal outcome of marriage founded only on romance," de Rougemont goes on, "is divorce, for marriage kills romance; if romance reappears, it will kill the marriage by its incompatibility with the very reasons for which the marriage was contracted." (de Rougemont, in Rubin, 1973, p. 192)

Another historian of love feels that we keep our ideals and our realities but that we keep them distinctly separate. "Americans are firmly of two minds about it all, simultaneously hardheaded and idealistic, uncouth and tender, libidinous and puritanical; they believe implicitly in every tenet of romantic love, and yet they know perfectly well that things don't really work that way." (Morton Hunt, 1959, p. 363)

Perhaps both observers are right. There is, however, no denying that our notions of what "love" is are colored with the brush of romance and shaped with marriage in mind.

Prepackaged Love

According to Zick Rubin (1973) we can be in love almost any time we feel the word *love* justifies or explains what we are doing. Many of us accept the concept of romantic love as it has been prepackaged for us by "True Romance" magazine, TV soap operas, movies, and romantic novels. The package is readily available to those of us who wish to wrap ourselves and the selves of others in layers of prefabricated expectations. In general the package looks something like this:

A man and a woman, young and beautiful, are drawn together by a strong physical attraction that tells them they are meant to satisfy one another's erotic and affectional needs. They are tossed about by the fury of passion and excitement and pain and fear, the two of them alone against the world and others who would intrude, forever and everlasting. Obsessed with one another to addiction, they are willing to risk all to retain the feeling of being in love. They are scornful of reason or harsh realities—the two of them, in love with love.

In this package we can also see expectations for behavior and attitudes appropriate to those "in love." Here, somewhat exaggerated, are some of the expectations we find associated with romantic love. (Notice that Jill and Bill could easily change places. Men admire, control, and serve women; women indulge and exploit men, and so on):

Admiration: Jill stands in awe of everything Bill does; she is impressed by his looks, his intelligence, his wit. She is devoted to him.

Indulgence: Bill gives Jill everything a woman could ask for—furs, diamonds, car, house, and so on. He takes care of her every material need and responds to her every whim.

Control: Jill must know and approve of everything Bill does. If he doesn't comply she whines, cries, or rages that he doesn't love her. He can't stand to see her cry or scream, so he lets himself be controlled.

Exploitation: Bill takes advantage of Jill by promising her that he loves her so that she'll be waiting when he wants company, sex, or a back rub. If something else comes along he doesn't think twice about standing her up, but when he's with her he really does love her.

Obedience and service: Jill obeys and serves Bill in every way she can. His word around the house is law. She takes care of all his physical and emotional needs and does not dare to challenge or question him.

Loyalty: Bill, in his undying devotion for Jill, ignores her bad habits, housekeeping, and cooking. He flares in anger when anyone else criticizes her in any way.

Michael Weisbrot

Kindness and consideration: Jill tries so hard never to say an unkind word to Bill. No matter how tired she is or what she wants she will try to please him and consider his needs first.

Possessiveness: Bill demonstrates his love for Jill by his jealousy. He loves her so much he can't bear to think about losing her to another man. He is always on guard that another man might take her away.

Sexual intimacy: Jill and Bill say they love each other, yet there is little in their lives they share besides sex. They rarely talk to each other about feelings or hopes or things which interest them. They love each other passionately.

Fidelity: Bill feels he is a good mate to Jill. He is her one and only. He has been sexually faithful since the day he said he loved her. As long as he is true to her with his body he loves her.

Pain: Jill loves Bill so much it hurts her. He is her heart's desire; she yearns for him, worships him, cries for him constantly when he is gone.

Romance: Bill is never so much in love with Jill as when they are in a romantic setting—just the two of them, with candles and soft music in the background. He is fond of recalling the day they met—the day the world stood still and bells rang and he knew.

Happily ever after: Jill and Bill, once in love, will live in loving bliss the rest of their lives. Their love will conquer all obstacles and they will never have to say "I'm sorry."

| EXPLORATION 7.8 Romantic Love | Have you learned to expect any of the above from love? Which expectations have been met in your love relationships? Do you feel any of these expectations are appropriate to, or would foster, an intimate relationship? |

Infatuation

Prepackaged love promises much when we first see it in fairy tales and other "happily-ever-after" stories. And the package it comes in does contain something good for most of us, even when we're grown. But it takes a lot of experience to sort the substance from the wrapping. If we're lucky, we find, among other things, that the package contains the ingredients of intimacy.

The first exciting flush of love is called infatuation. Infatuation can be an intimate contact. The connection is an acutely emotional one. We meet someone, connect, and feel enriched, enlivened by the experience. At other times infatuation is not intimate: someone comes along and we unconsciously project part of our selves onto them. Jung describes this as a projection of the *anima* (for a man) or *animus* (for a woman) (see Chapter 6). The only intimate connection here is between two aspects of personality — one aspect we know; the other, which attracts us, we don't. We cannot see that the objects of our infatuation are more than what we project onto them. We are firmly convinced that the anima or animus we are attracted to *is* the other person. Projection can be onto a real person or onto an "image" (a movie or rock star, for example). Whether we connect with a real other or with our own unconscious projections, the powerful emotions of infatuation are quite the same. If we, as most of us do, label these feelings "love," we then have love's romantic package of expectations, dreams, wishes, needs, and desires for the future. Calling these feelings love summons the expectation that they "should" last. Unless the conditions for intimacy accompany the emotions, we are bound to be disappointed. The romantic ideal of unrequited passion becomes a reality; we suffer a "broken heart."

Photograph by Charles Gatewood.

EXPLORATION
7.9

Infatuation

Recall the times in your life when you have been infatuated. Look at each one in turn, if you have had several. What were your feelings at the *beginning* of these experiences? Did you change your behavior, change, for example, your eating or sleeping habits? Did others notice changes in you? Did you talk to anyone about what was happening to you? Did you call it *love*? How long did these early feelings last? In what direction, when, and under what conditions did they begin to change?

Have your infatuations been mutual? That is, was the object of your affections in love with you? Can you *see* any reason for believing that you were in love with a projection of yourself? Was, for example, the person real or a type — football or movie star, etc.? Do you always find attractive the same qualities, physical or psychological, in the people that figure in your infatuations? Did any of your love objects fail to meet your expectations of him or her?

Love and Sex

Romantic love has always been associated with sexuality. It is a common belief that love is a necessary or sufficient condition for "healthy" or respectable sexual relationships. A few centuries ago, tradition set a love-marriage requirement for sexual intercourse. Today we may be persuaded to drop marriage as a necessity, but we have not been eager to drop love (see Chapter 8). Love, as much as pleasure or reproduction, justifies sexual intercourse. We need to feel we are in love to have sex; sex strengthens the feeling that we are indeed in love.

Under many circumstances (excluding rape), sexual intercourse is a perfect intimate contact. Attention is focused and there is a great deal of physical contact and emotional connection. Sexual situations make intimate contact easy; intimate contact may be one of the important pleasures of sex. Many people find sexual intercourse a vital contact for enriching, maintaining, or strengthening their relationship. If, however, sexual contact is the only type of intimate contact a couple makes, it carries a heavy burden. Sex is a poor substitute for intellectual intimacy, for instance. We may be led to believe that we "know" the person we sleep with, but physical knowing and sharing are only one kind of knowledge.

When we take sex either as a justification or as a signal of love, we can be led into the same expectations, needs, and demands that infatuation makes us liable to. Sexual fidelity in particular has come to be an important demand of love. We covet sexual exclusiveness in love more than emotional or intellectual exclusiveness. A love relationship is more threatened when one partner makes sexual contact outside the relationship than when emotional or intellectual contact is made "on the side."

Perhaps it is the association of love and sex which accounts for the way many relationships change when they evolve from platonic to sexual. One common change is in the expectations we have of ourselves or of our partner. We expect a kind of behavior ("love behavior") of those we sleep with that we do not expect from friends. Another change may be in the quality of intimacy a couple shares. A brother-sister type of friendship between a man and a woman can be close, warm, and intimate in every way except sexually, because of the taboo against sex between "brothers" and "sisters." Should the man and woman in this kind of relationship become sexually intimate, it will be difficult to retain the quality of their previous intimacy. Sex changes our intentions as well as our expectations.

Love's expectations and needs can be persistent in our love relationships. We want the object of our love to be loving, patient, kind, loyal, faithful, or whatever else we have learned is a sign of love. We need that other person to keep us from being lonely. We want commitment and promises for the future, a guarantee that love won't end. The needs and expectations associated with love are strong, as Doris Lessing recognized in *The Four Gated City* (1970, p. 301):

But to herself she was able to say precisely what she feared. It was the rebirth of the woman in love. If one is with a man, "in love," or in the condition of loving, then there comes to life that hungry, never-to-be-fed, never-at-peace woman who needs and wants and must have. That creature had come into existence with Mark. She could come into existence again. For the unappeasable hungers and the cravings are part, not of the casual affair, or of friendly sex, but of marriage and the "serious" love. God forbid.

Lawrence Durrell explores the meaning of "love" in *Justine* (1957, p. 68):

"Damn the word," said Justine once, "I would like to spell it backwards as you say the Elizabethans did God. Call it *evol* and make it a part of evolution or revolt. Never use the word to me."

Some of us decide, either because "love" has lost its meaning or because it has so much unwanted meaning, that we will discard the concept. Our problems with love are not so much the word we use but the expectations we have learned. Most of us are not as concerned with what to call intimacy as how to achieve it; our concern is with learning how to be intimate.

HONESTY AND TRUST

The twin cornerstones of intimate relationships are honesty and trust. Being honest is being yourself and disclosing yourself as you really are. It is knowing and accepting both your strengths and limitations. Honesty is what you give of yourself to another. Trust is also a gift, one of the most valuable you can bestow on another person. Trust inspires trust; when I trust you, you become more trustworthy. To trust is to be vulnerable, to choose not to defend against possible hurt. Trust and honesty allow whatever can be between two people to be.

The gifts of honesty and trust will build the self-knowledge and self-respect, open communication, mutual respect, and concern necessary for any intimate relationship—between husband and wife, brother and sister, between lovers, and between friends. These gifts are given without expectations; they do not come from a deficiency but from an abundance of care. When given, they can lead one to feel vulnerable and even naive compared to the demands our more sophisticated, nonintimate relationships make of us. Even when these gifts have been given and the relationship doesn't last, we are enriched:

Two imperfect people can create a perfect process out of which everything can be dealt with and turned into growth. The process is not dependent on outcome: The relationship might continue—strengthen and deepen—or the couple might leave each other, and go separate ways. However, if they move away, they will do so through the process they have built and therefore neither will feel he or she has failed. They will understand that one or both have grown to a different place where they no longer fit with each other. When the pain and hurt of separation has been expressed and passed, each will feel warmth and gratitude for the connection which helped both of them continue their growth. Even though the relationship could not continue, each used it to learn and grow and therefore experience it as positive. I have seen people use even very painful relationships to promote their individual growth. My experience is that if they could have found an easier way to facilitate their necessary growth, they would have done it. I don't believe people put themselves through very painful situations unless that is the only way they can learn what they need to know (Luthman, 1972, pp. 151–152).

EXPLORATION 7.10 Honesty and Trust	As you read (preferably aloud) the following statements, imagine what you would feel actually saying them to someone. What would you feel on hearing them?

Honesty:

I will reveal myself to you as I really am without letting the possibility of your judgement stop me. I will disclose honestly and openly. When I want something I will ask for it. You are free to say "yes," "no," "maybe," or "later."

I will recognize that I cannot change my feelings by an act of will, by thinking, wishing, or ignoring them in the hope that they will go away. I own my own feelings and emotions, whether they are "good" or "bad."

I will establish my own boundaries. I am in charge of myself. I will know and let you know what I can be and do, what I want to be and do in this relationship. I will do something because I want to do it, not merely because you want me to. Then I will not resent you.

I will make my statements about me, my likes, dislikes, and limitations. They are not "things" you have deposited in me:

I am bored   rather than you bore me.

I am angry   rather than you make me so angry.

I am happy   rather than you make me so happy.

I am irritable   rather than you irritate me.

I do not intend to hurt you. My intent is to give you all that I can, knowing that sometimes I am able to give you more than I am at other times.

I see differences and disagreements between us as opportunities for us to grow and change. I welcome you as being different from me, as not liking everything I like. I do not want to change you nor do I seek to change or control your feelings.

"I cannot in any honesty commit myself to love you all of my life. I cannot control or predict how I will continue to feel. I can only honestly commit myself to follow through with you on whatever comes up between us." (Luthman, p. 132.) I take responsibility to express myself fully and to hear you out until all our feelings are in the open and clear. When and if I leave it will not be in a huff of unfinished business.

Trust:

We have a commitment to contact. I have faith that we can and will make intimate connections. Both of us will be spontaneous, express our feelings, and leave room for mistakes and errors.

I trust that you will listen to and hear what I have to say and that you will pay attention to my expression of feelings even if you don't agree with me or are upset by what I do or feel.

I trust that you will establish and keep your own boundaries; that you will care for yourself. Your boundaries are not ultimatums or attempts to control me. They are the establishment of your needs. If I ask you for something which violates your boundaries or is beyond your capabilities you will say "No" rather than saying "Yes" and resenting me. I can be angry or withdrawn because I know that you will take care of yourself. If I yell or retreat, you will see and know me, rather than attacking or clinging to me.

I trust that you are giving what you are able to give at any one time. You have limitations, abilities, and emotional states which determine what you can give, and so do I. Being tired, preoccupied, frustrated, attentive, excited, or joyful will determine how much we give at any moment. We do not expect each other to be more intellectual, emotionally demonstrative, or outgoing than we are.

I trust that you do not intend to hurt, to be unthoughtful or unkind, or to wrong me. If you do something which hurts me it is for some other reason than that you want me to be hurt. I will always assume there is something other than the wish to "get me" behind the way you act.

I trust that you do not want to change me and that you will not try to change me.

I trust that you are committed to your own growth, and to my growth.

(This exploration is summarized from Luthman, 1972.)

When love beckons to you, follow him,
Though his ways are hard and steep.
And when his wings enfold you yield to
him,
Though the sword hidden among his
pinions may wound you.
And when he speaks to you believe in
him,
Though his voice may shatter your dreams
as the north wind lays waste the garden.

. . .

But if in your fear you would seek only
love's peace and love's pleasure,
Then it is better for you that you cover
your nakedness and pass out of love's
threshing-floor,
Into the seasonless world where you
shall laugh, but not all of your laughter,
and weep, but not all of your tears.

Love gives naught but itself and takes
naught but from itself.
Love possesses not nor would it be
possessed;
For love is sufficient unto love.

Kahlil Gibran
(*The Prophet*)

MAXIMIZING INTIMACY

A capacity for intimacy is greatly enhanced in those who are finding their
separateness and wholeness, who are free of stereotyped sex-role prejudices, who have a mature perspective about sexuality, and who have developed competence in emotional and interpersonal relationships. It
follows that many of the methods suggested in other chapters of this
book can be helpful in actualizing one's potentials to make intimate connections.

Other means for maximizing intimacy are Transactional Analysis;
couple, marriage, or family counseling; and experimentation with new
forms of intimate living.

Transactional Analysis has as one of its major goals the maximizing of
intimacy. TA, as it is often called, is usually conducted in a group setting
where participants can come to understand a variety of social intereac-
tions and the ways in which many of them prevent intimate contacts. As
Eric Berne points out in *Games People Play* (New York: Grove, 1964),

much of our time is taken up by rituals or games — activities which maintain interpersonal relationships but which also substitute for intimate connections. Games are (in the TA framework) unconscious transactions in which players are able to avoid closeness and, at the same time, get an emotional "payoff." Those interested in TA and Berne's theory of personality will enjoy *Born to Win: Transactional Analysis with Gestalt Experiments,* by Muriel James and Dorothy Jongeward (Reading, Mass.: Addison-Wesley, 1971) and *I'm OK — You're OK* by Thomas A. Harris (New York: Harper & Row, 1969).

Family, marriage, and couple counseling have become, over the past few years, important resources for those who wish to gain insight into their close relationships and to improve interpersonal communication. No one theory or method unifies the approach taken by marriage and family counselors; basically they hold change to be most likely when both or all members in a relationship are involved in counseling rather than just one individual. Some counselors use Gestalt techniques, others use TA, and many use techniques such as role-playing and psychodrama. In psychodrama, developed by J. L. Moreno, members of a group (a couple or a family) act out situations, each taking the different participant roles. Those interested in psychodrama will find more information in J. L. Moreno, *The First Psychodramatic Family* (Boston: Beacon, 1964).

A noted pioneer in family counseling is Virginia Satir, who discusses communication and esteem in troubled families in her books *Conjoint Family Therapy* (Palo Alto: Science and Behavior Books, 1964) and *Peoplemaking* (Palo Alto: Science and Behavior Books, 1972). An excellent discussion of couple therapy is Shirley Luthman's *Intimacy: The Essence of Male and Female* (Los Angeles: Nash Publishing, 1972). An increasingly necessary form of family counseling is divorce counseling. Mel Krantzler is a counselor who sees the end of a relationship as an opportunity for personal growth and for developing the capacity to improve future relationships. His book, *Creative Divorce* (New York: M. Evans & Co., 1974), provides valuable perspectives on living through the breakup of a marriage and improving ways of relating.

It is increasingly evident that intimate relationships are not necessarily those legitimized by marriage. In the last few years many people have experimented with alternatives to traditional marriage and have successfully developed intimate life-styles by modifying or discarding concepts of conventional marriage. One approach has been a redefinition of a marriage relationship to accommodate increased personal growth in both partners. Nena and George O'Neill have described such an approach in their book *Open Marriage: A New Life Style for Couples* (New York: M. Evans & Co., 1972). An excellent discussion of both traditional and innovative partnerships is Carl Rogers' *Becoming Partners: Marriage and its Alternatives* (New York: Dell, 1972).

SUMMARY

1. Intimate connections are physical, emotional, or intellectual contacts between two people who intend to be intimate, who both give and receive, and who are of equal status. We grow through making intimate connections.
2. There are many instances in which we do not intend to be intimate: we fear closeness, we are alienated, we make transactions for production, profit, or fun. We cannot be in intimate contact when we are not open to mutual give and take, when we need others to fill our deficits or when we do not relate on an equal basis.
3. Intimate relationships give us the greatest chance for intimate connections. These relationships are characterized by: self-knowledge and self-respect, mutual respect, open communication, and concern.
4. "Love" is a word with many meanings. Modern romantic love brings with it many expectations that make intimate relationships difficult and that sometimes hide intimacy.
5. The gifts of honesty and trust, given without expectation, will enrich our lives and our relationships.
6. Many techniques maximize our potentials for intimacy. One of the most useful is Transactional Analysis. Others include marriage and family counseling and alternative life-styles.

Suggested Readings

Bach, George R. and Deutsch, Ronald M. *Pairing*. New York: Avon Books, 1970. A popular and worthwhile book for singles who are searching for intimate relationships. Gives good descriptions of how our expectations and faulty communications can lead to exploitation.

Falk, Ruth. *Women loving: A journey toward becoming an independent woman*. New York: Random House and Berkeley: The Bookworks, 1975. A beautiful, moving, and highly personal exploration of one woman's growing love feelings for other women and for herself.

Fromm, Erich. *The art of loving: An enquiry into the nature of love*. New York: Harper & Row, 1956. Fromm considers love a human capacity—one that requires knowledge and effort in its performance. In this now classic volume he describes the theory and practice of love and argues against cultural barriers to its achievement.

James, Muriel and Savary, Louis M. *The heart of friendship*. New York: Harper & Row, 1976. A guide to the art of making and keeping friends, including chapters on expectancies, needs, transactions, and stresses in friendships.

Koch, Joanne and Koch, Lew. *The marriage savers*. New York: Coward, McCann & Geoghegan, 1976. An investigative report including interviews with counselors and their clients in the field of marriage counseling.

Montagu, Ashley. *Touching: The human significance of the skin*. New York: Columbia University Press, 1971. Physical contact between humans is considered vital for healthy development; it is a need expressed in various ways in different cultures but always forms a necessary component of our lives.

Ramey, James. *Intimate friendships*. Englewood Cliffs, N.J.: Prentice-Hall, 1976. A new look at alternatives to traditional marriage with convincing arguments that group marriage, multi-adult families, and intimate networks are increasingly satisfactory and practical bases for intimacy.

Rubin, Zick. *Liking and loving: An invitation to social psychology.* New York: Holt, Rinehart and Winston, 1973. An entertaining, well-written, and comprehensive overview of loving and liking as seen by a researcher in social science.

Radley Metzger's "The Lickerish Quartet," released by Audobon Films, Inc.

THE QUEST FOR A SEXUAL PERSPECTIVE

Everyone has sex before marriage. We're born with it and express it in our relationships from infancy on (Hettlinger, 1975, p. 57).

The quest for a sexual perspective is the search for a personal viewpoint that enables us to enhance our sexual potentials. In this quest we must first discover what we have learned about the place of sex and its meaning in our lives:

What have I learned about sex from legal, religious, medical, and commercial sources?
What are the prevalent attitudes about sex, love, and marriage?

Another part of a sexual perspective is an understanding of the physiological potentials of human sexual response. A third aspect is clarifying personal choices and finding the basis on which we make sexual decisions.

What turns me on?
How do I feel about my potentials for sex without a partner?
What am I communicating when I share sexually with a partner?
How many partners? Which sex? How do I choose?
What about pregnancy?

Sex can be a source of frustration and guilt if our perspective is narrow, based on incorrect information, or if it does not allow us to be honest with ourselves and others. When our perspective allows us to enhance our sexual potentials, sex becomes one of life's greatest pleasures. The acceptance of our own sexual behavior and a respect for others are the milestones in this quest.

Sexuality is not a wild horse that must be tamed and then exercised periodically. It is a potential with which we are born and which must be developed and nourished. It is every bit as important to be concerned about fulfilling our sexual capabilities as about fulfilling our intellectual or artistic capabilities (Katchadourian and Lunde, 1975, p. 13).

Sex can refer to making babies, making out, making love. It can also include dirty words, dirty jokes, genetics, prostitution, and venereal disease. It means choosing to mark an "M" or an "F" on an application form, choosing a partner, and choosing the color of a baby blanket, pink or blue. Sex is sensual, genital, and intellectual. It is the major appeal of advertising. It is intercourse. And it is more, much more.

Wherever we find it, at the center of all our concerns or at the periphery, sex is a part of life. Indeed, to be human is to be sexual, as well as to be intellectual, emotional, and mortal. And to be sexual is to be able to continue the human species. For sex is basically a means for reproducing our own kind. It is all the other things we have mentioned because, as human beings, we are more than the sum of our biological mechanisms.

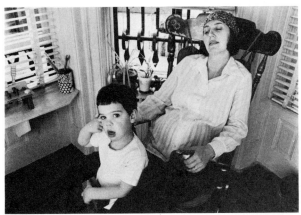

Michael Weisbrot

The reproductive function of sex does not mark the limits of human sexuality. The human animal has a sex organ that is unique: the human brain. This structure mediates all our sexual responses and assumes the highest importance in our sexual system for three reasons:

1. It allows us to be free of rigid, genetically determined sexual responses;
2. It gives us the capacity to include a rich and varied symbolism in our sexuality; and
3. It enables us to learn, choose, change, and be responsible for our sexual behavior and for the meaning of sex in our lives.

Being Free

The sexuality of nearly all animals is rigidly programmed. Through the genetic coding inherited from their parents, lower animals are directed by their instincts to court, mate, build nests, and care for their young. Thus certain animals perform complex sexual rituals which have never been learned but which are nevertheless enacted exactly by every individual of a species. During a courtship dance, the peacock fans his showy tail feathers as an expression of his genetic program. He does not select this display because he has learned that it will win him the favors of a hen. Nor does the display stand for his desires, his loneliness, his love for a chosen partner, his interpretation of what hens like to see, or for his reading of the latest fashion trends. He is merely responding by instinct to a sexual stimulus. Inherent or innate behavior such as this is the keystone of sex among nearly all nonhuman species.

The sexuality of the human species is free of rigid ritual, instinctual patterns, and blind adherence to sex drives. What we learn, think, and feel about sexuality and sexual behavior takes precedence over our involuntary, genetic, or hormonal tendencies. This is not to deny the biological component of human sexuality. In comparison with other animals, human sexual imperatives are psychological, social, and cultural rather than physiological. The wide variations in what we do sexually (how, when, with whom) and the range of importance that sexuality has in our lives attest to the power of our brains to modify the biological bases of behavior. We can choose to abstain from sex completely, or we can make the pursuit of sexual experience our primary concern. We can prefer homosexual to heterosexual activity, masturbation to intercourse, marital sex to nonmarital. We can find sex a joy or an evil, or an uninteresting duty. In this view, we all enjoy "free sex."

Symbolic Sex

The human ability to symbolize, to let one thing stand for another, accounts in large part for the pervasiveness of sexuality in our lives. Erotic literature, film, and art, sexual jokes, pornography, sexual advertising, and our sexual dreams and fantasies are among the human creations demonstrating our unique ability to have sex in our heads. We are able to experience sex at the slightest suggestion. Consider the number of long, straight, rigid, erect objects that have been seen as phallic symbols, making the number of penises in our lives countless. The human potential for experiencing sex owes its vastness to our ability to talk, think, and see sex in many situations. We do not need partners to have an extremely rich and varied sex life.

Photograph by Norfolk and Western Railway.

Human Sexuality Is Learned

Human sexuality is not natural and it is not unnatural. It is learned. The key to understanding the significance of learned sexuality is in the nature of the human female's sexuality. A woman's sexual receptivity is not regulated by her reproductive cycle. She need not wait until she is fertile to have intercourse; she can seek and enjoy sex at any time. Furthermore, human females alone among female animals are unmistakably orgasmic. We can obtain intense physical pleasure without having to reproduce.

By virtue of the human female's evolution, human males are freed from the uncontrollable, frenzied, reactive sexual behavior seen among other mammals. Although his sexual responses do not, physiologically speaking, differ widely from those of the apes, the human male is not genetically bound to do his part toward perpetuating the species with every periodically receptive female. He too can seek sex for pleasure, or for the other reasons humans pursue it, at any time. From a biological point of view, men as well as women can choose their sexual behavior.

Many of us, however, learn to believe that we have little or no choice in sexual matters, that we *must* do this and we *must not* do that, because to go against these imperatives would be "unnatural" or would impair physical health. We learn, in other words, that we are not responsible for our sexuality. We learn that sex is not learned. On the other hand, some of us learn to positively value and affirm sexuality in our lives. We learn to go beyond "the assumption that one can do no wrong as long as one does nothing at all." (Katchadourian and Lunde, 1975, p. 13) We learn that choices can be made.

The freedom to choose behavior does not mean that human sexuality is uncontrolled. Sexual behavior is restricted and monitored through learning. What we learn are our culture's standards for sex. We learn what to do, what not to do, when to do it, what to call it, and what to feel about it all. We even learn what questions to ask about sex.

CULTURAL GUIDELINES FOR SEXUAL BEHAVIOR

Our culture has already tried to answer certain fundamental questions about sexuality for us. It gives us, for instance, criteria for judging positive and negative aspects of sexuality. It gives us guidelines about integrating sexuality into our interpersonal relationships. Without an awareness of the answers we have already received from our culture, we cannot know if these are acceptable starting points from which to pursue our individual lives. Let's look briefly, then, at several of those institutions and popular notions about sexuality that provide the cultural context within which we must make our choices.

Right and Wrong: Law

Many sexual behaviors are subject to legal restriction. Sex laws in America today embody an ethical point of view which has its origins in ancient Judeo-Christian traditions. It is this ethical point of view that sex laws are designed to preserve, unlike criminal laws which have been made to preserve social order. The heart of this legal/religious view is

© Photography by Chris Rollins.

that the only purpose of sexual activity is reproduction (Katchadourian and Lunde, 1975, Chapter 16). Thus, although the stringency of sex-related laws varies somewhat among the states, they are consistent in prohibiting sexual activities that are not between legally married, heterosexual couples engaging in coitus. If you engage in sexual activities that cannot result in the birth of a baby, such as masturbation or oral-genital sex, you are, in this view, not only morally wrong but can be judged criminal as well. If caught in a nonreproductive-sex crime, the penalty is often quite severe, such as New Jersey's $5000 fine and 20 years in prison for sodomy (anal intercourse) (Wilson, Roe, and Autry, 1975, p. 159). Because most of us are ignorant of such laws they do not directly influence our sexual lives—if we are heterosexual and married.

Sex laws in several states are coming under attack for being unrealistic and outmoded. That they still exist in such detail and number speaks for the strength of the tradition out of which they grew and for the vigor with which they are defended.

Good and Bad: The Church

Most of our views about sexual behavior come from religious teachings or church doctrine. Western religions take a generally negative stance on nonreproductive sex, compared with the religions of other parts of the world. Several beliefs can be detected behind this religious interest in controlling sexuality. Among them are the conviction that only by restricting the sexual propensities of humans is it possible to stabilize the family. Another belief is that only by giving up pleasure in this world can one pursue God's work, redirecting energies that might have gone into sex toward more spiritual tasks in this life and the next. Whatever their doctrines, Christian churches have generally condemned sexual pleasure, and the result to our attitudes in the Christian West has been a firm association between sex, sin, and guilt. This association has been strengthened by notions that virginity is to be prized, that lust is dangerous, that the flesh is weak, the fleshly passions evil.

Today, many churches are taking a new look at the realities of sex, and by so doing are freeing many people to acknowledge that their personal needs for sexual expression differ from those allowed by traditional Christian doctrine. Many otherwise religious people, responding to the conflict between doctrinal restrictions and personal needs for enhancing their sexual lives, have come to ignore or discard church views on sex.

Healthy and Sick: Medicine

Sexual behavior is frequently judged for its healthiness or unhealthiness. Those sexual practices that are distasteful, unusual, or presumed harmful very easily assume the label "sick." Naturally enough, people who engage in "sick" sex become, by this kind of diagnosis, sick people.

The medical profession has done little to provide us with clear, unbiased criteria regarding the worth of such judgements. During the last century, to take a blatant example, doctors were of the opinion that masturbation could cause virtually any ailment from warts to madness. The popular expression of this opinion still causes many people to worry about "self-abuse," although few doctors would now condemn it.

Another medical view being changed as the result of contemporary studies is that toward homosexuality. Until quite recently (December 1974), the American Psychiatric Association listed homosexuality as a mental illness, despite a large body of evidence to the contrary (Freedman, 1973). Even now, however, self-doubts, fear, and guilt take a physical toll on many homosexuals faced with the widespread condemnation of their behavior, just as adolescent masturbators used to (and perhaps still) suffer by thinking that they are sick and despised. In and of themselves, homosexuality and autoerotic behaviors are neither diseases nor "sick."

The prevalence of social diseases, primarily the venereal diseases, in the United States leads to medical and personal problems for many. Cultural restrictions must be overcome in order to allow all people, married or not, to feel free to seek treatment without fear of censure.

BOX 8.1

SEX ISN'T SICK, BUT VD *IS* A DISEASE

1. Venereal disease is epidemic in the United States.
2. Of all contagious diseases, including mumps, measles, and TB, *only* the common cold is more prevalent than VD.
3. *Anyone* whose partner has VD can catch it through sexual contact. (This includes genital, oral, and anal contact.) VD does not prefer the promiscuous, the homosexual, the prostitute, the poor, the degenerate, the unmarried, or the young. VD grows in any warm, moist, dark membrane of any human vagina, urethra, throat, or rectum.
4. VD does not always present clear, distinguishable symptoms, even in men.
5. VD is easily curable with penicillin and other antibiotics. Much VD is preventable by the use of condoms.
6. If you are sexually active (have sex with more than one partner, or with a partner who does) get regular VD checks every 3 to 6 months at your public health department or VD clinic. Don't ignore VD.

(A reference book on this subject is *The VD Book*, by J. Chiappa and J. Forish, Holt, Rinehart and Winston, 1976.)

Private and Public: Commerce

In a culture that treats nonreproductive sex to silence, privacy, repression, denial, and guilt, it is sometimes surprising to note that sex is a moneymaker. But there's no denying it: sex is big business in America. Not only can one readily buy sexual titillation and sexual services, but

Michael Weisbrot

one is daily seduced by a large number of products that are advertised by means of consciously chosen sexual overtones. Across the country, from coast to coast, barely covered human breasts are a constant feature in advertising (but it is considered improper for a mother to nurse her baby in public). Prostitution, pornography, and advertising sell sex to the buying public and in the bargain perpetuate a variety of sexual contradictions and incongruities.

Our society is two-faced toward sex. Sex is supposed to be good, beautiful, and loving when one is in bed with one's spouse. The same sex acts are dirty, shameful, and criminal if one is in bed with a customer. Sex is despicable if sold openly, but it is not to be given away either. From the magazine racks of our most respectable supermarkets and drug stores we are allowed a wide selection of "soft core" pornography (nudes and seminudes), detective magazines promising by their covers the most imaginative sex crimes, and smart fashion magazines that show you how to dress so as to appear that you can't wait to get your clothes off. But "hard core" pornography, depicting explicitly what you only imagine when reading soft-core, must be bought for high prices at the specialty stores of big cities. The distinction between the wares and the kind of store in which they are sold glosses over the uniform appeal they have: buying any kind of "pornography" is a purchase of impersonal, sex-object arousal.

Only recently has the American public seen the birth of a human baby on TV. Some of the public, that is: the program was shown late at night to spare children the sight of human sexuality in action. We do not seem so delicate when it comes to human violence. Every evening American children are treated to countless prime-time instances of murder and lesser savagery, every week, year in and year out. The two-faced character of our society is further illustrated by the use of sex in the advertising media. While impressing on their children that sex is something sacred to be kept for marriage, the adult world has no hesitation in taking full advantage of erotic responses to sell everything from chutney to automobiles.

My point is not that society should be less open about sex. It is the commercialization of sex combined with the attempt to deny its honest expression that I deplore. While our society uses sex to sell its goods in the marketplace it fails to recognize the tensions this climate produces (Hettlinger, 1975, p. 4).

It is apparent that our culture's attitudes provide the field on which we play out a number of conflicts about sexuality. Legal and religious standards for behavior set more negative than positive guidelines, and are thus restrictive on balance. Medical and health standards about sex are a confusing mixture of knowledge and moral judgement. Advertising, on the other hand, taunts us with endless suggestions that we can, like the beautiful people in the ads, attain a perfect sex life. No matter what our intellectual or moral background, it is likely that each of us has learned to feel some measure of guilt about sexual behavior. To escape any such feelings we would have had to grow up outside our culture, untouched by the belief that certain aspects of sexuality are inherently evil. But we have grown up *within* the culture, not outside it, and the conspiracy of silence about sex in which we find ourselves involved inevitably leads to worries about what's normal, what's right, and about the adequacy of our sexual performances.

Lack of communication between partners about sex is a natural outgrowth of certain assumptions about men's and women's sexuality. If you believe that males are, by nature and status, totally and constantly sexual, whereas females are, by nature and status, asexual—that is, *non-sexual*—then there is no need to talk about it. That's just the way life is. Such an attitude underlies the *double standard* (one standard for women's behavior and another for men's), to which our culture, among others, has been a long-standing subscriber. The situation is not one in which truthful and open expressions of sexuality take place easily.

EXPLORATION 8.1

Sexual Learning

Finding answers to the following questions will give you a great deal of knowledge about your sex education up to now.

1. What are the sex laws in your state?
2. What are your church's views on sexual morality (or the views of your parents' church)?
3. Did your doctor (or your family doctor) take courses in human sexuality as part of his medical training?
4. How aware are you of, and in what ways influenced by, commercial sex?

SEXUALITY, MARRIAGE, AND LOVE

How should sexuality be, and how in fact is it, related to marriage and love? The search for the correct answer to this question generates a greater diversity of opinion than perhaps any other current sexual topic. The right and proper combination of sex, love, and legal marriage will often be prescribed differently by a young woman, her male partner, their parents, their friends, and the neighbors. Each party will deliver a recipe based on individual beliefs, the diversity of which can be simplified into the three major ideals of our culture.

1. *Marriage is the precondition of sex;* love catches a ride if and when it can, but it is not necessary.
2. *Love is the precondition of sex;* marriage is appropriate but not necessary.
3. *Consent is the precondition of sex;* pleasure does not require either love or marriage.

Each of these three views defines the purpose of sexual expression differently, each has its own implications for sexual behavior, each requires us to make important choices and decisions, and each leads us to certain expectations about sex in our relationships.

The view that marriage is the only appropriate condition for sexual behavior is the most traditional of the three views, and it supports most prevailing legal and religious standards. At the heart of this ideal is the notion that sexual intercourse is for the purpose of reproduction. Sexual intercourse is both the privilege and the duty of married couples; sexual intimacy is proper only when we have made a legal, life-long commitment to one member of the opposite sex. The important decision in this veiwpoint is the choice of a marriage partner.

In this view, sex is integrated into a marriage relationship. One's sex partner is one's partner in life and sex is only one of many shared activities, including the rearing of children. This view clearly restricts both premarital and extramarital sexual activities. A traditional variation has been to give the husband tacit approval for extramarital sexual affairs or visits to prostitutes, although the wife is strictly forbidden any other relationships. When the purpose of sex is reproduction, sexual fun is optional; neither sexual pleasure nor love is required in marriage, but both are usually expected.

Many expect the recital of marriage vows to transform the suppressed passions of courtship into loving, exciting, marital bliss. In fact, this does not always happen. It can be difficult for a woman to become, overnight, sexually active in a pleasurable way when she is used to vigorously defending her chastity. It can be difficult, too, for a man to learn to perceive his wife as sexual when he has known her only as virginal and "pure."

Viewing sex only as a necessity can inhibit sexual experimentation in search of pleasure. Indeed, intercourse may lead to feelings of guilt in those who have, for most of their lives, been told that it is at best a duty for a good wife or husband. The guilt that accompanies nonreproductive expressions of sexuality can be profound, prohibiting a couple from indulging in the spice of variety that makes sex a joy instead of a burden.

The second ideal emphasizes the necessity of love for sexual intercourse. How far one should go depends on the *quality* of the relationship, not the legality of it. Couples who are engaged, or in long-term relationships, can choose to express their love, care, and commitment through sex. This situation is today the most common in which premarital sex takes place, according to a recent survey (Hunt, 1973). Many couples also carry this view into their decisions regarding marriage. The absence of legal marriage as a precondition for sexual intercourse allows couples who feel close to one another a release for their sexual tensions and a means to express their intimacy. It is expected that full sexual expression will strengthen the relationship, and it often does.

The important decision to be made, in this view, is whether or not one is in love. It is a short, frequently taken step from "sex requires love" to "sex equals love." The degree of sexual intimacy between a couple may actually define for them the feelings they share. Whether in marriage or out, it is assumed by many Americans that sex and love belong together, and are virtually interchangeable. This equation is so strong that many of us take for granted that two people making love are in love. Sexual activity becomes a barometer of love in a relationship. Thus, "I love you" becomes an acceptable way to say "I desire you physically."

The third ideal on which people base their opinions about sexuality, and make their decisions about sex, is that sexual behavior needs no justification. Sexual pleasure is the purpose of sex, and it requires neither

Michael Weisbrot

love nor marriage to be achieved. Casual sexual encounters are by nature recreational and they imply nothing about how the participants feel toward each other, whether they could live together for a lifetime, or whether in fact they will ever see one another again. Changing partners, one-night stands, and sexual experimentation do not, in this view, carry the stigmas of promiscuity.

Sexual hedonism, as this ideal is sometimes called, does not carry a price of guilt, and yet it is not without morality. The line between what one should and should not do is usually drawn at the limit of what partners agree is pleasurable for them. Such an agreement need not abandon the concepts of consenting adults, privacy, and respect for another. Other than a mutual decision to have fun, however, partners owe each other nothing. A spokesman for this approach to sex, Albert Ellis, feels that sex, like sports, is an activity that can be enjoyed for the physical excitement it gives, without the condition of an enduring relationship or the promise of fidelity.

The important decisions to make, in this view, are about pleasure. Participants should know what they enjoy and what they don't enjoy, and how to communicate this to a partner. They should be free of expectations that the relationship will be anything more than a sexual one. Sometimes those who seem to participate in recreational sex are attempting to be fashionable, sophisticated, liberated, nonchalant nonvirgins by denying their needs for intimacy.

Those who believe in the exclusive propriety of married sex may find the idea of recreational sex abhorrent. Those who feel the need for love in the act of making love may recoil from the idea of sex-as-sport because it seems cold, calculating, or self-indulgent. Traditional views of women make it difficult to accept a woman whose life is casual. She may threaten men with the assertiveness of her advances; other women may question her motives; either might disparage her initiative as nymphomania. (Nymphomania, incidentally, is a relative term. The word refers to women who seem to have greater sexual desire or assertiveness than the name-caller has. One might well call these women "lucky.")

nymphomania

No one of these viewpoints about sex, love, and marriage suits all of us. Nor will our individual attitudes be right for all others. A young woman's parents may guide their own sexual behavior by the traditional view that sex belongs in marriage. But this view may not guide their daughter if she feels that sex is primarily a pleasurable activity between consenting adults. And in turn, her attitude may not be the one held by her partner. He may feel that she is the only one for him, and may expect, because she agrees to sexual intercourse, that she loves him and only him. If the woman, her parents, and her partner are not clear about their viewpoints, if they cannot or do not communicate these viewpoints, and if each cannot tolerate a view other than their own, sex will become a source of conflict among them.

Each of us has learned our attitudes about sexual activity in our interpersonal relationships. Our beliefs give meaning to sex in our lives. Our criteria for sex may be clear to us or just beyond the limits of our awareness. Our friends or partners may share our standards or operate on different ones. The quest for values in sexuality seeks to discover, examine, accept (or change) personal sexual standards to suit us. For most of us, this process means coming around to an attitude that affirms our sexuality and, by the same token, forsakes the guilt associated with it.

**EXPLORATION
8.2**

**Which
Values
for Me?**

Give the following questions some thought. Think about your responses in the light of what you have just read. When you meet in class, share what you have discovered about your values. Groups of six to eight are convenient for this kind of discussion. Listen for the experiences and values of others which resemble yours, and for those which are dissimilar.

1. How, if at all, have you modified the values you learned from your parents? Why did you make the changes you did? How have your sexual experiences helped define your attitudes relative to those of your parents? Are you, or were you, comfortable discussing sexual matters with your parents?

2. Given your personal set of values, what kinds of decisions do you have to make about sexual activity? (Choices, for example, about time, place, partners, the quality of the relationship, etc.) Do you make the same kind of decision in all situations or are you more likely to choose, for example, recreational sex at one time and romantic or love-based sex at another? What kinds of decisions are your friends making about their sexuality?

3. What conflicts about sexuality do your attitudes produce? How do these compare with the conflicts your classmates describe?

4. How tolerant are you of others' values? Of their behavior? If you, for example, engage in casual sex, how do you react to another's preferring to remain a virgin? If you believe that your sexual contacts should be confined to marriage, what do you think about mate-swapping?

5. How is sexuality integrated into the rest of your life? Does it take the major part of your time and energy? No part? A share that suits your evaluation of its importance to you?

6. In what ways does your thinking reflect the sexual double standard? For instance, do you feel that men have undeniable sex drives that must be satisfied, while women are naturally asexual?

SEXUAL RESPONSE

human sexual
response cycle

Every generation of our species has engaged in sexual behavior. But it is only within the last decade that we have learned what happens in our bodies as they respond to sexual stimulation. The human sexual response cycle (Masters and Johnson, 1966) refers to the several physiological reactions that accompany sexual stimulation. This cycle of response is divided into phases, each of which is characterized by specific reactions. Although individuals show considerable diversity in the time it takes to complete a phase, and in the intensity of physiological reactions within it, all healthy human beings are able to complete the cycle.

Keeping in mind that the phases of the sexual response cycle are seldom clear-cut, let's now look more closely at each.

Excitement Phase

The variety of events that can begin sexual arousal are virtually limitless. More often than a single isolated event, a combination of stimuli are usually involved, such as visual excitement plus fantasy plus physical contact. This phase can last anywhere from a few minutes to several hours, producing a rapid surge of tension or a very gradual buildup. The term *foreplay* is a common expression of the physical stimulation of initial excitement. When this phase is taken merely as a prelude to orgasm its unique delights may be lost. To rush through "the preliminaries" on the way to orgasm may interfere with one's potential for sexual pleasure. Arousal in itself, in the awareness of its sensations, can be exquisite if it does not always signal the start of a race to the finish.

Plateau Phase

The plateau phase is reached when continuous stimulation of the male's penis or the female's clitoral area produces a state of intense excitement throughout the body. If the preceding phase began in a playful, experimental manner, by this time mind and body have become focused in a direction unmistakably sexual. Whether reached by self-stimulation or through interaction with a partner, the plateau phase is one of height-

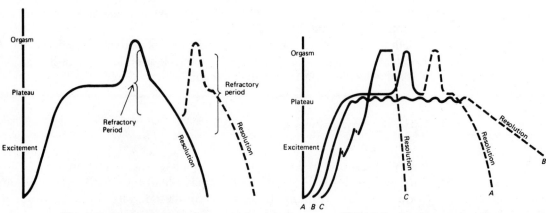

The male sexual response cycle.   The female sexual response cycle.

ened immediacy. One's attention is often concentrated in genital sensations. If stimulation is reduced or interrupted, however, the cycle may revert to the excitement phase or cease altogether. Continuing, effective stimulation for a period of from 30 seconds to 3 minutes after reaching plateau will initiate the orgasmic phase.

Orgasmic Phase

Orgasm is an extremely concentrated involuntary reaction lasting from 3 to 15 seconds. In both men and women, orgasm sometimes involves most muscles of the entire body and always initiates rhythmic contractions in the muscles of the pelvic area. As a physical event, orgasm is the same process for both men and women, no matter what the stimulation leading to it. The muscular contractions during this phase diffuse fluids that have accumulated in the female and expel semen that has collected in the male. Women have the capacity to experience repeated, or multiple, orgasms, one after another, as long as they are effectively stimulated and until they are fatigued.

An experience as intense and consuming as orgasm does not translate easily into words, and indeed the commonest description of it is "indescribable." Since not all orgasms are such monumental occurrences, however, evidence may sometimes be sought to establish whether or not it has been reached. There is little problem here with men, their ejaculate providing proof enough. Women do not ejaculate and as evidence must rely on their awareness of what is taking place in their own bodies. Female orgasms vary in intensity and length more than male orgasms, and females are more susceptible to psychological interference. Those who know they have had orgasms — and not all women are sure that they have — say that the experience is more than simply pleasant. Most will agree that they also feel a release of tension throughout their bodies and sensitivity of the clitoris. Because of the variable nature of the female orgasm, it is possible for women to fake orgasms if they feel the need to do so.

Resolution Phase

refractory period

During the last phase of the sexual response cycle, the body returns to a nonexcited state. This is a gradual process that is not complete until about half an hour after orgasm. Men experience a refractory period during this time, lasting from minutes to hours, during which they are physiologically incapable of having another orgasm. Women have no such period and can, with effective stimulation, reach orgasm again immediately. If a woman has not reached orgasm before stimulation stops, her body will require several hours to return to its preexcitement phase. It takes this long for blood and other fluids that have engorged her entire pelvic region to diffuse throughout her body.

Although orgasm is the culmination of the sexual response cycle, it is not its end. The resolution phase can provide opportunities to savor the pleasures just past in a mood of total relaxation.

Potential Troubles

The sexual response cycle is a human potential available to anyone. We know, however, that a large number of us do not regularly fulfill this potential in an easy and pleasurable way (Masters and Johnson, 1970). It is true that sexual gratification is subjective; one person's trouble may be another's satisfaction; what fulfills one may leave another sadly disillusioned. Aside from this subjective component, though, there are a few generally recognized and treatable "problems" in sex. For men, the most common difficulties are unreliable erections (not being able to achieve or not being able to sustain one) and premature ejaculation (reaching orgasm without, in the individual's or the couple's view, sufficient time in earlier phases). The most common difficulty for women is failing to experience orgasm at all, or failing to achieve orgasm in certain situations. Another female problem is with pain acting as a barrier to sexual enjoyment.

Most *sexual dysfunctions* (inadequacies in sexual response) have psychological causes rather than organic ones. Unacknowledged feelings that sex is dirty or sinful, conflicts about getting out of control, a lack of awareness of one's bodily sensations — these are the kinds of causes that are often found. Important too is performance anxiety — the fear that we won't be able to make it happen the way it is supposed to happen, with a clap of thunder, a crash of symbols, a chorus of angels, and a rainbow of heavenly light. When one's head is busily weighing and measuring what is happening against one's expectations, trying to achieve the perfect union, and fighting down fears of failure, one's body is bound to respond in an erratic way to the mix of messages it is receiving. In a society that in many ways draws an equation between sexual performance and self-esteem, that places a high value on sexual expertise without a balancing emphasis on the open expression of one's sexual needs and preferences, it is small wonder that many of us feel pressured and inadequate.

PERSONAL CHOICES

Sexual response is not involuntary. We are not sexual machines provided with ON buttons and OFF buttons to be pushed by circumstances or hormones. Humans make sexual decisions; we never lose the potential for making choices even when we are not aware of that potential. Within the limits of our culture and the limits of biological possibility, we make choices about what to respond to sexually and how to respond. We give meaning to our sexual experiences, and we choose the partners who share them with us.

Turning On

"I turn on myself. This doesn't mean just that I dig who I am and the way I look and feel and taste and smell—it also means *I* am the one who decides how emotionally and sexually excited I am by someone." (Rush, 1973, p. 159)

This woman has discovered in herself something that is true for all of us. Sexual arousal is not passive. It is an active process of integrating sights, sensations, sounds, odors, and fantasies in a sexual way. When this organization of experience produces a tingle of erotic excitement, we say that we have been turned on. The truth is we have turned ourselves on.

EXPLORATIONS
8.3

Turning On

a. This exercise has elicited many valuable insights from my classes. Divide the class into two groups according to sex. Men use one chalk board and women another, or divide a single board in half. (The best situation is provided by having boards at opposite sides of a room.) Each member of each group is to write an answer to the question, "What turns me on?" Be as candid as you can. When everyone has contributed an item, step back and have a look. Consider the variety of responses, the differences between the two lists and the similarities. Are there any items that surprised you on the opposite-sex list? On your own list? Are there many that you fully expected?

b. On a 3 x 5 card indicate your gender by putting either "M" or "F" in the upper left-hand corner. On this card write your responses to the questions below. Have the instructor or a class member sort the cards by gender and read the responses aloud. Discuss the responses as a group. If there are any differences between responses of men and women, what might account for them? Are there similarities? Is there a wide range in responses, or do people in your class seem to respond in similar ways?

Sexual arousal: How do I feel about being sexually aroused? (Is it always OK? What does my body feel like? Is it always enjoyable? Sometimes threatening? Pressured? Uncomfortable?)

Situations: Do I sometimes feel I shouldn't be turned on? (When? Why? Do I ever avoid situations in which I think I might turn on? Which?)

Fears: What fears have I experienced about becoming sexually aroused? (Losing control? Anticipation of pain? Interruptions? Discovery? Pregnancy? Feelings that arousal is inappropriate, such as getting an erection in public? Other?)

Turn offs: What turns me off? (How? When? Always or just sometimes?)

To the very brink of orgasm, human sexual response can be controlled, and is therefore the responsibility of the individual. Although we may not be aware of the ways in which we *eroticize* our experience of the world around us, it is nevertheless correct to say that we make choices, consciously or unconsciously, about what we will consider stimulating. Likewise, we decide *how* to react to particular stimuli, positively or negatively. And in doing so time and again we develop tastes and distastes, a repertoire of turn-ons and turn-offs.

Sex Without Partners

There are times in everyone's life when a desirable partner for erotic activities is not available. There are other times when we simply prefer private, solitary experiences. We all have the potential to be erotic by ourselves. The chief means to solitary sexual pleasure, although they can also be shared, are erotic fantasy and masturbation.

The range of sexual experience that can be created by the mind is virtually limitless. We can create any sort of sexual encounter we can imagine, from fingertip caresses over a dime-store counter to mass-participation sex in Yankee Stadium. These fantasies, as well as our erotic dreams, can give us pleasure, and they can make us anxious. Is there something wrong with me because I have these wicked thoughts? No, there isn't, for all of us weave something of a sexual nature into our daydreams and play variations on erotic themes in our sleep. Moreover,

"Ready-made Bouquet," Magritte (*private collection*).

both day and night fantasies are substitutes for action, not acts in themselves. We don't have to do anything about them, and in fact most would be far less exciting if we acted them out. Sexual reveries offer an uncomplicated, quiet, readily available avenue of sexual pleasure.

Much has been said about masturbation and, for the last 200 years, most of it has been bad. Today, we know that masturbation is not harmful. And even when it is thought to be somehow dangerous to health or morals, it continues to be a universally practiced form of sexual outlet. Nearly all men and more and more women masturbate at some time or other. For many people it is a way to learn about their own sexual responsiveness. An advantage of masturbation is that it allows individual exploration of erotic sensations without a partner, which may help to relieve inhibitions and pressures. This freedom can be self-serving in the best possible sense.

Sharing Sex

What I think is this; all the misconceptions about sexuality will straighten out if everyone simply grows up. For a grownup human being, what's good in bed is to be with another human being one truly cares about. And what one cares about in bed is exactly the same as what one cares about out of bed—honesty, imagination, a little mischief, and a lot of kindness (Perry, quoted in Pierson and D'Antonio, 1974, p. 70).

Having sex with someone else is sharing. Time is being shared, and so is physical space. Sexual sharing is also body contact, a give and take of physical stimulation, the buildup of sexual tension and its release. Being physically exposed in someone else's presence can entail a sense of shared vulnerability as well.

An act of sexual intercourse involves psychological risks because of the expectations, desires, and hopes each partner holds for the experience or for the relationship. Sometimes one partner is risking more than the other by having a greater emotional investment in the situation. Getting sexual or emotional satisfaction at the expense of such a partner's expectations and needs is to sexually use that partner. A man can take advantage of a woman's need to be loved in order to obtain sexual gratification. A woman can use a man sexually in order to bolster her image of sexual desirability. In either case someone is liable to get hurt, not by sex *per se,* but by the hidden motives it serves.

It is often difficult to acknowledge the needs which lurk in the shadows of our passion. Our motives are not always noble. If we acknowledged them we might not feel good about ourselves, or others might not accept us. We therefore choose to keep our true feelings obscured or unexpressed. Whether our partner is a new one or a spouse of many years, sexual intercourse can express many and diverse motives. Through sex we could be saying:

I love you.
I need physical contact, stroking, to be held.
I want you to love me. Please love me.
I will sleep with you so you won't leave me.
I'm lonely.
I know you. I will get to know you better if we sleep together.
I need to get rid of my (sexual) tension.
I'm performing my duty (as a husband, as a wife, as a lover).
I'm totally at your will. I'm powerless; take me.
I've got power over you.
I'm proving that I'm not inadequate (or homosexual).
I'm proving that I'm desirable.
I'm angry (at you, at women, at men, at the world).
I hate you.

Sex can be used as a substitute for love, affection, getting to know someone, as an expression of power, duty, anger, and as proof of adequacy, desirability, potency. When we are getting sex but are wanting something else we open the door to resentment, feelings of failure, and self-defeat.

It is important to *know* what you want in order to *get* what you want. Just as it is valuable to recognize emotional needs in order to meet them, it is valuable to attend to your sensual needs in intercourse. A first step, not always easily taken, is to become aware of bodily sensations. This means feeling them, not thinking about them; in the words of Fritz Perls, physical awareness means to "lose your mind and come to your senses." Knowing what feels good to you requires experience. This is especially true for a woman, because her sexual anatomy is less accessible than a man's. Women may have to engage in purposeful exploration and experimentation to find out what they like sexually.

A second step is being able to ask for what you want. To be open and honest about asking your partner to give you pleasure is somehow more difficult than asking someone to pass the butter at the dinner table. It is necessary to feel that your sexual requests are acceptable — and to know that even if acceptable, they may not be gratified. It is also necessary to be able to ask without conveying rejection or criticism of your partner, and without fear of being thought aggressive.

Sharing also means listening and giving. Alex Comfort prefaces the *Joy of Sex* with this advice:

There are after all only two "rules" in good sex, apart from the obvious one of not doing things which are silly, antisocial or dangerous. One is "don't do anything you don't really enjoy," and the other is "find out your partner's needs and don't balk them if you can help it." In other words, a good giving and taking relationship depends on a compromise (so does going to a show — if you both want the same thing, fine; if not, take turns and don't let one partner always dictate). That can be easier than it sounds, because unless your partner wants something you find actively off-putting, real lovers get a reward not only from their own satisfactions but from seeing the other respond and become satisfied. . . . Finding out someone else's needs and your own, and how to express them in bed, is not only interesting and educative but rewarding, and what sexual love is all about (1972, pp. 15–16).

Sharing sex can also be sharing fun:

It is quite characteristic of self-actualizing people that they can enjoy themselves in love and in sex. Sex very frequently becomes a kind of game in which laughter is quite as common as panting. . . . It is not the welfare of the species, or the task of reproduction, or the future development of mankind that attracts people to each other. The love and sex life of healthy people, in spite of the fact that it frequently reaches great peaks of ecstasy, is nevertheless also easily compared to the games of children and puppies. It is cheerful, humorous, and playful (Maslow, 1970, pp. 194–195).

EXPLORATION 8.4

Communication and Sex

Giving clear messages

a. Imagine a potential sex partner (a real or imagined person—it doesn't matter) sitting in a chair opposite you. You want to go to bed with this person and you are going to give him or her a clear, straight message as to your motivations.

The first is a need to give love. You dearly love this partner and desire to share this love physically. Tell him or her *out loud*. How does it feel to say this? (Pay attention to your heartbeat, your palms, feelings in your stomach, etc.)

Now you have a different reason. You need to be held. You need someone to cuddle, cradle, and stroke you. Say it *out loud*. How does this feel?

Continue verbalizing to your imaginary partner through the list on p. 206.

Now visualize your imaginary partner's responses. Can he or she hear you? Are your feelings and needs being accepted? Or are they being negated (e.g., "No, you don't hate me.")?

Trade places. Can you hear someone who is being clear with you?

Discuss this question in class: What would happen if *everyone* could be clear about motivations for sex?

b. Suppose, now, that someone has asked you to have sexual intercourse, but you don't want to. List *all* the possible reasons you can think of why. For example, you find the person physically unattractive; you wish to remain a virgin; you just masturbated and aren't up to turning on again, and so on.

Which of the reasons on your list could you be honest about?

Which might lead you to make excuses?

Discuss in class any problems you have met in turning down sexual advances.

Are there any differences between males and females? Between married and single students?

Choosing Partners

We choose our sex partners. Our genes do not control this choice, but neither are we completely free in it. We pick from those people who qualify according to the social values we accept. Our culture provides us with several standards for choosing, the most obvious being that which leads us to seek out someone who conforms physically to a generally accepted measure of sexual attractiveness.

Another standard for choice asks whether your partner in sex will be your partner in other activities. Is this the person with whom you wish to raise a family, share housekeeping, or to whom you would divulge your innermost self? If so, life-style, social and economic status, education, race, interests and ideals — these and other factors become pertinent. As nonsexual activities are shared, they lend relevant dimensions to the rational and emotional choices we make about sex partners.

We can also choose, theoretically, how many partners to have at one time, although our culture is geared to the promotion of sexual monogamy. We are encouraged by precept and institution to enjoy one partner, or one partner at a time. We frown on promiscuity, idealize fidelity, and make sexual jealousy a major emotional theme of life. The cultural foundations of jealousy rest on monogamous ideals. A basic premise of monogamy is that we somehow own the person of our choice, that we must (or should be able to) control that person in a way that secures exclusive sexual rights over him or her. This possessive ideal often leads us into insecurity about being able to hold onto a partner in the sexual arena, traditionally a highly competitive one. We learn to fear that a monogamous commitment will not be honored by a chosen partner and to guard against our fears with suspicion, doubt, and the withholding of trust. Monogamy in practice is not without its problems, but it is still a powerful ideal.

serial monogamy

Many people have today openly abandoned the one-partner-for-a-lifetime norm in favor of serial monogamy. This refers to the practice of having one partner for a period (sometimes years) and then making a different liaison for another period of time. Sometimes the switch necessitates divorce, sometimes a less formal move from one household to another. Yet others are directly challenging the confines of sexual monogamy through participation in group sex and swinging. Those who violate the monogamous ideal by "playing around on the side" have always been encouraged to be discreet.

Gender is another consideration in choosing a partner. The majority of us decide for a partner of the opposite sex. So many things in our world say boys belong with girls, and men with women, that we find it difficult to see heterosexuality as optional and not inevitable. Heterosexuality is the preferred, but not necessarily free, choice in cultures that are popularly and legally intolerant of homosexuality. In other societies

"Sleep," Courbet. Musée du Petit Palais-Paris. Photo Bulloz.

and at other times in history we find greater leniency in choosing either opposite-sex or same-sex partners. Heterosexuality and homosexuality are both human potentials.

Why, in the face of such strong and traditional sanctions, do some choose partners of the same sex? The answer to this question is not known; neither biological differences nor specific environments reliably account for homosexual preferences. What is known is that people who make homosexual choices are no more "sick" than those who do not. They do not have diseases, mental or physical, nor do they need to be cured because of their sexual preference. In fact, they are often not obviously different from anyone else except in this one aspect of their lives.

Sex preference is not a once-and-for-all choice. In the 1940s, Kinsey found that up to 37 percent of males and 13 percent of females had at least one homosexual encounter by the age of forty-five. Those who had consistently and exclusively maintained homosexual choices accounted for less than 5 percent of the population. These figures have remained stable in subsequent surveys. We seem to persist in labeling people homosexual, lesbian, or bisexual even though these labels obscure a diverse reality. Kinsey felt that :

Males do not represent two discrete populations, heterosexual and homosexual. The world is not to be divided into sheep and goats. Not all things are black nor all things white. It is a fundamental of taxonomy that nature rarely deals with discrete categories. Only the human mind invents categories and tries to force facts into separated pigeon-holes. The living world is a continuum in each and every one of its aspects. The sooner we learn this concerning human sexual behavior the sooner we shall reach a sound understanding of the realities of sex (1948, p. 639).

See Chapter 10 for another discussion of homosexuality.

Photograph courtesy of The Farm.

Pregnancy and Parenting

Every woman has the potential to decide if and when her body is to be used to shelter and protect a new member of the species, and if and when her life will be devoted to rearing a child. This potential is maximized by rational decision-making. The rationality of her choice will be based on the fact that, unless she or her partner is sterile, every act of unprotected sexual intercourse introduces a probability of conception. Nature has ensured that this is usually a high probability. If a woman and her partner choose not to conceive, one option (the only 100 percent effective choice, in fact) is abstinence. Since no temporary form of birth control yet devised is totally effective in preventing conception (although several approach 100 percent), a couple engaging in intercourse is taking a risk. This risk is minimized by the deliberate and careful use of birth control.

Studies of abortion patients have shown that their decision-making process before conception is often irrational. This is probably true of many parents as well. What contributed to these irrational choices? One thing may be a lack of knowledge about how conception takes place and how to prevent it. A rational decision is an informed decision including knowledge of what birth control options are available, what the possible

EXPLORATION 8.5 Birth Control	Prepare a report on one or more methods of birth control to share with your class. Present information on the pros and cons, side effects, how and when to use the method, the woman's responsibility, the man's responsibility. Include information about abortion and sterilization for both men and woman. You may find it interesting to research the history of birth control methods used in other cultures.

side effects are, how to use the method, and importantly, what the failure rates are. Even when informed, it is possible to be careless and forgetful. The erratic use of birth control is itself a decision — an *irrational* one, perhaps based on a subconscious desire to become pregnant. Carelessness can also result from accepting the erroneous belief that since pregnancy didn't result before, it won't happen this time. Conception is not the inevitable result of sexual intercourse, but the probability of it is constant.

EXPLORATION 8.6

Sexual Attitudes

The most valuable way to enhance sexuality is to clarify our sexual perspectives, to be conscious of how we feel about the many aspects of our sexuality. The intention of this exploration is not to change any of your attitudes. Rather, it gives you the opportunity to express whatever values you hold about many of the topics in this chapter and some additional ones. You will be able to identify your perspectives and to actively listen to others, and you will become aware of the diversity of viewpoints in your group.

Split up into groups of six and write each of the following topics on a separate card:

Prostitution	Sex and love
Pornography	Sexual jealousy
Masturbation	Premarital sex
Sexual double standard	Extramarital sex
One partner for a life-time	Recreational sex
Group sex	Bisexuality
Sexual fantasies	Homosexuality
Promiscuity	Abortion
Interracial sex	Birth control

Do this in each group of six people. When the cards are ready, place them face down in the center of your group. One person draws a card, reads it, and responds if he or she chooses. If not, that card is returned and another drawn. In responding, tell:

How you feel about this topic for yourself, for others in general, and for people close to you.

How your emotional responses to this topic compare with your intellectual responses.

Others in the group will listen to each response and respond also if they choose. Remember, the object is not to change anyone else's view, only to clarify it. When one person has finished, the next will draw a card and respond. (This exploration is adapted from *Values in Sexuality* by Eleanor Morrison and Mila Underhill Price, copyright 1974 Hart Publishing Company, Inc.)

RESPECT FOR OTHERS

As with any area of life in which we make choices, not all of us will make the same sexual decisions. Some choose to mate for life, others do not. We may choose to have sex alone, with others, or not at all. We may choose to be turned on by different events. In order to be free in our own choices we must also realize that others will not be choosing what we choose. If our perspective is one that forces others to agree with us or does not respect their choices, it is a limited perspective (see Exploration 8.6).

MAXIMIZING SEXUAL POTENTIALS

During the last fifteen years, basic research in biological, social, and psychological aspects of sexuality have added substantially to public knowledge. Sex laws are gradually being changed to reflect the range of human sexual potentials. The new feminism of the women's movement has proved to be a positive force in liberating women from traditional inhibitions and sexual misconceptions. It has freed both men and women by challenging woman's traditionally low sexual status. Gay liberation groups have been working to correct social and legal discrimination against lesbians and homosexuals. Public health facilities, such as venereal disease clinics and prepregnancy counseling services, are contributing to healthy sexuality. A particularly good book about sexual issues today is Richard Hettlinger's *Human Sexuality: A Psychosocial Perspective* (Belmont, Ca.: Wadsworth Publishing Co., 1975). A highly recommended resource about many aspects of women's sexuality and the changing nature of women's views is *Our Bodies Our Selves, a Book by and for Women* by the Boston Women's Health Collective (New York: Simon and Schuster, 1973). Also recommended as comprehensive and valuable are two pamphlets published by the Montreal Health Press: *Birth Control Handbook* and *VD Handbook*. For individual copies send 25¢ handling to P.O. Box 1000, Station G, Montreal, Quebec H2X 2N1.

Educating and reeducating about sex follows several paths. For instance, some large cities have sex "hot lines" where one can call in anonymously and receive correct answers to a sex question. We have an increasing number of formal courses in human sexuality at all grades in school and on TV. Many excellent textbooks are on the market; the most comprehensive is *Fundamentals of Human Sexuality* (2d edition) by Herant A. Katchadourian and Donald T. Lunde (New York: Holt, Rinehart and Winston, 1975). A refreshingly realistic book for children and their parents is *Show Me! A Picture Book of Sex for Children and Parents* with photography and captions by Will McBride and explanatory text by Dr. Helga Fleischhauer-Hardt (English language adaptation by Hilary

Davies. New York: St. Martin's Press, 1975). A unique educational approach is offered by the National Sex Forum in San Francisco. Their Personal Sexual Enrichment/Education program is a four-week course using video cassette tapes in conjunction with a counselor and the Sexual Attitude Restructuring Guide (San Francisco: National Sex Forum, 1975). Through this program one learns how to replace sex-denying attitudes with sex-affirming attitudes.

Another kind of reeducation is therapy. A variety of therapies deal with sexual problems, including psychotherapy, marital counseling, and behavioral therapy, aimed specifically at reducing anxiety in sexual situations. An innovative and intensive program for the treatment of sexual dysfunctions was developed several years ago by Masters and Johnson at their Reproductive Biology Research Foundation. This is a two-week residential program for couples. Many sex therapists use techniques and concepts developed by Masters and Johnson. If you are interested in sex therapy you might want to look into Helen Singer Kaplan's *The New Sex Therapy: Active Treatment of Sexual Dysfunctions* (New York: Brunner/Mazel Publishers, 1975) and *The Pleasure Bond* by William H. Masters and Virginia E. Johnson in association with Robert J. Levin (New York: Bantam, 1975).

There are also available today several ways of enhancing sexual pleasure on your own, without enrolling in an course or getting into formal therapy. Many books describe techniques for increasing body awareness, relaxation, and the acceptance of pleasuring. One popular technique is massage. Sharing a body massage with a partner is a delightful way to relax muscles, to stimulate circulation, and to increase enjoyable sensations. Massage also serves to enhance both the giving and the receiving of joy. For many massage is a good way to relearn that warm, caring, contact with someone is pleasurable in itself, and that it does not require justification by sexual intercourse. A fine introduction to massage is George Downing's *The Massage Book* (New York: Random House and Berkeley, Ca.: The Bookworks, 1972).

SUMMARY

1. Humans are free of instinctual sex patterns. We can learn, choose, change, and be responsible for our sexuality.
2. We learn about sex from legal, religious, medical, and commercial sources. These sources do not always encourage the honest expression of sex.
3. Today we find several opinions about sex, love, and marriage:
   When marriage is the precondition of sex, the important choice is that of one's marriage partner.
   When love is the precondition of sex, the important decision is whether or not one is in love.
   When consent is the precondition of sex, the important choices are about pleasure and communicating one's desires.
4. Among the most important processes in coming to a desirable sexual perspective is clarifying sexual values.

5. The human sexual response cycle is a series of physiological responses to erotic stimulation. The cycle is basically the same for males and females. It consists of four phases: excitement, plateau, orgasm, and resolution.
6. Sexual problems are often psychological in origin.
7. Humans can choose:
   to be turned on by some stimuli and not others
   to have sexual experiences alone through erotic fantasies or masturbation
   to share sexual experiences with others
8. A first step in sexual sharing is being aware of what feels good. A second is being open and honest in asking for what one wants. A third is being able to hear "No."
9. We choose the number and the gender of our sex partners.
10. We are able to decide rationally whether reproduction is or is not the desired outcome of sexual intercourse.
11. We make our own sexual choices; we can allow others to make theirs.
12. Social change and reeducation about sexuality are tools for maximizing sexual potentials.

Suggested Readings

Barbach, Lonnie G. *For yourself: The fulfillment of female sexuality*. Garden City, N.Y.: Doubleday, 1975. A step-by-step program for women who seek greater fulfillment of sexual potential; particularly of interest to those who have not yet achieved orgasm.

Brecher, Edward M. *The sex researchers*. New York: New American Library, 1971. A history of sex education and research over the past century from that of the early pioneers Henry Havelock Ellis and Freud to Kinsey and Masters and Johnson, including many fascinating but lesser-known works.

Brecher, Ruth and Brecher, Edward M. (Eds.). *An analysis of human sexual response*. New York: New American Library, 1966. A series of analyses of Masters and Johnson's book *Human sexual response* by several authorities in the social sciences.

Comfort, Alex. (Ed.). *The joy of sex: A gourmet guide to lovemaking*. New York: Simon & Schuster, 1972. *More joy of sex: A lovemaking companion to the joy of sex*. New York: Simon & Schuster, 1974. These two volumes provide a comprehensive and sophisticated guide to enhancing sexual pleasure. (The illustrated editions with drawings by Charles Raymond and Christopher Foss are recommended.)

McCary, James L. *Sexual myths and fallacies*. New York: Van Nostrand, 1971. A very readable and most informative look at over eighty common and uncommon misconceptions about human sexuality by a foremost sex educator. Highly recommended for accurate information on many sexual topics.

McCarthy, Berry W., Ryan, Mary and Johnson, Fred A. *Sexual awareness: A practical approach*. San Francisco: Boyd & Fraser Publishing and the Scrimshaw Press, 1975. The authors invite couples, through a series of partner exercises, to gradually move toward improved self-awareness, pleasure giving, and enjoyment of sexuality.

Delta Airlines Photo

Michael Weisbrot

WOMAN: FEMININE
MAN: MASCULINE

Sally glances at the clock as she reaches for another cigarette. 5:45. She looks around the kitchen, where it seems she has spent most of her adult life. The counter tops are tidy, the floor shiny, dinner is simmering on the stove. An ad in the magazine before her shows a woman her age packing the kids into a new station wagon. A smear of jam on the refrigerator door; her never-quite-finished landscape painting on the wall. "Why didn't I ever finish it?" she wonders. From the next room her waking child begins to whine. Sally finishes her drink with a long swallow as she heads for the living room.

Marc squints in the glare of automobile chrome. It's hot, and his lane of cars hasn't moved for ten minutes. This afternoon in the manager's office he got the promotion at last. Sally will be pleased. But his boss won't forget that incident two years ago. Why? There had been the pressures at home and work, and then Dad's death. I broke down and cried that day. Every time my record is reviewed there is a question about my strength, as if I couldn't take responsibility. I won't cry again, but will I ever live that day down? No answer. Marc turns on the radio to catch the 5:45 news.

Much of the time we may not even notice. But sometimes we do and we wonder, as Sally and Marc, why? Why do some of our potentials go unrealized? Why do we restrict ourselves? Why do we live such predictably female and male lives?

The quest for personhood starts with the questions and answers of this chapter:

What are masculine traits? What are feminine traits?
What are the images of men and women in our culture?
What are sex roles?
What are the roles I have been assigned and am expected to live for life?

TRAITS

Every culture considers certain qualities masculine and others feminine. For instance, many Americans would agree that the traits in the left-hand list below are generally considered feminine and the traits on the right masculine (Bardwick, 1972, p. 100).

subjective	objective
intuitive	analytic
passive	active
tender-minded	tough-minded
sensitive	rational
impressionistic	unyielding
yielding	intrusive

receptive	counteracting
empathic	independent
dependent	self-sufficient
emotional	emotionally controlled
conservative	confident

As in most other cultures of the world, in the United States we would also tend to agree that the qualities in the right-hand column are in general considered more desirable than or superior to the left-hand traits. Now the real world is not as tidy, not as clear-cut, as the lists may suggest; there is always some leeway for either sex to display opposite-sex characteristics. On balance, however, women have more room to be masculine than men do to be feminine. An active, confident woman is not as suspect as is a yielding, emotional man; a tomboyish girl is tolerated more than a sissyish boy.

It is important for males that they not cultivate their feminine qualities. No matter how masculinity is defined, and the definition changes from era to era, there is a standing injunction that men be *not-feminine*. The more masculine a man is, the less feminine he is. Men learn to recognize and preserve the differences between masculine and feminine; and they learn to reject that in themselves which is thought womanly. True, it is important that women be feminine, but they do not have to avoid masculinity with the same degree of fearful dedication with which men avoid femininity.

IMAGES

Assumed differences between men and women are fossilized in many of our cultural products. Our literature, arts, religion, music, TV programs, and advertising all present us with stereotyped images of the sexes. Taken out of their contexts, as below, these images are ludicrous caricatures of human beings. Yet these images, even when distilled, are recognizable and influential representations of females and males. We become so used to having men and women presented to us as they are below (although usually in less extravagant distortion) that we tend not to question their correctness.

Madonna

The Madonna is the woman to be worshiped from afar. She is a goddess, the ideal of feminine perfection—unattainable and unreachable. She radiates a soft glow of purity, goodness, and innocence. In her calm beauty she seems to stand aloof and silent above the baseness and meanness of ordinary life. She attracts us by her unsullied spirit and perfect countenance. Her power rests on our freely given adoration. She is the "fairest

of them all" — Snow White, Cinderella, the Angel, the Homecoming Queen. She reigns supreme as the Christian Mary, the virgin who mothered a god.

Mother

Mother embodies enduring love, sacrifice, strength, and devotion. She is a warm caretaker, living selflessly for her offspring. She is the keeper of home and hearth. Her breast is the source of milk and honey. Mother's work is never done: cooking, washing, mending, ironing, kissing scraped knees, soothing ruffled feathers, and inspiring achievement. She gives to others, she does not want or take. She is strong enough to nurture herself as well as those dependent upon her.

Because she is strong, Mother commands respect. Traditional respectability, wholesomeness, and the incest taboo protect Mother from sexuality. She is an asexual woman.

Whore

The sexual woman excites both fear and contempt. She is a lusting temptress, evil, hungry, depraved, and unclean. She seduces men and then castrates them. She is a "heartless bitch — luring men eternally toward spiritual death, making them come up against what they most fear and hate in themselves . . ." (Gornick, 1971, p. 78) She is the "living symbol of the obstacles God puts in man's way as man strives to make himself more godly and less manly." (ibid., p. 77.) She is Eve bearing forbidden fruit, whom men are unable to resist. He must therefore hate and defile her, transform her into a witch, a shrew, or a harpy. In this way he can fight his fascination with her. Men are obsessed by the whore but never marry her. She is not legitimate. She cannot be possessed. For she possesses her own sexuality and is, therefore, the only image of woman with power, a power at once sexual and evil. As *la femme fatale* her cunning ways are capable of snaring all but the most wary man.

Venus

Venus is a body, a shell, a receptacle. She is the passive sex-object woman. As the object of men's erotic desires and fantasies she has changed her proportions over the centuries but has never lost her basic form; robust or slender, her only noteworthy attributes are breasts, hips, and legs. (In some parts of the world a fuss is made over her slender ankle or the whiteness of her throat.) She is often presented in two dimensions, a flat, partially draped, air-brushed figure folded in three with a staple in her belly. She waits there, ready to unfold as the object of men's conquest, and then discarded when she gets old or when next month's centerfold comes out to replace her. She is young (age is Venus' mortal enemy), beautiful, and ultimately defenseless. Although she poses in the nude, she is never brazen or defiant. She is willing but not loose. She displays but never flaunts her body. She provides men with the opportunity for conquest, exacting only a minimum of manly persuasion before she succumbs. Beneath her naive facade there is always the glimmer of an invitation to play. However, Venus is doomed to endless teasing and provocation, for if she did give in or assert her own sexu-

"Venus," Titian. Alinari-Art Reference Bureau.

ality she would become a whore. Venus fills a need and when that need no longer exists or when she can no longer fill it her destruction is inevitable.

Lord

Man as a lord impresses by his size and strength. He towers over ordinary humans and by his monumentality he commands respect. He is authority, knowledge, wisdom, and law. He is a source of judgement in great matters. He rules as a stern but impartial master. He shows his displeasure with silence, rage, or a withering glare at those who stray from his lofty favor. To honor and obey this awesome authority is natural. We see his power in judges, presidents, professors, football coaches, fathers, generals, and priests.

His source of power is his ability to punish wrongdoing. The varieties of punishment are legion: imprisonment, humiliation, desertion, dismissal, threats, sulking, beatings, withdrawal of kindness, court martial, scorn, murder. All are coercions that intimidate with their promise as much as with their use. They represent the strength of one being over another. They are the privilege of natural and inevitable superiority.

Hustler

Hard work is the hustler's game. His goal is success. He may be a high school football player, an accountant for a large chemical firm, a woodcutter, a backpacker. He approaches his work in a fighting spirit, and he perseveres. He gobbles up obstacles to show his determination: rivers are forded, peaks climbed, sickness and discouragement overcome or ignored. The rule of the hustler is that in order to get the job done no amount of self-sacrifice or stoicism is too great. With a job to do, family and other personal affairs must be put aside. Life is tough, success eludes the timid. Self-indulgence, passivity, sentimentality—these erode the hustler's ability to carry out his duty. That duty is to succeed at work, to get it done, to rise in the world.

Don Juan

Don Juan is the beloved of the advertising and entertainment media. He is young, handsome, and fit, or he is older but suave, worldly, and smooth. He has been a Valentino, sporting slicked-down hair. In the mid-70s he is more relaxed, a casual but serious regular guy. The fashions change, in looks, language, and approach. What is constant in the image is its calculated attractiveness to women, its animal appeal.

The image of Don Juan follows changes in emotional fashions too. He may be attentive and passionate, smothering women with the heat of his attack. Or he may be "cool," as in the current mode, showing little or no sign of interest in making a catch, supremely self-confident that his looks and style will do the job for him, if not with this "chick" then with the next.

When he does go into action, Don Juan is irresistible. Having coolly chosen someone physically worthy of his effort, he begins his performance. His is a controlled and graceful conquest of the futilely, insincerely resisting woman. He is a technician, calm even in the heat of battle, and when he is in good form his pitch is irresistible—whether he's on the make or selling cigarettes.

Released by Metro Studio.

Dagwood

The image of Dagwood is neither fearsome nor contemptible. At worst, this bumbling, hapless man is looked at with resigned tolerance. He is Tom Sawyer grown up from an irresponsible lad to a man with the same boyish incompleteness. He shuffles through endless medicine commercials, a Kleenex at his nose, his wife following him with a worried look. We see him at sleep on the couch or in front of the TV, wherever Daddy is being made the butt of a joke. He drops dishes when he washes them, or can't bring himself to wash at all. He is happiest at his workbench, watching pro football, fishing, or discovering his ring-around-the-collar has disappeared. Bachelor or married, he can't seem to say no when asked to do something for a woman. So he hides, tells lies, or hangs his head.

Loved by those who enjoy his boyishness, Dagwood is also held in gentle contempt for never having grown up. He needs a mother to care for him, and so he marries one. Dagwoods are adult Boy Scouts who need help packing their gear for the big important adventure of work in the outside world, and who return to get their knees and egos bandaged before setting out once again. They never grow out of the urge to sulk when scolded and to make amends by helping Mommy with her housework. They are tolerated and loved, as little boys, because they do the work of men.

EXPLORATION 9.1

Images

Observe advertisements, TV, music, movies, and other media for one week. Bring to class the examples you find of woman as Madonna, Mother, Whore, and Venus and those of man as Lord, Hustler, Don Juan, and Dagwood.

Do you have any trouble recognizing or understanding these images? The media present us with part of our cultural tradition. We learn from these sources what to expect *women* to be; what to expect *men* to be. Expectations also become what *ought* to be: ". . . we understand who people are only in terms of what we think they ought to be. This is basic to the entire experience of a human being." (Janeway, 1971, p. 70)

SEX ROLES: IN GENERAL

Notions of maleness and femaleness are the offspring of sex roles. Roles are the parts we play in life. They are our scripts, written according to the expectations of others and of ourselves. Sex roles are those roles comprising the thoughts and behaviors which represent our images of men and women. They embody what we think a man or a woman ought to be, how men and women ought to act. Roles govern the way men behave, the way women behave, and the ways in which men and women relate to each other.

Here is a closer look at the characteristics of sex roles and some of their functions.

1. Sex roles are *assigned;* we don't choose them. As soon as it is seen that we are either male or female, the cultural machinery goes to work to teach us appropriate behavior. We learn what is expected of us as boys or girls and, ideally, behave accordingly. We then learn what is expected of us as men or women and, ideally, behave accordingly. Sex roles interact with other assigned roles, such as age roles.

2. Sex roles are patterns of *activity.* They comprise our behavioral responses to masculine or feminine expectations. Sex-role behavior embodies the characteristics of male and female images. Women, for example, take care of kids, wait for doors to be opened, and shave their legs; men support their families, open doors for women, and shave their (own) faces. Sex-role behavior includes such subtle activities as posture, tone of voice, and ways of expressing concern for others.

3. Sex roles, like other roles, are always played in relation to other, *complementary,* roles. A man acts as he believes a woman expects him to in a particular situation, or at least feels he should act that way. A woman does the same. Sex roles thus reinforce each other, as do husbands and wives, mothers and children, doctors and patients. Sex roles balance each other; they are reciprocal but not interchangeable.

4. Sex roles are *defined by society,* by the people among whom one lives and whose cultural traditions one shares. There is a tacit agreement, vague as it sometimes is, about the proper fit between role and image, activity and quality. Rebellion against this agreement is as predictable (but not as prevalent) as conformity to it. Whether it is more "masculine" to work in a steelmill or to stay home and knit cannot be established without reference to the culture.

5. Everyone plays *several roles in a lifetime* and often several at one time. Conflicts among roles happen when a situation requires behavior appropriate to two or more different roles, as "... when to forget the cleaning and play with the baby; when to let the baby cry and make love to your husband; when to insist on some quiet time for self-renewal and go collect seashells ..." (Janeway, 1971, p. 88)

The advantages of sex roles are in the regularity and predictability they give to social life. Role-playing smooths ordinary interpersonal behavior by reducing the number of choices one must make about "how to be." Sex roles sort out from the entire range of human potential those actions which are suitable. They help us to know easily, habitually, when to sit or stand, to laugh or cry, what to wear, what to consider as an occupation. Sex roles reduce confusion in society and in the individual mind.

The disadvantages of sex roles are the other side of this same coin. In order to simplify behavior, sex roles limit our alternatives of action. New or inappropriate behavior is inhibited, slowing social change. Individuals who feel constrained to exhibit only those characteristics assigned to their sex are denied roughly one-half their potentials as human beings. An individual who adopts a role that denies him or her full human status, according to Elizabeth Janeway:

... will cease to be a performer and become a puppet, moved wholly by the demands of his role and feeling that his fate has gone out of his control. Society can survive that for a while, for the puppet still acts and still expresses the meaning of his actions. But the individual is no longer a person, only a bundle of prescribed gestures with nothing inside to tie them together; and too many of these robots a changing society cannot afford, for they do not adapt to change (Janeway, 1971, pp. 82–83).

Besides considering the advantages and disadvantages of sex roles, it is instructive to compare the benefits and rights one gains in a role along with the obligations and prohibitions. According to studies by Barbara Polk and Robert Stein (1972) and Janet Chafetz (1974), women's roles consist mostly of prohibitions, some obligations and benefits, and only one right (the freedom to express emotions). Men's roles, however, are heavily weighted by obligations, with some proscriptions, benefits, and rights. Generally, women's roles mold women by setting out what they *can't* do; men are molded by what they *must* do.

Male dominance has been the rule in this country and throughout the Western world for many centuries. Men occupy most positions of consequence in the government, sit at the head of most major corporations, and preside over the highest courts in the land. President, congressman, judge, general, governor, administrator, symphony conductor, professor, mayor, policeman, doctor, lawyer—these positions of prestige are occupied almost entirely by males. To point to the occasional woman who has held political or financial power merely reminds us how unusual it is for a woman to have this kind of power at all. It has been a fact of life that social and financial success, measured by the power they command, are male prerogatives.

Men not only crowd the corridors of public power, they also hold substantial control at home. Even if it can no longer be said that a man's home is his castle, or that he is a king, still it is a man who carries the status of head of household. His family assumes his name, inherits his socioeconomic position, and lives in a place convenient to his work. A man's responsibility to work gives him control over the family income. And whether he is authoritarian or not, a man is considered the central figure in his family.

Along with dominance and social superiority, men have taken on responsibilities: responsibilities to prevent or win wars, to control pollu-

Smithsonian Institution
Photo No. 65638, Division of Political History.

tion and the stock market, to produce art and technology, and to dispense justice. Men have traditionally borne the weight of civilization on their shoulders and set standards of normality by their example.

Despite dramatic changes in the last century in what is expected of men and in the nature of men's work, the theory and practice of male superiority persists. Men continue to be taught and to learn those psychological qualities necessary for power and control.

In her now classic study of cross-cultural sex roles, *Male and Female*, Margaret Mead noted that ". . . maleness in America is not absolutely defined, it has to be kept and re-earned every day, and one essential element in the definition is beating women in every game that both sexes play, in every activity in which both sexes engage." (1949, p. 303)

Perhaps the need to "beat women in every activity" is not as strong today as it was when Margaret Mead wrote this in the late 1940s; but it is still detectable. And though men and women today are not as often portrayed as contestants in the battle of the sexes, they are still perceived as opposites. Dorothy Sayers has written: "The first thing that strikes the careless observer is that women are unlike men. They are the 'opposite sex'—(though why 'opposite' I do not know; what is the 'neighboring sex'?). But the fundamental thing is that women are more like men than anything else in the world." (1947, p. 142) Emphasis on male/female differences, rather than human similarities, was fostered by ignorance of sexual biology. This emphasis has withstood the attacks of new knowledge and remains a strong rationale for the continuance of male domination.

**EXPLORATION
9.2**

**Role
Reversal**

An excellent way to get in touch with the influence of sex roles in our society and in ourselves is to imagine reversing them. That is, to ascribe masculine attributes and norms to women or to try out feminine stereotypes on males. This exercise (by Wells, quoted in Rush, 1973, pp. 126–128) will give you a sense of what it might be like if females were put in traditional men's roles. It is most effective as an exercise if you close your eyes, turn off your analyzing intellect and feel your responses, while someone else (your instructor) reads it aloud to you. After you finish, collect your feelings and discuss with the class what you have discovered.

Woman—Which Includes Man, Of Course: An Experience in Awareness

There is much concern today about the future of man, which means, of course, both men and women—generic Man. For a woman to take exception to the use of the term "man" is often seen as defensive hair-splitting by an "emotional female."

The following experience is an invitation to awareness in which you are asked to feel into, and stay with, your feelings through each step, letting them absorb you. If you start intellectualizing, try to turn it down and let your feelings again surface to your awareness.

Consider reversing the generic term Man. Think of the future of Woman which, of course, includes both women and men. Feel into that, sense its meaning to you—as a woman—as a man.

Think of it always being that way, every day of your life. Feel the everpresence of woman and feel the nonpresence of man. Absorb what it tells you about the importance and value of being woman—of being man.

Recall that everything you have ever read all your life used only female pronouns—she, her—meaning both girls and boys, both women and men. Recall that most of the voices on radio and most of the faces on TV are women's—when important events are covered—on commercials—and on the late talk shows. Recall that you have no male senator representing you in Washington.

Feel into the fact that women are the leaders, the power-centers, the prime-movers. Man, whose natural role is husband and father, fulfills himself through nurturing children and making the home a refuge for woman. This is only natural to balance the biological role of woman who devotes her entire body to the race during pregnancy.

Then feel further into the obvious biological explanation for woman as the ideal—her genital construction. By design, female genitals are compact and internal, protected by her body. Male genitals are so exposed that he must be protected from outside attack to assure the perpetuation of the race. His vulnerability clearly requires sheltering.

Thus, by nature, males are more passive than females, and have a desire in sexual relations to be symbolically engulfed by the protective body of the woman. Males psychologically yearn for this protection, fully realizing their masculinity at this time—feeling exposed and vulnerable at other times. The male is not fully adult until he has overcome his infantile tendency to penis orgasm and has achieved the mature surrender of the testicle orgasm. He then feels himself a "whole man" when engulfed by the woman.

If the male denies these feelings, he is unconsciously rejecting his masculinity. Therapy is thus indicated to help him adjust to his own nature. Of course, therapy is administered by a woman, who has the education and wisdom to facilitate openness leading to the male's growth and self-actualization.

To help him feel into his defensive emotionality, he is invited to get in touch with the "child" in him. He remembers his sister's jeering at his primitive genitals that "flop around foolishly." She can run, climb and ride horseback unencumbered. Obviously, since she is free to move, she is encouraged to develop her body and mind in preparation for her active responsibilities of adult womanhood. The male vulnerability needs female protection, so he is taught the less active, caring, virtues of homemaking.

Because of his clitoris-envy, he learns to strap his genitals, and learns to feel ashamed and unclean because of his nocturnal emissions. Instead, he is encouraged to keep his body lean and dream of getting married, waiting for the time of his fulfillment—when "his woman" gives him a girl-child to carry on the family name. He knows that if it is a boy-child he has failed somehow—but they can try again.

SEX ROLES: IN PARTICULAR

The major roles played by men and women are familial or occupational. Traditional women's roles are based on reproductive capacities and are home-centered; men's roles are basically productive. Traditional men are providers. In early adulthood both men and women prepare for the roles they will occupy during the middle years of life. The primary task for men is to gain vocational training. This is the *apprentice* role. A woman prepares for her future roles by securing a husband; she is a *husband seeker*. The next set of roles are marriage centered; he becomes a *husband*, she a *wife*. The third set are parental roles, *father* and *mother*.

As you read the following generalized accounts of men's roles and women's roles, explore your understanding of them by asking the following questions of *each:*

EXPLORATION 9.3

Sex Roles

a. In what ways do *you* think this role is a positive force in the development of personhood? What are its negative contributions; those which limit the development of human potentials?

b. In your class and among your acquaintances there are men and women playing all of these roles. Divide your class according to the sex role now most important in each person's life. Within these groups discuss your answers to the following questions:

What are the satisfactions of your life?
What are the major conflicts in your life?
When your life draws to a close, what will have been your greatest success?

Supplement your personal exploration by asking people outside of your class these same questions. (There may be few mothers or fathers in your class. If so, talk with one or two outside of class and share their comments when you discuss the roles.) After you have held your small-group discussions, share your perceptions with the entire class. What themes emerge? What do men and women playing the same roles have in common? What were the kinds of successes foreseen? For example, were rearing children or climbing the career ladder equal measures of success for both men and women?

Apprentice

Our culture does not provide for a formal rite of passage into adulthood. Men spend many years treading water in society until, by marrying, fathering, or becoming self-supporting, they gain grounds for being recognized as adults. During this long transition period there is always someone (father, professor, sergeant, or foreman) to remind a male that he is still only a boy, a freshman, a private, a helper, or a junior member

Ford Foundation Photograph.

of the firm. A young man's promise is in the future, and he cannot easily escape the fact that, like it or not, he is expected to prepare for it.

A young man's future rests on the choices he makes as an apprentice, in particular on his vocational choices. The first primary task of the apprentice is to secure the training or credentials necessary to his occupation. The number of potential occupations in our society is staggering, and many of them require lengthy and highly specialized training. So pressure is on a man to choose his goal early in life, to stick with his choice, and to waste as little time as possible before jumping into the job market. The bewilderment and confusion of the young man who cannot decide, who flounders in indecision is expressed by Biff, in Arthur Miller's "Death of a Salesman": "I just can't take hold, Mom, I can't take hold of some kind of life."

Those who do take hold find a large part of their identity in their chosen vocational role. A man's work can define who he is even before he gets his first position. Even while he is in school, an apprentice's attitudes and tastes, his demeanor, and his circle of friends will be influenced by his vocational aspirations. When he has decided on a career he has chosen a certain social status and taken the first step toward achieving economic security.

Part of the apprenticeship of many men is served in the armed forces. Here is a shortcut to becoming a man. But not all men join with this in mind: some join to get away from the pointlessness of studies, some to become independent of parents, some to begin a career, and some to serve their country. The services promise, and sometimes give, an immediate taste of interesting work, travel, adventure, and pay. They also offer a crash course in the essentials of masculinity. One learns the importance of strength and guardedness, the virtues of obedience and discipline, and the comradely feeling of shared hardship and commitment.

U.S. Army Photograph.

Legally armed and trained to kill, or to stand behind those who do, the military apprentice also learns of the need to get the other guy before he gets you, and of the right of the strong to dominate others.

The focus of the apprentice's life is his preparation for a stable, responsible adulthood. But he is also expected to think about finding a wife. Often, wary of being trapped too soon in a serious relationship, pressured to create an image of himself as a lover, and unprepared to be emotionally vulnerable, a young man may seek casual and superficial relationships at first. This role does not encourage in him attitudes which would contribute to intimate relationships. Because women demand it, he may learn to say, "I love you," in order to get sex and attention, but he is faced with the question (which, according to Shulamith Firestone, faces every normal male): "How do I get someone to love me without her demanding an equal commitment in return?" (1970, p. 137) The apprentice is often prepared to forego intimate closeness, human contact, and emotional expressiveness, if necessary, in order to achieve financial security. It is the attainment of financial independence that will bring him freedom and personal security. He can then strive further for that financial success which will reflect his ultimate worth. His stability will be demonstrated to others when he makes his occupational commitment and when, sooner or later, he enters into a serious relationship with a woman—a relationship which leads him into marriage.

Husband Seeker

The first of the male roles in life requires a man to prepare himself for his occupational future. A woman in the complementary role is providing for her future by securing a husband. The criteria by which we make our mate selections are usually physical attractiveness and romantic attachment. It is therefore important to a husband seeker's success that she develop and enhance her physical attributes. She tries to be aware of and to meet contemporary standards of feminine beauty, and to cultivate a youthful appearance, for the young and the beautiful are often the preferred choice of men of all ages.

It is not enough to be alluring. A woman should also cultivate enough flexibility in her attitudes and avocations that she could become a suitable companion to any of several possible mates. She is not under pressure, as is her brother, to concentrate her interests in preparation for a salaried career and a climb up the ladder of vocational success. Advanced schooling and degrees are optional for the future wife and mother. In 1974 it was estimated that of all the well-qualified students who did *not* go to college, fully 75 percent were women (Gager, 1974, p. 523).

The husband-seeking years are often idealized as the most romantic and carefree years in a woman's life: parties, dating, beautiful clothes, candle-lit dinners, and hand-in-hand walks on the beach. This is an occasional reality shadowed, for many women, by conflict and disappointment. Many women fear time will run out before a suitable man is found. If a woman lets herself be absorbed in intellectual or artistic pursuits, she risks missing marriage altogether. Competition with other (seemingly more attractive) women is likely. Hours drag as women wait for telephones to ring; spirits fall when promising relationships fall short of marriage. A traditional woman is expected to battle sexual desires for control of her virginity. (If I succumb, to my desires or to his, and then if he leaves, what do I have to offer?)

A profound consequence of spending one's youth and early adulthood in husband-seeking is that one delays the formation of an individual identity. An authority on identity, Erik Erikson, supports a traditional view by suggesting that a woman should leave part of her identity unformed while she is seeking a husband. "Granted that something in the young woman's identity must keep itself open for the peculiarities of

Erik Erikson (*Harvard News Office Photo*).

the man to be joined and of the children to be brought up, I think that much of a young woman's identity is already defined in her kind of attractiveness and in the selective nature of her search for the man (or men) by whom she wishes to be sought." (1968, p. 283)

Erikson feels that marriage signals a woman's maturity, as well as allowing her to complete her identity. He says that ". . . the stage of life crucial for the emergence of an integrated female identity is the step from youth to maturity, the state when the young woman, whatever her work career, relinquishes the care received from the parental family in order to commit herself to the love of a stranger and to the care to be given to his and her offspring." (1968, p. 265) At traditional marriage ceremonies women are handed by their fathers to their husbands.

A husband-seeker succeeds by finding a mate. And the successful culmination of this search is as important as the mate himself, for marriage is still considered the only certain path to legitimacy for women. Throughout American history a woman has been, as she often is now, thought a failure if she is always a bridesmaid and never a bride. It is estimated that 97 percent of American women will be married at some time in their lives. In 1970 only 22 percent of U.S. women fourteen and older had never been married (Barnard, 1973, p. 122). To be a married woman is to be like most other women.

Husband

To hear the many jokes about marriage, you would think it an arrangement designed specifically for male torment and frustration. The fact is, as many studies have shown, marriage often treats men much more handsomely than it does women (Barnard, 1972).

Marriage is one of the most stabilizing forces in a man's life. When a man marries he is expected to, and usually does, settle down and begin fulfilling his purposes in life. Husbands may mourn the carefree days of bachelorhood, but they also recognize that marriage brings a kind of security to their lives through routine, the acceptance of responsibility, and participation in a household. A married man has a wife who traditionally does his cooking, cleaning, mending, laundry, and keeps his house in order. He has a mate to give him emotional support. He has opportunities for an intimate relationship and for a regular sex life. Becoming a husband establishes a man in his community as a respectable, responsible, normal heterosexual male.

Traditionally, husbands are defined as men who, first, provide for, and second, maintain a relationship with their wives. It is the obligation to be a provider which occupies most of a husband's time and energy. A man's identity as a husband is often inseparable from his identity as a breadwinner. A husband's self-esteem and status come not from his being a married man but from his job. To be a good husband is to be a good provider and, conversely, the man who earns little income or who is out of work fails not only as a worker but often as a husband as well. It

Photograph by T. O'Reilly.

is often difficult for a husband to let his wife support the family, unless he is in school and the situation is temporary. There are men who become angry when their wives attempt to work. Their images as husband-providers are threatened on the one hand, and they are faced on the other hand with the inconvenience of losing the support services that their wives provide. These husbands would rather work overtime, or at a second job, than have their psychological and domestic worlds upset.

Responsibility for supporting a family, with or without children, limits a man's freedom. A husband-provider must go to work day in and day out, whether he feels like it or not. In many respects he has lost the opportunity to pick up and go when he wants, to keep irregular hours, and to be his own man. Today not all husbands are driven by a compulsion to be the sole breadwinner for the family, although few are willing to give up the role of provider altogether. Millions of men have wives who share the financial burdens of the family by working outside the home. In 1974, 43 percent of married women worked, an increase of 80 percent from 1950 (Van Dusen and Sheldon, 1976). Although a working wife can take the strain off family finances, her absence from the home may call for the husband's sharing in the housework. Many men are poorly prepared to do domestic work; their interest in cooking and other home arts may have been stifled early in life, their opportunity for practice limited, or their attitude that they won't do "women's work."

A man will have related to women in a number of ways before he marries, but these relationships will not necessarily have taught him how to be a woman's companion. With his mother he learned how to be a son, dutiful or otherwise. Other women may have been for him teases, sex objects, image enhancers, conquests, creatures to please, entertain, and even to fear. He may find women so foreign, incomprehensible, and contradictory that setting up a household with one is, to him, like going off to live with an unknown species. In the past, men managed their estrangement from women by dominating and controlling them. Today's man cannot in good conscience treat his wife as property, but often he does not find it easy to develop and maintain genuine intimacy with her.

A major obstacle to male-female intimacy is a cultural environment that gives higher status to men than to women. So long as a husband holds more power, or is given social, political, or economic superiority because he is a male, and so long as his wife is thereby dependent on him, intimate connections between husband and wife will often be limited. A related concern is the emotional restrictions on couples in a superior-inferior relationship.

Compounding the inequality of the genders is the fact that our sex role stereotypes have left virtually the entire realm of emotional expression and human caring to femininity. It is difficult to imagine a genuine loving relationship involving the stoical, unemotional, instrumentally oriented, dominating, aggressive, and competitive creatures of the masculine stereotype . . . It is, of course, equally difficult to imagine a male developing deep respect for the scatterbrained, passive, dependent, vain creature who would be "feminine." (Chafetz, 1974, p. 166)

What happens in marriages that have failed to provide continuing warmth, intimacy, and genuine human relatedness? When emotional bonds break down, a couple is saddled with their unfulfilled expectations of each other. A husband may feel himself nagged and belittled for his lack of caring. His wife turns to the children for emotional sustenance. A common response is for the husband to withdraw. He buries himself in his job and spends less time at home. He uses his obligation to work as an escape from demands that he prove himself a good companion. About 40 percent of married men have extramarital relationships. We don't know what percent resort to physical violence: wifebeating, not restricted to the "lower" classes, goes unrecognized in the statistics of family life.

It is not at all inevitable that couples become involved in such unhappy circumstances. There are husbands who can make intimacy the

Michael Weisbrot

focus of their marriage. These are men who relate to women as fellow human beings, who actively share in the making of a home, who do *not* live according to sex role stereotypes, and who care as much about caring as they do about earning. They may not be considered "successful" men, but they are often successful human beings.

Wife

As a youngster I assumed that the only reason a man married was to have a family. A man was Mr. Somebody with or without a wife. But with women, the difference between Miss Nobody and Mrs. Somebody was apparent. I didn't need my eyeglasses to see that marriage gave a woman status she often couldn't gain on her own. A wedding made a woman eligible for those legal, social, economic, and psychological benefits which nearly everyone agreed she should properly want.

Important to most women who marry is the opportunity to develop a sustained, monogamous relationship with their husbands. A good marriage can yield intimacy and reliable companionship, and can grow into a mutually satisfying partnership of many years. A woman's sexuality is legitimized through her marriage, and *only* through marriage in the eyes of tradition. Married, she can rightly be seductive, sexually assertive, and free in her sexual responses to her husband.

Being a wife is never quite as romantic as being a bride. Starry-eyed girls dream of their wedding day for years, and wives often look back on it as their one moment of triumph, romance, and significance. Throughout the day, with its festivities and ceremonies, the bride is the focus of attention. The rest of her marriage, by contrast, may often be made up of routine, repetition, and subordination. She becomes the mistress of a house, no part of which is hers alone. The rooms of a home are hers only

Michael Weisbrot

to share (the living, dining, and bedrooms) or as places in which to work for the family (kitchen, sewing, and laundry rooms). A wife seldom has a room of her own where she can be physically or psychologically by herself.

A wife's role enables her to be the supportive center, the heartbeat, of the family establishment. The support she gives to the marriage usually is not financial. It is emotional and practical. She keeps the family on an even keel, rescues, soothes, prods, and reminds. She is expected to know where everyone's possessions have got to and to keep track of upcoming appointments with doctors, dentists, and friends. She controls the household by her involvement in everyone's affairs, which she must do to keep the home in material and emotional order. Having taken charge in this way, a wife is indispensable.

In performing her duties as a traditional housewife a woman has considerable leeway. For example, she can wax the floors with any brand of wax she likes, and at any time of day she chooses. Most housewives are self-employed, being both their own boss and their own staff, though unpaid in either position. The housewife's freedom to make her own schedule of work, to relieve the monotony of work by relaxing, to operate without a supervisor, to putter in a garden in the morning and to read or catch the TV serials at noon — this freedom is envied by salaried men and (for that matter) by many women working outside the home.

Contemporary housework requires little physical exertion, few skills, and minimum ingenuity. Most of a housekeeper's time is spent cleaning, cleaning again, and recleaning. From detergents to vacuums, from self-cleaning ovens to automatic washers, the modern housewife is equipped with an array of labor-saving cleaning aids unknown to her grandmother. She should have more free time than her grandmother did, but she doesn't. The housewife of the 1970s spends the same number of hours cleaning as her counterpart did in 1900; her house is much cleaner than her grandmother's was.

Among the advantages to a wife in a traditional family is not *having* to be gainfully employed outside the home. Conventional wives are supposed to be supported by conventional husbands. Wives can spend money they don't earn themselves. In many traditional families, wives are the chief buyers, bookkeepers, and budget-makers. They are in charge of routine maintenance expenditures. A wife can learn to be a shrewd consumer, how to balance a budget, where to find bargains in food, clothing, or shoe repair. In most families, however, a wife does not purchase large items (cars, houses, vacation trips, etc.) on her own.

A wife's fortune is tied to the success of her husband. If he is a good breadwinner, she will be financially secure. If he makes a poor living, or if hard times come, she suffers along with him. Unless she finds time, energy, and a job — thus becoming a working woman as well as a wife — a woman has no means to supplement the family's income. As a wife she puts in an average of 99.6 hours a week (Benston, 1971). Even if she had the strength to put in overtime, she couldn't turn *any* of her time into dollars. She can increase the patience, support, and encouragement she contributes to the family enterprise. She can wash the dishes faster, clean the house better, and cut down on household expenses. Still, none of these heroic efforts will directly increase the amount of money coming in. Her labor is not worth cash in itself, although it may enable her husband to work harder, or to put in overtime, to gain a promotion or an increase in *his* paycheck. The all-American notion that the hardest workers get the greatest rewards simply does not fit the situation of housewives. The idea assumes the freedom to compete for rewards, but the role of the housewife is to support her competitive husband.

Money isn't everything, of course. But dollars *are* a primary reward for achievement and a measure of personal worth in this society. Women who become housewives cannot earn *independent* financial reward. As long as women stay in their own homes, their goods and services are traded directly for food, clothing, shelter and a husband's services. *If* a housewife sold her domestic services outside her own home, she would find herself among the lowest paid workers in the country — cleaning women. A housewife is a worker who never gets a promotion, a paid vacation, sick leave, or a higher-status title.

A wife's dependence is not only financial. Many modern housewives are also instrumentally dependent, that is, they cannot get many of their chores done without help. To keep a home running many things must be maintained, repaired, and built. Women are traditionally ignorant of even the rudiments of plumbing, electricity, mechanics, or carpentry. In a modern American home this can be a real handicap. Instead of being taught how to do household maintenance, a wife has learned how to get her husband (or outside help, usually male) to do these jobs. She is often helpless, feels stupid, and sometimes frightened, when facing mechanical problems on her own.

DEAR ABBY: My husband makes me feel like such a dummy every time I ask him a question that I've quit asking him. However, right at this moment I am sitting here puzzled and in tears, so I decided to write to you.

My basement is flooded, and I can't do my washing. My husband went on a fishing trip, and he never told me what to do if the water in the basement comes up so high it covers the pump.

Should I wade down there and unplug it, or will I get electrocuted?
                                        IN TEARS IN KANKAKEE

DEAR IN: First, you are no dummy for asking. When electricity is involved with water, DO NOT TOUCH ANYTHING! Phone your power company and ask them to come out and turn off the power to your house.

Wives are habitually busy doing things with and for their families rather than for and by themselves. Often they fear doing things on their own or feel guilty for wanting to be alone. Some women are not aware of the strength and pervasiveness of their psychological dependence. They experience feelings of entrapment in their own homes, homes in which they realize uneasily they have "everything a woman could ask for." The following letter and response illustrate a common inability to even imagine a wife's engaging in certain activities on her own. Neither "Homebody" nor Abby considers the possibility of a wife going to movies, church, dancing, out to dinner, concerts, camping or fishing *without her husband*. Abby's advice is the same advice women have always been given: stay in your place, learn to enjoy it, and don't complain. Adjust.

DEAR ABBY: My husband is a 43-year-old handsome hunk of man with a peach of a disposition. He's a TV repair man and does very well. We have two children, and I must admit he is a good father.

My complaints: He can't go to a movie because he hates to sit still for that long. He won't go to church for the same reason. He won't take me dancing because he thinks dancing is foolish. He doesn't like to go out for dinner because it's too expensive. He refuses to go to band concerts because he doesn't like that kind of music.

Camping is too rough and fishing is boring. He WILL go deer hunting, but he won't take me because "men don't take their wives." He won't go for a walk with me because he might miss his favorite TV programs.

The only place he likes to go with me is to bed and he's very good in that department.

I'm 38 and tired of staying home all the time. Any suggestions?

HOMEBODY

DEAR HOMEBODY: Count your blessings. A man with a "peach of a disposition" who is a good father can't be all bad. Build a social life by inviting a few friends in. You don't have to go "out" to have a good time.

Father

Fatherhood consists of two distinct and separable activities. The first is fathering. Fathering a child is usually taken to be the act of sexual intercourse which results in a woman's pregnancy. Since fathering is rarely the certain or predictable outcome of any particular sex act, and because biological fathering is finished sometime before a man knows it has happened, *paternity* can be conveniently distinguished from the *social-role* behaviors assigned to men who are called fathers. These social behaviors are the second kind of fatherhood activities.

Biological fathering is an act which few men actively control. The control they do have is negative: they can prevent pregnancy by using condoms or sterilization, or by relying on a woman to protect herself. The passive part men play in reproduction may be one reason men have often sought to control women. The passivity of the man's role is reflected in the difference between fathering a child and mothering it.

By a long (now weakening) tradition, men have been excluded from the event which marks the beginning of their social role as father: childbirth. This tradition kept a father-to-be waiting anxiously while the baby's mother and her doctors delivered in isolation. Now, when fathers are present in delivery rooms, they can share in the birth of their children and the process is stripped of its mystery and exclusiveness.

After the birth of his child a father's social role begins. Most men who accept the role discover that they usually are not the primary parent. Parenting is frequently equated with mothering even by behavioral scientists, who study child-rearing practices by observing only the mother's behaviors. From the point of view of society at large, men are secondary parents because of the all-encompassing parental role given to mothers. Behind this assignment lies the erroneous belief that women possess some genetic, inborn maternal instinct which makes them better fit to parent. In truth, neither women nor men are born knowing how to care for children. Still, some people insist that women have certain necessary psychological qualities that men can never achieve. This notion becomes a rationale for the exclusion of men from full participation in the care and nurturance of their children. One result of this exclusion is that the role of father is imprecisely defined.

The usual fathering behaviors spring from the obligation to protect and provide. Most fathers carry out their obligations by extending and continuing the same breadwinner function they had as husbands without children. With children they are legally obligated to be providers until their children reach adulthood. As the jubilant new father proudly passes out his pink- or blue-banded cigars, the last thing on his mind may be the enormity of the financial burden he has just acquired. If he has two children he wants to send to college, and if his wife stays at home, he will have to come up with between $80,000 and $150,000 in the next few years (Chafetz, 1974).

The obligation fathers have to provide financially for their children is strong enough that it persists, morally and legally, even when the relationship between a man and the mother of his children has ended. When a husband and his wife are divorced, the parent-child relationship is not legally dissolved, but is divided between the parents. This allocation usually respects the traditional provider role of the father by charging the mother with physical custody of the children and continuing the father's responsibility in the form of child-support payments. The rationale for this division rests on nothing more solid than a sex-role stereotype: men are fitter providers and women fitter parents.

Even in continuing marriages, many fathers today spend so much time tending to their financial obligations that they often appear to their children as familiar but temporary visitors. What can a man do as a father if he is only home sporadically, if he has been led to think of himself as incompetent in caring for children, or if he has only the vaguest notions of what fatherhood or good fathering is? He can try to live up to the image of father as an authority figure, friend, or a teacher. He can also serve as a model of masculinity and male roles for his children. But these functions, too, will be disturbed by his being so often away from the home. It seems common enough that, instead of modeling themselves after their father's actual behavior, children often settle for images created by Mother, the media, and folklure to understand who Dad would be if he were home.

The role of father as strict, demanding, authority figure and disciplinarian is less fashionable than it used to be, particularly among middle-class families. Fathers, because of their status as head of the household and their physical stature, may indeed command subservience from their children, but it is often the mother who does more actual disciplining. Being a demanding critic is certain to conflict with being a friend to one's children. While many fathers would rather be good guys who play ball and go fishing with their kids, they often lack time for a sustained relationship with them. Intermittent attempts at friendship may not succeed, leading dads to try to secure allegiance, love, affection, and respect by giving their children material goods. Instead of patience, tenderness, or nurturance children get clothes, toys, money, and cars. While the kids are learning to accept material gifts as substitutes for closeness, dads are able to feel that, because they are good providers, they are good fathers.

In all that he does as a father, a man must coordinate his role as father with his role as husband and his relationship with his children's mother. Again there are conflicts. In order to carry out his obligation to see that his children are physically cared for and properly protected (particularly in his absence) he is cast as a supervisor to their mother. But, often, from the beginning of the fatherhood role, it is the father who is actually mother's helper. Many fathers approach their infant children with bewilderment or even hidden panic if required to take care of them for even a

Michael Weisbrot

day. They have been taught to express distaste for duties like diaper changing and feeding. While they may do some odd jobs if requested by the mother, they rarely assume an equally shared responsibility for child rearing. They are assistant parents. Besides having to be a supervisor and assistant at the same time, fathers can get caught in an emotional power struggle, competing with their wives for the children's affection and with the children for the wife's attention. Because the mother-child bond is so strongly supported by social and professional values, and because the man's role of provider is so dominant, most men find this competition a losing battle. Not only do fathers lose by being shunted to the fringes of the family, but the family itself becomes far less than it could be as a source of warmth and affection for all its members.

Mother

A woman who becomes a mother fulfills the reproductive potential of her body and meets the primary social expectations of womanhood. During pregnancy, there is often little for a woman to do except maintain her health, wait, and experience the profound changes in her body chemistry and shape. When her child is born, a woman cares for it as she has learned to do. Unlike other animals, human females do not have maternal instincts to aid them in caring for and rearing their offspring. Women must somehow pick up the skills of mothers, together with the knowledge of what is "good" mothering according to their culture.

Today many women take on this role, which will occupy roughly eighteen to twenty years of life, with little or no training or preparation. Nuclear families give girls few opportunities to practice mothering skills, to see real live babies being reared by real live mothers, or to know what motherhood means in reality as opposed to its image in the media. Anxiety, confusion, and inconsistency in carrying out the role of mother can be expected when women have scant experience, or education, in child development and the effects of various child-rearing practices.

It is common today that a woman carries the greatest share, if not the total burden, of parenting her children. She rarely has grandmothers, aunts, sisters, or older children around to assist her. If her husband works long hours outside the home, she is quite alone and without support or relief for hours and days at a time. If something goes wrong, if her children get into trouble or do not turn out well, she is often the first to be blamed by teachers, judges, therapists, grandparents, fathers, and neighbors—even if she has done her best in the given circumstances and with the given children. If her children turn out all right, on the other hand, it is rare that her influence is emphasized.

The role of mother gives a woman the opportunity of daily participation in the development of her child. She can join in a close, trusting, loving relationship. Through this bond she can develop and express her

Photograph courtesy of B. and E. Misher.

potentials for caring and caretaking. The duties of motherhood require that she draw as fully as possible on her potentials for patience, responsibility, and affection. As she does, she and her child can build the closest of human relationships, one which lasts for many years and which provides a woman with many rewards.

No matter how ordinary a woman considers herself, or how unspecial she is to others, she is an extraordinary being to her child. She doesn't have to change, put on airs, or be especially pretty or intelligent to be loved. If she loves her child, she finds that love returned unconditionally. Until her child approaches adulthood, and occasionally beyond this time, she receives spontaneous and unsolicited love.

Unfortunately, many of the activities a woman does in the course of caring for children are, in themselves, menial, boring, repetitive, unrewarding, and unfulfilling. Further, many are performed mechanically and are devoid of human interaction. For example, the job of keeping furniture, clothes, car, and person free of the sticky residue left by small fingers and spilled liquids is a chore which neither requires, conveys, nor begets love. Yet it is something mothers do again, again, and again, as with picking up the same toy over and over, and driving children to the same places week after week.

Taking on a twenty-four-hour-a-day, seven-day-a-week job as a mother severely cuts into one's opportunities to do nonmothering things. For many years, all such activities are planned around the children, squeezed in here and there as possible. Without making special and costly arrangements, the mother of young children will rarely have a single block of free time longer than about fifteen minutes. She must be constantly prepared to drop whatever she is doing to attend to a scraped knee, a hungry stomach, a fight, a soiled diaper, or to the thousands of discoveries and delights of her children. A simple task, such as writing a letter, can stretch into a day-long project. There is little time or place for privacy in a mother's life, until the children are off to bed or in school. Peace, quiet, and solitude are strangers to most mothers' lives. Being constantly "on call" and continually occupied with child rearing can prevent a mother from developing other potentials. Going to school, engaging in creative activities (such as art, music, writing, dance, etc.), running for political office, or making commitments to any long-term activity outside the home will inevitably bring conflicts into a mother's life.

From the first few weeks, when mothering goes on round the clock, to the onset of adulthood, there is indeed a gradual decline in the number of hours a woman must devote to being a mother, but not much reduction in the responsibility she carries. A large part of a mother's energy goes into anxiety about her children's safety and well-being, concern for the best social and educational opportunities for them, and worry about whether or not she is doing a good job as mother.

Mothers spend the most productive years of their lives caring emotionally and physically for others. For many women this is most fulfilling, but often a combination of guilt and a lack of opportunity, or energy, effectively prevents some women from caring more for themselves. Children and husbands thrive on motherly nurturance, but they are usually unable, in their roles, to give emotional support to mothers in the same measure. Mothers are often unmothered persons.

Subcultural Variations

Sex roles are played with variations according to the socioeconomic status of the family and, sometimes, its ethnicity. A family's circumstances and values are not always those of the white middle class (the position described in the previous sections of this chapter). An adequate

Michael Weisbrot

discussion of the complex issues contributing to any variations is beyond the scope of this chapter, but it is important to touch, even briefly, on three aspects. The first is the influence of a man's occupational level on the way he plays his roles and achieves masculinity. The second is the influence of poverty on a family and, in particular, on the woman's role. A third consideration is that of some ethnic definitions of sex roles and the impact of racial discrimination on the family.

Masculinity, male roles, and the relative importance of family and work differ according to a man's socioeconomic status. A man's property and prestige determine the style in which he is dominating, powerful, and controlling, the ways in which he gains respect and enhances his self-image. Potential and real power of some kind are standards by which men are judged. Wealth gives a man power. Financial security, stability, and respectability are sources of power for the less-than-wealthy. Without these a man must rely on a dominating appearance or physical prowess. How a man is manly depends in large part on how much money he has.

Although broad generalizations, the following examples (from Hacker, 1975) illustrate the ways in which socioeconomic factors influence males' roles at work and in the family.

A man of wealth can be a "true gentleman," living gracefully and luxuriously. His masculinity is softer, more sophisticated, than men of lesser means, but his male roles are just as surely masculine. He demonstrates control without having to sweat, as when he carefully orders a bottle of expensive wine or discusses the bidding tactics that won him his Picasso original.

The business executive is near the top of the social caste system. He expresses his masculinity through a singular devotion to his career. His work is clean and the force he exerts on others need only be strong enough to keep himself in control of his position.

The middle-class man is often subordinate to other men in his job, although he is sometimes self-employed. He can most easily demonstrate his masculinity through his role in the family. He can feel manly when taking his family to the mountains for the weekend, or, even, when helping his wife with the dishes.

The blue-collar worker's job seldom is intrinsically interesting, and is often dirty. It is stable, however, and he can be a reliable, hard-working, respectable provider. He contributes to the family also by mowing the lawn, clearing the snow from his sidewalks, and visiting his in-laws regularly.

The less education a man has the more likely it is that sex roles in the family will be rigidly defined. The lower-middle-class man may constantly struggle to make ends meet, but he, too, can prove himself by performing as a diligent and conscientious provider. He brings home his paycheck weekly, but usually disdains any household chores. He is satisfied to have his wife run the family as long as he retains the appearance of authority. He often enjoys spending his weekends hunting or fishing with his buddies.

Without working-class status or a stable job, how well does the marginal man express his masculinity? How well can he perform the roles of husband and father? He will never be a successful man (as measured by wealth) and will have to struggle to be an adequate man. He can best, and sometimes only, prove himself adequate by being physically strong, by dominating women, or by demonstrating his sexual prowess. He must fight to gain any sense of power. He lives for today, to survive. Living for the future makes no sense at all to him; he must get what he can, when he can.

Poverty, or a low standard of living, means a harsh life for women. Compared to affluent wives and mothers, poor women have fewer resources with which to manage a home. They must supply more energy in just making do for their families. Lower-class women often live in poor health with many children and little education. The American family pattern in which women must depend on men as breadwinners means disaster for women whose men cannot or do not provide adequate financial support. In order to maintain a relationship and a family with a man who is not financially stable, a woman must go to work outside her home. Often work is more available to her than to her uneducated or unskilled husband, but it is work at the lowest-paid, most menial jobs in society—such as domestic service jobs. If a poor woman cannot cope with rearing her children, caring for her husband, and working outside the home, she may become a welfare mother, caught in a vicious circle with never enough money to better her condition.

Each ethnic subculture in our society has its own cultural definition of women's place in the family and their status relative to men. For example, for centuries Oriental cultures have maintained male dominance and authority over women. The proper roles of Japanese and Chinese women require submission and deference to men. The Chicana's culture also makes her subordinate to Chicano men, whose manhood is proven by *macho* behavior, which demonstrates his superiority and dominance. La Raza peoples respect women who are mothers, and motherhood is the perpetual condition of many Spanish-American women.

The blacks in this country lost most of their African family tradition when they were brought to this country. Black family life evolved in a slave culture which prevented both the nuclear and extended families from easily becoming stable living groups. A black woman, as a slave, did not dare become financially dependent upon the father of her children, nor could she count on marriage to prevent her from being separated from the black man. The black woman's adaptability, strength, and independence have enabled her race to survive, but it has also led to contemporary conditions in which she may be alone in shouldering the burdens of rearing and providing for the economic welfare of her children. Compared to white women, the black woman "remains single more often, bears more children, is in the labor market longer and in greater proportion, has less education, earns less, is widowed earlier and carries a relatively heavier economic responsibility as family head than her white counterpart." (Murray, 1975, pp. 359–360)

The minority male lives within the same masculine value system as the white male, a value system which obligates him to achieve a sense of power. But he is barred from access to many of the means to power by discrimination and prejudice. One of the conspicuous effects of racism on the minority male is the limitation it puts on his ability to achieve power through wealth or even through being an adequate provider. The struggle to get and keep a decent paying job has withheld from many minority men a means of surviving and a means of achieving "manhood" as well. A few careers, such as in sports or the entertainment field, are more open to the minority man, but the dream that has been most elusive to him is that of achieving a respectable, solid, secure life-style which will bring him dignity and allow him to retain his own cultural values. As racism and discrimination wane, this dream should come within the reach of more and more minority men.

The minority male is hampered by stereotypes of both masculinity and of race. He learns, for example, that men are tough, but that black men are tougher (or sexual superstars, or unstable, or inferior in intelligence, or whatever). His task becomes one of defining himself as an individual and, at the same time, either accepting (and trying to live up to) racial stereotypes or rejecting, fighting, or proving the exception to them.

SUMMARY

1. People are neither all masculine nor all feminine. *Masculinity* and *femininity* refer to certain qualities or traits. Males are expected to have traits which are *not* feminine.
2. Our expectations for self and others are influenced by cultural images, or stereotypes, of men and women.
3. Sex roles are assigned patterns of activity defined by society. Male and female roles are complementary. Among the advantages of playing sex roles is stability; among the disadvantages is the limit they place on the actualization of potentials. In general, men are limited by what they *must* do, women by what they *can't* do.
4. Men are allowed and required, through the roles they play, to assume power, dominance, and control. Women's roles are opposite and not powerful.
5. As an *apprentice*, a man prepares for his future. It is important that he get vocational training and begin his career; a relationship to a woman is a secondary concern. He learns to strive for financial security. As a *husband seeker*, a woman devotes herself to being attractive. She may be expected to stall the formation of her identity until she finds a mate; she may not be considered fully mature until she is a wife. Marriage is her security.

6. A *husband* is a breadwinner. His obligations to be the family provider and to control his emotions often restrict the quality of companionship he may achieve with his wife. A *wife* runs a household. She takes care of the family's domestic needs. She does not have to be employed but she has no means to responsible independence. She is financially, instrumentally, and often emotionally dependent.

7. A *father's* role is usually passive. He may assist his wife in child care, rule the family, or try to buy affection, but he often misses important contacts with his children as he goes off to work every day to provide for them. *Mothers* carry the greater share of parenting. They devote the productive years of their lives to caring mainly for others.

8. There are variants of the traditional sex roles in ethnic subcultures and according to socioeconomic status. The manner in which a man demonstrates his power and the ability of a woman to run a household usually depend on how much property and prestige the man has.

Suggested Readings

Books on women's roles

Andelin, Helen. *Fascinating woman.* New York: Bantam, 1974. Based on the principle that men and women are different and that each has God-given roles in life. A woman's place is in the home; a man's function is earning the daily bread.

Dector, Midge. *The new chastity and other arguments against women's liberation.* New York: Coward, McCann & Geoghegan, 1972. An outspoken critic of women's liberation argues that women's real difficulties stem from their having too much freedom, too many choices.

Firestone, Shulamith. *The dialectic of sex: The case for feminist revolution.* New York: Bantam, 1971. A thought-provoking statement of radical feminist theory, which argues for the elimination of women's traditional family roles.

Friedan, Betty. *The feminine mystique.* New York: Dell, 1964. Important for its historical role in beginning the current women's movement, this book also provides an excellent description of middle-class women's roles and the institutions that perpetuate the mystique of femininity.

Janeway, Elizabeth. *Man's world, woman's place: A study in social mythology.* New York: Dell, 1971. An examination of women's traditional roles with a reasoned plea for discarding the myth of female inferiority.

Books on men's roles

Andelin, Aubrey P. *Man of steel and velvet.* Santa Barbara, Ca.: Pacific Santa Barbara, 1975. A companion volume to *Fascinating woman.*

Farrell, Warren. *The liberated man.* New York: Bantam, 1975b. One of the best books currently available on masculinity, the male value system, and consciousness-raising among men.

Petras, John W. (Ed.). *Sex: male/gender: masculine: Selected readings in male sexuality.* Port Washington, N.Y.: Alfred Publishing Co., 1975.

Pleck, Joseph H. and Sawyer, Jack (Eds.). *Men and masculinity.* Englewood Cliffs, N.J.: Prentice-Hall, 1974. Petras and Pleck are two anthologies containing selections on men's socialization, relationships, and changing roles.

Tiger, Lionel. *Men in groups.* New York: Random House, 1970. Using anthropological and ethological studies, Tiger proposes a theory that males have an innate propensity to "bond" with each other and therefore hold the dominant positions in society.

———. *Unbecoming men.* Washington, N.J.: Times Change Press, 1971. A collection of short, personal accounts by members of a men's consciousness-raising group.

Michael Weisbrot

10

THE QUEST FOR PERSONHOOD

Once upon a time there lived a species of mammal that came in two sizes, large and small. The Smalls' bodies were built to carry Littles, and Smalls gave much time and energy to the care of these Littles. Now Smalls were able to do Other Things, besides taking care of Littles, but Other Things were not thought appropriate for them. In fact, Smalls had to pay penalties when they did Other Things instead of what they were supposed to do. Other Things always needed doing: building, protecting, and providing. And since the Bigs did these Other Things, Smalls became dependent on Bigs. The Bigs, responsible for so many Other Things, were terribly burdened. Many Bigs did not want to be so big, but they had no choice in the matter and were required to pay penalties when they didn't do what Bigs were supposed to do. These mammals, the Bigs and the Smalls, became convinced that one was born either a Big or a Small, and that was that. They could not see how much they were alike (for example, they were all able to do most Other Things), nor could they appreciate how special each of them was, individually. Then the world they lived in began to change, and they began to wonder if they too could change, and if life wouldn't be more enjoyable if they did.

The quest for personhood is the search for liberation from sex roles and stereotypes. It is the search for a concept of humanity that is broader than male: masculine or female: feminine.

In this quest we examine the lives of those who deviate from sex roles and stereotyped expectations. We also see the costs we pay as individuals and as a society for conformity to the stereotypes and roles set for us. We discover the historical functions of roles and ask:

Are sex roles appropriate in our changing world?
How is it that sex-role stereotypes persist?
How can we change our attitudes and maximize personhood?

DEVIATIONS FROM TRADITIONAL ROLES

Expectations define acceptable behavior. So do sex roles. Men and women who stray too far from either are usually penalized in some way. It is true that certain deviations from traditional expectations or roles are so common that we have become quite tolerant of them. Most men, for instance, now have social permission to wear their hair long; generally speaking, women may wear pants. But these are superficial transgressions. Radical departures from sex-role stereotypes often exact high costs. Consider what happens to men and women who are not husbands or wives, who, either because of choice or circumstance, are single, widowed, or divorced. What happens to men and women who do not choose sex partners of the opposite sex but prefer relations with their own sex? And what happens to women when they work outside the house and to men who drop out of the provider role?

Unmarried and Widowed

We live in a couple-oriented society. Choosing a single life is to choose
to swim against a strong current. Friends, parents, the media, even the
income tax structure—all encourage one to become a legal spouse. The
unmarried female or male is often subject to matchmaking schemes,
made to feel like a third wheel, pitied, left out of couple- and family-
oriented activities, forced to pay higher taxes, and faced with the possibility of growing old alone. Social and legal conventions geared to facilitate married life make it difficult, if not impossible, for the unmarried to
participate in a home-centered life-style or to rear children. In a society
which offers greater status and rewards to the married, the choice to
remain unmarried is not a "free" choice. But it may be the choice that
allows an individual the best opportunities to actualize his or her potentials. Not all of us are cut out for married life; not all of us will choose to
devote ourselves to the tasks of rearing or providing for children. And
these people should not be coerced by convention into a life that is not
right for them.

If living a single life by choice is difficult, it is even more difficult to
be married one day and then, suddenly, widowed the next. The death of
a mate is a grievous loss in itself (see Chapter 14), but the surviving
spouse also loses the role by which much of life has been defined.
Because sex roles are complementary, each partner of a married couple
specializes in taking care of certain life needs. A man who loses his wife
has lost his domestic and emotional support—maybe the mother of his
children. Can he cope with his emotional loss and begin learning how to
clean and cook for himself and a family? A widow may be faced for the
first time in her life with supporting herself, and perhaps her children.
She often has no idea how to manage money, let alone earn it. It is a rare

Michael Weisbrot

woman who will not be a widow; women, on the average, outlive men by six to eight years. Yet, if she followed a traditional sex role, she lived as though someone would *always* be there to take care of her. Many widows live in poverty as well as loneliness. Traditional sex roles do not provide realistically for widowhood or old age (see Chapter 13).

Divorced

The number of divorces in this country has doubled in the last ten years and continues to rise. One out of every three marriages comes apart (World Almanac, 1976). Traditionally, divorce meant that husband and wife had failed. They hadn't tried hard enough, hadn't played their married roles assiduously enough. Our divorce laws still require some-one to assume responsibility for failing when a divorce is contested. Even if they are spared legal blame, divorced people often carry a heavy load of guilt for their imagined and real misdeeds in a marriage that didn't last "until death do us part." Divorce, no matter how common, is a trauma. It calls for major changes in one's life-style. It forces the dissolu-tion of a home and a division of property. A common condition of the divorced person, male or female, is loneliness. Once accustomed to liv-ing closely with a partner, whether intimately or not, life alone is not always easy. The bed is cold night after night, and still feels empty when shared with a stranger. Meals eaten by oneself are tasteless. Friends who were "ours" line up on "her" side or "his" side, or stop calling.

Divorce cannot be the same as starting life anew. The remnants of marriage roles linger. If there are children the job of rearing and support-ing them remains. The husband's role of provider for the wife is con-tinued, in theory at least, by the provision of alimony. Alimony is an ac-knowledgement that a woman, as a traditional housewife, has foregone the education and work experience necessary for her to support herself. To keep the state from having to care for indigent divorcees, the courts traditionally pass this obligation on to the ex-husband. He is supposed to support her until she remarries. Actually, alimony is awarded only in a small percentage of divorces, and is paid in even fewer. (According to an American Bar Association study, 87 percent of men are no longer meet-ing court-ordered payments ten years after divorce.) (Deckard, 1975).

Three-quarters of the divorces in this country involve children. The courts reflect tradition by awarding these children to their mothers (stereotypically the better caretakers) and require fathers to provide for them with childsupport payments (men are better providers). Fathers are allowed, not required, to visit their children. The visiting father has even less opportunity to pursue a relationship with his children than he did when he was married. He shells out money monthly and comes by on Saturdays to take the kids to the park. He is both deprived of and spared their daily care and nurturance.

A divorced mother becomes a single parent. She is fortunate if she can make ends meet while staying at home to care for the children who now belong entirely to her. Many divorcees must go to work, and therefore must have their children cared for. But by whom and where? It is estimated that the number of places in licensed day-care centers in America is 1 million (U.S. Department of Labor, June, 1975b); there are at least 8 million children who have single mothers. If a single working mother does find a place for her children, she will have to use a large part of her paycheck for their care. Families without a male provider suffer in a society which assumes everyone is being taken care of by husbands and fathers.

Homosexuality

Perhaps no deviation from traditional roles is as costly as choosing a sex partner of one's same sex. Most people consider homosexuality obscene, perverted, immature, sick, or criminal. Behavioral scientists have not yet come up with fully convincing explanations to counter popular prejudice. (Why, for example, do so many people choose homosexuality in a culture that despises it, or why do researchers [e.g., Kinsey, 1948, 1953] find three times as many male homosexuals as female?)

Homosexuality is often, and erroneously, believed proven by "feminine" mannerisms or physical characteristics in men; lesbians are wrongly imagined to be burly and masculine. Homosexuals are confused with transvestites (people who dress in opposite-sex clothing) and transsexuals (people who wish to be the opposite sex). Actually, homosexuals are rarely, if ever, in doubt about their gender. Whatever sexual activities he engages in, the male homosexual knows he is not a woman; a woman who makes love with another woman does not believe she is a man.

It is impossible to distinguish most homosexuals by the way they look or act in public. Most are single, but some are husbands and fathers, or wives and mothers. Some carry traditional sex-role behaviors into their homosexual relationships, one partner the provider and the other the homemaker. Homosexual men have more short-term, or exclusively sexual, relationships with their partners than do lesbians. This may reflect the same double standard seen among heterosexuals: men are allowed and expected to be more promiscuous than women. But male homosexuals also have companionable and lasting relationships. Male-male and female-female liaisons can be as full and as loving (but not as legal) as male-female unions and, for some, much more satisfying.

Because of the sanctions against homosexuality, some homosexuals loathe their own behavior. Their parents did not purposely bring them up as homosexuals; like most parents they were probably careful to discourage any signs of femininity in their sons and forceful in encouraging their daughters to be interested in men. These lessons are now carried by homosexuals as a heavy burden of guilt. Not all are ashamed of their choices, but even those who are self-accepting have had to struggle with negative attitudes to become so.

Michael Weisbrot

Males, in general, are anxious about homosexuality. They keep careful watch against it, in themselves and in other men, as though it might attack without warning. This guardedness comes in part from the suspicion that homosexuality is a disease. More importantly, it springs from the male sex role and its implication that men either cannot or should not control their sexual impulses. This notion, according to the double standard, requires a man's female partner to say "No" in order to control the man's constant and insatiable sexual appetite. Given this perception of an uncontrollable sex drive, it is not surprising that men feel uneasy when they get physically close to or feel attracted to another male. Anxiety of this kind is an obstacle to establishing genuine, intimate relationships between heterosexual men.

Dropping Out

Men who drop out of the provider role usually do so either before they begin it or after they have been at it for a number of years. At whatever point in his life a man rejects the task of breadwinning, if he continues to be out too long, and if he is not independently wealthy, he will find the question of support for himself and his family, if he has one, a difficult one.

The young man who drops out of school or college is often treated with tolerance; if he is not out for longer than a year or so, he might even be encouraged. But usually parents' viewpoints are steadfastly directed toward academic and financial success for their sons, and they see a lack of education as a handicap. The longer a young man stalls before dropping back in, the more he invites loss of support and even hostility from his parents. He may eventually find, should he want to try, that he is barred from getting back into school or from getting a good job. Of course not all young men have higher education or status as their own goals.

Even so, they compromise the male tradition when they decide not to jump on the success bandwagon.

Around the age of forty, many men begin reexamining their lives. Some find themselves in a rat-race, others in a rut. They come to realize that things aren't going to change. If a man is not progressing toward success by this age, it isn't likely that he is going to achieve it. Some men just take off, leaving job, wife, and family. Running away is rarely applauded by family, community, church, or state, but it is seen as a solution by some men, for a while at least.

Men who want to leave their jobs but not their families usually have serious problems. It is very difficult for most men to change careers after they have become established in one line and after the chance for schooling is over. Sometimes the solution lies in the family's lowering their standard of living. Many find they don't need so many and such expensive things that the trade they make of money for time and peace is well worth it. Self-employment, farming, crafts, and communal living have been the answers for some men. Our society does not offer many second career options nor does it provide many good part-time jobs. Part-time work or a job that a husband and wife can share equally would help many men live happier and longer lives. A relatively recent attempt at solving these problems is for the husband to exchange roles with his

Photograph by Charles Biasiny.

wife. She goes out and earns a paycheck while he stays. home and becomes a house-husband. Men who have written about this experience (for example Roache, 1972) report that their views on the ease of housework and the joys of mothering change radically. Housewives may find that they enjoy working outside the home, but few can make the same salary that their husbands did.

Women Who Work

Millions of American women will not be found at home or with their children, at least not during the work week. In 1974, 53 percent of all women between the ages of 18 and 64 were in the labor force. In fact, if we count all women over the age of 16, there are now more women in the labor force than there are women keeping house. Most working women are married; over two-thirds of them have child-rearing responsibilities in addition to their jobs.

Why do women work? The U.S. Department of Labor says, "Women work for the same reasons men do. The millions of women who were employed in 1974 were working not only for economic reasons but also because their talents and skills were needed in the economy." (Women's Bureau pamphlet, May, 1975a) In 1974, 70 percent of working women were single, widowed, divorced, separated, or had husbands who earned less than $9999. Women work because of economic need. They must support themselves and others.

What do women do in the labor force? Seventy-seven percent of all working women are clerical workers, service workers outside the home, sales workers, private household workers, or operatives (factory workers). These same occupations employ only 38 percent of male workers. Fifteen percent of working women are professional and technical workers; most professional women are teachers, nurses, and other health workers. Only five percent of women who work are managers and administrators.

The majority of women who work have jobs rather than careers. They often work at dead-end jobs, mostly serving and caring for others. Their work usually offers little opportunity for advancement either in status or pay. Waitresses do not become headwaiters, secretaries do not become corporate executives, nor do nurses become doctors. Working women perform very necessary and supportive jobs, as do wives and mothers. The work of the nation would grind to a halt if women did not do their jobs.

The work women do outside the home is characteristic of much of women's work: it is significant but often undervalued. On the payroll a woman can earn, on the average, only 62¢ for every $1.00 earned by men. A study published in 1973 (Levitin, Quinn, Staines) reported that fully 95 percent of a sample of working women were earning less than they deserved. Some of the salary differences between men and women are due to women's having less education, less time on the job, less responsibility, and fewer hours of work per week. When these factors were discounted it was found, in the 1973 study, that the average woman was paid $3458 a year less than she should have been. Some women were earning nearly $12,000 less than men with comparable experience and skills. One can justly say that a working woman pays a penalty of $3458 a year, every year she works, for being female.

Many problems can arise in a family whose woman works outside the home. If housework continues to be the woman's responsibility, where does she get the time and energy to do it? If her husband shares this work, can he reconcile it with his own masculine image? If a housekeeper must be hired, who pays? Not all of the support services provided by a wife and mother, such as emotional support, can be hired out. Can the family with a working mother and a working father survive without one woman's constant nurturance? Who gets up in the night and stays home from work to nurse a sick child? Who has time to be a Den Mother or to attend the PTA? Who arranges for child care and transportation? Can adequate child care be found? Working women with families must continually make decisions about which of their many duties and responsibilities they will meet and must put their energies into resolving the conflicting demands of their several roles. They often find themselves feeling guilt, resentment, and depression when they are unable to do all that they "should" be doing.

A woman desiring achievement, self-development, and status outside the home faces many obstacles beyond those she must meet in gaining an education. She will have to display those "unfeminine" qualities of tenacity, discipline, assertiveness, devotion, single-mindedness, and talent considered necessary to career men. If she marries, she and her husband may be at odds if her work commands an equal or higher status and salary than his. The relationship may be strained if an advancement re-

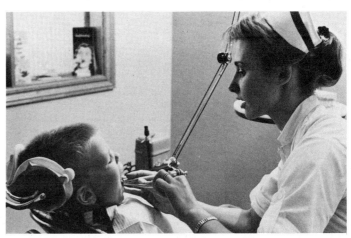

Copyright by the American Dental Association. Reprinted by permission.

quires her to move away from the site of her husband's career. If a career woman wants to become a mother, she must weigh the effects on her work of "dropping out" for a few years against the effects of being absent from her child at this crucial time. If she chooses for her career, she may feel either that she is missing many of the joys of motherhood or that she is selfish; if she chooses for her child, she may jeopardize her career. Extraordinary adjustments must be made for a two-career family to survive in a society built around the traditional sex-role division of labor.

The single, widowed, and divorced do not have ready-made traditional sex roles to guide their behavior or to help them gain acceptance. Not only do they have to define their own social behavior, they are often outcasts in a society which does not recognize their needs. This is also true of homosexuals, who carry a stigma for their sexuality. Husbands and wives face many difficulties in their attempts to step out of house-woman, provider-man roles. People who are suffering for not being the men and women they are supposed to be are frequently advised to adjust to traditional sex roles. Those who deviate pay by suspecting there is something wrong with themselves rather than with the traditional roles.

EXPLORATION 10.1
Deviating

Sit in a circle. Each person in turn completes the following sentence:
    If I were single all my life, I would most want or need . . .
After everyone has responded, discuss your responses. What was the most often-stated need or desire? Did women and men respond differently? What is the likelihood that you would get what you want?

Repeat, completing each of the following sentences:
    If I were widowed at thirty-five, I would most want or need . . .
    If I were a divorced person, I would most want or need . . .
    If I were a homosexual, I would most want or need . . .
    If I were a man who chose not to play the provider role, I would most want or need . . .
    If I were a woman with a family working outside the home, I would most want or need . . .
If possible, invite people who are single, widowed, divorced, homosexual, dropped out, or working mothers to come to your class and talk about how they see their lives and what they most want and need.

THE COST OF CONFORMING

Just as we pay for deviating, we also pay for conforming to sex-role stereotypes. When a woman who has talents and an interest in developing them through a career stays at home to keep house, she pays with unrealized potential. When a man devotes the prime of his life to getting ahead and drops from a coronary attack at age forty-five, he pays with his life. When a woman devotes her youth to her husband and her children and finds them gone when she is forty-five, she pays with depression, loneliness, and often poverty for the next thirty years.

Personal Growth and Relationships

We may pay by being stymied in our growth when we guide our lives by sex-role stereotypes. In Maslow's hierarchy of needs (Chapter 3) physiological needs are basic, followed by needs for safety and security. Sex roles serve these basic needs admirably. Men and women work together, dividing tasks so that they and their children remain alive, safe, and physically secure. The next level of needs are for belonging and love. Families are the primary groups in which these needs are met. According to traditional sex roles women belong to and in families more than men do. Women's roles, and the requirements of femininity overemphasize the importance of having belongingness needs satisfied. These needs may become the singular focus of a woman's life if she devotes herself to her husband and to her children. The post-industrial family does not, on the other hand, offer as much to men. Men must leave the family for the major portion of every day. And when men spend their energy in being masculine, they often waste their potentials for getting and giving love when they are home.

The next level of needs are esteem needs. Men gain esteem through their occupations and by being adequate for successful providers. Conforming to ideals of masculinity gives men status and power. Gaining and preserving esteem is the primary focus of many men's lives. Women do not get much esteem through housework and often they are not provided with much status as mothers (except, perhaps, by the advertising media). Instead, women's esteem traditionally comes through their relationships with men; it is through *belonging* rather than through being or independent action that many women achieve success, status, and respect. Most female human beings are frozen into belonging; most male human beings are frozen into esteem. Neither of us is completely free to pursue all of our human growth needs. We often pay a price in our failures to create and sustain genuinely intimate male-female relationships. Recall (Chapter 7) that intimate connections may be difficult between people of unequal status, when one person is in a dependent role (woman) and the other in an independent role (man). Can one human who feels it necessary to be superior and unexpressive connect in equal ways with another, opposite, human being who has learned to be weak and unimportant?

As they are currently being played, sex roles can contribute to human devastation. Men's roles are more lethal than women's (Jourard, 1971). Males are placed under stress we would never subject a machine to. Having to be tough, objective, and emotionally unexpressive and with-

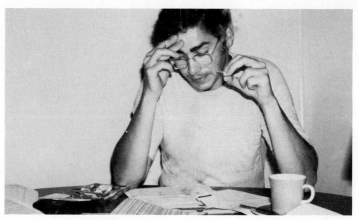

Photograph by T. O'Reilly.

out vulnerability results in constant, unrelieved body tension. The pressure men are under to strive, to succeed, and to provide for themselves and their families takes its toll in heart attacks, ulcers, hypertension (high blood pressure), suicide, alcohol, and drug use. Stress and tension kill millions of men. Men's roles also encourage them to take risks, to live hard and fast, to be adventurous. It is not surprising that males are victims in 69 percent of all accidental deaths. Almost three-quarters of all automobile accident victims are men (World Almanac, 1976).

Women who play traditional roles don't die quick deaths. Females live longer than males, but as a result of often being cast in helplessly dependent roles they are more often sick, both physically and mentally. Women make 69 percent of all suicide *attempts* in this country (Chesler, 1972). A recent study of marriage by Jessie Barnard (1972) provides evidence that the role of the American housewife is particularly harmful. After reviewing a number of surveys comparing the health and happiness of working men and women, both married and single, Barnard concludes that ". . . it is being relegated to *the role of housewife rather than marriage itself* which contributes heavily to the poor mental and emotional health of married women. . . . In terms of the number of people involved, the housewife syndrome might well be viewed as Public Health Problem Number One." (Barnard, 1972, pp. 51–52. Italics added.)

Psychologist Sandra Bem, who has been studying rigidly sex-stereotyped men (those who are very masculine) and women (the very feminine), says there is "considerable evidence that traditional sex typing is unhealthy. . . . High feminity in females consistently correlates with high anxiety, low self-esteem, and low self-acceptance. And although high masculinity in males has been related to better psychological adjustment during adolescence, it is often accompanied during adulthood by high anxiety, high neuroticism, and low self-acceptance." (Bem,

1975, p. 59) Each gender comes to have high anxiety and low self-acceptance when playing totally traditional roles.

EXPLORATION 10.2

Women and Men

It has been said that women are parasites. A parasite is an animal or plant that lives in or on another organism from which it derives sustenance or protection without making any compensation. Is this an appropriate analogy?

It has also been said that women are addicted to men. Gloria Steinem has used the term "Man Junkies." Is the comparison of women to habitual drug users correct?

The relationship between men and women has been described as "symbiotic," this biological term referring to the union between two dissimilar organisms in a close association which is advantageous to both. Do you feel this is an apt way to consider women's traditional relationship to men? If so, is the union equally advantageous to both partners?

Social Loss

Not only do we pay as individuals caught in a scheme that can damn us if we do and damn us if we don't conform, we pay as a society for the sex roles which demand so much from us. Roughly half the human potential, talent, skill, and possibility is denied in one way or another when it is "natural" for all women to run the home and "natural" for all men to run the world. The proscriptions and obligations of sex roles limit the pool of human potential. The world has missed those women who could have been political leaders, symphony directors, inventors, architects, and physicists had they not been excluded from scientific, political, and artistic communities for lack of training and opportunity. Countless homes and families, too, have gone without the interest, care, and devotion their men would have provided had those men not been so pressed to provide a living. Society pays when maleness sets the standards, when men *must* run the world, and *must* be masculine.

A society in which male standards predominate sees these standards reflected in crime and in a distortion of human sexuality. American men commit more crimes than women do. Men account for the majority of arrests for every type of crime except prostitution (a crime for which the man pays and the woman is arrested). Overall, five times as many men as women are arrested. Many situations contribute to criminal behaviors, but among them is the masculine emphasis on power, courage, strength, and force.

Male crime is encouraged when men have easy access to and an acceptance of weapons as a means to extend their power. Merely holding a gun or a knife gives a man power. Men, who are expected to control (or

Photograph courtesy of the New York City Police Department.

more accurately, to suppress) emotions, commit more crimes of passion and violence than do women. Without permission to vent feelings by crying or other harmless expressions of frustration and vulnerability, men can let emotional tensions build to the point of violent eruption. The masculine emphasis on success as measured by material goods and money, and on competition, are direct contributors to crimes against property (such as theft, burglary, and vandalism). Male crime is by no means limited to lower-class men or violent illegal behavior. Some male criminal activities are syndicated by efficiently and highly organized groups. And, as America has recently witnessed, men in the highest levels of government can engage in criminal activities in the attempt to preserve their power.

The justice system is almost totally male throughout—from legislators who make laws and police who arrest lawbreakers to judges who pass sentence and the majority of offenders. It is a system which catches and punishes predominantly those men who are disadvantaged. It helps competition thrive by marking the losers. Clarice Stoll feels that ". . . the criminal justice system operates so that one group of men can intimidate and punish another group of men." (1974, p. 174)

Human sexuality has been discussed at length in Chapter 8, but here it is necessary to point out how sexuality is affected by sex roles and the sexual double standard. Active sexuality is proscribed by traditional women's roles: women should not be sexually aggressive. Women are often required by their traditional roles to become sexual objects for men's pleasure and to trade sex for financial support. Feminine sexual inhibitions prevent many women from full sexual fulfillment, enjoyment, and orgiastic release. Sexual pleasure is traditionally seen as a male prerogative, sexual performance his obligation. Men *must* be sexual, powerful, ever-ready performers. Men, afraid not to be masculine, are often inhibited from being open, loving, and affectionate with their sex partners. Masculinity may block a real human sexuality that would transcend these obligations.

It is primarily men (rarely, if ever, women) who resort to extreme sexual deviance: child molesting, exhibitionism, voyeurism, incest, fetishism, and rape. Rape is a complex topic, one too complicated to cover adequately here. But it is important to note that the rapist is usually a man particularly molded by male programming. Most rapists are normal, red-blooded, men who know their victims, and plan their attacks in advance (MacKellar, 1976). They are men who have learned to use sex to express aggression, and believe that it is their right to sexually dominate women, or weaker men, and who feel their sexual activities need not be self-controlled. Many of our movies and books, pornographic and otherwise, present women as wanting or needing rape, and reinforce rape as an appropriate male behavior.

The world as a whole is convinced that masculine standards and male behaviors provide a scale of normalcy by which we all can be measured. Recently, a group of mental health experts was asked to describe a "healthy human being," a "healthy man," and a "healthy woman." The healthy human being and the healthy man were described in similar terms. But the researchers found that ". . . clinicians are more likely to suggest that healthy women differ from healthy men by being more submissive, less independent, less adventurous, less competitive, more excitable in minor crises, having their feelings more easily hurt, being more emotional, more conceited about their appearance, less objective, and disliking math and science. This constellation seems a most unusual way of describing any mature, healthy individual." (Broverman, et al, 1972, p. 322) The qualities which define normal people are qualities which women have difficulty developing within traditional women's roles; they are the qualities of men in male roles.

EXPLORATION 10.3

Sex Roles and Potentials

Answer the following:
These are the potentials my sex roles have encouraged or allowed me to actualize:
These are the potentials that may have been prevented actualization by my sex roles:

STABILITY AND CHANGE

Sex roles took shape under conditions of life radically different from those of the modern world, and some of the functions they served in ancient times are still being served, even though life is not what it used to be. Let's look at why and how sex roles have functioned before examining the kinds of changes which might herald the day when we no longer have such rigid sex-role stereotypes.

So long as men and women have played their complementary roles, the social order has been stable. Work has been done, children have been born and reared, and the family has endured as the most solid cultural institution. This stability, letting us predict our lives and our relationships without a great deal of confusion, gives us a sense of security as individuals and as a society. We can feel that we know where we stand in relation to others and as members of a well-ordered world. The strength of sex roles, their resistance to change, comes in large part from the comfortable predictability they lend to our lives.

Family roles provide the means for men to have, care for, and control their offspring. If women were at liberty to mate with whomever they chose and then to move on, impregnated, men would not *have* children at all. To perpetuate themselves, men must be able to know for sure that their sperm caused a woman to be pregnant. By supporting a tradition whereby wives should be sexually monogamous and stay at home, men have tried to ensure that they, as well as their women, can say of an infant: this one is *mine*. There has never been a way to control biological immortality, blood lines, or property as certain as this.

Contemporary sex roles in America are a legacy of traditional divisions between the sexes which grew out of a reproductive imperative. When the struggle to survive as a species was desperate, when social groups were threatened by high infant mortality and short life spans, reproduction had priority over most human activities. Women were at the mercy of their reproductive potentials; they were expected to bear as many children as they were capable of conceiving. Without effective means of birth control there was almost nothing they could do, short of sexual abstinence, to avoid giving birth every year of their fertile lives. As a consequence, motherhood was the destiny of most women.

Life Has Changed

Whereas sex roles for both men and women once suited the conditions of life, those conditions have changed. There have been changes in the family and in the nature of work.

If we think of the world as a stage upon which we all are cast to play certain roles in the drama of life, and if we step back and look at that drama as it is currently unfolding, we find that it is just not being played as it was written. The theme of the play is the family, and the script is written as though we all lived in a monogamous, nuclear family group. This is the family in which the father is the breadwinner, the mother is the housewife and caretaker of children, and in which parents confine their sexual relations to each other. This is more and more becoming a storybook family. It has been estimated that less than 19 percent of us live in such a family. "Most of us live in single household, or dual-working families, or childless couples, or post-childrearing couples, or extended families or in some other type of household." (Ramey, 1975)

Perhaps the greatest single change for women has been the increasing availability of means for controlling reproduction. Among the consequences of easy birth control has been, of course, a decline in the birth rate. In the last decade the birth rate has dropped from 19.4 to 14.8 births per 1000 population (World Almanac, 1976). A new world is opening up to women who have the option not to be occupied with reproductive obligations. Whereas a woman at the turn of the century devoted 18 years of her life to child-bearing and child-rearing, the average woman in 1975 spent only 10 years with these duties (Ramey, 1975). But birth control is not without side effects, and its use does not answer the question: If I don't have (so many) children, what else can I do with my life?

The nature of work has changed dramatically in the past decades. Just as it is no longer necessary for a woman to bear child after child, it is no longer necessary for a person to be a Hercules to get jobs done. It is enough if one can follow instructions and operate labor-saving machinery. Along with the mechanization of work has come the increasing distance between workers and the fruits of their labor. The factory worker assembling an automobile, the foundry worker remote-controlling the production of steel, the broker managing the money of a client 3000 miles away, the farmer loading his silo with tons of grain that his family cannot use and which he cannot sell because of international disagreements, and the housewife popping TV dinners in the oven—these examples illustrate the widespread alienation of men and women from their work.

Nevertheless, tradition, expectations, and the old family roles persist. Women still learn to develop those interpersonal skills that will get them a mate; they learn that their bodies are to gestate and protect; they learn that they best fulfill themselves when they nurture and support others. Men still learn to protect, defend, and provide for dependent women and children; they learn that it is important to be strong and to avoid any display of emotional weakness; they learn to take charge of nuclear, monogamous families.

Why—when women are no longer destined to bear children, when men do not have to be physically strong or dominant, when people do not live the life-styles for which our roles prepare us, when life has changed so radically—do we persist in such habits? To answer these questions, we must consider, again, the assumptions we make about the nature of women and the nature of men.

Sex Roles Persist

Sex roles and the separateness of "masculine" and "feminine" are based on a belief that men and women are basically different. Whether we feel the differences are as striking as those between day and night, or see them merely as shades of gray, our attitudes assume that men and

BOX 10.1

He is playing masculine. She is playing feminine.

He is playing masculine *because* she is playing feminine. She is playing feminine *because* he is playing masculine.

He is playing the kind of man that she thinks the kind of woman she is playing ought to admire. She is playing the kind of woman that he thinks the kind of man he is playing ought to desire.

If he were not playing masculine, he might well be more feminine than she is —except when she is playing very feminine. If she were not playing feminine, she might well be more masculine than he is—except when he is playing very masculine.

So he plays harder. And she plays . . . softer.

He wants to make sure that she could never be more masculine than he is. She wants to make sure that he could never be more feminine than she. He therefore seeks to destroy the femininity in himself. She therefore seeks to destroy the masculinity in herself.

She is supposed to admire him for the masculinity in him that she fears in herself. He is supposed to desire her for the femininity in her that he despises in himself.

He desires her for her femininity which is *his* femininity, but which he can never lay claim to. She admires him for his masculinity which is *her* masculinity, but which she can never lay claim to. Since he may only love his own femininity in her, he envies her her femininity. Since she may only love her own masculinity in him, she envies him his masculinity.

The envy poisons their love.

He, coveting her unattainable femininity, decides to punish her. She, coveting his unattainable masculinity, decides to punish him. He denigrates her femininity—which he is supposed to desire and which he really envies—and becomes more aggressively masculine. She feigns disgust at his masculinity—which she is supposed to admire and which she really envies—and becomes more fastidiously feminine. He is becoming less and less what he wants to be. But now he is more manly than ever, and she is more womanly than ever.

Her femininity, growing more dependently supine, becomes contemptible. His masculinity, growing more oppressively domineering, becomes intolerable. At last she loathes what she has helped his masculinity to become. At last he loathes what he has helped her femininity to become.

So far, it has all been very symmetrical. But we have left one thing out.

The world belong to what his masculinity has become.

The reward for what his masculinity has become is power. The reward for what her femininity has become is only the security which his power can bestow upon her. If he were to yield to what her femininity has become, he would be yielding to contemptible incompetence. If she were to acquire what his masculinity has become, she would participate in intolerable coerciveness.

She is stifling under the triviality of her femininity. The world is groaning beneath the terrors of his masculinity.

He is playing masculine. She is playing feminine.

How do we call off the game?

(Roszak and Roszak, 1969, pp. vii–viii)

women are not the same. We hold one set of expectations for a female and another set for a male. Psychological and social characteristics are often one with physical characteristics; it is natural for men to be manly and masculine, natural for women to be womanly and feminine. Gender and gender expectations are a fundamental element of personhood. Very few of us ever confuse our own gender and we never forget the sex of another person. We may forget a name, an age, or hair color, but not a person's sex.

I am a woman. I have no desire to change my sex. I do, however, feel often that my life as a human being might be richer and fuller if less were contingent on that single aspect of my being. Too much of my life is dependent on what I have learned to be and what others hold to be true of me because I am female. My genes have dictated the form of my body, but my society has often imposed on my entire being qualities, expectations, and demands of femininity and sex roles that are supposed to be natural and correct for a human with a female anatomy. By this imposition I am less than I can be, as are all my fellow humans. We are less than human when our destinies are a function of our anatomies.

How can one be a male person or a female person without abiding by sex-role stereotypes and expectations? There is no answer to this question and will be none until we believe more in humanness than we do in maleness and femaleness. We do not know how to be merely human. As Janet Chafetz says, "We need a vision of what it would mean to be a society not of feminine and masculine creatures, but comprised of humans. The truth of the matter is that we have no real notion of what it means to be human, divorced from notions of masculinity and femininity." (Chafetz, 1974, p. 201) Until we fashion such a vision we are often stuck playing masculine and feminine, not knowing how to call the game off (see Box 10.1).

MAXIMIZING PERSONHOOD

Roles that cast us as stereowomen and stereomen make a travesty of humanness. *Sexism* is the belief that certain traits or behaviors are characteristic of only males or females; these behaviors are often interpreted in such a way as to ridicule the opposite sex. Sexism contributes to the reduction of opportunities for one-half of the human population and, at the same time, burdens the other half with onerous obligations. *Feminism,* the belief that women, being as human as men, are entitled to rights and privileges equal to men's, has always had a more sympathetic audience with women than with men. However, it is feminism that is leading our masculine-oriented society to a new humanism.

Critical views of sex-role stereotypes gained popular support with the publication, in 1963, of *The Feminine Mystique* by Betty Friedan. This was one of the first statements of the idea that there is nothing wrong with a woman who doesn't adjust to society's expectations but there is something wrong with a society that tries to force her to do so. Betty Friedan brought to public awareness the "problem which has no name" —the hardships imposed on women who try to live by "the standards of feminine normality, feminine adjustment, feminine fulfillment, and feminine maturity." (p. 26) The women's movement has certainly not been a revolution in any traditional sense. Women have no single spokeswoman, they remain largely unorganized, they are split into factions, they have a range of goals designed to satisfy women's diverse needs, and they suffer a backlash in which women themselves participate.

Men, despite their overwhelming advantages in jobs, pay, and power, are also beginning to examine their sex roles and the influence of masculinity in their lives. It is only recently that these have been seen as obstacles to personhood for men. For most of human history, the frustrations suffered by men have been put down to the anger of the gods, fate, an inhospitable environment, poverty, religious and racial discrimination—all external and constant forces. The elusiveness of success has been explained by the individual man's lack of strenth or courage, independence, or self-sufficiency. It is becoming clearer that the source of frustration in men's lives can no longer be exclusively sought in nature or individual shortcomings, although these may be formidable barriers.

Many men can see in their roles and the pressures to be masculine justification for Thoreau's observation, made over a hundred years ago, that "the mass of men live lives of quiet desperation." A young man, growing up in the world today can say:

I, a twentieth-century male, feel trapped, suppressed, suffocated by an uncaring, stereotyping . . . society. My individuality is labeled queer and my interests unnatural because the idea of seeing a baseball game . . . does not send me into euphoric ecstasy. I feel bitterness for the conforming role nature has forced me to bear . . . (from Chafetz, 1974, p. 59).

Public and Private Changes

In order for females and males to actualize the full range of potentials we have as humans, we need a society which provides a wide range of options, choices, and chances to live a full human life. Alternatives will be available when there are legal, medical, educational, and occupational opportunities for all, regardless of gender, and when there are social services sufficient to make our options viable. But alternatives alone are not enough. Given opportunities, we need then to make our own personal and private decisions, to actively choose among alternatives. We need to change our attitudes about women and men, feminine and masculine.

The most needed social changes are those which will ease and eliminate the unequal division of obligations and prohibitions now allotted to men and women and, simultaneously, will equally distribute human rights among us. Men and women must have equal legal rights in every area of the law and we must also assume equal responsibilities as citizens. There must be social changes that will give men and women opportunities for equal sharing of family and home responsibilities. For instance, when women get paid as much as men do for working outside of the home, then men will be free to become housepersons if they wish. Part-time jobs (with full pay pro-rated and fringe benefits) and staggered working hours will allow parents to share equally in domestic work. Working men, working women, and their children need child-care centers located conveniently, preferably where the parents work. Reliable, safe birth control for both men and women will allow us to plan for every child and for assuming our parental roles. Our society is moving, however slowly, in the direction of making these kinds of services available, but it will be some time before all of us in every socioeconomic class can benefit. One of the most influential powers behind the achievement of these changes is the National Organization for Women (NOW) founded in 1966. "The purpose of NOW is to take action to bring women into full participation in the mainstream of American society *now,* exercising all the privileges and responsibilities thereof in truly equal partnership with men." (Deckard, 1975, p. 330)

The public, social changes necessary to allow people of both genders to develop full potentials will come when we eliminate our stereotypes about men and women. Changing these attitudes, many of which are

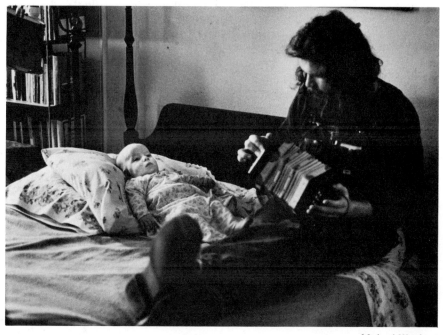

Michael Weisbrot

Photograph by R. Dian.

supported by tradition and by contemporary culture, is exceedingly difficult. Our stereotypic viewpoints often lie outside the reach of our awareness.

Women will not be liberated by being allowed to assume men's sex roles; men will not be liberated by being forced into women's roles. We need new viewpoints which are not based on female/male differences but on individual uniqueness. One such concept is that of androgyny (from "andro," meaning male, and "gyne," female). An androgynous person is one who has both male and female potentials and who is not limited by the label "male" or "female." Each of us finds situations in life which require us to be assertive, decisive, and self-reliant, and situations in which we would best be tender, intuitive, or sensitive to others' needs. Traditional sex roles and stereotypes restrict our responses; "androgyny greatly expands the range of behavior open to everyone, permitting people to cope more effectively with diverse situations." (Bem, 1975, p. 62)

As beneficial and necessary as attitude changes are, it is also necessary to change the ways in which we behave. It is one thing to say we believe that men and women should have equal human rights or that men should express their emotions and women should be assertive, and another thing to put these attitudes into practice. In a study of men's attitudes, for example, Warren Farrell found that the "closer proposed changes in gender roles came to the home environment, the more the men opposed it. For example, 82 percent of the men were in favor of the Equal Rights Amendment (ERA), which few men see as affecting their personal lives. However, . . . it was virtually impossible for men to accept giving dolls to their sons." (1975a, p. 218)

Attitude, behavior, and social changes begin with an awareness of the many ways in which we live according to traditional sex-role stereotyping, particularly those ways which are close to home. For some years

androgyny

now women have been meeting in small informal groups to raise their own consciousness about their lives as women. Consciousness-raising is the process of changing viewpoints, of seeing the subtle and more obvious problems caused by sex roles, of sharing, and of supporting others in change. More recently, men have joined men's groups for the same purposes.

In order to raise your own consciousness I suggest that you break up into discussion groups of men-only and women-only. (If you have a large class, form more than one same-sex group so that everyone has a chance to talk. Eight is an ideal size.) There are several values in beginning with members of your same sex: it will be easier to talk freely, it will help you see the ways in which you are both similar and different from others of your gender, and it can enrich your appreciation of your same-sex peers. Mixed groups can perpetuate traditional competition among women and among men.

After you have explored the topics suggested (some or all of them) you should then get together and share your explorations in a larger mixed group.

EXPLORATIONS 10.4 Personhood

Women

Because women have not had many options in the past, part of our heritage is a lack of experience in making decisions about our lives. In order not to be passive subjects of cultural proscriptions, women must learn how to decide, make choices, and take responsibility for the consequences of having chosen this instead of that. As you discuss the following questions, notice how you might feel unable or unwilling to make decisions that determine the way you live.

Am I aware of all the skills, talents, and aptitudes I possess and that I might develop in a vocational way? Are there careers I have not considered because they require lengthy training or a substantial commitment on my part? Are there jobs I might be good at if I didn't feel they were unfeminine? Do I undervalue my intellectual or academic potentials?

How self-sufficient am I? How well do I keep myself and take care of my own needs? Do I manage my own money and make decisions about how I want to spend it?

In what ways do I depend on men to do things for me? Do I let men do things for me that I could just as well do myself? Do I play "poor little helpless me" when I want some help from a man? Do I ever suggest that I would be willing to give myself sexually for a man's favor?

Can I say "No" when someone needs my support or services if I feel their needs impose on my own? Can I be assertive w.thout feeling guilty?

What are my feelings about sexuality? In what circumstances do I want to share my body: only within a marriage or a love relationship? With close friends? Acquaintances? Strangers? With no one? Does my sexual behavior reflect my sexual values 100 percent, all the time? Do I let circumstances or someone else decide for me?

How do I answer the following questions when I'm in a close relationship with a man: Do I *need* this relationship to make me a whole person? Will I be destroyed when it ends? Am I able to supplement my devotion to this relationship by engaging in activities with other people and by myself, or have I imprisoned myself?

When I'm not in a close relationship do I ever feel that if I were in love or married my problems would be solved or that I would be happy?

Do I *want* a husband? Children? Do I *need* either to make my life whole or for security? Is a family of my own necessary for my survival or well-being?

If and when I'm a mother, can I share equally with a man in all aspects of rearing children? Can I share in all aspects of homekeeping? Do I feel some part of a house or some jobs are exclusively mine or that men are incompetent to do "women's work?"

How do I feel about other women?

Men

Warren Farrell, author of *The Liberated Man* (subtitled *Beyond Masculinity: Freeing Men and Their Relationships with Women*) has observed in the several men's groups he has begun that men find it very difficult to talk to one another on an intimate basis about their deepest needs and their insecurities. Masculine values lead men to condescension, intellectualization, anxious laughter, put-downs, obsession with sex, and to interrupting one another. Openness, warmth, empathy, and contact are difficult for most men to achieve with each other. As you discuss the following questions (adapted from Farrell's "Guidelines for Consciousness-Raising" *Ms.*, Feb. 1973, p. 15ff) keep the first question uppermost in your mind.

What do I feel most vulnerable about? What about me do I want to keep hidden from you?

At what times in my life have I felt rejected by individuals or groups? What do I do to prevent rejection? Do I talk more or clam up?

What are my views about women? Do I feel superior to or contempt for women? Do I treat women as sex objects? Do I like my women friends or my wife to look nice as a reflection of my good taste or attractiveness?

Do I feel I have to be an expert in some certain area(s) (for instance, cars, math, stereos, electricity, etc.)? How do I feel about this; do I resent it? Do I let others, especially women, pressure me to seem to know everything?

What pressures do I get from my peers to be a leader?

Do I feel competitive in school, at work, with my woman friend or wife?

Do I know anybody who has had a vasectomy or an abortion? How do I feel about these?

Do I share equally in all kinds of work where I live? What kinds of work do I leave to my woman friend, wife, mother, sister? What gets left undone because I don't do it?

How do I feel when I'm with children? With infants?

Do I think children should succeed as a reflection of their parents?

Who talks most in a serious conversation: me or my woman friend or wife? What have I *learned* from listening to others?

What are my attitudes toward sexuality? Homosexuality?

What pressures do I feel to be a breadwinner? To achieve status through a job? To get rich?

When are emotions helpful? What are my fears of expressing emotions? When did I last cry? Would I like to be able to cry more? What are the purposes of crying?

How do I feel about other men?

SUMMARY

1. The single, widowed, and divorced, homosexuals both male and female, men who drop out, and women who work — all are in some sense deviants from traditional sex roles and stereotypes. All pay, in one way or another, for *not conforming*.

2. The penalties for *conforming* to traditional sex roles may be a slowing of personal growth, a diminution of intimacy in male/female relationships, and threats to one's physical and psychological well-being. Society as a whole loses certain potentials of both women and men when they conform and loses also from the crime and extreme sexual deviance that may result when men try to conform.

3. "Normal" for everyone is primarily defined by male sex-role standards.

4. The historical function of traditional sex roles has been made obsolete by the ready availability of birth control methods and by the changing nature of work in industrial society.

5. Sex roles and stereotypes persist because we continue to think of men as "masculine" and women as "feminine" — each the opposite of the other.

6. The women's movement, consciousness-raising activities by both men and women, the increasing acceptability of androgenous modes of life, and the institutional changes that are resulting from these are all contributing to the knowledge that we can live without traditional limiting conceptions of masculine and feminine, female and male.

Suggested Readings

Chafetz, Janet S. *Masculine/feminine or human? An overview of the sociology of sex roles*. Itasca, Ill.: F. E. Peacock, 1974. A well-written look at the theories, history, function, and future of sex roles.

Duberman, Lucile. *Gender and sex in society*. New York: Praeger, 1975. Addresses the question of psychological and social differences between men and women.

Kaplan, Alexandra G., and Bean, Joan P. *Beyond sex-role stereotypes: Readings toward a psychology of androgyny*. Boston: Little, Brown, 1976. An excellent collection of articles and research reports focusing on alternative conceptions of sex roles.

Maccoby, Eleanor E., and Jacklin, Carol N. *The psychology of sex differences.* Stanford: Stanford University Press, 1974a. A scholarly review of a large body of evidence concerning intellectual and behavioral differences between males and females. The authors conclude with a summary of unfounded beliefs, four established differences, and several ambiguous areas needing further research.

Money, John, and Ehrhardt, Anke A. *Man & woman, boy & girl: Differentiation and dimorphism of gender identity from conception to maturity.* Baltimore: The Johns Hopkins University Press, 1972. Drawing from many disciplines (genetics, embryology, endocrinology, anthropology, and others), the authors present a theory of gender differentiation which combines biological and social contributions to gender development.

Morris, Jan. *Conundrum.* New York: Harcourt, Brace, Jovanovich, 1974. An autobiographical account of the transsexual changeover from man to woman; at age 46 "James Humphry" became "Jan," thus actualizing his life-long conviction that "he" was a "she."

Sheehy, Gail. *Passages: The predictable crisis of adult life.* New York: Dutton, 1976. Describes stages of adult life for contemporary men and women in the United States, revealing the possibilities of growth in various adult roles.

Stoll, Clarice S. *Female and male: Socialization, social roles and social structure.* Dubuque, Iowa: Wm. C. Brown Co., 1974. Examines the consequences of being female and being male given the roles, rewards, costs, and identities that accompany biological gender differences.

National Education Association Publishing, Joe Di Dio.

11

THE QUEST FOR COMPETENCE

Reason's whole pleasure, all the joys of
  sense,
Lie in three words—health, peace, and
  competence.

Alexander Pope
(Essay on Man)

Living is a test of ability. Every day our capacity to survive, to perform, and to grow is challenged. Absorbed as we are by living, we rarely take stock of our abilities:

What can I do?
What do I need to do?
What do I want to do?
What do I do well? How do I know?

The questions are simple enough; the answers do not come easily. The quest is to know and value our abilities and to find the worth of life.

Doing well is only partly the result of ability. We need also to *feel* competent, to be reasonably secure in the knowledge that we will be able to meet the demands of the future, for a sense of competence leads us to successful performance. We do our best when we have a positive regard for who we are and what we can do. To value ourselves is to believe we are worthy of challenges, of success, and of reward. "Competence means fitness or ability. The competence of an organism means its fitness or ability to carry on those transactions with the environment which result in its maintaining itself, growing, and flourishing." (White, 1960, p. 100)

As with all species, human abilities vary among individuals. Some of us are "more fit" than others owing to individual combinations of genetic and social influences. And like other species, there are certain minimums of fitness below which humans cannot survive and grow into maturity. But above these lowest limits, humans show a tremendous range of abilities which develop in our individual responses to the demands and opportunities of our culture.

PHYSICAL, EMOTIONAL, AND INTELLECTUAL COMPETENCE

Nothing we do in life is purely intellectual, purely emotional, or purely physical. Living is an integrated process requiring all kinds of skills and abilities. Every activity or experience is a combination of thought, feeling, and action. And it is through our capacity for integrating these abilities that we achieve. While we can consider physical, emotional, and intellectual competence separately, it is well to remember that these are inseparable functions. As Jacob Bronowski has put it, ". . . every man, every civilization, has gone forward because of its engagement with what is has set itself to do. The personal commitment of a man to his skill, the intellectual commitment and the emotional commitment working together as one, has made the Ascent of Man." (1973, p. 438)

Michael Weisbrot

Physical Competence

Being able to walk, run, move gracefully, breathe deeply, sleep well, see, hear, and taste; having good muscle and hand-eye coordination; having the full use of a body that is in top condition—these enhance all that we do in life.

It is not necessary to have a "perfect" body in order to be competent. There are many individual differences in physical potentials and in the development of these potentials. Almost everyone has some kind of physical handicap or deficiency—either undeveloped physical potential, a physical defect such as imperfect vision, or temporary ailments which reduce ability. Some of us suffer permanent impairments such as a loss of vision, hearing, or a limb. But because we can compensate, and because physical perfection is not necessary to competence, these impairments do not have to be handicapping (unless society discriminates against us for having them). We have potentials to develop the acuity of one sense if we lose another, to live rich and rewarding lives with our scars and losses, as long as our sense of worth and self-acceptance has not been destroyed. Helen Keller, Beethoven, Franklin Roosevelt, and many others have taken advantage of the possibilities for compensation.

During childhood and youth we develop many physical skills, those of both large and small muscle proficiency. We are physically active when young but many of us become more and more sedentary as we get older; we no longer maintain our physical capacities. Unless we are in a profession such as dance, athletics, or music, many of our physical potentials decline from lack of daily exercise. We all have physical limits, even the professionals, but we rarely approach our upper limits of proficiency as adults.

Bodies work best when they are cared for, maintained properly, and given rest and exercise. A good body can be abused by improper nutri-tion, the overuse of drugs, or too little rest. Poorly maintained bodies are much more susceptible to disease and prone to accidents than those which are taken care of. If our bodies are abused or neglected, resistance and resilience are lost. Chronic and unattended physical problems sap us of energy and vigor. In this culture we are most apt to think about health when we don't have it. We are not awfully concerned with proper health care habits or preventive medicine. We are concerned more with cosmetic than with physical condition.

hypochrondriac

Illness, even life-threatening illness, can be a signal that something is wrong with the way we are living. It has been recognized for many years that one of the benefits of getting sick is the attention that others pay us. The label hypochondriac is given to people who create or develop symp-toms just to get attention and care. We are now beginning to see that sickness has another benefit: it can force us to "get off the merry-go-round" before we spin ourselves to death. Illness can be, and often is, an indication that we are striving too hard, that there is more stress in our life than it is possible to bear. It may even mean that we have packed too much change into too short a period (Holmes and Masuda, 1972). Getting sick gives us the opportunity, if we take it, to pay attention to ourselves, to examine the way we are living, and to reorder our priorities.

EXPLORATION
11.1

Physical Competence

Think about the ways in which you like your body, the ways in which it pleases you.
How do you take care of your body and your health?
How do you feel about your body when you use it? When you push or stretch it toward the limits of your physical potentials?
How do you regularly use your body? Abuse it? Take a good look at yourself in a full-length mirror.
  As you regard yourself, answer this question: This is how I feel about my body:
What physical activity would you like to do but don't?
  Why don't you do it?
When do you get sick? In what ways might illnesses be useful to you?

Emotional Competence

Emotional competence is the awareness and the constructive expression of emotional states. Emotions do not occur in our hearts or guts. Emo-tional states are manifest throughout our bodies, in many internal organs, in posture, facial expression, and muscular tension. We become aware of emotional states with our brains. The cortex must pay attention to and give meaning to the various signals in the body. Emotional competence is the ability to express emotions directly and spontaneously as well as the ability to control emotional outbursts.

Emotions give life its flavor, variety, and vitality. Emotional states let us know that we are alive. When we express our emotions, others know we are alive. Emotional states are also preparations for action. Even before we can understand a situation intellectually our emotions can warn us that something is wrong (that we are being threatened, that we have lost something of value, or that our goals have been thwarted, for instance). Emotions act as clues. Having and being aware of a wide range of emotions—fear, joy, anger, sadness, surprise, ecstasy, calmness—is an important part of self-knowledge.

Emotions are neither good nor bad. But we have all learned that there are "appropriate" situations and behaviors for the expression of emotional states. As children we learn to inhibit the expression of our feelings; part of growing up is learning to moderate anger, love, hostility, and other strong emotions. We learn rules about when and with whom to show affection. Most of us are urged to suppress contrary emotions, the ideal being never to let anger, for example, or fear, or disappointment show. As we learn suppression we may also learn not to acknowledge to ourselves what we are feeling. Then we may gradually cease feeling all together.

When emotional states are long-lasting, overwhelming, or pent up, they can disrupt our lives. When we are aware of moderate amounts of fear, anxiety, or other contrary emotions we can use them constructively. These emotions get us going. They act like the spark plugs in a combustion engine: without them we couldn't get started.

On the other hand, a lack of any restraint or unreliable control of emotions reduce us to childish, immature patterns of behavior. Control is not the same as suppression. Control is the ability to delay or contain emotional expression when we want to, to react to situations with the appro-

Photograph courtesy of The Farm.

priate emotion and intensity, and to let go of emotions when they have served their purpose.

We are not emotionally competent if we hang on to guilt, regrets, or resentments from the past or when we are overburdened with worry about the future. Being emotionally competent is being able to deal with the present, letting the present situation determine our emotional reactions.

EXPLORATIONS 11.2

Emotional Competence

a. Answer the following questions:

Are there any emotions which are taboo for me — that is, feelings I am not comfortable expressing?

Are there some people with whom I curb my emotional expression?

In which situations do I feel I ought to suppress my feelings?

How do I express anger, joy, sadness, excitement, or other states?

When do my emotions frighten me? Are there times when I feel unsure of my ability to control my expression?

b. Here are suggestions about how to better integrate feelings (adapted from James and Jongeward, *Born to Win.* Addison-Wesley, Reading, Mass., 1971, pp. 200–209):

First: Exaggerate the way you express an emotion that is bothersome to you. If you are troubled by depression, make your whole body express "I'm depressed." Look in the mirror. Make the saddest face you can. If you cannot control anger, make an angry face. If fear overwhelms you, make a fearful face. Show an emotion in the most extreme way possible, using your whole body. Move around, make sounds to demonstrate how sad, or angry, or afraid, or whatever you are.

Second: Become aware of how your body *feels* when you are depressed, angry, afraid, and so on. Where are you holding your tensions? What is your breathing like? Your jaw? Your stomach? Your forehead? Your shoulders? When you find tension increase it, hold it for a few moments, and then let go — relax completely.

Third: Reverse your feelings: do exactly the opposite of what you were feeling. Feel joyous, mellow, fierce, and so on.

Fourth: Develop a fantasy in which you are in complete control over what might be making you depressed, angry, or afraid. If there are other people in your fantasy tell them to get off your back (if you are depressed) or shout at them (if you are angry), or turn to the people you fear and tell them you are not afraid.

Fifth: Assume responsibility for your own feelings by saying "I am letting myself be depressed." "I am allowing myself to be angry." "I am afraid."

One of the most troublesome emotions in this culture, with its emphasis on polite and rational interpersonal relationships, is anger. An angry response every so often is inevitable, but we have all been socialized—some of us more than others—not to display anger. Every time we are angry and fail to find an outlet for our hostility we store some tension in our muscles, add stress to our stomachs or respiratory systems, and may even set the stage for skin problems such as eczema. Years of unexpressed anger (and the unexpression of other taboo emotions) take their physical toll. Sometimes we learn to cope with anger (which we do nor dare express directly) by indirect expression or displacement, or by turning it back on ourselves. Indirect expressions of anger can be nagging, whining, or harping. We blow off steam or maliciously gossip about someone else when we are afraid to confront them directly with our anger. We tease with the pretense of harmless and innocent fun, but with the aim of hurting just a little bit. Anger is displaced when it is directed at someone more vulnerable than we are rather than at a source of anger that is more powerful (for example, kicking the dog when you are angry at your boss). Turning anger inward is thought by some to be the cause of depression. We feel helpless, weak, and ineffectual when we cannot confront the source of our anger. The energy of our hostility turns to self-resentment.

Intellectual Competence

In general, we acquire information incidentally as we live and intentionally through formal education. We often consider information valuable if it has use-value; that is, if we can put it to work for us in some way. The value of a certain kind of information is, to some degree, determined by cultural and social demands. Most of us have little use for knowledge of how to track wild game, just as an early American Indian would have had little use for a bus schedule. However, we are also creatures who enjoy having knowledge for its own sake and to play with (as in crossword puzzles and trivia games).

We do need material to think with. Bits of information (facts) and the concepts by which facts are organized are the raw materials of thought.

Photograph by Michael Heron.

We can probably store many millions of bits of information in a lifetime and still not overtax our brains; it is estimated that we use only a fraction of our intellectual potential. More vital than facts are the concepts and categories by which they are arranged. The more relevant and flexible our concepts, the more easily we can assimilate and understand new information (see Chapter 12).

Intellectual processes are what we do with knowledge, the ways in which we manipulate information to meet our needs. We use information in solving problems, making decisions, and planning ahead. We have abilities for rational/deductive thinking and intuitive/inductive thinking. These processes are necessary for intellectual competence.

Many inadequacies in intellectual skills do not result from lack of information, but in our misuse of it. One malfunction is seeing the elements of a problem or situation incorrectly. We come prepared in our minds to encounter certain circumstances and are not easily dissuaded from our "set" by the true nature of the situation. A common source of error is habitual thinking. We assume that one situation is just like other, similar, situations we have met in the past. Another way of putting a situation into an inaccurate or inadequate concept-category is by stereotyping or prejudging. When one's mind is already made up it does not perceive reality. Other intellectual problems we have are not the result of intellectual incompetence but of either physical or emotional deficiency. Fatigue and anxiety, for example, can lead to poor intellectual performance.

The largest share of formal schooling in America is devoted to the acquisition and rational application of knowledge. "Intelligence" is thought to be a primary, if not the paramount, ability. IQ scores are taken by many as a measure of aptitude and personal worth. We come to believe that we can solve all our problems if we "think" about them long enough. We strive to be bright. We learn in school and at home to live in our heads. By contrast, physical training is secondary and emotional training is usually ignored in formal education. This is unfortunate, for many of our failures in life stem from inadequate emotional competence, and we miss much of the zest of life when both our emotions and physiques are allowed to go flabby from disuse.

EXPLORATION 11.3 **Intellectual Competence**	Do you show your intelligence all the time? Ask yourself, "Do I act intelligently" when taking exams? In emergencies? On the job? With my friends? With my family? Do I sometimes act stupid or inadequate? Or do I try to bluff—act smart when I don't feel it? How important is it that others see me as intelligent? Stupid? Could I be more competent if I decided that I was "OK" intellectually? What advantages are there in appearing dumb? Do I possibly control others by appearing to know less than I do? By seeming incompetent do I get out of working hard or accepting responsibility?

GAMES: PLAY AND WORK

Any structured activity can be considered a game if it has these characteristics: roles to perform, a goal to be reached (which lets us know when the game is over and who won), and rules about the ways and means of reaching the goal. Some games also include competition and payoffs. Some games we play merely for the fun of playing. Fun games, or play, are not "real"; that is, we design them to provide pleasure and we know that they are only games (Kinget, 1975). If a game has a purpose beyond fun, it is a life game. It is work rather than play. Fun games and life games can be equally demanding, challenging, and useful for developing competence. What is work for one person may be play for another, the difference being how and why the game is being played. Our society traditionally values work above play; doing things just for the fun of it is often considered childish and self-indulgent. It is easy for us to neglect play or to feel guilty about engaging in "nonpurposeful" activity.

EXPLORATIONS 11.4

Play

a. Make a list of the fun games you engaged in during the past week, those things you did freely and solely with the expectation of having fun. *Were* they fun? How did you feel about doing them? Did you play more fun games than life games this week? What kinds of competence did your play allow you to demonstrate?

b. This is a classroom exploration that has no purpose beyond having fun: it is play. The whole class participates and there is no goal, no competition, no winners or losers. It allows childlike spontaneity, physical activity, laughter, and relaxation. Let yourself go! Play! (You may want to remove your shoes so you can run faster!)

Arrange in a large circle as many chairs as there are students. The instructor (who plays too) will whisper to each student one of the following designations: "Apple," "Peach," or "Pear." Then the instructor moves to the center of the circle and calls one of the following:

"Apples"
"Peaches"
"Pears"
"Fruit-basket-turn-over"

Whichever group is called, each member must leave his or her seat and take any other vacant seat. The call "Fruit-basket-turn-over" signals everyone to leave his or her seat. After making this call, the instructor joins in the search for a seat; one person will end up in the center without a chair. This person becomes the next caller. The game is over when the instructor says "The game is over."

(I am indebted to Dr. Valda Robinson of Hillsborough Community College for suggesting this exercise.)

Work, a life game, is much more than going to a job. Robert White defines work as those ". . . serious, stable, lasting concerns of human life." (1960, p. 135) Work is serious because it has a purpose. This purpose can be the gaining of something tangible, such as money or material goods. Work can also have as its object an intangible goal, such as love or acceptance or self-actualization. What are the life games that we are expected to play in this society, through which we develop and manifest competence?

Self-Maintenance

Self-maintenance is usually done to enable us to do other things. It tends to become a series of routine chores, tasks that seldom call into question our competence, jobs in which we do not seek pleasure. It is not common to think of self-maintenance as a lasting concern of life. However, there is potential for deriving pleasure, and a sense of satisfaction and competence from keeping our lives and selves in good running order. There is also potential for stress, worry, or frustration when we do not achieve proper maintenance. Inadequate self-maintenance can damage everything else we try to do. It can also be an indication that we do not value ourselves highly.

Some of us take care of ourselves by ourselves, for the most part. But it is becoming ever more common for us to buy, barter, or trade for many of the services necessary to self-maintenance (for example, car repair, housework, medical care). The details of self-maintenance vary with time, technological development, and geography. Basic to all societies, however, are the tasks of providing one's food, shelter, clothing, and health.

Very few Americans produce their own food, build their own houses, or even make their own clothes. We buy (rent or lease) what others have produced. We also buy our medical care. This situation has dramatically affected the nature of the skills required for self-maintenance. Instead of developing potentials for growing, making, and creating we need to be competent money-makers and consumers. The skills (and joys and pleasures derived from using these skills) required in taking materials and turning them into products for our own use are less and less in demand. Many of us are incompetent at the arts of preparing food, maintaining, repairing, or decorating our homes and clothing, and physical fitness.

Contemporary American living requires competence in those self-maintenance tasks that define a "middle-class" way of life. These skills of consumption include:

Transportation: We need to get from here to there and back again efficiently and quickly. We ride, fly, drive and hitchhike, all of which require specific skills. We must manage to buy and maintain the cars and other vehicles which many of us feel we must own.

Michael Weisbrot

Ordering and caring for possessions: We accumulate large quantities of things which we spend time and energy in sorting, storing, cleaning, recording, and disposing of.

Financial accounting: Since much of our livelihood depends on the exchange of our time and energy for money and, in turn, the exchange of money for things, competent self-maintenance necessitates a scheme for keeping track of our financial resources. We need to be able to balance the checkbook.

Clock watching: We consult clocks in order to know when to work, eat, sleep, conduct business, and make interpersonal transactions. We also regulate our activities according to a weekly calendar. We are competent if we can plan our time, make appointments, know various schedules (for classes, TV programs, buses, holidays, etc.) and if we can be "on time" when we choose to be.

EXPLORATION 11.5 **Self-Maintenance**	Consider what you *do* to maintain yourself. What kinds of skills and abilities does your self-maintenance require? What are you responsible for for yourself? How does your self-maintenance reflect your individuality, your personal style or competence? Is your responsibility for yourself (or lack of it) in certain areas dictated by sex roles? Is self-maintenance ever a fun game for you or is it all work? Are there areas of self-maintenance in which you are a competent producer as contrasted with a consumer? Do you feel different about things you produce than you do about things you buy?

What do you feel helpless about? Fill in the blanks:
    I can't take care of _____ by myself.
    I feel helpless when _____. |

Learning and Education

Learning is said to happen when experience (whether it's touching something too hot, reading a book, or repeating a verse over and over) results in a more or less permanent change in behavior. Basic to this formula is curiosity, which leads us to try to understand ourselves and the world around us. Curiosity seems to be innate in human beings, as anyone who has observed the "unmotivated" explorations of an infant will testify. But curiosity can be dulled, and it often is, as we develop routine, habitual ways of behaving. The ability to learn requires that a certain amount of curiosity be kept alive, which is to say that the more routine our experiences become, the less we are likely to learn.

Education is the formal survival technique of culture. It is the transmittal process by which culture survives from one generation to the next. Education is also a means for living competently. Learning and education can be either fun or work (or both) depending on whether we pursue them for pleasure or because we have to. Much of our formal education is not fun precisely because it is a compulsory, standardized experience. School is supposed to prepare us for the future, to train us for specific jobs, and to give us formal qualifications. Education is reserved for youth, shaped to fit the school years, and judged by its success in getting us degrees, certificates, or jobs. One can be competent in school and at learning, although the two do not necessarily require the same abilities. School may be where we learn how to learn, but it may also be a place where we learn only how to get good grades.

Higher education provides specialized training, offers a general education, and gives many students the opportunity to discover aptitudes and make a commitment to an occupation. By the time we finish college, we are supposed to have decided what we want to do, to have received the training needed to do it, and to be ready to settle into an adult life. As far as the traditional educational system has been concerned, the opportunity to do all this comes only once. In this system few of us are free to pursue education for very long or to delay making decisions about a career. The threat of the future too often interferes with learning and the pleasures of learning. The notion that education is a once-in-a-lifetime process belonging to youth is changing, however. There are more and more opportunities for us to continue formal education all our lives.

Occupation

Earlier *work* was characterized as a structured activity that has a serious goal or purpose, and which is a lasting concern in life. The Special Task Force on Work in America (1972) defines work as "an activity that produces something of value for other people." (Coleman and Hammen, 1974) This latter definition of work I take to mean *occupation*. In an oc-

**EXPLORATION
11.6

Learning**

Do you enjoy becoming more competent? Learning new things? Do you recall the last time you got a kick out of learning something new? (Was it when you were feeling good about learning and about yourself?)
How do you feel about yourself when you know you know something?

Do you ever think you will stop learning? Fantasize a time in your life when you have stopped changing. Why, when, how would this happen? What would life be like?

Explore the situations in which you feel you learn the best and contrast these with situations in which you do not learn well or easily. How do you feel when you learn easily? What do you do?

As a college student do you ever feel conflicts among different goals in learning, getting a degree, or passing certain tests of your achievement? For example, are there times when you feel forced to study material you think is irrelevant to your own goals or interests? Do you feel pressure to learn faster or slower than you would pace yourself? Are you better when you follow instructions or when you are free to set your own pace? Does academic competition (for grades) stimulate your mastery of subject matter? What can you as a student do to make conflicts about learning and school less frustrating? Would a change in any of your attitudes about learning and schoolwork help?

Fill in the blank with as many things as you need to:

For me, school is _____.

Some years ago, I was associated with a research project on the effects of college on students' personalities. The study found that most students fall into one of the following three stages of "occupational identity" (Henry, 1972):
Decided: Decisions about education and occupation were made before college. People in this group had always known what their goals were, perhaps since grade school but certainly since high school. College for them was the means to achieve that goal; education would give them the skills they needed to succeed. They had no difficulty in choosing courses or majors.
Deciding: Students in the second group spent much of their time and energy making choices. They had diverse interests and experimented in several majors. They took much time reformulating ideas, seeking knowledge of themselves, and looking into the job market. They were often in conflict, worried, or excited about the range of opportunities in college.
Identity achieved: After a period of exploration, experiencing, and sorting out, people in this group made a choice of one plan and rejected many others. Not many reached this stage until the end of college, but some students had matched their knowledge of themselves with their knowledge of an occupation before graduation.

Do you find yourself in any of these three groups? Discuss with your class the various considerations that students meet with in deciding on an occupation. Do you come up with categories different from the three given above?

Grumman Photograph by Bob Setles.

cupation (job, career, or profession) we produce goods or services in return for money. An exception to this rule is the occupation of housewife, a job which is not performed for cash.

There is a popular, if idealistic, belief in America that we are free to choose our occupations. We are not expected, as in some cultures, to follow the trade or profession of our parents. We are also free to change our occupations when they no longer suit us. However, as we know, this freedom is not evenly distributed throughout our society: our race, sex, age, and economic level may influence the number of options we actually have.

An occupation rewards us in several ways, but the rewards are not necessarily true measures of competence.

Pay: Many of us are not paid for doing our jobs well; we are paid for an adequate (or even mediocre) performance. We are paid for many reasons: for putting in eight hours a day on the job; according to how long we have been on the same job; for the responsibility we are potentially able to assume (even though we may never assume it); for having been elected, for being rich, for looking right on the job, for having the right name. We usually can't keep a job unless we produce at some minimum level of output or quality, but above that (unless we work on a commission) many of us are not financially rewarded for increased competence. In conditions such as these, it is not to show or to increase our competence that we perform. Our goal is money.

Occupational identity: One of the crucial bits of information we exchange in becoming acquainted with someone is our occupation. It is important for most of us to have an occupational status and identity which is congruent with the rest of our identity. (It is incongruous, for example, for an atheist to be a minister.) It is usual in this society to seek high status occupations, for what we do is taken as an indicator of who we

City of New York, Department of Sanitation.

are. The more prestigious our occupations and titles, the more respect we can command. Some garbage collectors like to be called Sanitary Engineers; some instructors are always called Professor.

Realization of potentials: Adults spend one-third to one-half of their lives working at their jobs. Occupations can, but do not always, offer challenge, support, and time enough for us to develop our abilities and enrich our lives. It is important that our interests and aptitudes match the kind of work we do, although it is sometimes difficult to know what a particular job will offer and which of our potentials it will draw on until we start it. Occupations can tap many of our competencies and still be very routine and uninteresting if we are not challenged to develop our abilities further.

Security: Having and keeping a job is vital to personal security for most of us, especially for those whose primary role in life is to be a breadwinner. Because self-maintenance depends so much on consumption, the loss of a job may mean that we are incapable of providing for our basic necessities. If occupational identity is the identity by which we chiefly define ourselves, then we cease to exist when we lose our occupation.

Security comes not only with having a job but also, in this country at least, with the status of one's occupational position. The common expectation is that a good employee will work his or her way up the ladder of success, gaining in wealth and status with every promotion. There is security in the belief that hard work and competence will be rewarded: this is the American Dream. One critic, however, has suggested that our hierarchical occupational structures and systems of job promotion combine to foster *in*competence in the world of work. It is Laurence J. Peter's Principle that "In a hierarchy every employee tends to rise to his level of incompetence." (1969, p. 25) That is, workers in organizations are promoted from a job they do well to the next higher job level, where they are not competent. For example, a good teacher will, because of his or her excellence in the classroom, be promoted to school principal and turn out to be an incompetent administrator. According to Peter, organizations are always staffed by people doing work that is just beyond their level of competence.

Some people do not seek identity, fulfillment, or security in their occupations. All they expect from work is money, and they work only to get

---

EXPLORATIONS
11.7

Occupation

a. Think about what your ideal occupation would be. What is important to you about a job or career? List several of the goals and requirements you seek and put them in order of their priority for you.

b. Now take a realistic look at your work life as you presently see it. Do a history and projection of your occupational life by listing all the important jobs you have ever had, the one(s) you now have, and then project into the future. What kind of work will you probably do for the rest of your career?

For your past and present jobs:

1. List the values, rewards, opportunities for growth, and the development of potential you found or are finding in this type of work.
2. List the drawbacks of these jobs. What do you know you dislike about the jobs you have had?

For the occupation(s) you are considering:

1. What factors led you to choose the occupation you are thinking about? Think of all the possible influences.
2. How well do you know what it is like to work at this occupation? Do you have a realistic or an idealistic picture? What are your sources of information and how reliable are they (counselors, people on the job, your own experience, books, movies, other)?
3. List the advantages of this type of work, including the competencies (skills, abilities, talents) you will develop as well as the pay, status, opportunities, and other rewards.
4. List the disadvantages of your proposed career. What about it will not suit you?
5. How well does your intended career match your ideal career? For instance, if your ideal career involves working with people, does your intended career give you the opportunity? Think of all the ways your plan is like and unlike your ideal.
6. How will this occupation affect how you think, who you meet, where you live, your emotional life, your physical well-being, your life-style in general?
7. When you retire, how do you expect you will feel about having spent a large portion of your life at this occupation?

c. If you had a guaranteed income would you work? Why?

it. To those who value ambition, perseverance, and the pursuit of lofty goals, working just enough to get by is incomprehensible. But those who seek jobs only for the money may find identity, fulfillment, and security in other ways.

Friendships, Interpersonal Relationships, and Social Roles

The work of relating to and interacting with others cuts across many of life's pursuits. This work begins in the family and then shifts into the larger world. We take on family and then social roles, and in both we develop our social competence. We become colleagues, neighbors, friends, and acquaintances, each role requiring distinct social skills. We have a few close relationships, many superficial ones, and vague awareness relationships with thousands. Stanley Milgram estimates that "in a ten-minute walk in midtown Manhattan it's possible to contact (however briefly) 220,000 other humans." (Poland, 1974, p. 2)

Being competent at playing social roles is not the only ability we need in interpersonal relationships. Most interpersonal relationships depend on communication. Competent communication is sending accurately and receiving accurately both verbal and nonverbal messages. Nonverbal communication includes physical distance from others, body orientation (which way we face, how we hold our heads, etc.) and posture, gestures and movement, facial expressions, tone of voice, where and how we touch others, and the clothing we wear. Nonverbal communication is always more ambiguous than verbal communication: one nonverbal expression has many potential meanings. Some of the trouble we have in interpersonal relationships stems from ambiguity and some of it stems from inadequate receiving (listening). Some of the trouble arises because the verbal and nonverbal messages do not agree (as when

Photograph by T. O'Reilly.

someone says "I love you," but never touches the other in a loving way). According to some observers, continual disparity between verbal and nonverbal messages leads to schizophrenic behavior in the receiver (Bateson, 1972).

Many of us, according to Eric Berne, have learned to play interpersonal games with ulterior (hidden) motives. On the surface, the transactions made in the games Berne describes (see Chapter 7) are rational, but they conceal the underlying motive to "prove" one or both players incompetent. The payoff in such games is the reinforcement of a sense of incompetence. For instance, in the following game (Kick Me) the student and instructor conduct a logical transaction, but the payoff is that they confirm the student's lack of competence and worth:

Student: I stayed up too late last night and don't have my assignment ready. (Ulterior: I'm a bad boy, kick me.)
Instructor: You're out of luck. This is the last day I can give credit for that assignment. (Ulterior: Yes, you are a bad boy, and here is your kick.) (James and Jongeward, 1971, p. 30)

EXPLORATION 11.8

Communication

Try these different modes of communication with a partner.
1. Communicate with words alone. Sit back-to-back with your partner making sure that you cannot see or touch each other. Carry on a conversation this way for about five minutes about anything you would like to discuss.
2. Turn around and face each other, but do not touch. Carry on your conversation for another five minutes or so listening, talking, and watching each other.
3. Stop talking and join hands. Now communicate *without* words using sight and touch only. Notice how you feel (Silly? Serious? Frustrated?) The only requirement is that you keep silent for five minutes more.
4. Now review these fifteen minutes of communication. Share how you felt. Were you comfortable? Which mode allowed you to communicate best? To receive best? Did your feelings change as you changed modes?
(Adapted from Adler and Towne, 1975, pp. 200–201.)

Creative Self-Expression

We have the potential to be creative in everything we do. We each experience the world in an individual manner and for the most part behave in a style unique to each of us. But habits in perception, thinking, and behaving have a way of blunting experience and blurring our individuality. We often express our uniqueness in any of a variety of media: words, movement, music, paper and ink, paint, clay, fibers, metals, and so on. However, creative *self-expression* does not always require an audience,

EXPLORATIONS
11.9

**Creative
Self-Expression**

a. What skills have you developed to express yourself creatively? Do you write poetry, sing, dance, play a musical instrument, work with your hands at a craft? How do you feel about your skills, about performing, about what you can say in your medium? Do you sometimes concentrate so intently that you are oblivious to others, or are you always aware of their judgement? How do you feel when you are expressing yourself?

b. Create something. Everyone in class takes a card and creates one or two sentences containing these three words: scramble, charge, rifle.
Sign your card with your signature.
How does what you have just created express YOU? Is there anything characteristic of you in what you have written? Pass your cards around the class. Notice how others have expressed themselves. Does one's use and choice of words represent individuality? Does one's signature? Can you feel OK about your creation without comparing it to others or are you apt to rate your efforts relative to those of others?

nor does it require that we put on a show. Creativity is a process whose value is in the "doing" rather than the "done." It is work with an intangible goal and it is play when we engage in it for the pure pleasure of doing. Self-expression is certainly a serious, lasting concern of life, but it is also an activity which can never be real if we are coerced or forced by someone else to do it. It comes from inside us.

In order to express ourselves in a creative way we often find that we must acquire new skills. We need to make our hands and bodies, and our materials, work for us. The development of this ability can often take years of experience, perseverance, and practice. Perhaps the most frustrating times in life are those when we wish to express something but

National Education Association Publishing, Joe Di Dio.

cannot find the right words, movements, sounds, or shapes. To be able to do so easily and reliably is the reward of practice.

Occasionally we can be creative in our occupations or self-maintenance, but the goal of making money, achieving status, or being finished "on time" can interfere with the process of creativity.

Values and Morality

Values include the spiritual, political, and aesthetic beliefs which govern our behavior. They are frameworks in which we think, act, and feel; they are guides to our decisions and plans. Our personal relationship with a creator and the spiritual universe, our political and social ideologies, and our appreciation of beauty also give us something outside ourselves in which to believe. Of all the work we do in life clarifying our values may be the most serious, the most difficult. And the results may be the most intangible. Values cannot be seen, and sometimes it is difficult to articulate them, yet they are always with us determining what we do. The work of defining values is personal work; we cannot adopt someone else's (like a hand-me-down coat), for values grow out of our own experiences. Those values that we blindly accept from others, without critical evaluation, rarely serve us well.

Morality is a set of ideals by which we judge what is good and bad or right and wrong. Lawrence Kohlberg suggests that moral judgement follows a developmental sequence through life. Each stage in the sequence has a distinct moral orientation. For example, consider the following situation, one of several Kohlberg has used in his research on moral development:

In Europe, a woman was near death from cancer. One drug might save her, a form of radium that a druggist in the same town had recently discovered. The druggist was charging $2,000, ten times what the drug cost him to make. The sick woman's husband, Heinz, went to everyone he knew to borrow the money, but he could only get together about half what it cost. He told the druggist that his wife was dying and asked him to sell it cheaper or to let him pay later. But the druggist said, "No." The husband got desperate and broke into the man's store to steal the drug for his wife. Should the husband have done that? Why? (1969, p. 379)

EXPLORATION 11.10 Values The Rokeach Value Survey (1970, p. 34) is an instrument designed to measure values. Use the following two lists to clarify the importance of (1) the guiding principles in your life and (2) the means whereby these principles might be achieved. For each list, separately, select the value you think most important and write a "1" on the parallel blank. Rank the next most important item "2," and so on, through the list of values. Do the same with the second list. In this exploration you are forced to rank the goals and means in order of their importance to YOU and YOUR life.

Goals	**Means**
1. A World at Peace ____	1. Honest ____
2. Family Security ____	2. Ambitious ____
3. Freedom ____	3. Responsible ____
4. Happiness ____	4. Forgiving ____
5. Self-respect ____	5. Courageous ____
6. Wisdom ____	6. Helpful ____
7. Equality ____	7. Broadminded ____
8. National Security ____	8. Clean ____
9. A Sense of Accomplishment ____	9. Capable ____
10. A Comfortable Life ____	10. Self-controlled ____
11. Salvation ____	11. Loving ____
12. True Friendship ____	12. Cheerful ____
13. Inner Harmony ____	13. Polite ____
14. Mature Love ____	14. Independent ____
15. A World of Beauty ____	15. Intellectual ____
16. Social Recognition ____	16. Logical ____
17. Pleasure ____	17. Obedient ____
18. An Exciting Life ____	18. Imaginative ____

Pick out the three most valued goals and the three most valued means (those with the lowest numbers). How are you living your life as a reflection of your goals? Are the means you have selected as most important qualities or attributes you see yourself developing?

What would the world be like if everyone had the same goals as yours? How do you live your life, day by day, to show what you value most?

In establishing levels of moral development it is important to know why one feels an act is right or wrong; why Heinz should or should not have stolen the drug. (Before reading on, what would your response be?)

These are the stages of moral development set forth by Kohlberg along with examples of the responses to the above problem. (Again, the question is: Should the husband have stolen the drug?)

"No. He would go to jail for stealing."
Stage 1: Orientation to punishment; good is not punished, bad is, and one obeys in order to escape punishment.
"Yes. He needed to save his wife's life so she could cook for him and take care of him."
Stage 2: Orientation to satisfaction of one's needs; good is self-pleasing or gratification.
"Yes. His wife would be proud of him."
Stage 3: A conformity orientation to gain the approval of others and good relations; good is what pleases others.
"No. Stealing is against the law."

Stage 4: Respect for authority to achieve law and order; good is following the rules, doing one's duty, being respectful.

"Yes. The druggist was not being fair so Heinz had to steal."

Stage 5: Orientation according to agreements which groups construct and which bind all parties — the social contract; good is what has been determined by a whole society.

"Yes. A human life is more important than the druggist's profit."

Stage 6: Orientation is a set of self-chosen, abstract ethical principles of justice, respect, and dignity such as the Golden Rule of situation ethics; good is determined by the most ethical or loving thing to do.

EXPLORATION
11.11
Values Clarification

Many situations do not present us with a clear "right" thing to do, feel, or think, particularly unexpected events. Consider the following two vignettes (from Simon, Howe, and Kirschenbaum, 1972, pp. 201 and 203). What *could* you do? What *would* you do? Compare your possible responses with your class. Are there any responses which illustrate one of the six stages of moral development?

1. At a picnic, there is a giant punch bowl. One of the little kids, much to everyone's horror, accidentally drops his whole plate of spaghetti into the punch. What would you do?
2. You're late. Your dad said you had to have the car back by midnight or it would be real trouble for you. Two blocks away from your house, you hit a dog who runs across the street. What would you do?

The manner in which we manifest competence in self-maintenance, learning and education, occupation, interpersonal relationships, creative expression, and values determines our own personal style of living. Through our participation in fun games and life games we grow in competence and realize our potentials. The games may remain the same but how we play them changes as we grow. Changes in life-styles reflect growth and allow us to develop further competencies. There is no end to becoming competent and there is no one unchanging life-style that will allow us to grow.

Just when I think I have learned the way to live, life changes and I am left the same as I began. The more things change the more I am the same. It appears that my life is a constant irony of maturity and regression, but my sense of progress is based on the illusion that things out there are going to remain the same and that, at last, I have gained a little control. But there will never be means to ends, only means. And I am means. I am what I started with, and when it is all over I will be all that is left of me (Prather, 1970, p. 24).

MASTERY

We do not do all things equally well. Some work and play we are content to do adequately; in other cases we are motivated to master the activity. The motive to mastery is a growth motive; it is a wish to do better, to enhance our knowledge, skill, or talent. It is a desire to be more than merely competent. The desire to do things well is a peculiarly human desire; we have the ability to conceptualize or imagine how we can act and the possible results of our actions. We have the ability to experience satisfaction and pleasure in doing.

According to Jerome Kagan (1971), mastery motivation is founded in our uncertainty about whether we can really do what we imagine or hope we can. If we are certain of *either* success or failure, we are not motivated to mastery. Our aspirations must lie within the realm of probability and possibility. With a sense of probable success we know that we can attempt a task without becoming hopelessly frustrated or bored. This sense leads us to differentiate what is too difficult and what is wishful thinking from what is reasonably challenging. We seek to master that which is just slightly beyond our reach. When we expect some possibility of success we are willing to take risks which will stretch our potentials. When we feel too challenged we retreat or become overwhelmed; when we feel too little challenge, we lose interest, begin to err, or quit.

Mastery contributes to our individuality. Part of our identity, our knowledge of ourselves, rests on the particular profile of talents we develop. One way we know we are different from others is by knowing we are better at certain things than they are, and, of course, that others are better than we are at other things! The more unique the skill we choose to master, the more individuality we acquire. Kagan says, "There is

U.S. Geological Survey, Department of the Interior

minimal advantage in acquiring a talent that everyone possesses." (1971, p. 51)

There is an old saying that anything worth doing is worth doing well. Not everything is *worth* mastering. When we believe that what we seek to master is worth our while we can engage in the activity sincerely, genuinely, and honorably. The process of work or play will have meaning for us. If we do not believe that an activity has this utility for us, that it dignifies us, or that we can take pride in the accomplishment, there is not much point in putting out the effort to do it well. "What people really need and demand from life," according to Thomas Szasz, "is not wealth, comfort or esteem but *games worth playing*." (de Ropp, 1968, p. 11) A game worth playing is worth sustained effort and self-discipline. It is worth months or even years of practice and sometimes almost imperceptible improvement. It is worth mastery.

EXPLORATION 11.12

Games Worth Playing

Consider: What are the games worth playing in my life? Of what can you sincerely say, "*This* is worth living for" or "*This* is worthy of *me,* my life, my energy, my risking"?

Now ask: Do I play these games every day? Do I sometimes let other games take my time and energy? Is there any way I can redirect myself or put more into the games I consider worth playing?

Evaluation of Competence

How do we know when we have been competent, or when we have mastered an activity? We measure our performance against a goal or expectation. This goal can be a possibility, a requirement, or a desirable outcome. It can be very clear or somewhat ambiguous. It can be: make it work, do it well, do it perfectly, get the right answer, make it beautiful, get it done, win, enjoy. The goal can be our very own or someone else's expectation of us, or even our expectation of other's expectations. We can judge how well we have done against the performance of others in the same situation, against our past achievements, and against our aspirations.

feedback   The result of comparing performance with a goal is feedback, either negative (we aren't doing or haven't done well) or positive (our performance meets the expectation). Feedback comes from both the process and the product. Process is the doing, product is the outcome or end result. Products give us and others something to judge; they are tangible and "public." *Product feedback* is the basis for deciding success and failure, winning and losing, better or worse. All too often it is the product which leads us to judge our activity as competent or incompetent. If the bread rises, the car runs, the answer is right, the grade is "A," the socks fit, or

Michael Weisbrot   Michael Weisbrot

if the game is won—we feel competent. If not, we have failed. *Process feedback,* in contrast, is intangible and "private." It is the awareness of the experience of doing. For example, process feedback is: the enjoyment of kneading bread dough, procrastinating about changing the spark plugs, the headache while doing a math problem, the satisfaction of working on a paper, starting to knit a pair of socks but never finishing them, the playing of the game. Process feedback can tell us a good deal about our competence, our fears, our goals, and ourselves when we pay attention to it.

SENSE OF COMPETENCE

A sense of competence is the result of repeated experiences of positive feedback. Each activity-feedback sequence in our life contributes its outcome to the rest; its results serve as a "set" for other encounters with aspiration and it becomes part of our self-image. Nobody gets positive feedback from every activity in life, but we can build a reservoir of positive experiences to draw from. A sense of competence is also referred to as self-acceptance, self-esteem, positive self-regard (Carl Rogers) and I'm OK—You're OK (Thomas Harris).

Few of us begin adulthood with a large reservoir of self-confidence. We have been children. By most measures of competence, a child is not as able as the adults around him. Children often learn through observation and from negative feedback that they are not as physically, emotionally, or intellectually competent as adults. According to Thomas Harris, we learn as children to feel I'm Not OK—You're OK; this is a position many of us do not change. Many of us bring this feeling to adulthood. We continue to devalue ourselves by evaluating our competence as less than the competence of others. We feel powerless or helpless. The extreme sense of this position is: "My life is not worth much." The position of self-confidence is I'm OK – You're OK. We come to this view when we make deliberate decisions to value ourselves, to take responsibility for our adulthood, and when we believe in our competence. We then feel "Life is worth living." (James and Jongeward, 1971)

Some of us reach adulthood with a well-developed sense of competence. In researching the antecedents of self-esteem, Stanley Coopersmith found that high self-esteem results from parental acceptance, the setting of limits, and freedom for individual action within those limits (Coopersmith, 1967). Acceptance is an appreciation of who a child (or adult) is independent of what he or she does. Behavior and products are judged without implications as to the worth of the person. Goodness does not depend on good acts, and failures or mistakes do not mean a person is unworthy. Because it is very difficult for children to set their own limits, or to have any realistic notion of what might be possible or appropriate, the child whose parents establish clearly defined and enforced limits has an advantage. He or she has a basis for evaluating performance. As adults we all set our own limits and have our own expectations of ourselves, a process which is much easier if we have had limits as children. Within limits, children (and adults) need to be able to risk and have their efforts respected. There must be equal room for success and failure.

How can we come to a sense of competence even though we fail? One way is to focus on our processes rather than our products. Another is to refuse to give the power of evaluation totally to others. A third is to make positive use of negative feedback.

negative feedback

Focus on the process   Over and over we are told that it is the playing of the game, not the winning, that counts, but we know very well from many experiences that winning *does* count. It is also true that *how we play* is important to how we feel about ourselves and to the satisfaction we get from an activity. An orientation that ignores process awareness in favor of product awareness is analogous to dying without having lived. Awareness of process lets us know in what ways we are competent. One can get an "A" on a biology exam by knowing biology or by cheating; the product is the same. In the one case we are competent in biology (or taking biology tests), in the other we are competent at cheating, and it is perhaps helpful to be able to know the difference (even if the biology teacher doesn't).

Evaluating ourselves   Many times we rely on others to evaluate our competence. We had to do so as children and we continue to do so as adults. It is difficult for anyone else to evaluate accurately *how* we do something (the process). Usually all they can judge is the product.

Others may not use the same criteria of success that we do. No matter what the response of others to our work (for others cannot judge play), whether it is silence, rejection, praise, equivocation, or encouragement, we are in a position of I'm not OK – You're OK when their power to judge is greater than ours. Kagan says, "Perhaps psychological maturity should be defined as that time in life when a person has established such a well-articulated understanding of himself that he can decide on the quality or morality of an action *without showing it to anyone or comparing it with the actions of others.* A few fortunate adults come close to attaining this precious state; most do not." (1971, p. 51, italics added)

Using negative feedback   Negative feedback is essential for change. As long as we get positive feedback we continue doing the same thing that produced it. Positive feedback contributes to our sense of competence and it feels *good.* We need it. Negative feedback rarely feels so good but we also need it in order to improve both *what* we do and *how* we do it. We can find out what went wrong and have the option of correcting ourselves. Failures broke the trail for every scientific discovery made in history. The success of science is due in large measure to a method which does not ignore error or negative results. Negative feedback from the process is as important to competence as a negative outcome. Procrastination, headaches, high anxiety, and apathy are examples of negative process feedback. These states can signal that somehow the goal is not right. Perhaps there is not enough challenge. Perhaps we have taken someone else's expectations or aspirations for us as though they were our own. Perhaps we don't feel our activity is a worthy game. Negative feedback gives us the chance to examine our motivation and our techniques of work and to understand why the process is uncomfortable.

However instructive it is to discuss the value of failure and the necessity of negative feedback, in the "real world" rejection, fear of failure, anxiety, depression, guilt, shame, and all the other emotions which can accompany failure are potential contributors to a sense of incompetence. These emotions can be powerful and continual supports to a lack of self-acceptance. They can also be merely temporary states with no power to erode our foundation of positive self-regard, if that foundation is solid.

Even when we fail we can know that *we are not failures* if we

believe in the worth of what we do
choose realistic aspirations
make the doing as valuable as the outcome
make a deliberate decision to feel life is worth living
judge for ourselves the quality of our work and the pleasure of our play

A sense of competence allows us to risk, to venture into the uncertain, and to accept the challenge and possibility of success and of failure.

<table>
<tr>
<td>

EXPLORATION
11.13
Sense
of
Competence

</td>
<td>

Consider several areas of important activity in your life right now. Answer these questions:

(*Process*): *What* am I doing? How do I feel when doing _____? What can I know about myself from the way I approach this task, the way I execute it? Do I like being sloppy, neat, orderly, vigorous, active, deliberate, thorough, quick? Do I like the way I am when I am doing _____? Do I feel good? Do I feel angry, irritated, resentful, peaceful, intense, absorbed? What activities do I do *just to do* them (not to finish, win, get something)?

(*Evaluation*): Of what can you honestly say: "I am satisfied with what I do"? Do I *need* others' evaluations? Are their judgements about my work more important than my own? Is it OK for me to make mistakes? Not to do everything "just right"? Do I escape responsibility and activity by telling myself I just can't help it, nothing is my fault? Do I have many good intentions that never become good deeds? Is it OK to try?

(*Negative feedback*): The next time you get negative feedback ask yourself: How can I use this feedback to grow, to become more competent? If I paid more attention instead of ignoring or disregarding negative feedback, becoming angry or defensive, how could I improve? (Be aware that not all feedback is useful for improving competence. Hearing that you are a poor speller, for example, is not as helpful as knowing which word is misspelled.)

</td>
</tr>
</table>

MAXIMIZING COMPETENCE

> God grant me the serenity to accept the things I cannot change,
> Courage to change the things I can,
> And wisdom to know the difference.
>
> Reinhold Niebuhr

Becoming more competent, achieving mastery, and a sense of competence are realized in diverse ways. Sometimes we seek improvement in a single skill; sometimes we desire to be more competent in a particular area of life, such as social relationships; at other times we need to completely reorient our self-concept to allow ourselves a sense of competence. The goal will, of course, determine which method is most effective. Below are only a few examples of techniques, both general and specific, which are used in the promotion of competence.

behavior modification   ***Behavior modification***   These techniques change behavior by manipulation of reinforcements so that the individual can lead a more competent life. Three types of behavior modification are:

1. Desensitization—the process of gradually eliminating fear or strong negative emotional reaction to situations. Another response can then be substituted.
2. Aversion therapy—the process of creating a strong negative reaction which will prevent unwanted habitual behavior such as drinking, smoking, or muscle tics. (Aversion therapy is essentially opposite to desensitization.)
3. Shaping behavior—the use of positive reinforcements to create new behavior patterns and to increase competence.

Behavior modification is successful in altering some kinds of unwanted behavior patterns. It has the advantage of being a briefer treatment than many traditional psychotherapies, with which it is sometimes used. A good resource is Albert Bandura, *Principles of Behavior Modification* (New York: Holt, Rinehart and Winston, 1969).

psychosomatic

Psychosomatic approaches   Many techniques for improving competence are approaches that, in theory and practice, are based on the recognition that the mind and the body are not separate.

One of the oldest practices taking this holistic view is Yoga, specifically Hatha Yoga, which is concerned with the physical aspect of well-being. It is basically a series of movements, postures (called *asanas*), and breathing exercises. A practical and instructive book is Richard Hittleman *Introduction to Yoga* (New York: Bantam Books, 1969).

Two theoretically similar systems of therapy are Reichian therapy and Bio-Energetics, both relying on the theories of Wilhelm Reich, who was a radical disciple of Freud's. Reich felt that psychological repression and political suppression were manifest in body tension and blocked energy. Many of his ideas have been incorporated in Bio-Energetics, a form of therapy designed to release trapped tension. An interesting analysis of Reich's thinking is *Salvation Through Sex: The Life and Work of Wilhelm Reich* by Eustace Chesser (New York: Morrow, 1973). The best known works on Bio-Energetics are by Alexander Lowen, specifically *The Betrayal of the Body* (New York: Collier Books, 1967).

Another related approach is Structural Integration or *Rolfing* (after Ida Rolf, its creator). This is a method of deep-muscle manipulation and body realignment. It works to remove postural and muscular tension resulting from years of accumulated stress. Other body-reformation methods are the Alexander technique (developed by Dr. F. M. Alexander) and Polarity therapy, pioneered by Dr. Randolph Stone.

Of course there are many ways to improve well-being by keeping physically fit. Jogging, bicycling, massage, relaxation techniques, breathing therapy, and sensory awareness techniques are among the many approaches to increasing physical competence. Some of these techniques are practiced in groups, some individually. Many are most beneficial when practiced regularly, even daily.

There has been recent widespread interest in techniques known gen-

biofeedback

erally as biofeedback. This is the term given to the use of electronic instruments to amplify and report changes in body functioning which usually escape notice and were previously considered beyond voluntary control: heartbeat, blood pressure, muscle tension, brain waves, and so on. With information (feedback) it is now known that we can quickly learn to modify these functions, thus actively participating in the reduction of bodily manifestations of anxiety and stress. A comprehensive resource is Barbara Brown, *New Mind, New Body — Biofeedback: New Directions for the Mind* (New York: Harper & Row, 1975).

Reevaluation approaches   There are several similar, but essentially unrelated, types of therapy with the goal of reorienting self-evaluation.

Alfred Adler (an early associate of Freud's) was one of the first personality theorists to note psychological difficulties stemming from feelings of inferiority. Adlerian-based therapy is aimed at reducing feelings of helplessness through the development of realistic self-appraisal and a sense of competence. One of Adler's best known works is *What Life Should Mean to You* (New York: Putnam, 1959).

The therapy of Albert Ellis stresses the problems created by our inability to live up to impossible standards. Rational-emotive therapy, as Ellis calls his approach, is aimed at the formulation of more realistic and attainable goals and encourages the formation of rational living patterns. A statement of Ellis' approach is in *Reason and Emotion in Psychotherapy* (New York: Lyle Stuart, 1962).

Reality therapy, developed by William Glasser, encourages one to assess current behavior, critically evaluate it, and make realistic plans for change. Therapy is directed toward increased self-competence. For more, refer to *Reality Therapy* by William Glasser (New York: Harper & Row, 1970).

Three other programs which lead to increased competence are:

Assertiveness Training: teaches how we can claim our legitimate rights without hostility or disregard for others. Assertiveness is a key to avoiding the oppression of passivity and the oppressiveness of aggression. See R.E. Alberti and Michael Emmons, *Your Perfect Right* (2d ed.) (San Luis Obispo, Ca: IMPACT, 1974).

Parent Effectiveness Training: A technique developed by Thomas Gordon (*Parent Effectiveness Training.* New York: Peter H. Wyden, Inc., 1970) for improving communication between parents and their children. Parents are encouraged to use active listening and to send "I . . ." statements to their children. The goal is competent parents who will help children build a sense of competence for themselves.

Values Clarification: This is a systematic approach to the process of valuing. Its objective is to help students become aware of their feelings and beliefs so that choices and decisions are based on conscious value systems. A book of exercises designed for individuals is *Meeting Yourself Half Way: 31 Values Clarification Strategies for Daily Living* by Sidney B. Simon (Niles, Ill.: Argus Communications, 1974).

Educational and vocational counseling Educational counseling in high schools and colleges is sometimes limited to guidance in scheduling classes. But many college counselors are trained to deal with a range of learning, personal, and emotional problems and are specialists in vocational counseling. Counseling often includes (1) assessment of the counselee's personality, ability, aptitude, and vocational interests, (2) information about various vocations such as the type of work involved, education and training requirements, and the job market, and (3) help in setting goals and decision-making. Most colleges and universities provide free or low-cost educational and vocational counseling to students as part of their student services. If you have not already done so, find out about the counseling department on your campus. Many students are surprised at the wide range of services offered.

Nonprofessional self-help groups There are a number of groups which rely on the supportive aid of members to maintain competence in surmounting particular problems. The model for some of these groups is Alcoholics Anonymous, which has been successful in curbing drinking problems. Other groups based on this model—those who "have been there" helping others—are: Synanon, for drug-related problems; Weight Watchers, for overeaters; Parent's Anonymous, for potential child abusers, and Delancey Street, for former drug users and ex-convicts. Two interesting books are: *Tunnel Back: Synanon* by Lewis Yablonsky (New York: Macmillan, 1965) and *Sane Asylum: The Dramas of Delancey Street* by Charles Hampden-Turner (San Francisco: San Francisco Book Co., 1976).

SUMMARY

1. The ability to maintain ourselves, grow, and realize our potentials is competence. We have physical, emotional, and intellectual abilities, all of which together contribute to how well we perform. To be physically competent we need to develop physical skills and to take care of our bodies. To be emotionally competent we need to be aware of emotional states and to control the expression of our feelings. Intellectual competence is the ability to acquire and make use of knowledge.

2. Most of our activities are games. Fun games (play) are those which we engage in for pleasure. Life games (work) have a purpose. Among life games are:

    self-maintenance — being self-sufficient

    learning and education — the life-long process of change and the acquisition of knowledge of our culture

    occupation — producing something of value in return for rewards

    friendships and interpersonal relationships — communicating and relating with others

    creative self-expression — expressing who we are through our activities

    values and morality — defining what we believe in; what is good and right

3. Mastery goes beyond competence: it is the ability to do well that which we feel worth doing.

4. Competence is evaluated by comparing performance to a goal or expectation. This comparison results in feedback. Feedback can be positive or negative.

5. Product feedback is based on the outcome of our work. Products can be judged by self and by others. Process feedback is the experience of doing. Process usually is not judged by others, only by oneself.

6. A sense of competence comes from repeated experiences with positive feedback. It is a feeling of confidence in ability and high self-esteem. It is a reservoir of positive self-regard.

7. We increase our sense of competence, even when we are not perfect, by:

    focusing on the process, on how it feels to do what we do

    assuming responsibility for judging and evaluating ourselves

    paying attention to and using negative feedback in order to change

8. Ways of maximizing competence include behavior modification, physical fitness and body therapies, reevaluation therapies, vocational and educational counseling, and nonprofessional group support.

Suggested Readings

Deacon, Joseph John. *Joey*. New York: Scribner, 1974. The autobiography of a man with cerebral palsy. Joey, born in 1920, has never walked or talked. The only person who can understand him is his friend, Ernie, who cannot read or write. Ernie listened to Joey's story and repeated it to Michael, who wrote it and repeated it, letter by letter, to Tom. Tom learned to type and produced the manuscript at the rate of 4 to 6 lines a day. A monument to the human potential for transcending handicaps and to the possibilities of cooperative effort.

Langer, Ellen J. and Dweck, Carol S. *Personal politics: The psychology of making it*. Englewood Cliffs, N.J.: Prentice-Hall, 1973. Suggestions for increasing competence by examining one's approaches to situations, improving skills in obtaining and using information, and gaining control over self and the situation.

Luce, Gay Gaer. *Body time*. New York: Bantam, 1973. A book about the role of biological time cycles in human behavior. Reviews experimental work and suggests the importance of attending to bio-rhythms in explaining and arranging our lives.

Samuels, Michael and Bennett, Harold. *The well body book*. New York: Random House and Berkeley, Ca.: The Bookworks, 1973. A demystification of the practice of medicine, including sections on the diagnosis and treatment of disease, and practical suggestions for keeping the body in a state of well-being.

Toffler, Alvin. *Future shock*. New York: Random House, 1970. Change is occurring at an unprecedented rate in our society. Familiar social cues to behavior are lost, leading to disorientation, dislocation, and an inability to deal competently with the world.

Williams, Robert L. and Long, James D. *Toward a self-managed life style*. Boston: Houghton Mifflin, 1975. A practical guide to the use of behavior modification techniques for increasing competence in health, sports, studying, career planning, and interpersonal relationships.

"Time is a River Without Banks" (1930-39), Chagall.

12

THE QUEST FOR UNBOUNDEDNESS

To see a world in a grain of sand
And a heaven in a wild flower,
Hold infinity in the palm of your hand
And eternity in an hour.
William Blake
(*Auguries of Innocence*)

As children our conscious experience of the world is not bound by the many restrictions a grown-up life brings. As we have seen in Chapter 4, a child's consciousness has not yet been confined to the limits of ordinary states of consciousness. But as adults most of us are bound—the nature of our experience conforms to ordinary reality. Certain of our potentials for consciousness have been developed; others seem to have been neglected at least in present-day Western life. Ronald Laing comments:

As adults, we have forgotten most of our childhood, not only its contents but its flavor; as men of the world, we hardly know the existence of the inner world: we barely remember our dreams, and make little sense of them when we do; . . . Our capacity to think, except in the service of what we are dangerously deluded in supposing is our self-interest and in conformity with common sense, is pitifully limited: our capacity even to see, hear, touch, taste and smell is so shrouded in veils of mystification that an intensive discipline of unlearning is necessary for *anyone* before one can begin to experience the world afresh, with innocence, truth and love (1967, p. 26).

The limits of the human potential to experience varying states of consciousness are unknown. It is known that experience is limited by the way we live, think, and by what we expect consciousness to be. There is increasing evidence that over-controlling, in order to stay within the confines of ordinary consciousness, is as destructive as are some of the means by which we alter body chemistry in order to escape reality.

There is no obvious reason why one should spend his lifetime solely in the two traditional mind-states: the problem-solving conscious state and the "recovery" sleep state. Most of us, in fact, wander off the narrow path and spend time in free-association (wool-gathering), browsing through our memories, and enjoying flights of fantasy; . . . So our reduction of human existence into an alteration of consciousness and unconsciousness—waking and sleeping—is a local (Western) oversimplification.

There are other modes of conscious and subconscious experience which can enrich our lives; and on the condition that they do not rob us of our sanity or endanger others, there is no valid reason why they should not be known (Christian, 1973, p. 174).

In this chapter we consider these questions:

What is ordinary consciousness?
What is nonordinary consciousness?
What are the consequences of being bound in ordinary consciousness?
How and when can consciousness be altered?
Why are some means to reaching altered states of consciousness preferable to other means?

Consciousness can be likened to a house of several rooms. Each room in this house differs from the next in access, furnishings, and mood. Each has windows offering a unique view of the world. In *The Master Game*,

Robert de Ropp suggests that some of these rooms are secret. They are "vast chambers full of treasures with windows looking out on eternity and infinity. Man does not enter these rooms, or does so only rarely. They are locked. He has lost the key." (1968, p. 30)

The quest for unboundedness is the search for the key, the means to enter our secret rooms. We search for the ability to move at will and with ease throughout our "house." When we can do this, we are freed to use our entire being instead of remaining confined in a single, narrow, stuffy, corner of it. A "bound" life is lived in one room. The walls of this room are the boundaries of our awareness or consciousness as these have been erected and reinforced by our experience. Sometimes we are comfortable in a single room, sometimes intimations of what lies beyond make it a prison.

HUMAN POTENTIALS: STATES OF CONSCIOUSNESS

Nature decrees that we alternate periodically between waking and sleeping states. This alternation is necessary for biological survival. During sleep our awareness is greatly reduced from what it is during wakefulness. Relatively speaking, we experience so little during sleep that many people claim they experience nothing at all. It is now known, however, that everyone dreams every night—not all night long, but at fairly regular intervals throughout the night, about every 1½ hours. Along with sleeping, dreaming seems to be a biological necessity. It has been found that during dreams the brain repairs and restores itself. It has also been found that people deprived of dream periods experience irritability and anxiety. If one has been deprived of dreaming for a night, the chances are that the brain will make up for lost dreams the next night (Calder, 1970).

Photograph by R. Dian.

Dreams are elusive. We don't recall them easily, accurately, or sometimes at all. They are the stuff of another room, and memories of them are seldom carried intact across the borders of wakefulness. Dreaming belongs to an altered state of consciousness. Dreaming and the remembrance of it are often blocked by everyday, ordinary consciousness.

Most of our waking hours are known through "ordinary" consciousness. Later on this will be considered in greater detail, but for now ordinary consciousness can be described as the experience of making sense of the world. This is the state of mind we are in as we try to communicate with others, as we try to organize our experiences such that they can be understood by someone who has not had them firsthand. Although most of the time we are aware in an ordinary way, every so often we experience phenomena that resemble our dream consciousness. Here are some rather common examples of "nonordinary" consciousness which many of us have experienced:

Déjà vu (literally "already seen"): In a new situation, the feeling that one has been here before, although there is no way rationally to account for the familiarity. One explanation for *déjà vu* is that we experienced the situation in a former life or incarnation. Another, more plausible explanation is that there are enough familiar elements in the new situation that we generalize the familiarity over the entire scene.

Highway hypnosis: Driving along a stretch of monotonous highway; nothing interesting to distract one's attention; the steady hum of the motor and the drone of the wheels; sunlight filling the car with warmth: suddenly we return with a start from some other world and slam on the brake or twist the steering wheel sharply, hopefully soon enough to avoid a collision.

Hypnogogic states: States of transition between wakefulness and sleep. Voluntary control of consciousness is extremely difficult to maintain as attention drifts. Sometimes there is a kaleidoscopic turning of fragments of voices, visions, and thoughts. We may not be aware of this state, though we always pass through it on the way to sleep. This state can sometimes be experienced attending dull lecture classes right after lunch.

Strong emotional states: Strong emotions can lead to altered states of consciousness. One is panic. Reasoning completely deserts us, we are paralyzed by visions of disaster, and feel completely out of control. While in a state of panic I have become so detached that I was able to look at myself as though I were another person whom I could not control. Another emotional path to nonordinary consciousness is in the profound esthetic experience that sometimes occurs while listening to music or viewing a work of art or scene of nature.

Orgasm: As sexual excitement builds, awareness often narrows to exclude extraneous noise and shifts to distort our sense of time. Orgasm can trigger inner visual experiences such as vivid images or colors.

Fever: As the body reaches temperatures of over 103 degrees one may experience hallucinations and disengagement from the body. "Real" reality becomes indistinguishable from made-up reality. Control over thinking and experiencing is difficult.

"Aha" experiences: Brief moments of sudden insight or illumination are sometimes experienced when we let go of a problem with which we have been struggling. Such insight can also come during hypnogogic and sleep states.

Not everyone experiences altered states of consciousness such as these, but many people do. There will be a more complete discussion of nonordinary consciousness later on, but for now notice that in each of these examples the state is brief, transitory, and unexpected (that is, to a large extent, uncontrollable).

EXPLORATION 12.1 Altered States of Consciousness   Recall and describe a recent altered state of consciousness which you have experienced. What was it like? How much of it can you remember? Share with others in your class. How much variety is there in experiences?

ORDINARY CONSCIOUSNESS

Ordinary consciousness is the familiar shape we impose on our experience to make it understandable. If we did not make some sense of our experience the world would seem a jumble of chaotic, unrelated sensations. It takes a long time to put the world in order; we work at it for most of our childhood years and even into adulthood. Although our experience never becomes fully comprehensible, we are usually able to manage it with the habits that develop during our long training. We repeat the same mental and perceptual processes over and over again until they are strong enough to bend even the most uncommon experience into familiar shape. To revert to our metaphor of a house, over the years we build sturdy walls around the room of ordinary consciousness. (Beyond these walls are nonhabitual modes of experiencing.) We then see the world only as it is revealed to us in an ordinary light.

We construct reality. Very briefly, this is how we do it:

data reduction   ***Data reduction*** Every waking moment, a great number of forces (or energies) impress themselves on us. Light, smells, sound, taste, gravity, fatigue, memory, hunger, and so on — all are within the range of our attention. Our immediate problem is to reduce to manageable proportions the number and kind of stimuli that could be input for our system. What is important to us must be sorted out, selected, and distinguished from what is not important. Importance may change from moment to moment, by the hour, daily, or more slowly. A stop sign is not important to a four-year-old, who may therefore not even see it. The muffled noise upstairs is not important to the downstairs tenant, who is absorbed in a book. One notices many tasty items at the grocery store when shopping on an empty stomach, items that do not seem to exist when one shops right after dinner.

The operation of our sensory and nervous systems provides for some sifting of input. The brain, for example, responds to *changes* in intensity or quality of stimulation. If the energy level or form of a stimulus does not change, the stimulus soon disappears from our awareness. This process is called habituation. Habituation can affect any of our senses. I noticed few birds until an enthusiastic friend called my attention to them. Before that they were as invisible as the gravel in the driveway and as noiseless as the highway that hums incessantly near my home. But once my input of bird shape, sound, color, and so on was intensified, my brain registered the change, and I now see them everywhere. The same process is at work when you learn that the radio has been on only when someone turns it off, and background noise becomes silence.

Data reduction is accomplished also by the limits of our sense receptors (located in the eyes, ears, nose, etc.). Each receptor has a range beyond which it cannot detect stimulation or change. Our visual system, for example, responds to only a narrow band of the energy waves in the electromagnetic spectrum, that is, to visible light waves. We cannot see X-rays, gamma rays, or radio or TV waves, even though these forms of energy surround us.

Brain direction   A large part of sifting or filtering information is done under the direction of the brain. Since the nervous system can cope with only limited amounts of information at one time, the brain acts as a director of our experience. It is continuously making decisions about where attention is to be focused, which stimuli should be highlighted, where there should be silence (nonreception). The brain does this even while we sleep, so that a mother may sleep through a thunderstorm but will wake the moment her baby starts crying several rooms away. Under the brain's direction, the various sense organs collect data and pass it on to the higher centers of the nervous system. As it is passed along nerve channels information is further refined, filtered, and changed. By the time it reaches the cortex (the central processing area of the brain) it has been stripped down and coded into electrochemical energy.

Meaning   By processes not yet fully understood, incoming information is put in order, classified, and integrated by the cortex. In some way new information is matched with information already in storage in the brain. When a match is made, that is, when the new information fits, it *means* something to us. If there is no fit, if there is nothing in the brain's storage

habituation

long-term memory

which matches, the new information seems simply to disappear. The storage in the brain has been called long-term memory. Long-term memory contains memories in the form of concepts, language and mathematical symbols, expectations, and other categories. Some concepts we have in common with other members of our culture; some are the unique result of individual experience. Some concepts are specific and precise, others are general and vague.

EXPLORATION 12.2

Concepts

Rather complex concepts are often called to mind by a single word or some other symbol. Think, for example, of everything you could say about the animal symbolized by the word *dog*, or about the position indicated in the phrase *in front of*. For each of the following symbols write down the first thing that comes to mind. (Do one at a time without looking ahead.)

1. +   10. □
2. −   11. △
3. ÷   12. 12
4. ×   13. ß
5. #   14. 14
6. A   15. ( )
7. ß   16. "
8. C   17. –
9. 0

Compare your responses with those of others in your class. Did anyone write "ex" for #4? For #5 did you write "number" or "pounds?" How many of you wrote "zero" for #9 and how many "Oh"? Did anyone see the symbol for #7 as the same as that for #13? What about #2 and #17?

How would you explain or justify your responses if you were called on to do so? What were the contexts in which you placed the symbols in order to get one meaning rather than another?

There are many complex factors that determine which concept will be activated and therefore what the meaning of a stimulus will be. Long-term memory is similar to a vast, idiosyncratic, instant-access library of concepts, the organization of which is not entirely understood. Some psychologists believe that "experience" is composed of the activation process and the resulting concept, not of a thing or event outside ourselves.

Experience Takes Place in the Brain

Consciousness is a personal construction to which stimuli, brain functions, and previous experience all contribute. The process takes place in the brain with such rapidity and so habitually that we cannot recognize that anything is happening at all. The same process works in ordinary consciousness as in nonordinary consciousness. From this perspective, you can see that the act of living is one of continuously "making up your mind."

Human beings experience in a very adaptable way. We can control experience so that there is, usually, a minimum amount of confusion in our lives. Independent of the order or chaos which exists in the world, we *impose* an order and meaning on it. Thus the world comes to be predictable and manageable. Because we are able to be selective in our awareness we do not need to respond to every stimulating thing in our environment. The human brain selects, according to our needs, what to pay attention to. We can shut out irrelevancies as we strive to reach our goals, both momentary and long-term.

Most of the time our experience is accurate, our constructions are well-grounded in reality. We can be aware of both ourselves and of that which is outside ourselves, and we can keep the two separate. Even though an experience occurs in the nervous system (primarily in our brain), we can point to those elements of the experience which exist in our environment.

We usually share this outside reality with others. The concepts with which we organize information are largely shared concepts. Other people use the same words, symbols, and ideas that we do and, as a result of many years of communicating, we come to know the same world others know. In fact, we come to assume that others are experiencing the same way we are, but, as we all know, this assumption often proves to be mistaken.

THE CHARACTERISTICS OF ORDINARY CONSCIOUSNESS

Ordinary consciousness is a function of culture. Some cultures define "ordinary" experience differently than do others. For instance, it is "normal" to experience ghosts in some cultures, but not in contemporary Western cultures. Our culture discourages us from forming the concept of "ghost" because our scientific ways of knowing have not established the existence of ghosts. We instead must try to match ghostly experiences with some other scientific explanation—eyestrain or trickery, for example.

Ordinary consciousness has these qualities:

1. *Object-centered.* We strive to be objective and realistic in our experiencing. Scientific thinking requires that we strive to experience ourselves separate from what we observe in our environments.

2. *Reality is based on sensory information.* What is "real" to us is what can be touched, seen, heard, tasted, smelled. We believe in the existence of that which can be documented by our senses or, preferably, by

an instrument such as a camera or tape recorder. We are skeptical of unproven phenomena such as UFOs, ESP, abominable snowmen, or reincarnation.

3. *Analytical.* We look for the differences among things, discriminate this from that. We break processes, systems, ideas, down into steps or parts. We tend to classify and organize things into groups according to similarities and differences.

4. *Reason and logic.* We use both inductive thinking and deductive thinking. In the first, we formulate general rules from our observations of particular instances. In the second, we start with a notion of general applicability and against this we measure particular instances for their logicality or illogicality.

5. *Linearity.* We experience one idea or process after another, sequentially; they do not occur simultaneously. We are trained to express our ideas in complete sentences of subjects and predicates. Time is taken as linear: the past precedes the present, which is followed by the future. Events happen "before" and "after." We impose cause-effect sequences in explaining things (this happens *because* that happened).

6. *Controlling experience.* We tend to regulate our experience so that it does not deviate widely from the reported experience of others. We seek experiencing which is communicable and which others have described to us. We often strive for predictability and seek to minimize surprises.

In 1890, the psychologist William James noted the strength of ordinary consciousness and commented on the potentials we have for nonordinary experiencing:

Our normal waking consciousness, rational consciousness as we call it, is but one special type of consciousness, whilst all about it, parted from it by the filmiest of screens, there lie potential forms of consciousness entirely different. We may go through life without suspecting their existence; but apply the requisite stimulus,

William James (*Library of Congress Photograph*).

and at a touch they are there in all their completeness, definite types of mentality which probably somewhere have their field of application and adaptation. No account of the universe in its totality can be final which leave these other forms of consciousness quite disregarded. How to regard them is the question—for they are so discontinuous with ordinary consciousness. Yet they may determine attitudes though they cannot furnish formulas, and open a region though they fail to give a map. At any rate, they forbid a premature closing of our accounts with reality (1950, pp. 288–89).

EXPLORATION 12.3

Ordinary Consciousness as a Construction

Break the class up into groups of 5 or 6. Each group goes out into the campus or nearby neighborhood for a half-hour's observation. You'll want to pick a spot where there is considerable activity, such as the student lounge or a playground, perhaps another classroom. Each member of a group takes detailed notes of what he or she sees during the half-hour, or writes them out immediately after. Along with sights, note thoughts that cross your mind, events that caught your attention, sounds, times when your mind wandered. Now, compare your notes with those of others in your group. What did each of you see in the same spot? Did everyone experience the same reality?

CHARACTERISTICS OF NONORDINARY CONSCIOUSNESS

William James' problem of how to regard nonordinary consciousness is still with us. Neither centuries of experiencing, nor many notable poetic and scientific descriptions, nor contemporary interest in nonordinary consciousness, have brought us totally satisfactory understanding. Much of the difficulty lies in the fact that we must use processes of ordinary consciousness (language, analysis, experiment, etc.) to examine something which, by its very nature, is probably beyond the reach of these approaches. Nevertheless, attempts to understand continue, and the results of these attempts will be the subject of this section.

Although nonordinary states of consciousness take diverse forms, they all seem to share a common origin, arising spontaneously as we stop trying to make the world make sense. When we are able to give up or unlearn our habits of ordinary consciousness, we can experience a qualitative shift in our patterns of mental activity. Sidney Jourard says, "I believe that anything which ends a searching, striving attitude toward the world triggers off an alteration in all modes of experiencing, even when the objective state of the world has not changed." (1974, p. 49)

Many of the following characteristics define states of nonordinary consciousness (from Ludwig, 1969):

1. *Alterations in thinking.* There are, in contrast to ordinary consciousness, disturbances in judgement, concentration, attention, and

"The Persistence of Memory" (1931), Dali.

memory. Reality ceases to be real, there is less reliance on objective reality. The distinction between cause and effect is blurred. The world does not have to behave according to physical laws such as that of gravity.

2. *The sense of time is disturbed.* The experience of time is altered so that it may bear little relation to clock time. Time may come to a standstill, accelerate greatly, or slow down. Chronology and the order of past, present, and future become unimportant.

3. *Experience of control is altered.* Sometimes there are feelings of impotency and helplessness, of losing self-control and one's grip on reality. There may be, on the other hand, a sense of greater control or power. There may be a sense of having conquered the world.

4. *Changes in emotional expression.* Here emotion does not have to be logical. It can be sudden and unexpected and unexplained. Laughter, crying, anger, fear, depression, joy, ecstasy, and other strong emotions may be experienced in the extreme and without inhibition. There also may be an emotional detachment or a lack of any emotional display.

5. *Body image change.* Various parts of the body may become distorted, larger, heavier, shrunken, weightless, disconnected, or otherwise "strange." Sensations such as dizziness, numbness, or tingling may be experienced. There may be a schism between the mind and the body such that one is able to stand outside the body observing oneself. There can be a dissolution of the boundaries between one's self and others, the world, or the universe, until a sense of oneness with all is reached.

6. *Perceptual distortion.* Sizes, shapes, textures, luminosity, and patterns of things and sounds may change. Imagery may be profoundly increased. Sensory experience—sound, smell, taste—can be sharpened or distorted. Sometimes we refer to these perceptual distortions as hallucinations, if they do not occur during sleep.

7. *Change in significance.* The trivial can become monumental in meaning. There may be an experience of great insight, illumination, or truth. This is an emotional experience which may or may not bear a rela-

tionship to "objective" truth. For example, under the influence of nitrous oxide, William James came to an ultimate "truth." He scrawled it down and eagerly read it on his return to ordinary consciousness. Here is his profound revelation (de Ropp, 1968, p. 62):

> Hogamous, Higamous,
> Man is polygamous.
> Higamous, Hogamous,
> Woman is monogamous.

8. *Indescribability.* There is often an inability to communicate the nature of the experience to others who have not shared it or a similar experience. There may be slight to total amnesia.

9. *Hypersuggestibility.* There sometimes seems to be an uncritical acceptance of commands, suggestions, or instructions. There may also be a tendency to interpret situations according to inner fears or wishes.

10. *Renaissance.* Occasionally one experiences rejuvenation, the feeling of having been reborn with a new sense of hope.

EXPLORATION 12.4 A Mind Game

(This exploration is an adaptation of one of the first of an ordered series of steps to altered states of consciousness in *Mind Games: The Guide to Inner Space,* by Robert Masters and Jean Houston, 1972. The rest of the mind games, taken in the order Masters and Houston have presented them, will help you to reach new levels of awareness.)

Do not do this exploration under the influence of any mind-altering drug. First, do the relaxation exercise in Chapter 1. Then have someone read the following to you slowly and evenly. Concentrate fully on the words you hear and on what you experience. If at any time you wish to return to ordinary consciousness, merely open your eyes.

You are having a dream, one you have had many times before. You are in a small room. There is a closed door at the far end. As you walk toward it, the door opens for you and you pass through. You are standing at the head of a stone staircase.

The staircase is ancient and winding down and around. You begin going down one step at a time, eager to go down in the dim light. You descend, deeper and deeper to the bottom, where you find a pool of water gently lapping the bottom step. There is a small boat waiting. Now, lying on the bottom of the boat, wrapped in blankets, you drift into blackness, rocking gently from the motion of the water. The boat drifts down, down as you feel the gentle rocking motion, back and forth. You listen to the soft water noises. Gradually the boat passes out of the darkness into warm sunlight.

You float downstream in the warmth, feeling a soft breeze, hearing the birds sing, smelling the fragrance of the flowers lining the bank. You feel a great contentment, serenity, and drowsiness. Gently you drift on, down and down. Be aware of all your sensations as you drift.

Your boat gradually approaches the shore and runs smoothly aground. You leave the boat and walk up the bank to a large tree. Sit there now, under the tree, and hear the birds, feel the sun, smell the air. You are in total harmony with this gentle world.

Feel yourself relaxed. Your body is totally relaxed and heavy. You are becoming heavier and heavier, very, very heavy, so heavy you cannot move, so relaxed you cannot move.

Now the heaviness begins to lift; you begin to feel lighter and lighter. You are your normal weight, and you continue to become lighter and lighter. You are as light as a feather. You are so light you can feel yourself rising just a little above the ground. You are floating in air a few inches above the ground. Slowly you settle back down once again.

You feel pleasant and refreshed. You are totally aware of your body now. You find, to your surprise, that you are growing smaller and smaller. You are shrinking as Alice did when she drank from the bottle in Wonderland. You are 4 feet tall, 3, and now 2 feet tall. Now you are only a foot, and then 6 inches tall.

Feel how it is to be half a foot tall, look about you from side to side and up to the sky.

You notice that you are now getting larger, taller and taller. You grow slowly to your original height, but you don't stop there. You continue growing up and up and up. You are 7, 8, and 9 feet tall. You feel a giant's strength, very, very big and powerful. Look around, see how it feels to be a giant.

But notice now that you are returning to your normal height and things appear as they did before. You feel your body becoming denser and denser. You feel as if you were made of rock. You are a solid stone. Now you are an ice cube, hard and cold. You begin to melt. Slowly you get warmer and warmer spreading out into a puddle on the ground. Feel yourself all wet and warmed. You begin to evaporate as the breeze flows over you. You become that gentle breeze yourself. You are blowing completely free, skimming over the tops of the flowers, over the grasses and the sand. You are a hot wind passing over the desert and now a cool breeze stirring the leaves. And now feel yourself slowly whirling, whirling, around and around until you become transformed into your own body again and settle down under the tree.

Sit and remember all you have experienced and know that you can experience any state, you can be any size or shape, become any substance. You can experience your body in any way at all.

In a minute or two you will be awake and alert. I am going to count backwards from 20 to 1. As I count you will become wider and wider awake with each number. You will feel refreshed and pleased with your journey. (Count slowly from 20 down to 1, pausing at 10 to say "You are now half awake, feeling more and more alive and alert." After "one": "You are fully awake. Open your eyes and feel totally alive.")

Are Altered States of Consciousness "Normal"?

There is an increasing acceptance of the inevitability and the positive function of altered states of consciousness. Some of this acceptance is based on theoretical speculation, some rests on recent discoveries about the functioning of the brain.

One investigator of altered states of consciousness, Andrew Weil, says that the periodic need to shift into altered states of consciousness is innate. This need is a normal and natural part of human life. He feels that occasional experiences of nonordinary consciousness are as ordinary as hunger and the desire for sexual fulfillment. He makes the point that much of child's play is a matter of altering consciousness. As we grow older, less physically active, and more occupied with the needs of ordinary life, we live less and less in nonordinary reality.

One source of evidence for the normality of altered states of consciousness is found in their inevitability. Whether we, as adults, intend to or not, we do experience them as dreams. lapses of attention, or daydreams.

For Abraham Maslow, the human potential for altered states of consciousness goes beyond the common phenomena of dreams and daydreams. In his book, *Toward a Psychology of Being* (1968), Maslow describes two types of thinking, or cognition. The first is a deficiency-motivated consciousness which corresponds closely to the driving, striving, goal-oriented aspects of ordinary consciousness. This cognition,

D-cognition

D-cognition, is the need to make sense of, to impose an order on, and to rationally understand the world. Another type of cognition Maslow

B-cognition

describes as B- (for Being) cognition. B-cognition allows the positive experiencing of altered states of consciousness that Maslow calls "peak experiences." B-cognition is a possibility for anyone who can relinquish immediate needs, roles, and projects. Peak experiences are moments of highest happiness, fulfillment, and satisfaction with oneself and one's life. In his studies of self-actualizing people, Maslow found them to lead lives rich in peak experiences. This would seem to indicate that not only are altered states of consciousness normal, they are an important part of a fulfilled life.

Recently, as a result of research on the functioning of the human brain, we seem to be finding some clues to the inevitability of and the potential for different states of consciousness.

LEFT BRAIN AND RIGHT BRAIN

Robert Ornstein, a psychologist who has written extensively about consciousness, writes that our understanding of the differences between ordinary and nonordinary consciousness has been furthered by the discovery that each side, or hemisphere, of the cortex is specialized in its functioning. "Both the structure and the function of these two half-brains in some part underlie the two modes of consciousness which simultaneously coexist within each one of us. Although each hemisphere shares the potential for many functions, and both sides participate in most activities, in the normal person the two hemispheres tend to specialize." (1972, p. 51)

The right side of the cortex controls mainly the left side of the body, and the left hemisphere controls the right side of the body. The two hemispheres are joined by a large bundle of fibers called the corpus

corpus callosum

callosum. In people who are right-handed it has been found that the *left* hemisphere is predominantly involved with analytic, logical thinking, especially in verbal and mathematical functions. It operates in a linear way, processing information sequentially, something like a computer.

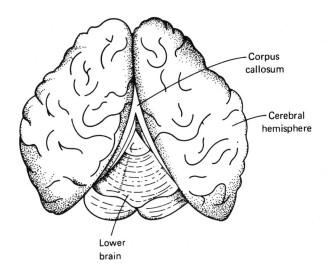

The *right* hemisphere is quite limited in its language ability; it can only process the simplest of words or ideas. It seems to be the side of the brain specializing in holistic, relational, and simultaneous operations. It is responsible for our orientation in space, artistic endeavor, body image, and the recognition of faces. The right hemisphere can readily integrate many inputs at one time. No computer yet devised can simulate this type of processing. ["This right-left specialization is based on righthanders. Lefthanders, who are about 5 percent of the population, are less consistent; some have reversed specialization of the hemispheres, but some have mixed specialization—e.g., language in both sides. Some are specialized in the same way as righthanders. . . . At least in very young people each side does possess the potential for both modes." (Ornstein, 1972, p. 53, footnote)]

Each side of the cortex is specialized, having its own long-term memory, concepts, and its own way of processing information. Each side can function independently of the other. Communication between the two (via the corpus callosum) is only necessary in the performance of certain specific tasks. This has been demonstrated by experiments with people whose corpus callosum has been severed surgically. Their functioning is only impaired when they must use language (and other left hemisphere functions) to describe what their left hand is doing (the left hand is controlled by the right hemisphere).

It is not clear just how the left and the right hemispheres of normal people share and coordinate their functions. Do we alternate from one mode of functioning to another? Do we use both simultaneously? It is quite likely that each hemisphere functions in both ordinary consciousness and in nonordinary consciousness. It may be that the left hemisphere controls ordinary reality while the right directs nonordinary states. That we use the right hemisphere in ordinary consciousness is evident when we tackle such tasks as describing a circular staircase (try doing it with just words—no gestures!), or learning how to perform highly coordinated skills (riding a bicycle) with only verbal instructions.

Perhaps one fact keeping us tied to ordinary consciousness is that the left hemisphere of the brain dominates the right. We become proficient with our right hand (the 95 percent of us who are right-handed) at a very early age and from then on we do little of importance with our left hand. We reach first with the right, we do intricate work with it, while the left serves as a mere assistant. Now, if the left hemisphere of the brain dominates the right hemisphere in a manner similar to this, the functions of the right brain must become secondary. The right-brain functions of holistic, spatial, simultaneous, artistic thinking do not ordinarily get much chance to work. It is probably true that each of us has a vast right-hemisphere potential lying dormant. One left-right brain researcher, Sperry, says, ". . . our educational system and modern society generally (with its very heavy emphasis on communication and on early training in the three Rs) discriminates against one whole half of the brain." (1975, p. 33)

EXPLORATIONS 12.5

Right and Left in Action

a. Divide into pairs. Ask your partner the following questions and observe which direction his or her eyes move, i.e., to the right or to the left:

Divide 144 by 6, and multiply the answer by 7.
Which way does an Indian face on the nickel?
(Chances are that with the first question the gaze will shift to the right, and that while thinking about the spatial question of the Indian, it will move to the left.)

b. For this next demonstration you will need a wooden dowel and a clock. Have your partner balance the dowel on the index finger of each hand, one at a time. Generally, the preferred hand will be best at this task. Now ask your partner to speak while balancing the dowel first on the right hand and then on the left hand. In an experiment by Kinsbourne and Cook (1971), the balancing time of the right hand decreased when the subject was asked to talk because it is difficult for the brain to coordinate two tasks at once. However, the balancing time of the left hand *increased* as the subject talked. Why? The left hemisphere was occupied in speech and no longer seemed to interfere with the left hand.

INDIVIDUAL DIFFERENCES IN CONSCIOUSNESS

It is a truism that people differ in what they are conscious of, how they become aware, and how they see and interpret things. Perhaps you had one parent who was exceedingly rational, a hardheaded thinker, while the other was intuitive and dreamy. You learned by observing them relate to the world that there are differences in consciousness. Some of us seem more inclined to experimental modes, others to speculative, others to artistic ones.

Carl Gustav Jung based his personality types on just such differences in consciousness. First he distinguished between introverted and extraverted orientations. After Jung coined these words, they became popular and their meanings changed. Usually we speak of extra- and introversion in a social way, referring to gregariousness and shyness. Jung, however, was referring to an objective, outer-directed, extraverted manner of viewing things and to a subjective, inner-directed, introverted manner. Some of us are nearly oblivious of our psychological and physiological functioning; we focus on the outer world of things and ideas. Others of us turn our thoughts and attention inwards, focusing on our own emotions and body states.

According to Jung, both introverts and extraverts can function in any of four modes of consciousness. Two modes are rational and two are irrational. The distinction between the two is that rational functioning is a process with an aim or goal; irrational functioning is immediate and aimless. The two rational functions are *thinking* (the process used to answer the question, "What is this?") and *feeling* (the process used to answer the question, "Is this agreeable or not?"). Thinking, for Jung, is rational, analytical, and logical. Feeling is evaluative and judgemental. It is coming to some conclusion as to the value of something. We are sometimes referring to this process when we use the words "belief," "value," or "attitude." Do we like it or not? Is it good or bad? Worthy or unworthy? This is the feeling function and it is as rational in the Jungian framework as thinking is.

The two irrational functions are *sensation* (the process used to answer the question, "Does this exist or not?") and *intuition* (used as an immediate approximation for "Whence did this come and where is it going?"). Sensation is the function of noticing what exists around and inside us. Sensation can be a function much like a photographic plate that immediately and accurately takes an impression of the world. Intuition is vague, imaginative, and sometimes visionary. It is a hunch not necessarily backed up by or necessitating further thought. It is not explainable, does not come from reason or logic. We simply have it.

Jung felt that each of us has an ascendent, or dominant, function. The other three functions are less available and sometimes occur unconsciously. If the sensation function, for instance, is predominant over the others, a person will ever be aware of details, changes, and conditions in his or her environment, either internal or external. Without a strong thinking or feeling function, however, a sensation-oriented individual will not be able to make much sense of things or stay with anything for very long. Sensation-oriented people are impressionable but their impressions don't have much meaning, nor do they last.

A full description of Jung's types is beyond the scope of this chapter. Should they be of interest to you, I suggest *Jung's Typology* by von Franz and Hillman (Zurich, Switzerland: Spring Publications, 1975).

introverted
extraverted

EXPLORATION
12.6

Four
Functions

Begin with an orange.

1. *Think* about this orange, about oranges in general. What do you know about this fruit—how it grows, its tree, its harvest, its marketing and purchase? What is it used for? What does it do? Think about all that you know of this orange.

2. How do you *feel* about this orange? Do you like it? Does it please you? What is good and bad about this orange? Is it better or worse than other oranges? Than other kinds of fruit? How do you feel about this orange?

3. Smell the orange. Close your eyes and feel it. Turn it over in your hand, *sense* its weight and texture. Open your eyes. Look at its color, shape, texture. Slowly peel the orange, focusing all your attention on experiencing the orange. Listen to the sounds you make with it. Eat the orange, one section at a time. Taste every bite. Feel the tartness and the sweetness and the juiciness in your mouth. Sense the orange.

4. Where was that orange before you got it? Before that? Where did it come from? Who had it before? Where do you suppose it was grown? Where was it three months ago? Last week? Where is it now? Where is it going? Where will it be next week? Three months from now? What is the significance of your having had this specific, particular orange? Make some guesses. Use your *intuition.*

Which step of this exploration was the easiest for you? Which might be most characteristic of you and your way of approaching things? Each is a valid way of functioning; each gets us different knowledge of oranges and of the world.

Jung felt that psychological health and the realization of our full power came from being able to achieve a balanced use of the rational and irrational functions, from being both introverted and extraverted. Again, we can see that ours is a culture which rewards extraverted thinking far more than any other modes of consciousness. We are not using our full psychological or brain capacities if one form of consciousness is strongly dominant over the other. Andrew Weil, who calls ordinary consciousness "straight thinking" and nonordinary consciousness "stoned thinking," says, "Straight thinking is straight in the way an interstate highway is straight: it does not follow the natural contours of reality" (1972, p. 57).

SOME CONSEQUENCES OF LIVING IN ORDINARY CONSCIOUSNESS

Trying always to live in ordinary consciousness does not lead to a rich nor even to a benign life. The effort can lead us into some peculiar and not altogether desirable states, if it is unrelieved. One of these states is

Michael Weisbrot

boredom. Consistently rational, orderly, predictable experiencing is dull, dull, dull. Millions of us are bored to tears with monotonous, tedious, unvariegated living. (One observer, Estell Ramey, (1974) considers boredom the most prevalent American disease.) Boredom is painful and we will go to extreme lengths to escape it. Children will act up in class; adolescents will form gangs to provide themselves with diversionary mischief; people will act with hostility to one another just to get a novel reaction; some folks will eat when they've nothing else to do, and many will consume oceans of alcohol in an attempt to sparkle things up a bit. We develop physical symptoms with no organic causes and let doctors treat us with tranquilizers. Approximately 15 percent of the population of the United States takes Valium. (One of the effects of tranquilizers, incidentally, is to interfere with dreaming.)

Paranoia and depression are fed by unrelieved ordinary consciousness. Paranoia is not peculiar to mental patients. Many of us live daily with both reasonable and unreasonable fears. The more unfounded our fears the more we anticipate catastrophe just around the corner. The word paranoia was not even used until the mid-nineteenth century and now it is common. Its widespread occurrence is often the basis of much political pursuasion (Hertzberg and McCleland, 1974). Paranoia is based on the assumption that one is being persecuted and is supported by rigorous logic that interprets all information as evidence for the assumption. Paranoid thinking is extremely logical, certain, and allows no room for coincidence. Ordinary consciousness, with its dedication to keeping the self distinct from others, and its predilection for logic, fosters a paranoid viewpoint. Depression is much like boredom thickened by the addition of despair, pessimism, alienation, and passivity. Paranoia without its alertness resembles depression, another of America's most prevalent psychological states.

Ordinary consciousness, unrelieved, creates a tremendous amount of tension in life and in our bodies. It is singularly striving, goal-directed, and nonrelaxed. "Straight thinking" leaves little room for emotional experience or expression. Extraverted orientation excludes an awareness of inner states, so emotional conditions go unexperienced.

Another problem of ordinary consciousness (and of the society which trains so well for it) is a lack of creativity. We learn how, by rational means, to arrive at *the* right answer, but we do not get much training in how to use intuition and nonordinary consciousness to lead us to new and creative answers to problems.

SOME CONSEQUENCES OF EXPERIENCING ALTERED STATES OF CONSCIOUSNESS

The shift from ordinary consciousness to an altered state can give us relief from a demanding, energy-consuming life. The shift is like going on a mental vacation, getting away from the routine of ordinary consciousness. As with job vacations, some shifts of consciousness leave us refreshed, relaxed, and revitalized. At other times nothing seems to go right and we return drained, with fewer resources than when we started. Altered states of consciousness can renew us or they can create problems in our lives, depending on circumstances which are not entirely understood or predictable.

Periodic altered states, such as peak experiences, can be extremely valuable. They seem to produce benefits that carry over into daily consciousness. One benefit is the ability to *transcend,* to rise above the persistent differentiation and categorizing of everyday living. In altered states there sometimes comes a sense of unity or oneness with everything, with other people, with nature and the universe. One's sense of self is expanded. The orderliness and categories we usually impose on the world seem to disappear. Transcendence brings a feeling of *serenity,* a calm sense of harmony. Another positive aspect of nonordinary consciousness is sensual *acuity.* Experience comes with greater clarity. Perception is richer. It is as though the lens of life had been adjusted for a finer focus.

Altered states of consciousness can also be "bad trips." They have been described as nightmares and decents into private hells. The consensus of opinion among researchers, observers, and participants is that the negative aspects of nonordinary experiences are not inherent in the alteration; nor are they necessary. The more one *needs* to order reality by the principles and processes of ordinary consciousness, the more likely that letting go will be experienced as negative chaos. The confines of ordinary inhibitions and the mechanisms of control are gone, but so are the comforts. Nonordinary reality may be a relief from ordinary reality, but it is not an escape from self. Those aspects of the self which have been pushed into unawareness because they are uncomfortable or threatening can be the focus of clarity reached in altered states. The ability to control awareness, to keep rejected material rejected is often lost when one enters a nonordinary state.

Altered states are states of being out of touch or out of contact with ordinary reality. Energy and attention are directed not outward but inward. It is difficult to communicate with others and be responsible to (or for) them when one is out of touch. Often we are not dependable, reliable, or even understandable when in nonordinary states. When we are off on vacation we usually don't get much work done. The same is true of being off in an altered state: goal-oriented, sustained perseverance is impossible. Decisions and commitments are not easy to come by in nonordinary consciousness. One cannot keep one's nose to the grindstone. While periodic adventures into altered states are tolerated in this culture (as are short vacations), our orientation toward productiveness and communication means that we will not be rewarded for staying out of touch too long. We are likely to be punished. Besides falling out of favor with those among whom we live, we may be denied our freedom of movement, and access to the ordinary world. Long-term loss of contact with reality (ordinary reality, that is) is the most common definition of schizophrenia. Although schizophrenia and other mental disorders are not fully understood at this time, there are many who consider psychoses as permanent alterations of consciousness.

HOW TO ALTER CONSCIOUSNESS

Altered states of consciousness are the antithesis of ordinary consciousness. In a culture which demands self-control, being in touch with "reality" (ordinary reality), rationality, and predictability in daily performance, altered states of consciousness are seen by most to be undesirable, frightening, and punishable. To live a meaningful, socially responsible life we are discouraged from "letting our minds wander," from daydreaming, fantasizing, hallucinating, or experiencing delusions. Instead of being valuable, altered states of consciousness are to be avoided or, worse, hidden or kept secret.

Non-Western and "primitive" cultures have been more conscientious in their endeavors to alter consciousness. Many have traditional rituals, both sacred and secular, with and without the use of drugs, to develop highs. These religious, mystical, and ritualistic ceremonies are not given much status in technological, industrial, scientific cultures such as ours.

We generally alter consciousness by accident, by experiment, in the course of relieving pain, or by escaping the demands of ordinary consciousness. Consciousness is altered accidentally when it is not our intention to remove ourselves from the confines of ordinary reality. For instance, we do not intentionally sleep to dream, we sleep to refresh and renew our energies. Most of us do not *intentionally* sit down to day-

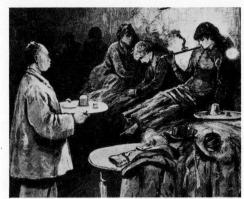

The Bettmann Archive.

dream. The experimental alteration of consciousness has become prevalent in the last fifteen or twenty years. People have experimented with mind-altering substances for years: William James with nitrous oxide, Freud with cocaine, Aldous Huxley with LSD. More recently, in many laboratories drugs, hypnosis, sensory deprivation, and many other techniques have been tested scientifically. Reaching altered states of consciousness by way of attempts to escape the "real" world began in earnest after the discovery of various anesthetics (in the mid-1900s) and mind-altering drugs (in this century). Escape is probably the most prevalent contemporary route to altered states of consciousness.

Whatever the motivation, altered states of consciousness are most likely to be produced under one of the following four conditions. The examples given are some of the ways Western, Eastern, and primitive cultures reach altered states of consciousness (from Ludwig, 1969):

1. Decreased alertness or relaxation. These are states in which active, striving, goal-directed thinking is minimal:
   daydreaming, fantasy, reverie
   autohypnotic (self-induced) trances
   profound esthetic experiences
   creative insight (the "aha!" phenomenon)
   free associative states during psychoanalytic therapy
   music trance (absorption in music)
   floating on water or sunbathing
   nostalgia
   mystical, transcendental or revelatory states attained through passive meditation (some labels for these states are: satori, samadhi, nirvana, cosmic-consciousness)
2. Reduction of outside stimulation or restriction of body movement:
   solitary confinement
   sensory deprivation
   prolonged deprivation while at sea, in the arctic, or on the desert
   highway hypnosis

   hypnogogic states (the transition between wakefulness and sleep)
   sleep
   immobilization in a body cast or iron lung
3. Increased stimulation, body movement, or emotional states as a result of
   "sensory overload," strenuous physical activity, or exertion:
   brainwashing
   hyperkinetic trance (frenzy reached in a highly emotional group or mob set-
      ting)
   religious conversion and healing trance during revivals
   inner conflict leading to heightened emotional states (amnesia, panic, rage,
      etc.)
   acute psychotic states
   bewitchment and demoniacal possession
   shamanistic and prophetic trance states during tribal ceremonies
   fire walker's trance
   ecstatic trance from whirling or howling (practiced by dervishes, holy men of
      the Islam religion)
4. Alterations in body chemistry or neurophysiology:
   hypoglycemia (abnormally low blood sugar level, spontaneous or as a result
      of fasting)
   hyperglycemia (diabetic reaction)
   dehydration
   thyroid and adrenal dysfunctions
   sleep deprivation
   hyperventilation
   fever
   auras preceding migraines or epileptic seizures
   ingestion of poisons (toxic agents)
   abrupt withdrawal from addicting drugs (e.g., alcohol, barbiturates)
   pharmacological agents: anesthetics, psychedelics, narcotics, sedatives, and
      stimulants

   The following two explorations will be most beneficial if you work at
them each day over a period of a few weeks. The first will aid you in
achieving altered states of consciousness while awake; the second will
provide a way of capturing dreams, those elusive altered states of sleep.

**EXPLORATIONS
12.7**

**Altering
Consciousness**

Concentration

a. You breathe in and out every minute, but you probably rarely pay any sustained attention to your breathing. In this exploration you are to concentrate
your full attention on your ordinary, regular breathing pattern — and block out
awareness of *everything* else. Breathe normally and naturally. Let your mind
watch your breathing, in and out, in and out. Just concentrate on each breath
without any attempt to regulate or control your respiration. Be aware of all the
changes and of the rhythms for five to ten minutes. Forget everything else in
your surroundings, everything else you feel except breathing.

You will find, at the beginning, that it is extremely hard to concentrate your attention. It is amazing how the mind wanders away. You begin to think of things, hear sounds outside, feel other sensations. You may be disappointed at first, but if you practice twice a day for five to ten minutes you will gradually become able to do it. You will be able to concentrate for longer and longer periods with no awareness of the external world. It will not even exist for you. You may experience moments of total joy, happiness, and tranquility. You will lose yourself completely.

(Adapted from Claudio Naranjo and Robert E. Ornstein, *On the Psychology of Meditation*, 1971, p. 146.)

Dreams

b. The greatest difficulty with dreams is that they are so easily lost. Here are a few techniques you can use to help you remember them. To begin with, set your alarm for about two or three hours after you go to bed. When it goes off, lie quietly, stay awake, and try to remember what you were dreaming. Have a notebook and pencil at your bedside to make notes of the high points of the dream. Try to get the whole dream situation down in outline. If you try for all the details now you'll forget something further on. It may take some effort to force yourself to stay awake long enough to record your dream, but it is the only way. If you simply wake up, recall the dream, and then tell yourself you'll take notes in the morning, you will forget. (You'll forget, too, if you decide to remember as much as you can when you wake up naturally to go to the bathroom.) You cannot trust your memory to remind you. Your notes, however, will remind you, even if you have completely forgotten that you dreamed at all.

An easier method of recording is to have a tape recorder by your bed. Set it up so that, without turning on the light, you can reach over and switch it on, report what you remember, switch off, and go back to sleep. With the tape recorder too, in the morning you will be reminded by your own voice of dreams you have no idea you dreamed.

Now that you have a dream in your notes or on tape, how can you explore it further? One approach is to search for what triggered it off. Look for something in the dream situation that happened to you recently; a sight or sound, a snatch of conversation, perhaps an unexpected meeting with an old acquaintance. Next, go into the dream itself. First of all, go through the content of the dream to see what it says to you. Then, recall the mood you were in, either in the dream or in the morning when you woke. What were your morning feelings after the dream: were you cranky, exhausted, sad, exhilarated? Work back and forth between the triggering event, the content of the dream, and your mood.

Just before you awake in the morning you will have your longest, most complicated dreams. If you're interested in getting to the bottom of these, don't jump out of bed. Stay there and run through the dreams as thoroughly as you can. Try not to move around or to think about what lies ahead that day. Don't be in a big hurry to come alert.

MAXIMIZING: KEYS TO THE ROOMS
OF CONSCIOUSNESS

There were doors all round the hall, but they were all locked; and when Alice had been all the way down one side and up the other, trying every door, she walked sadly down the middle, wondering how she was ever to get out again.

Suddenly she came upon a little three-legged table, all made of solid glass: there was nothing on it but a tiny golden key, and Alice's first idea was that this might belong to one of the doors of the hall; but, alas! either the locks were too large, or the key was too small, but at any rate it would not open any of them. However, on the second time round, she came upon a low curtain she had not noticed before, and behind it was a little door about fifteen inches high: she tried the little golden key in the lock, and to her great delight it fitted!

Lewis Carroll
(Alice's Adventures in Wonderland)

The first step in finding the key to unboundedness is to make a positive decision to do so. This decision should be based on valuing altered states of consciousness as potentially worthwhile, enriching experiences. The most effective approach is to seek to express one's consciousness potentials, not to look for ways to escape the demands of daily living. In choosing to explore our consciousness, many of us will struggle with the competing requirements of work and pleasure, self-absorption and responsiveness to others, or between "outer" reality and "inner" reality. This will be especially difficult for those who have internalized the virtues of productivity, responsiveness, and extraversion. Compulsiveness and conformity are rigid barriers to exploration, doorless walls around the room of ordinary consciousness.

Michael Weisbrot

A key is a technique that works. It is one which is reliable, one which can be counted on to unlock the door every time it is used. Not all keys are easy to come by; some require both perserverence and practice. Once discovered, however, the best keys are those which do not require that we depend on other people, on circumstances, or on things and substances.

Any technique making use of something material or external to the individual will tend to produce dependence, will tend to lose its effectiveness over time, and will limit one's freedom to get high. Any method requiring things, for example, ties a person to his thing—whether they be glowing coals, biofeedback machines, or tabs of LSD. [Better methods are those] that one can use by oneself any time, anywhere. . . . The person who can get high by himself is at a great advantage. (Weil, in Rosenfeld, 1973, p. 6).

The best keys are also ones which do not deplete our energy or lead to destruction.

Drugs

Whether or not to use chemical substances to alter consciousness and achieve unboundedness is a controversial question. Unfortunately, the controversy sometimes is over the legality of drugs rather than over whether or not they are effective, reliable keys. Legal restrictions on drugs are not based on whether chemicals make good or poor keys. Drugs are usually restricted for medical, political, and social reasons. Many legal drugs such as nicotine, caffeine, and alcohol are both toxic and addictive. When the issue of drugs focuses on legality some other issues tend to be obscured.

Effects   A drug is "any substance which by its chemical nature affects the structure of function of the living organism." (Nowlis, 1971, pp. 8–9). Drugs used to alter consciousness are commonly classified according to the effect they produce on the central nervous system. One group, the depressants, lowers the activity of the brain, producing effects from mild euphoria to oblivion, stupor, and death. This group includes alcohol, opiates, barbiturates, and tranquilizers. Another group, the stimulants, increases activity in the nervous system. This group includes amphetamines, cocaine, and benzedrine. A third group, the psychedelics, affects the brain in ways not clearly understood. The psychedelics (or mind expanders) probably disturb the balance of excitation (energy release) and inhibition (energy blocking) in nerve pathways of the brain and, possibly, affect the energy regulating systems of the brain (the hypothalamus). Drugs which alter consciousness seem to act by affecting the energy level of the brain: slowing energy transfer down, speeding it up, or liberating it.

With some drugs, notably the psychedelics, the liberating of chemi-

depressants

stimulants

psychedelics

cal energy in brain nerves leads to a serious depletion of energy. Biochemist Robert de Ropp writes:

It is not spiritually lawful to take psychedelics merely for "kicks" or to use them as substitutes for the special kind of inner work that alone can produce lasting results. Those who use the drugs in this way suffer a penalty imposed not by flat-footed tax collectors disguised as "narcotics agents," but by the impartial forces that regulate a man's fate. The penalty takes this form: *he who misuses psychedelics sacrifices his capacity to develop by persistently squandering those inner resources on which growth depends.* He commits himself to a descending spiral and the further he travels down this path, the more difficult it become for him to reascend. Finally, the power to reascend is lost altogether (1968, p. 44).

While the exact biochemical effects of mind-altering drugs are not known, there is ample evidence that drugs are not a reliable way to change consciousness in a positive, growth-fostering manner. Drugs can bring on "bad trips" and can result in no experiential effect whatsoever.

Dependence   Any kind of drug, from caffeine to heroin, can produce psychological, if not physiological, dependence. Whether the drug can be purchased in the supermarket for under a dollar, raised in the back yard, or must be purchased from a dealer at a high price, one *has* to have "it" to get there. A key that is outside oneself is not as valuable nor as reliable as one that is inside.

Overuse   Drugs cannot be used regularly without losing their effectiveness. This is another reason why drugs are not a reliable key; they lose their potency. One either has to take larger and larger doses or accept weaker and weaker highs. (The first option is almost always chosen.)

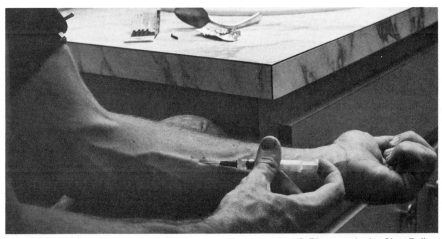

© Photography by Chris Rollins.

Illusion   Andrew Weil has pointed out that drugs reinforce the illusion that altered states of consciousness are *caused* by the drugs, when in fact highs are the result of what is happening in the central nervous system. Holding onto this illusion is holding onto the cause-effect sequence of ordinary thinking, and thus impoverishes rich relationships among events that might be perceived. Getting there with drugs may seem the only way to get there to a drug user, but there are hundreds of ways to get high.

There are many reasons why people use (and abuse) drugs, including curiosity, doctor's orders, addiction, rebellion against antidrug laws, to escape from reality, and to alter consciousness. Human beings have been using drugs for centuries, but large numbers of Americans began using them to alter consciousness only in the last ten to fifteen years. The American experience with mind-altering drugs has not been a total success. Perhaps this is because we want so much from drugs, or because we often use them without first experiencing positive altered states of consciousness without them; perhaps it is because of an ambivalence about the propriety of drugs, or because we use them in ways which deplete our energy and inner resources. Weil gives these suggestions to those who wish to use drugs to enhance growth through altered states of consciousness:

1. Use natural drugs in natural ways. Try the coca leaf rather than cocaine, beer and wine rather than hard spirits; moreover, introduce drugs into the body in natural ways. Intravenous injection of any chemical is an unnatural route of administration and thus, to my mind, an unreasonable practice.

2. Use drugs ritually. It does not matter what the rules as long as they are acceptable and consistent with other beliefs. Such rules might concern times and places for using drugs and should define the purposes for which drugs are taken.

3. Seek advice from persons who *know* what they are talking about. The best guidance comes from analogs of tribal witch doctors — that is, from persons qualified by virtue of their own experience. Of course, drug experience in itself does not necessarily confer this kind of authority. But academic degrees and membership in professional societies by themselves certainly do not confer it.

4. Use drugs for positive reasons. The Indians use altered states of consciousness for positive ends, not for such negative goals as escape from boredom or anxiety. Many Americans take drugs for escape, or for no reason at all, and I suspect this difference is a final key factor in our having a drug problem. (1972, p. 95)

Without Drugs

The means to expanded consciousness are many and diverse. The ability to concentrate or focus attention in some way is a necessary component to most. Attention can be focused on a sight, a sound, sensation, or on an activity. The ability to achieve reliable concentration usually requires practice, repetition, and determination. One technique of concentration is meditation.

Meditation is, essentially, sitting quietly and doing nothing. The meditator stops his or her mind from continual vacillation between the past (remembering) and the future (planning ahead). The constant stream of thoughts and daydreams which usually keeps the mind busy is stopped. Many meditators find it helpful to focus on some meaningless object such as a candle flame, a sound, or on breathing, in order to shut off the internal dialogue of ordinary consciousness. The sound is sometimes a *mantra,* meaningless syllables (for example Shar-rim or Om) repeated rhythmically.

Trancendental Meditation (TM) is becoming more and more popular in the United States. Its founder and leader is Maharishi Mahesh Yogi. This meditation requires only brief training and gives the practitioner a secret, indivitual mantra. One of the advantages of TM is that it is easily incorporated into most people's daily lives. Once mastered, all it requires is a quiet place, free of interruptions, for about twenty minutes once or twice a day.

Increasing numbers of Westerners have found new ways of living their lives and new value systems in the ancient philosophies of the East. Practical experience in Eastern disciplines is commonly acquired under the direction of a master, or *guru,* who is a spiritual teacher. The following books are introductions:

Needleman, Jacob. *The new religions.* New York: Doubleday, 1970.
Watts, Alan. *Psychotherapy East and West.* New York: Mentor, 1961.
Baba Ram Dass (Richard Alpert) and the Lama Foundation. *Be here now.* New York: Crown, 1971.

The philosophies and practices which have been most successfully imported to this country are briefly described below.

Buddhism has come from Japan (as Zen Buddhism) and from Tibet. In Zen spiritual enlightenment and realization of inner self are achieved primarily through meditation. Also from Japan are the martial arts; aikido, karate, and judo are the most popular in the United States. Their use to alter consciousness depends on the user's dedication to seeking through them inner peace and enlightenment.

From Hinduism and Tibetan Buddhism we have adopted several forms of yoga, traditionally the means to achieve unity with the godhead. In addition to Hatha Yoga (described in Chapter 11), Kundalini, Hare Krishna, and Tantric (sexual) Yoga are popular.

The mystical tradition of Islam (also called Muslim or Moslem) is Sufism. Influential Sufi leaders are Meher Baba and Indries Shah. The teachings of Georges Ivanovitch Gurdjieff have much in common with Sufism and have appealed to many Americans. Another related movement, combining Sufi with Tantric Yoga and meditation, is Arica, which came to the United States from Chile.

From China the religions of Taoism and Confucianism have given us the *I Ching* (The Book of Changes) and the meditative technique of Tai Chi Chuan. Tai Chi is moving meditation, a series of slow movements in which the body weight is constantly shifting in coordination with deep breathing. Tai Chi is flowing and beautifully relaxed.

Another route to altered consciousness is sports. It is not uncommon for athletes to experience ecstasy from pushing themselves to their limits. Competitive athletics and individual sports require extreme focusing of attention and physical strength. Some nonordinary experiences reported are seeing auras (colored lights surrounding people), hallucinations, extrasensory perception, and surges of energy. *The Ultimate Athlete* by George Leonard (New York: The Viking Press, 1975) encourages the use of noncompetitive approaches to sports in attaining fuller awareness.

There are hundreds of other methods for changing awareness and expanding consciousness. Here are some of the means suggested in an excellent source book by Edward Rosenfeld, *The Book of Highs: 250 Methods for Altering Your Consciousness Without Drugs* (New York: Quadrangle, 1973):

fasting—for those in good general health
sleep deprivation—the record is 268 hours
sunbathing
prolonged sexual intercourse and masturbation
jumping up and down (Rosenfeld believes that experts in this method are all
    under eight years old.)
massage
silence—try it for two days
flower arranging
automobile destruction—make sure you recycle all the junk
gliding
skiing

If you want even more alternatives, *The Great Escape* (New York: Bantam, 1974) is full of wonderful suggestions, including:

"The Waterbed and How To Do It"
"How To Grow Things in Your Car"
"Whitewater Kayaking"
"Condor Watching"
"Frisbees: Still the Only"
"How To Win at Pinball"
"How To Set a World Record"
"Really Cheap Thrills in Los Angeles"
"Sand Sailing in the Mojave"
"Make a Dinosaur Footprint"

SUMMARY

1. There are many states of human consciousness. Wakefulness and sleep are only two among a wide range of qualitatively different modes of human experiencing.

2. Most of our waking hours are spent in ordinary consciousness, a state in which we maintain a sense of reality. Nonordinary states tend to be brief, transitory, and unexpected.

3. We strive, in ordinary consciousness, to make sense of the world. We impose an order on experience; that is, we construct reality, by means of the following processes: cutting down on the amount of information we respond to; responding to change; selecting some information as relevant and important; and ordering, classifying, and integrating information to give it meaning.

4. Experience takes place in the brain. Most of the time, experience is grounded in reality: we perceive accurately the nature of our environment and our perceptions agree with those of others.

5. Ordinary consciousness is defined by a culture. In our culture, ordinary experience is objective, based on sense data, analytical, reasonable, linear, and controlled.

6. Nonordinary consciousness is defined by several characteristics, among them altered thought, distortions in the experience of time, changed sense of control, changes in emotional expression, and perceptual distortions.

7. Today it is thought that both ordinary and altered states of consciousness are normal and natural states. Both are constructions of the brain.

8. The two hemispheres of the brain, right and left, seem to function in distinctly different ways. For most people, the left controls language and operates in an analytical, linear, logical manner. The right has limited language ability and processes information in a more holistic manner. It is possible that one hemisphere (usually the left) dominates ordinary consciousness while the other (usually the right) dominates in nonordinary experiencing.

9. Jung distinguished two orientations to the world, extraversion and introversion, and four functions: thinking, feeling, sensing, and intuiting. It was Jung's contention that each of us tends to favor one orientation and use one or two functions more often, although the ideal personality approaches a balance.

10. Boredom, paranoia, and depression can be the outcomes of unrelieved ordinary consciousness.

11. Periodic experiences of altered states of consciousness can bring transcendence, serenity, and increased sensory acuity. Altered states of consciousness can also be frightening or unpleasant. The difference seems to depend on one's personality and the situation. Long-term altered states of consciousness are considered abnormal in most societies, including ours.

12. In contemporary Western societies the common conditions for altering consciousness are accident, scientific experimentation, the desire to relieve pain, and the need to escape. Escaping is thought to be the most common.

13. Altered states of consciousness are most likely when we are in a relaxed, nonalert state, when outside stimulation is decreased, when stimulation is increased, or when body chemistry is altered.

14. Keys to nonordinary consciousness are methods which are reliable, nondestructive, and do not require a dependence on substances, situations, or other material conditions. These methods are of maximum benefit in enriching life and actualizing our consciousness potentials.

15. There are several practical reasons why the use of drugs does not maximize unboundedness: drugs change energy levels in the brain; many deplete the body of energy; using drugs to alter consciousness is being dependent on drugs rather than on inner resources; drugs lose their effectiveness with use; and drug use fosters the illusion that nonordinary consciousness is caused by drugs. Drug use which is unnatural, haphazard, uninformed, and motivated by a desire to escape does not lead to unboundedness.

16. There are hundreds of positive methods for attaining unboundedness. Most rely on concentration. Meditation, study and practice of techniques from Eastern religions, and sports are among the most popular.

Suggested Readings

Calder, Nigel. *The mind of man.* New York: Viking, 1971. An interesting presentation of current investigations by physiologists and experimental psychologists on the functioning of the brain. Integrates research from around the world.

Faraday, Ann. *Dream power.* New York: Coward McCann, 1972. Dreams are messages from ourselves to ourselves; we can become aware of and use these messages for increasing self-knowledge.

Fort, Joel. *The pleasure seekers: The drug crisis, youth and society.* New York: Grove, 1969. Describes the uses and abuses of a wide range of drugs from aspirin and nicotine to LSD and marijuana.

Lilly, John C. *The center of the cyclone: An autobiography of inner space.* New York: Julian Press, Inc., 1972. A personal account of experiences of higher consciousness and the several routes this innovative scientist explored in transcending the limits of belief.

Pearce, Joseph C. *The crack in the cosmic egg: Challenging constructs of mind and reality.* New York: Pocket Books, 1973. "Our *cosmic egg* is the sum total of our notions of what the world is, notions which define what reality *can be* for us. The crack, then, is a mode of thinking through which imagination can escape the mundane shell and create a new cosmic egg." (p. xiv)

Tart, Charles T. (Ed.) *Altered states of consciousness.* Garden City, N.Y.: Anchor/Doubleday, 1972. A now-classic collection of reports on many aspects of consciousness, including drugs, yoga, hypnosis, meditation, and brain-wave feedback.

Michael Weisbrot

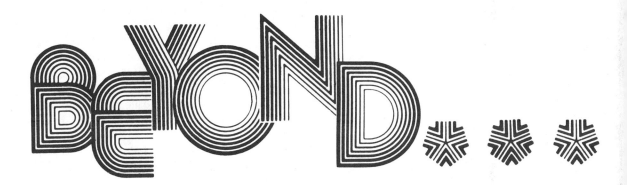

As humans we have a potential unique among all living things: we can imagine, at will, the past and the future. We can easily move our consciousness back and forth in time. We are not bound by the immediate present, or a particular situation, for we can create memories and dreams which transcend the here and now.

Our ability to think ahead allows us to plan, to hope, to dream, and to wish, and then to work to create the future. We can indulge in make-believe, exploring possibilities without making commitments. Our dreams remove us from the known and permit us ventures into the unknown.

What makes hope such an intense pleasure is the fact that the future, which we dispose of to our liking, appears to us at the same time under a multitude of forms, equally attractive and equally possible. Even if the most coveted of these becomes realized, it will be necessary to give up the others, and we shall have lost a great deal. The idea of the future, pregnant with an infinity of possibilities, is thus more fruitful that the future itself, and this is why we find more charm in hope than in possession, in dreams than in reality (Bergson, 1959, pp. 9–10).

Not only do we gain pleasure from imagining the future, we also modify our present according to our images of what the future will be. We can use foresight in evaluating the present. We make decisions based on our estimate of the consequences of our actions. We can abandon a course of action with the thought that we will be sorry if we don't. And we can tolerate discomfort and distress if we believe that, in the future, we will be glad we endured.

Our approach to the future often depends on how much of it we have left. The older we get, the longer our history and the shorter our future. Whereas the future of the young can be filled with many dreams and plans, the old face the reality that the beyond is no longer large enough to encompass all unrealized dreams. What pleasure then? To be without hope even with the shortest of futures brings despair. Certainly there are pleasures in reviewing the past with satisfaction and in achieving the integrity of a life well-lived (see Chapter 3), but at any age, what is life without a belief in the possibility of growth and change?

A view that old age is hopeless is not uncommon in our society. We live in a culture that attends more to rewarding the spirits, potentials, and promise of youth than to venerating the wisdom, experience, and insight of the aged. Most readers of this book know old age and death as events which happen to others. These are not usually among the thoughts of college students preparing for the future. Becoming old is not thought to be a good thing in itself, but it is necessary if we are going to avoid dying young. We want to live a long life, and die quickly, and avoid pain. Beyond these considerations, most of us pay little mind to the end of life.

Today the chances are that most of us will live to be elderly. And, as long as we are alive, we will want to grow and be able to hope. In Chapter 13 we consider the potentials of old age and the quests for separateness and wholeness, intimacy, sexual fulfillment, personhood, a sense of competence, and unboundedness during the later years of life. Chapter 14 is about death—not as an end to questing but as a moment of life which gives meaning to all that precedes it.

Photograph by Joe Molnar.

13

GROWING OLDER

The only way to avoid old age
is to die young.

We get older every day, but when are we old? Defining old age is not simply counting birthdays, as we shall see in the first part of this chapter.

At any age, *growing* old is not a matter of chance. It is a matter of living with the attitude that growth is always the outcome of experience. It is a matter of not becoming resigned to thinking we are finished with living before life is over. It is also a matter of developing potentials, not just during our childhood, but throughout middle-age and beyond.

There are milestones—markers of progress—in the quests we make during the later years. Those discussed in this chapter are:

- increasing self-knowledge and self-definition
- time for intimacy
- continued sensual and sexual pleasure
- opportunities to define personhood beyond the sex-role stereotypes that limit the young and middle-aged
- years of experience to contribute to competence and mastery
- a broadened range in states of consciousness

There are other possibilities for old age, too. There are conditions of isolation, loneliness, discomfort, despair, feelings of worthlessness, boredom, and situations of unrealized potential. It is not so much that aging, *per se*, deprives us of potentials. As we shall see, negative attitudes toward the old and expectations by which we limit our own growth are the most important factors in a stagnant old age.

The great American formula for old age is a pension, a hobby, and a little cottage by the roadside. All of these are in varying degrees contrary to the needs of the aging. Even the attitude behind this formula isolates the older person and seeks to deprive him of stimulation. ... The true need of aging is not the geriatric equivalent of a cradle. To the contrary, Nature's decree to the older person is: If you would keep your faculties, exercise them (Stonecypher, 1974, p. 346).

When we are children, every adult seems old. Some look older than others; the really old ones have gray hair. As a little girl I thought I would be old when I was forty-five. At thirty-five, with only ten years to go, I have revised that childish forecast. *When* will I know I'm old? Will I know when I can count sixty or seventy birthdays? Will it come to me one morning as I look into the mirror and see myself old? Perhaps I will become aware that I am spending my time doing the things old people do, and suddenly feel old.

WHAT IS OLD?

The longer we live the less our activities are predictable by our age. When we are young, chronological age is a fairly good index of behavior. I would, with confidence, bet that a two-year-old is walking and talking but isn't doing long division. And it's even money that a six-year-old is in the first grade. I have some chance of winning a wager that a randomly selected eighteen-year-old is a high school senior. But for ages past the teens I have less confidence. And as for the ages between fifty and eighty, I would not even make a guess about a person's looks or activities from his or her number of years alone. There are fifty-year-olds who look and act older than ninety-year-olds.

Could I guess someone's age knowing his or her activities? I'd do all

---

EXPLORATIONS 13.1

Age Norms

a. Read through the list of activities and characteristics below. What do you think is the appropriate age for doing them? First, put down the first age or age range that comes to mind. Then go through the list again and think of possible exceptions (for example, one could be getting married at age seventy-eight, but it's not usual) and note any activities which you feel would be quite inappropriate, impossible, or ridiculous for an aged person. Note also any activities that you feel are all right for old ladies but not old men, or vice versa. Compare your responses to those of others in your class. Do you all agree?

rides a bicycle	wears a bikini at the beach
travels around the world on a luxury liner	is in medical school
is learning Chinese	is widowed
eats breakfast	is earning his/her own living
drives a red sports car	has many friends
is expecting first child	is fun to spend an evening with
a couple living together, but not married	is living alone
is a grandparent	dyes hair
has preschool children	is attractive
wears bifocals	engages in sexual intercourse at least twice a week
is married, living with spouse	has a $20,000 mortgage on home
is a hospital volunteer	walks with a cane
	goes barefoot all day

b. Assumptions about the elderly

Do you ever make any of the following assumptions about older people?

they are set in their ways	living in the past
rigid	boring
fuzzy in the head	senile
lonely	disoriented
childish	can't be taught new tricks

c. Suppose you and a friend are planning to go to a party together. Your friend asks if he can bring along a friend. What would you say? Suppose he wants to bring his kid sister along? What if he wanted to bring his grandmother?

right for some activities if I could give an age range rather than a specific age. For instance, riding tricycles is appropriate for three- to six-year-olds, but I couldn't estimate a person's age by knowing he rode about in a car. Some activities have age norms based on social expectations and social roles. There is a time for riding tricycles and making mud pies, for going to school, for having children, and for retiring. In general, we share our culture's age norms and we use them to judge what we are supposed to be doing at certain periods in our lives. Some activities are restricted by developmental abilities (we don't expect seven-year-olds to bemoan the generation gap or seventy-year-olds to climb trees) and some by convention (it isn't right for a seven-year-old to wear lipstick or for a seventy-year-old to play with dolls, although both are possible). When people do what we regard as old-age activities we are apt to judge them old. The more middle-age activities people continue into their later years, the younger they will seem to us.

age norms

agism

Many of our old-age attitudes are formed by stereotypes, and many of the stereotypes are not flattering or pleasant. As a society we suffer from agism, the belief that the young are more important, valuable, and better people to be with than the old. Other cultures do better by their elderly by admiring their wisdom and respecting their experience. We are more prone to focus on the infirmities and weaknesses of age. Old age is feared; it is considered an ugly age, something we wish to forestall as long as possible. We lump old people together in a group and refer to them as Senior Citizens or Golden Agers, and few of us look forward to becoming one of them.

Attitudes about the aged are related to the modernity of society. Industrialization and related social conditions have a definite impact on the way a society views aging and treats its aged. The more modern the society:

the longer people live, the greater the number of years before one is considered old, and the larger the percentage of old people. (In 1900, 2.5 percent of Americans were over sixty-five. By 1975 there were 10 percent and it is estimated that there will be 20 percent of us over sixty-five by the year 2000.)

the more "old" is defined by the number of years one has lived rather than by life events, such as becoming a grandparent.

the more the responsibility for the elderly shifts from the family to the state.

the more likely it is that the old are retired from their lifetime occupations before death.

the more ambiguous are social roles for the old. In modern societies there is less clarity about what one is supposed to be or do when one is old.

the lower the status of the elderly. Status decreases with increases in urbanization, literacy (when we learn from books we don't rely on our elders for knowledge), the predominance of the nuclear (rather than the extended) family, mobility, and the rate of social change (the faster things change, the greater the likelihood that one will become obsolete in a lifetime). Status also decreases with age in societies which embrace individualism or some form of the Protestant Ethic (i.e., one's worth is relative on what one produces).

Michael Weisbrot

There are some characteristics shared by the aged in all societies. In every social group the aged are a minority, and they are regarded as a separate class. The old are always less productive and less physically active than the young and middle-aged. There are always more older women than men, and many of these women are widows. (There are 143 old women for every 100 old men in America.) Every society has some social or political leaders who are elderly (Cowgill and Holmes, 1972).

Perhaps the surest sign of old age is that one has come to *feel* old, whatever one's chronological age. When will we feel old? For some it will be when they notice physical symptoms—gray or white hair, wrinkled skin, or stiff joints. It may be when we conform to the age norms for the elderly. It may be when others begin treating us as one of the old folks.

> Age is a quality of mind—
> If you have left your dreams behind,
> If hope is lost
> If you no longer look ahead
> If your ambition's fires are dead—
> Then you are old.

(Singer, 1966, p. 192)

When we feel old will we stop living? Biologically speaking, we won't stop living until we die, but psychological questions about life in old age must be answered in terms of the life we live before old age. The potentials we actualize through our youth and middle age will be the ones we have in old age and the ones we can continue to develop. If we leave our potentials dormant early on they will remain so in our later years.

a. Answer these questions and discuss your answers in class: How many old people live in your neighborhood? Are you guessing or do you know? Do you know how they live? How well they live? Are they happy? (It is not unusual for the elderly to be invisible members of a neighborhood or for neighborhoods to be composed entirely of young and early-middle-aged persons.)

Is there any place in your community with a high concentration of old people? (Retirement communities, nursing homes, tenements or low cost housing developments, rooming houses, upper-class residential areas, parks where the old congregate.) Are the old integrated in your community or are they segregated in old-age ghettos? In what ways do the wealthy old appear different from the impoverished old or those in the middle economic class?

b. Spend some time observing old people. Go to a park or, better, arrange to visit an institution for the elderly. Answer as many of these questions as you can from your observations.

How do old people treat each other? How are they treated by the middle-aged and by children? (Do they have occasions to interact with children?) What do they do with their time? Do you see some who don't seem to be getting any attention, some who get it because they are demanding or hostile, and others who get attention because they are interacting and giving others attention? Can you guess the chonological age of any of them by looking? Are there any who seem interesting, whom you'd like to know, or would you just as soon keep your distance? What are your feelings after spending some time observing?

c. Think of all the old people you know personally. How much of your time do you spend with them? Are they your friends, acquaintances, or relatives? Do you spend time with any old person because you feel you ought to, or because someone else tells you you should, or because you want to? Do you feel responsible for any of them? In what ways? Do you learn anything from them? Do they learn anything from you? Do these people have any value to you: would you miss their company, companionship, or advice if they died tomorrow? Would you be relieved in any way? Would you notice?

d. What have you learned in Explorations a through c about your *own* old age? What do your reactions to old people tell you? Would you feel comfortable having other, younger, people regard you in the same ways you regard the aged? What do you fear most about your own old age? What do you look forward to? How do you want to be able to live when you are old? Do you want to be integrated in the community or to have a special place to share with other old adults?

In relation to physical, sexual, intellectual, and psychological functioning, . . . there is one rule that seems to be consistently true: *Use it or lose it*. Evidence is accumulating that indicates you are much more in control of how you age than is popularly believed. You need not accept the view of aging as deterioration; if you choose to continue to grow and develop as you grow older, you will very likely be able to do so (Joseph and Laurie Braga, in Huyck, 1974, p. vii).

Michael Weisbrot

Accepting that our quests need not end as we grow old, let's look at each of the quests we share and at how we can continue to grow even as we reach an advanced age.

SEPARATENESS AND WHOLENESS

One of the advantages of living a long life is that of becoming aware of the continuity of self. The years of one's life bring innumerable changes and yet one remains a distinct individual throughout it all. Most of us will live through a number of changes in clothing styles, political boundaries, governments, and technological developments during sixty, seventy, or eighty years. Our skin, hands, hair, and other parts of our bodies will all undergo transformations. Only the old can know at first hand, as the young cannot, that although superficial change is inevitable, such transformations do not destroy one's core identity.

The longer we live the more chance we will have to become separate. The experiences of living in various relationships, in various places, and with various things can teach us that we exist independently from the people and things around us. One of the changes often seen among the old is a lessening of emotional attachments to objects and people, and an increase in the attention given to the inner life (Neugarten, 1973). The old are sometimes seen as self-centered or introverted. But many have simply reclaimed and directed inward the energy that they once invested in the outer world of things and events.

A sense of wholeness, too, can be more readily achieved by those who have lived many years. More and more pieces in the Who-am-I puzzle fit together. Fewer and fewer questions remain unanswered, and fewer alternative paths present themselves. In old age we can look back over what life has been. We can see what life was about and accept that all that was had to be. Erik Erikson has referred to the achievement of wholeness in old age as Integrity (see Chapter 3). Triumphs and disappointments are put into perspective with the realization that these were the products of the life lived, the choices made, and the coincidental events of our era combined. What cannot be redone may be accepted with certainty and without regret.

Old age does not bring separateness to all people. Time passing, year after year, is not the critical factor in establishing integrity. *How* that time is spent is critical. The more our actions *throughout* life are directed by the real self, and the more we are able to fulfill our potentials, the more likely we are to enter our later years with integrity. Carrying regrets into old age brings despair. It burdens one with what should have, could have, and would have been, if only. . . . Perhaps the profoundest despair of all is born by those who approach the end of life wishing that they had had different parents, married someone else, chosen other work, or spent life differently than they did.

How can some people live the last years of life feeling that it has been right and good, and others feel the opposite? Margaret Huyck believes that the difference is in how well we know and accept ourselves:

Our self-concept, how we see ourselves and feel about ourselves in relation to the world, is the key to how we will grow older—whether we will simply age or will truly grow. If we feel good about ourselves and see ourselves as a growing, learning person, then we will *grow* older. If, on the other hand, we have very negative feelings, or if our self-concept is based on superficial characteristics (e.g., physical appearance, sexual attractiveness, or even the kind of job), then as the years pass, we are likely to feel less good about ourselves. For a growing person, time-passing is parallel with growth of the self—you become ever more who you really are; you continue to be more self-actualizing. For the person who is not really in touch or at peace with his real, inner self, however, time-passing can be seen as loss—of who he thought he was, or what was superficially valued by himself and others. Knowledge and acceptance of self is central to growing older successfully (1974, p. 133).

Growth as a person can continue as long as we are alive; it does not begin and end in childhood. The sixty-year-old person has been an adult for over forty years. During these years of daily living, each day has contributed to habitual patterns of thinking, perceiving, and acting. The habits which develop can be so rigid and inflexible that notions of self and the world are the same at eighty as they were at twenty. Or the patterns can be adaptable, allowing for change and growth. Life after sixty does not erase all that has come before. We continue to be the people we are as long as we live.

Some people seem to be ageless; we think of them as people first and as *old* people second. Others seem old before they should be. What is the difference? For one thing, the ageless are people who retain mental flexibility. They can accept new and various ideas (whether or not they agree with them) and they are open to learning. They are people who have appreciated life at every stage along the way. They continue to feel, "The age I like best is the age I am," without yearning to be younger or older. They are people who have the ability and courage to make commitments to values and to other human beings. Above all, I think, they are people who have enthusiasm, a zest for living and learning all their lives. I see students every day plodding through life. I sometimes look at their vacant, dull, humorless faces and wonder what kind of old people they will be if they cannot enjoy learning and living now. If you haven't got enthusiasm for life at twenty, when are you going to get it? When you are forty? Sixty? Eighty?

EXPLORATION
13.3
 	
Separateness
and
Wholeness
	How is your life, as you live it today, preparing you to look back in your last years and feel:
	
	    My one and only lifetime was right and good. I was the person I could be. I
	    am satisfied.

INTIMACY

Among the advantages of being old is having *time* for intimacy. There is time to sit and talk, time to listen, time to share. Hours are freed which were previously spent on a job, a family, or a social life, and getting-ahead activities. We are released from many of the responsibilities we had for others. We may have released ourselves from our need to keep relationships from becoming intimate. We are old and needn't play so many social and psychological games with others. We don't have to parent or to boss.

The value of intimate connections does not diminish as we grow older. Consider again the theme which threads through this chapter: if we don't make intimate connections easily when we are young and middle-aged, will we be blessed with them in old age? As we grow old we will find some conditions which favor connections and others which work against them. If we wait until life is drawing to a close before risking intimacy we will have missed much that life had to offer.

Photograph by John Swisher.

Those who have developed the capacities to be open, honest, and trusting earlier in life will find intimacy easier to achieve in old age than will those who have lived closed lives. For example, a man who pours all his young energy into his career may retain his ability to relate to others in those pragmatic ways appropriate to the business world. But his ability to touch and be touched in a human relationship will be undeveloped unless it receives attention as well.

Those who have shared in an intimate relationship during their adult lives will not only possess the skills needed for intimacy, they will have created a sturdy foundation for continuing intimacy with each other. Living through the crises and successes of life with another person provides an abundance of shared experience to enrich old age. These people will have made many intimate connections and will have stored their memories and understanding of each other in a sort of trust account. This account, like a savings account, builds interest and pays rich dividends. There is no way to measure the value of having grown through life with another, of having understandings which don't need words, or family jokes which don't have to be explained.

Growth, sharing, and companionship in old age are among the advantages of a life-long, intimate marriage. Most of us marry with every intention of staying coupled until "death do us part." Fifty years ago there was a high probability that our expectations would be met. Every year, as the divorce rates go up, we have more and more reason to wonder if we will be needed and cared for when we're sixty-four. Some of us decide within the first few years of marriage that the relationship is not surviving. Others spend twenty or more years together before they realize that two unconnected people are merely existing in the same household. The stale marriage of late middle-age becomes a crisis partly because we *can* expect to live to age seventy or longer. It is one thing to weather a decaying marriage for a few years, knowing that death will end it soon anyway, and quite another to face sticking it out for another twenty years. Some couples resolve the crisis by renewing interests and commitments with each other and, in so doing, grow in their intimacy. Others continue living lives devoid of contact, hoping that some spark will magically rekindle their love. Some dissolve the marriage on the chance of finding intimacy with new partners, or face the prospect of living out their life without an intimate relationship.

EXPLORATION 13.4

Intimacy

How is your life, as you live it today, preparing you to be trusting, honest, and genuinely intimate with others for as long as you live? Are you collecting a lot of "hush moments"?

No matter how successful we are in marriage and in other intimate relationships, the longer we live the higher the chance that aging and death will deprive us of intimate contacts. Some biological effects of growing older may become obstacles to intimate connection, such as the loss of hearing. Our social world narrows as hearing diminishes, as we are no longer able to move about freely and independently, as we become less resistant to disease. Many old people find financial conditions limit the maintenance of friendships. They must move out of the neighborhoods where they had friends. All these changes mean increased isolation. And again, the longer we live the higher the probability that relationships with spouse and friends will be severed by death. The likelihood that a woman will live the last few years of her life alone is very high.

There is no way of predicting with certainty how aging and the approach of death will affect one's life. We may be fortunate in keeping

Photograph by Dick Swift.

our health and friends until we die; or we may find ourselves alone with our memories. Many people say that the best way to prepare for the future is to make the present as rich in intimacy as possible, so that we may at least have the comfort of our memories. A friend once told me that he takes mental snapshots of the beautiful and intimate moments in his life (he calls them "hush moments"); when he is old, he will be able to review them over and over.

SEXUAL FULFILLMENT

Now it takes my wife and me all night to do what we used to do all night (Seventy-two-year-old man, quoted in Felstein, 1970, p. 147).

Most of us do not regard old people as sexual. Having lost many of the physical attributes that we consider sexually attractive, the old (we presume) have also lost their sexual desires. They are just not interested. Those who continue to be interested are often labeled "dirty old" men or women and excite more disgust among their families and friends than admiration. The assumption behind such repulsion is that sexuality is the perogative of the young and that among the old it is either silly, unnecessary, or both. Typical of this attitude was that of a student who told me she had fought with her parents because they would not let her sleep with her boyfriend when he visited. This same student was later appalled to learn that her grandparents had made love when they were guests in the house.

self-fulfilling prophecy
As with many attitudes that go unexamined, the belief that sex is inappropriate beyond a certain age can become a self-fulfilling prophecy. Sexual activity may be dropped from the routines of life when it seems unbecoming to one's idea of aged dignity. Or an old couple may continue to be sexually active from habit, all the while feeling that they shouldn't be, and they must never, in any case, discuss it. There are a growing number of people, however, who are continuing to enrich their lives with sexual intimacy so long as their health permits. These people appear to agree that "The only thing age has to do with sex performance is that the longer you love, the more you learn. . . . The things that stop you having sex with age are exactly the same as those that stop you riding a bicycle (bad health, thinking it looks silly, no bicycle)." (Comfort, 1972, p. 220)

The purpose of sexuality after middle-age is rarely reproduction. Women lose their reproductive capacity between the ages of forty-five and fifty-five. While men are fertile until the end of their lives, few old men engage in sexual intercourse in order to have children. The older generation engages in sexual activity for all the same reasons the young do: to share affection, to give and receive pleasure, to release sexual tension, and to prove they can do it.

The biological changes of aging usually affect sexual activity. For men, the changes are few, but they may be a source of great distress. Aging lengthens the refractory period (the necessary time between one ejaculation and the next) in most men. It may be lengthened to several hours, even a full day. It takes men longer to achieve an erection, though once achieved it can be maintained longer; this is usually enjoyable for both men and their partners. Ejaculation is not always virorous in older men, and may be a mere dribble. The effect of aging on man's potency — his ability to get an erection — may limit his range of sexual activity. He may consider himself a failure when his penis no longer responds as quickly or as reliably as it did when he was younger. Or he may accept his ability for what is is and enjoy his sex life.

Aging women undergo sexual changes primarily because their ovaries stop producing estrogen. This leads to several body changes. Skin tone becomes less firm. The walls of the vagina become thinner, and the uterus shrinks. The natural lubrication of sexual arousal decreases in many women and, because of increased sensitivity, intercourse may be painful without artificial lubrication. However, women do not lose the potential for orgasm.

menopause

When the ovaries stop estrogen production, menopause follows. Some women find this a very trying time. For a couple of years the regulating mechanisms for hormone levels are not working properly. Women sometimes experience "hot flashes," mood swings (not too different from adolescence, another period of hormonal imbalance), and depression related to the loss of conceptive potential. But sometimes too women don't even notice that menopause is happening until it is over. The end of reproductive possibilities is taken by some as a sign that sexual functioning should also end. Others are relieved of worries about pregnancy or birth control. They may find their sexual interest greatly enhanced.

Men do not experience menopause nor do they undergo a sudden shift in hormone balance. But some men do have periods of depression and sexual malfunction in late middle age. The symptoms resemble those a woman shows during menopause. They seem to appear when a man can no longer deny obvious indications that he is old and getting older. His hairline has receded and he is balding; his sexual vigor is diminishing and his potency is not as reliable as it used to be; he may feel stress on the job, at home, and in his relationships; friends are having heart attacks; the children are leaving home; there are fewer and fewer occupational opportunities. His wife is looking old. There are constant reminders that he is no longer young and that death is not so far away.

What contributes to a long and satisfying sex life? Contrary to an ancient belief, sexual capacity does not get used up. The opposite is true: the more regular and successful sexual activity has been in earlier life, the better it will be when we are older. If sexual activity becomes only sporadic and incidental in middle age, it may cease altogether in old age.

"Individuals who lead active sex lives in their youth and throughout adulthood appear to carry this pattern into their old age." (Katchadourian and Lunde, 1975, p. 80) As long as one expects to find pleasure in sexuality, feels good about his or her own sexual functioning, and is reasonable in recognizing that it may be an activity of several hours rather than a few minutes, sex in the later years can be rewarding. Ivor Felstein concludes his book *Sex in Later Life* on this encouraging note:

Franz Schubert, who never came to enjoy the longer life, composed a delightful quartet in D minor, in whose second movement the tempo is marked "andante, con variazioni." I can think of no better instruction for marital maintenance of sexual interest and pleasure than Schubert's musical advice: a steady pace, with variations on the theme (1970, p. 143).

EXPLORATION 13.6

Sexuality

How is your life, as you live it today, preparing you for being sexually fulfilled throughout your life?

PERSONHOOD: FEMALE AND MALE

The attitudes of a youth-oriented society and the double standard combine to work considerable mischief on the process of aging in America.

Both men and women are affected from their schooldays onward by pressures to be physically attractive. As a youngster, the models of beauty and virility that one looked to belonged to peers or to adults whose age group one would join in time. As one passes middle age, however, and enters old age, it becomes clear that there is no more looking forward to becoming physically anything more.

Youthful models of attractiveness are especially hard for women to ignore. They are constantly reminded that they can continue to look young if only they will do something about their sagging tummies and chins, their softening thighs and behinds, their dulling hair and teeth. Women are encouraged to take care of these matters by the cosmetic and clothing industries who sponsor warnings about decrepitude and the signs of old age. That these industries thrive is indication enough that many women are willing to pay for the chance to wear, smear, eat, tighten, or dye—as indicated on the label—and to thereby conceal the physical signs of aging.

Men may buy toupees, begin to exercise, or sport youthful styles of clothing as they notice the telltale marks of age. But men have more than a single, youthful model to which they can refer in gauging their looks.

They can admire the gray hair of a distinguished judge, the leathery sun-tanned face of the Marlboro cowboy, or the "successful" paunch of the public official.

The high rate of divorce, coupled with the relatively early death of men, means that there are now more aging women living alone than there are men. The double standard makes this a difficult situation in that women have few prospects of finding a partner. Custom decrees that it is inappropriate for an old woman to date or marry a young man, al-though it is acceptable for old men to seek out younger women. This is in fact what men have generally done, often finding women who are their juniors in years more attractive than women who, though more experi-enced in many areas of life, may be considered less desirable because they are older.

Biological aging for men is a gradual process. If men stay in good physical condition their bodies do not give any sudden notice of age. But a woman's body, at some time between forty-five and fifty-five, sends out an unmistakable message that she is no longer young. The menopause (cessation of menstruation and reproductive capacity) tells her clearly, "You are now an old woman." Not only does a woman's *re*productive life come to an end in middle age, but her productive role may be over long before a man's. A mother's job is less important when her children are grown. Many women are retired from the work of rearing children by the age of forty-five or fifty. At this age a man is often at the prime of his ca-reer and has fifteen or twenty years to go. If he is one of our financial or political leaders he may have as much as thirty or forty years of work left.

As we move from middle age to old age, we begin to outlive middle-life sex roles. We don't cease being men or women, but we find that being "a man" or "a woman" has less meaning and that being "an old person" has more. Role differences based on men's bread-winning duties and women's child-rearing duties no longer support distinctions between men and women. These roles are the preoccupation of the young, not of the old.

Qualities regarded as masculine and feminine fade as we get old. As we near our sixties or seventies, biological changes tend to erase many physical and psychological boundaries between male and female. Men may accumulate fat and find their muscles weaker, their stature shrunk. Women's bodies cease producing the high levels of estrogen which have kept their skin soft and inhibited the growth of facial hair. Men often become more accepting of their affiliative, nurturant, and sensual capaci-ties while women are more receptive to aggressive and egocentric im-pulses (Neugarten, 1973).

Growing old is especially difficult for people whose identity has been defined by sex roles or by feminine and masculine stereotypes. Much of depression in the later years, for both men and women, is not so much the result of aging itself as it is the result of losing gender-related means of self-definition. The woman who continues mothering her adult chil-

Michael Weisbrot

dren and the man who turns into an aging Don Juan may simply be trying to hang on to roles which they feel make them "someone."

Some women and men find new roles as grandmothers and grandfathers. Most of us think of grandparents as "old" people, but it is not unusual to become a grandparent at forty, long before we ourselves would think we are old. Young grandparents sometimes resist accepting this role because they do not feel old enough to be Grandma or Grandpa.

Besides being "old," what are grandparents and what do they do? The role of grandparent in the United States illustrates the ambiguity of social roles for the aged in modern society. There are many ways of grandparenting. How the role is played depends, for example, on how far away the grandchildren live. In contrast to times past when three generations lived in one household, and elders had specific responsibilities for the young, it is not unusual today for grandparents and grandchildren to be separated by thousands of miles. When you rarely see your grandchildren, your role may consist of little more than carrying their pictures in your wallet and sending presents on their birthdays. Sometimes contact is made at Thanksgiving or Christmas; Grandma may get a chance to cook a large holiday meal and Grandpa to spin tales about the good old days. For those whose grandchildren live nearby, grandparenthood can mean a chance for fun on an outing now and then or occasional babysitting duties, the joy of contact with children without day-to-day responsibility for them. For others, especially for some grandmothers, the role may mean they have another generation to rear.

Children learn from their own experience what it means to be a grandparent. This is what grandparenting means to a third-grader in West Hartford, Connecticut (Huyck, 1974, p. 77):

A Grandma is a lady who has no children of her own, so she likes other people's little boys and girls.

A Grandfather is a man Grandmother. He goes for walks with the boys and they talk about fishing and things like that.

Grandmas don't have to do anything except be there. They're so old they shouldn't play hard. It is enough if they drive us to the supermarket where the pretend horse is and have lots of dimes ready.

Or if they take us for walks, they should slow down past things like pretty leaves or caterpillars. And they should never say, "Hurry up!"

Usually they are fat, but not too fat. They wear glasses and funny underwear. They can take their teeth and gums off.

They don't have to be smart, only answer questions like why dogs hate cats, and how come God isn't married.

They don't talk baby talk like visitors do because it is hard to understand.

When they read to us they don't skip words and they don't mind if it is the same story.

Grandmas are the only grownups who have got time—so everybody should have a Grandmother especially if you don't have television.

**EXPLORATION
13.5
Personhood**
How is your life, as you live it today, preparing you to be a person (female gender or male gender) when you are old and have no sex role by which to define yourself?

COMPETENCE

Perhaps nothing is as susceptible to the aging process as competence and the sense of competence. Biological, social, and psychological factors combine to give the old, more than any other age group, the message: "You are not as competent as you used to be."

What can we expect from our bodies as we age? In general, there will be a progressive decline in strength, endurance, agility, and resistance to disease. There are often losses in sensory acuity (seeing, hearing, taste, smell), especially after seventy. The body has less resilience; the arteries, lungs, muscles, and heart take longer to return to normal after activity, particularly when there has been a stress on the system. The body is less able to stand abuse of any kind: too much exertion, over-eating, lack of sleep, long periods of stress, and, of course, disease. The aged cannot bounce back as quickly as the young after a bout of the flu or a night on the town. It is often difficult to distinguish the natural progression of aging from the effect of illness. Some aged are more debilitated by disease than by age itself.

It is inevitable that we will have to confront some physical changes as we age. When these changes will occur and what they will be varies from one person to the next. Some will be subject to a disabling disease or injury which gets progressively worse with time. Others will remain active, alert, and involved until the day they die.

Michael Weisbrot

- A man at age sixty-seven has lost the ability to walk and has difficulty talking. He suffers from arteriosclerosis, is disoriented, and would be described as senile.
- A woman of seventy-five is in a hospital waiting out the last stages of cancer. She enjoys company and likes to watch TV, but is in more and more pain. She spends the last weeks of her life bedridden, sedated, and helpless.
- A man of eighty-five is out on the golf course every weekend. He is annoyed by his rheumatism and moves more slowly than he used to, but he fills his hours with the many interests he has developed in the twenty years since he retired.
- A woman of ninety-five lives alone, does all her own housework, makes pies and cakes every week, just as she used to, and tends her garden. She is never ill and will die peacefully in her sleep one night.

Among the many factors influencing competence in old age are inheritance, nutrition, and life-style. An especially important factor is what is expected of us as we get older. As we age, tasks requiring speed, agility, and strength become increasingly difficult. We often cannot compete favorably with younger people when these qualities are called for. However, older people can prove more competent than the young when asked to do work in which accuracy and judgement are important. Sometimes the old can compensate for slowness by spending less time in correcting errors. Older people are often more reliable than the young. Although they may not be abreast of the latest developments in a field, they do have a general knowledge of life that no young person can achieve. Years of living and accumulating experience lead to wisdom, common sense, and a broad perspective on life. When the aging are not considered competent, it is sometimes because they are not being asked to do what they can do well.

If our value to others is discounted, we find it difficult to retain a sense of competence. How easy is it to keep from feeling worthless when we are not wanted or needed? Often, in modern societies, the old find themselves sitting on the sidelines, expected to watch as other players take over the game. Can we expect them to sit without becoming depressed or feeling a loss of competence? My mother, having worked as a wife and mother for almost forty-four years, described her experience when these roles ended: "Everyone leaned on me all those years, and when they stopped leaning I fell down."

Most of us spend the first two or three decades of our lives learning, the next three to four decades doing (that is, productively contributing to society), and then at sixty-five or so we are retired. Our schools and our work schedules limit the amount of time we may give to learning or resting during that middle, productive period of life. Many of us become tired or bored years before we are sixty-five, but in order to make a living we must stick with a job until we reach the arbitrary retirement age. Others are fully competent and interested enough to work beyond age sixty-five, but they too are put out to pasture when a specified number of calendar years have passed.

Arbitrary retirement is a modern phenomenon. It is a useful device in an industrial society which has a larger labor force than it can accommodate, and in which the expected life span is long. It is a means of moving the older members of the work force out to make room for the younger. The work force itself resembles a large machine whose millions of parts are replaced on a schedule of assumed wear and tear. If some parts get worn out before they are due for replacement, they must wait. And those parts that improve and become more capable with experience? They must be discarded according to the schedule.

The meaning of retirement varies with a number of conditions: health, financial situation, the centrality of work in life, the development of leisure-time activities, and the importance of one's own productivity. The young and the middle-aged may dream of a perfect retirement, a time of leisure without stress and work pressures, a time to do all the enjoyable things that had to be postponed to pursue an occupation and to rear a family. This ideal life will be difficult to achieve without physical and financial resources. Some of us will find that aging and ill health prevent the "golden years" from matching our dreams. For many the loss of meaningful work activity seems to accelerate physical failures; there is a rapid decline in ability when we no longer feel useful and productive. Inactivity, mental or physical, results in deterioration. Most of us retire with the highest standard of living we have had in all our lives. We were used to scraping by when the family was young and when income was lower, but the last few productive years have accustomed us to a relatively comfortable life-style. Retirement means a cut in income to all but the very wealthy. There is less money; income is fixed. If inflation drives prices up, the buying power of those on fixed incomes must go

---

down. Even with retirement plans and Social Security it is very difficult for most workers to save enough to live without financial strain throughout the indefinite time between retirement and death. One-third of all aged have severe financial difficulties (*Time*, June 2, 1975). More than fifteen percent of those over sixty-five live in poverty (eleven percent of those under sixty-five live at or below poverty levels). Two-thirds of these old people are women (*World Almanac*, 1976).

> **EXPLORATION 13.7**
> **Competence**
>
> How is your life, as you live it today, preparing you to maintain your sense of competence and self-esteem as your abilities change, your body slows down, and you are retired? Will you have, and continue to play, games worth playing?

Whatever our material resources at retirement, the fact that it is not necessary to get up every morning and go to work brings changes to daily living. One problem for many is what to do with time. Now that time is unstructured, it can drag by hour after hour unless one is doing something productive. Years of living by a work ethic (time is wasted unless something is produced) make it difficult to shift to a play ethic (time is well spent if the process or the doing is rewarding in itself.) Husbands around the house all day, at loose ends, can be very disturbing to wives who have been used to having the house to themselves. They now have twice as much husband on half as much money, and a new way of life to establish. Retirement calls for many adjustments for most couples.

Perhaps more than any other single factor, it is what we do throughout our lives that determines how we will act when we do not have the

Florida Department of Commerce.

structure and demands of a job to regulate us. The interests and habits we form when we are younger will give hope and give our lives meaning when we are without deadlines and external pressures. Successful aging is not found so much in adding years to our lives as it is in adding life to our years.

UNBOUNDEDNESS

A common stereotype of the aged depicts them as gradually losing coherence of thought, becoming absentminded and unable to solve simple problems, becoming vague and dreamy, out of touch with everyday reality and, finally, turning senile. Observations of old people in all walks of life make it clear that this kind of degeneration will not be the fate of us all. Some, at a relatively young age, will indeed begin to lose the faculties of ordinary thinking. Others will remain mentally intact, lucid to their last moment. Most of us will fall in the wide range between these poles. Beyond this commonsense conjecture, however, it is difficult to predict the course that states of consciousness will follow as a person advances in years.

Interest in altered states of consciousness was only slight until about fifteen years ago. Since then, most experimental work has been done on younger adults. This would explain in part the lack of knowledge about altered states and the elderly. But there is something else to be noted here as a reflection of the conditions of age in America. Since consciousness became an important topic of study, experiments in mind-altering drugs have taken for subjects only adolescents and young adults. No matter that the old are the fastest growing segment of the population, and that many of the aged are unhappy; they have somehow escaped notice as potential sources of valuable information.

It might be assumed, because people now in their later years have spent most of their lives in ordinary states of consciousness, that the aged do not seek or easily attain unboundedness. This is a reasonable assumption, given the fact that the ability to alter states of consciousness improves with concentration and practice. Recall the maxim "Use it or lose it." Perhaps, because of disuse, the capacities for attaining and controlling altered states of consciousness disappear.

On the other hand, many of the routines and requirements which keep us in ordinary states of consciousness are relaxed in the later years of life. The elderly are not expected to continue intense, striving, goal-oriented thinking processes to the same extent as the middle-aged. In fact, the expectation is that old age brings increased detachment from the present, a tendency to live in the past with old memories. Perhaps some of the elderly, freed from the demands of "straight thinking," may be more able to indulge themselves in "stoned" thinking.

neurons

It is known that a few neurons (nerve cells) in the brain die off daily, so that a small part of total brain mass is dead by the time we reach old age. Unlike other body cells, which also die regularly, brain cells are not replaced by new cells. The older we get, the more of our brain is inert. With age there is also a decrease in the myelin sheaths which surround cells. These sheaths facilitate the transmittal of energy throughout our nerve networks. A decrease here might account for the slower response patterns of the aged. However, at this time it is impossible to say with certainty how changes in the brain contribute to psychological functioning. Perhaps a portion of the brain remains always untapped, reserved for use as necessary, and we are impaired in no way at all by cell degeneration. But it could be that for some people atrophy in the brain is related to changes in thinking. People who suffer from arteriosclerosis, a condition which deprives the brain of its blood supply, are subject to disordered thinking, lapses in memory, and even delusions. Why and how disease affects thinking and why some of us are victims and others of us not are subjects for further study.

We can also speculate that some people have their consciousness altered because of diminishing sensory input. Our sensory systems, our receptors of information about the world, become less efficient as we age. At sixty, we will not hear, see, smell, or taste as acutely as we did at thirty. It has been shown by experiment that a drastic reduction in sensory information leads to altered states of consciousness. When deprived of stimulation our nervous system appears to take off on its own, providing imagined sights, sounds, and nonordinary experiences. Something like this condition may be an effect of reduced acuity, as the aged come to pay (by default) increased attention to their inner rather than their outer experiences.

The interconnectedness of physiological change, habitual patterns of consciousness, and changes in social requirements for ordinary consciousness is not clear. If we regard aging itself as a process of becoming unbound, free to be fully conscious, it may be that our richest experiences of unboundedness will come when we are old. Perhaps we should look forward with eagerness, rather than fear, to a time when we can live more comfortably in states of reverie and dreaminess. Is senility perhaps nothing more than a natural alteration of consciousness?

EXPLORATION 13.8

Me — In the Future

Go back to Exploration 3.4 in Chapter 3. Redo this exploration, this time projecting yourself into the future, into your old age. Use the same arrows you used before. How far will you have extended them when your life is nearly finished? Are there any potentials you want to add — areas you are going to develop later in life (for instance parenthood)?

Will you be satisfied with this portrait when your life is ending? Will you have made it come true or maybe have gone beyond it?

MAXIMUM LIVING IN OLD AGE

The problems of aging are caused not by growing older but by inadequate social concern for the situation of the aged. Increasing demands for improvements in the situation have forced the confession that we know little about aging and old age. The study of biological, social, and psychological changes occurring with age is called *gerontology*. This is still a relatively new field, but it is already advancing our knowledge of the aging process and aiding people in human services jobs to meet the special needs of older people. Knowledge about the plight of the aged is being made public by associations of the aged themselves, formed for the purpose of bringing about political change at national, state, and local levels. The American Association of Retired Persons and the National Retired Teachers Association have over seven million members organized to lobby for legislation to benefit the aged. Locally, the Gray Panthers, a political caucus of the elderly, has organized to influence political decisions and express the needs of the aged for alternative lifestyles.

Although all of you reading this book are aging, few of you are aged. Old age is a part of your life only as some remote, future event or as a concern more and more families face: what do we do with our aged parents? This situation, more than any other, brings the problems of the old into sharp focus. Some problems associated with aging have solutions; others may not be easily or adequately solved.

After retirement, much time is spent at home. Some people are able to make their home in the house where they have lived all their lives. Those who have the money may be glad to move to retirement communi-

Michael Weisbrot

ties where the weather is favorable, youngsters with their noise and toys are excluded, housing upkeep is provided, and where recreational facilities are available. Others are able to move in with their grown children. But there are many families and homes that do not easily accommodate three generations. Disability and ill health create a need for nursing and home care, either occasionally or routinely. It is often necessary to send the elderly to nursing homes. The difficulties in these cases are in locating homes which provide humane care, paying for it (costs averaged $15,000 a year in New York in 1975), and managing one's guilt about putting one's parents away.

The desires of the old are various. Some want to live in the country, some in the city, some alone, some communally, some where they can be with younger adults and children, some in age-restricted neighborhoods. Some need occasional help keeping up their homes and themselves. Some need hot meals, some day-care, some total care. Those who can get out and about need to be able to do so. Trips to visit friends, libraries, and stores require accessible, safe, and inexpensive public transportation. Those who move slowly need crossing lights that allow time enough to cross streets. Those in wheelchairs need ramps. Is it possible for all the aged to live in a comfortable environment? The answer today is no. Our society down not provide sufficient options nor adequate environmental planning to meet the needs or the wants of our elders.

A fundamental concern for almost all of the elderly is providing financially for the years between retirement and death. Individuals and families alone can rarely meet these needs. Those who believe that only people who work deserve to be paid, believe also that accepting welfare is a sign of personal failure or inadequacy. "One of the basic issues of financial security is whether we, as a society, believe that adequate incomes, health care, and decent housing are the right of every member of society — or only those who are currently productive in ways the society values at the time. Our actions tend to reflect the latter viewpoint, and they contribute to the uncomfortable position of the elderly." (Huyck, 1974, p. 168)

Social Security, Medicare, and Medicaid programs ease, but by no means resolve, the money and health-care worries of the aged. Social Security is a system whereby younger, productive workers contribute some of their earnings to a fund from which the old and disabled may draw. Benefits are determined by income earned during one's lifetime and are not enough to live on. In 1975, the average old couple received $310 a month (*Time*, June 2, 1975). Housewives, who have no benefits of their own, must share their husband's benefits. The ability of the Social Security system to continue providing benefits to a growing proportion of old people is doubtful.

Medicare is a federal health insurance program for the aged which helps pay hospital and doctor's fees when illness occurs. It is not a plan for preventive medical care. Medicaid is public assistance for those who require nursing-home care. A few hospitals in the country have programs of regular medical care to out-patients, including home visits to the elderly. The cost of this preventive care is substantially lower than nursing-home care, but it is available to only a few.

As vital to old age as finding a place to live is finding a reason to live. Our society seems to have very little need for old people. There are a few federal and local programs that encourage the elderly to contribute their skills and talents. Among them are the Foster Grandparent Program, Retired Senior Volunteer Program, Senior Corps of Retired Executives, and the Green Thumb Program, which pays older rural workers for doing community-service jobs. Some communities sponsor employment bureaus for the aged. There is a need for more part-time jobs. If there were positions available for those who wanted to work less than a full day, both the young and the old could mix leisure and work throughout life. Making retirement a function of desire and worker ability, rather than of birth date, would solve some retirement problems.

Among the most positive approaches to maximizing life in old age are those which encourage the old to renew their lives, to establish new identities now that they have outgrown parental and occupational roles. We need to provide lifelong learning and growing opportunities. One pioneer program is the SAGE (Senior Actualization and Growth Explorations) Project. SAGE urges older adults toward actualization through techniques such as deep breathing, relaxation, biofeedback, yoga, massage, meditation, tai chi, art and music therapy. SAGE views aging as a creative process and finds that even its oldest participants grow, develop, and find new interest in life through these methods.

A new program for the elderly at the College of Marin, near San Francisco, is serving as a model for other community colleges. This is the Emeritus College, a special college curriculum offering both credit and noncredit courses to community residents over the age of fifty-five. Before the development of Emeritus College, the College of Marin served fewer than 100 senior citizens a semester. There are now over 2000 older adults enrolled. The outstanding success of Emeritus College has been in bringing new interest into the lives of many older people and in changing the character of the entire campus. It is a delight to walk across our campus and see so many eager old faces among the young. Here are people of all ages making lifelong learning a reality.

SUMMARY
1. Behavior in old age is subject to age norms—stereotyped expectations of what people at certain ages ought to do. As chronological age increases, continued participation in middle-aged activities keeps a person feeling younger. We begin to be old when we feel we are old.
2. Our society suffers from agism, the social and psychological devaluation of the elderly. The situation of the aged is adversely influenced by conditions in a modern, industrialized society.

3. The more potentials we actualize throughout life and the more abilities we continue to use as we grow older, the more we have in old age.

4. Old age brings the opportunity to draw upon self-knowledge accumulated through the years. This consolidation of life experiences enriches and optimizes continued growth.

5. The elderly, freed from many social obligations, are able to further develop potentials for intimacy and, as much as any of us, the old need intimate contact to maintain well-being. Loneliness and isolation are not inevitable in old age; they are largely products of lives lived without previous intimacy and agism.

6. Although some biological changes with age affect sexual performance and decrease reproductive capacity, the potential for sexual fulfillment is basically curtailed by sex-negative attitudes and the lack of sexual activity.

7. The more youthful images of masculine men and feminine women are socially promoted, the more difficult it is to accept the physical signs of aging. A sexual double standard discriminates more against aging women. Traditional sex roles do not accommodate the aged; those who have taken their identity primarily from a stereotyped sex role will lose their source of self-definition in old age. The elderly person's role of grandparent is ambiguous in modern society.

8. Capacities for physical endurance, speed, agility, and strength decline with aging. But these losses are not as devastating to competence as a feeling of worthlessness, or forced inactivity, or the lack of means to achieve an adequate standard of living.

9. Very little is known about the relationship between aging and states of consciousness. Physical changes in the brain, habitual patterns of thought, changes in social expectations, and other factors may interact to determine the degree of unboundedness in old age.

10. Maximizing the process of aging includes research on all aspects of the aging process, provisions for living a wide range of life-styles, social and political concern for old people, and, most important, respect for the worth of human life at every age.

Suggested Readings

de Beauvoir, Simone. *The coming of age.* (Translated by Patrick O'Brian). New York: Putnam, 1972. An interesting account of historical views of old age with a pessimistic view of current attitudes.

Cabot, Natalie H. *You can't count on dying.* Boston: Houghton Mifflin, 1961. Describes research on over one thousand normal individuals over the age of fifty who came to the Age Center in Boston.

Cowgill, Donald O. and Holmes, Lowell D. (Eds.) *Aging and modernization.* New York: Appleton, 1972. A cross-cultural perspective on aging, including theory and attempts to discriminate universal from culturally dependent factors in the status of the aged.

Huyck, Margaret Hellie. *Growing older.* Englewood Cliffs, N.J.: Prentice-Hall, 1974. An optimistic and positive view of aging, including the concept that growth in the later years is a continuation of earlier growth.

Neugarten, Bernice L. *Middle age and aging: A reader in social psychology.*

Chicago: University of Chicago Press, 1968. Over sixty research articles covering a range of topics on the aging process and the aged.

Stonecypher, David D. *Getting older and staying young.* New York: Norton, 1974. A physician encourages us not to underrate the normal capacities of the elderly. Optimistic suggestions for preparing for old age and making the lives of the elderly meaningful.

United Nations/John Isaac.

14

DEATH

In all of our growth situations except one, we can look forward to new vistas, new goals, new projects, and new enriching relationships. When we look forward to that time of dreaded news when our own death becomes imminent reality, we draw back in fear and rejection. That is the one journey, the one labor few of us look forward to. Fear of that final separation, death, is natural. The thought of sleep without dreams, timelessness without concern and conversation with others is the most difficult thing we humans face (Imara, 1975, pp. 148–149).

We are afraid of death. It means so much, yet is inconceivable. We know death will come to us all, yet we are so often unprepared.

In this chapter we ask:

How do we experience death while we are alive?
How do the dying experience death?
What control do we have over how and when we die?
What can it mean to the living to know that death is inescapable?

That death will come to each of us is a certainty, but when? Why do some live long lives and others die almost before they've begun? Why do some linger on long past useful potential and others lose life in a matter of seconds? We will examine these questions and find no final answers.

Death is the end to which all quests bring us, when the ebb and flow, the games and work, the saying and doing of life are over. Death is the process by which a living thing ceases to be alive. Death does not touch the inanimate, only the living. Death is not an accident. It is the final stage of the life cycle, the "final stage of growth." (Kübler-Ross) Death is is the inevitable consequence of having lived; the end to which all of us come.

Death occurs over a period of time. Aging is a parallel process; we begin to age not when we have a certain number of years but at birth. The older we get the more rapidly we approach death. Living, then, runs side by side with the long process of death. The last short phase includes the event of passing from life to death. Not even this event occurs at once; various parts of the body die at different times. Nails and hair often continue to grow for several hours after life signs have disappeared from the heart, lungs, and brain.

Just as life can be defined by various criteria, so can death. The criteria by which death is defined do not always agree. The *medical* definition of death used to be, until the invention of resuscitators, the moment when the heart and lungs stopped functioning. Since in some cases heart and lung activity can be artificially sustained, other medical definitions had to be constructed. Today, doctors will often use the presence or absence of brain activity to differentiate life from death.

The contemporary medical definition of death requires that all four of the following conditions be met for twenty-four hours:

1. Unreceptivity and unresponsivity. There is a total unawareness of all stimuli; a condition of irreversible coma.
2. Absence of reflexes. The pupil becomes fixed and dilated.
3. Breathing and all other movements have ceased.
4. Unless the patient is under the influence of barbiturates or other chemicals which depress brain activity, death occurs when the electrical activity of the brain can no longer be measured by an EEG (electroencephalograph) (Hendin, 1973, p. 32).

Death can be defined *biologically* as that time when all activity of every body cell has ceased; when there is no longer any biological exchange with the environment. Using this measure, death frequently occurs after a person has been pronounced dead according to the medical definition.

A third definition of death is sometimes important to survivors, insurance companies, or parties in malpractice or criminal trials. This is the *legal* definition. Legal death occurs when the courts say it has occurred. Legal questions about cause of death—whether a person was killed or died naturally—require that the exact time of death be established. Since death is a process, this specification is arbitrary.

Other definitions of death are *psychological* and *social*. Life is over when consciousness ends or when the personality is extinguished. A person may cease to live in any meaningful way long before the medical or biological criteria are met. Psychological death comes with a belief that there is no hope for the future, that conditions are beyond control, or that one is helpless, lacking competence to cope with life. Research has shown that placing animals and humans in situations of helplessness and hopelessness accelerates death (Seligman, 1974; Weisman, 1972). Life is gone when hope is gone. Doctors cannot predict precisely how long a critically ill patient will live, even with a thorough understanding of the patient's medical condition.

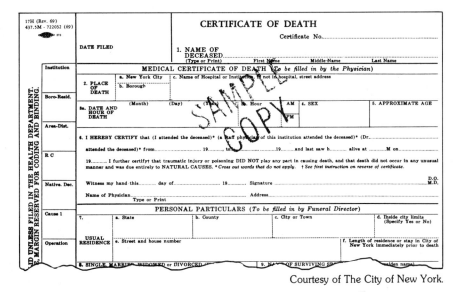

Courtesy of The City of New York.

WHAT DOES DEATH MEAN?

Determining whether we are dead or alive is perhaps not as important to us as what our death will mean—to us and to others. Joseph Mihalich has stated the meaning of death this way:

My death does not belong to me—it is the outer limit of my consciousness, the last of my possibilities. The meaninglessness of death for me is summed up in the phrase that 'my death is the one moment of my life which I do not have to live.' My death is not for me but for others; it is not my concern but the concern of others who will notice it and need to deal with it . . . (quoted in Christian, 1973, p. 477).

From what I know of death I believe that after I die it will be impossible for me to experience anything, anyone, or even myself, as I do today. I will not have the possibility of acting. Death will end the biological and social communication I have with the world. I will no longer make living exchanges with my environment. Life will not be my responsibility—nor will it be my privilege.

Will there be other, different possibilities after life is over? For the living, the answer to this question is a matter of belief. I cannot know, I can only feel, that there will (or will not) be an essence (or soul or spirit) of me to survive the physical body in which I live today.

Will there be nothing left? After I die my children will offer tangible proof that I existed. I will survive genetically for at least one more generation, because I contributed one half of their genetic material. The survival of "me" after that will depend on whether or not they reproduce. (But the genetic "me" is only what I inherited from *my* parents. Was it "me" at all?)

I will be left in the memories of others. Of all those people I contacted through my life, some will think of me from time to time. I will exist as long as my image lives in the minds of others. My words may be remembered. What others saw me doing may be remembered. What others thought of me will be remembered. The experience others have of me after my death will be immutable; I will no longer be around to

Michael Weisbrot

correct or amplify it. My input ends when my ability to communicate ends.

There will be some material left when I die. The chemicals constituting a human body were worth about $3.50 in 1973 (Hendin, 1973) — perhaps they will be worth $5.00 or more when I die — if someone wants to buy them. The matter of my body is not for sale, but it is in demand. Each living thing must die if something or someone else is to live. As long as I am alive, I monopolize a small amount of chemicals. These chemicals are then unavailable for use by other living things. When I die I will (with the help of bacteria) release carbon and nitrogen and other chemicals which will be recycled or used to maintain further life. Without death there would, in the long run, be no life. My death will promote further life.

EXPLORATION 14.1

Meaning

Answer the following question in as many ways as you can:

    What does death mean to me?

When we die we leave our things. We have been warned that we can't take it with us. What will happen to your things when you die? Do you have a Last Will and Testament directing others to use or dispose of your material possessions when you are no longer around to do so? If you were to die today would your things be a burden on someone else? Would others fight over your things? Would your belongings go where you would like to have them go?

The Experience of Death: For the Living

Although we die only once, we can experience death in several ways while we are alive. What death means to us may depend on the faces it has shown us.

To very young children, up to about age three, death means separation. Because a child cannot live independently, the absence of a caretaker, temporarily or forever, may be devastating. *Forever* has no meaning, but *now* does: what is not here now is gone. The important death for the young child is that of someone necessary to his or her well-being.

Between age three and about six, death seems reversible. Pets, friends, even siblings and parents who have died are perceived as having gone away only for a little while. They will return, like the flowers of spring or the sunshine . . . perhaps in the morning. Only gradually does the meaning of death come to include a sense of permanence. Until about the age of ten, when it can be understood in biological terms, death may be personified as the bogeyman, eerie ghosts, or skeletons (Hendin, 1973).

© 1976 J. Brian King.

Whether he or she understands death as a biological event or not, even the youngest child will be aware of the grief that accompanies it. Children feel loneliness, abandonment, fear that others or they themselves will die, and even anger when a significant person in their lives has died.

As children and as adults we may deny that death occurs. One way of denying death is to protect children from it. Children are sometimes not allowed to participate in the activities that go with a death in the family. They are kept away from the dying and from the dead. They may be sent away to relatives until it is all over. As a consequence, death may take on some strange meanings to children. I remember being banished from the kitchen when my mother and a friend were talking about the suicide of one of their friends. I was six at the time and for many years after the incident I had a morbid fascination with people killing themselves and with carbon monoxide poisoning. (Being sent out of the room didn't keep me from knowing what they were talking about.) A recent survey of children's textbooks showed that children get the message that death only happens to plants, animals, and historical figures. Many biology tests do not even mention death (Green and Irish, 1971).

Death is denied when it is referred to euphemistically. Instead of dying one has passed on, gone to rest, passed away or has been taken by the Lord. Animals are put to sleep. Death is not really final when the dead are as alive as the living on our TV and movie screens. We can still see John F. Kennedy, Marilyn Monroe, Humphrey Bogart, and many others just as we saw them when they were alive. Even the religious belief that death is only the entrance into life everlasting denies its fact.

Death is not real when it is removed from life and the living. These days people seldom die at home with their families and in familiar surroundings. The majority die in hospitals. The impact of death for survivors is muted. Death does not touch us nor do we touch the dead. I have never put my hand on a dead or dying person's body. For me death has been distant and removed. Is my lack of contact with the dead exceptional? I have been protected from death more than some (soldiers or morticians, for example) but I have not had to take any extraordinary measures to avoid contacting death in my life. In contemporary America it is easy to avoid any contacts with real death before one's own.

These American ways of denying death lead to and support the notion that death "happens to thee and to thee—but not to me!" (Kübler-Ross, 1969) We think of death as coming to others, to people we don't know, to people whom others love and need. Death is not for me or for mine.

Death in America is robbed of significance by its treatment on television and in movies. We are entertained by over 18,000 TV deaths before we are fourteen years old. Many thousands of these deaths are cruel, violent, and criminal. Yet we are emotionally immune to most of them. Death stripped of sorrow or grief serves to create suspense, to give police and detectives a crime to solve, and to affirm that the bad guys get it in the end. We experience these deaths as incidental. They are rarely portrayals of real lives ending or having any personal loss to anyone.

Alien death (in stories, biographies, autobiographies, and even fairy tales) is not always an impersonal, unfeeling event. Tender, moving, bittersweet accounts of the deaths of unknown and unreal people can provoke very real emotions; the sadness and the tears are certainly real enough even though the death is imaginary. As a child I cried over *The Little Match Girl* (a story about a destitute child who freezes to death) and as an adult I cried (as did most everyone else I know) on reading Erich Segal's *Love Story*. Whether we scoff at tearjerkers or admit the poignancy they have for us, it is only our response which is real, not the death. We can turn off the TV, walk out of the theater, or close the book, richer for the emotional experience, without loss from our lives.

Death has a place in almost everyone's fantasy life. Beginning in early childhood we bring death into our daydreams and nightmares. Sometimes we imagine our own death as a relief from our problems and struggles. Or we may express antagonistic feelings toward others by wishing them dead. Visualizations of death serve other purposes. Daydreams of all kinds, including those of death, help us prepare for the future. We can practice our responses and assess our abilities to cope with the possible loss of important people in our lives. We can become aware of our vulnerability and of our responsibilities to others. As a new mother I experienced chilling fantasies of the death of my infant. These made me increase my vigilant concern for my baby and reminded me of the importance of parental responsibility. At times in my life I have had fantasies of someone close to me dying. These scenes inevitably include my receiving condolences and sympathy from friends and acquaintances. I am always reassured by these fantasies that I do have friends who will support and care for me; I am not alone in my life. Fantasies of others' sorrow at my possible death serve the same function. Others *do* care about me.

The living experience death largely as fear. We fear pain, suffering, and loneliness in our own death. We fear our nonexistence, the loss of all our options and control. Death will be the end of everything and everyone we know; this is a fearful, almost incomprehensible state of affairs. We sometimes fear that the dead will return to haunt us, that their ghosts will seek revenge for our transgressions against them. We fear that death will come before we have finished our business in life, that we will die with sorrow, guilt, and regrets for missed opportunities. We see death as a punishment; it is a penalty exacted for bad deeds. Some religious views of death hold that there will be a continuation of punishment after death. We may be doomed to eternal suffering and damnation in the fires of Hell to pay for our sins during life. While a belief in everlasting Hell may encourage the living to live right, or to confess sins, it also greatly increases our fear of death.

The older we get the more likely it is that we experience death as the loss of a loved one or close friend. When death claims a parent, child, spouse, or friend, we feel its finality most acutely. Some vital and important part of our lives is gone. No matter how clear our memories of the dead or how great our longing, our relationship with them must change. There will be no more good times or bad times with them; there is no possibility of restoring or redoing. We are left alone with disbelief, panic, confusion, emptiness, memories, anger, and grief. We think of how we could have made life more pleasant and rewarding, but now it is too late. Grief is a normal reaction to death but we are rarely prepared for its severity or for its length. At first we may experience numbness, nothing at all. Then protest and yearning come. Insomnia, physical distress, and fantasies are common. Although the initial impact may diminish in a matter of hours or days, the grief process is often not complete for two to three years. Even after this time the feelings of loss, sorrow, and panic may return. "Death ends a life, but it does not end a relationship, which struggles on in the survivor's mind towards some resolution which it never finds." (Anderson, 1968, p. 277)

EXPLORATION
14.2
Your
Experiences

Consider your experiences with death and dying. What did you know of it as a child? What was your family's reaction to death? What has been your reaction to death as portrayed in books, on TV, and in the movies? Do any of these deaths have an emotional impact on you? What kinds of fantasies have you had about your own death or the death of others? What are your fears of death? Have you grieved at the loss of a relative or friend? Share your experiences in class.

The Experience of Death: For the Dying

Dr. Elisabeth Kübler-Ross, a psychiatrist, has been studying death and the terminally ill for ten years. As a result of many conversations with patients who know they are approaching death, she has been able to identify five stages in dying (1969). Insight into these stages is important for friends, relatives, hospital staff, and for the dying themselves. Each stage represents a normal response. Not all dying patients experience each, but for many these stages are steps leading to an acceptance of death.

Stage 1: Denial   The first response to finding that one has a serious life-threatening illness is disbelief: "No, not me." There may be a pretense of being healthy, plans for life when one is cured, feelings that a mistake has been made, that the diagnosis belongs to someone else. Denial is important to cushion the shock. It gives the person an extension of time before the reality becomes inescapable. Usually this stage cannot last too

Elisabeth Kübler-Ross
(*Courtesy of E. Kübler-Ross*).

long, for the course of disease does not indicate a return to health. Denial may recur occasionally as death approaches, but Kübler-Ross found that only one percent of her dying patients could delay facing death right up to the end.

Stage 2: Anger   Denial gives way to rage, envy of the living, and resentment. Anger is directed at the living—friends, doctors, nurses—and at God. The reaction is "Why me?" In this stage the dying can be unbearably complaining, demanding, and difficult. No one and nothing will curb their frustration and bitterness. Patients in the denial stage are far easier to deal with than those who have become angry. In many ways hospitals can and do encourage denial. It allows room for optimism, for talk of the future "when everything will be all right again." But the angry patient often disrupts hospital routines and arouses the anger of staff. Kübler-Ross reported a study which showed that terminally ill patients had to wait twice as long for a nurse to respond to their calls than did other patients. It is difficult to face a patient who is dying and who is incessantly critical as well. No matter how difficult the dying are to handle, if they can be allowed to express their anger and defiance, with understanding they can move to the next stage.

Stage 3: Bargaining   This stage indicates the beginning of acceptance. The stance becomes "Yes me, but." But if I promise to do this or that couldn't I have a reprieve or an extension of my life? Most often the request is made to God, but promises of good behavior and other favors are also made to doctors and nurses. Kübler-Ross says it doesn't matter what the promises are, they are never kept.

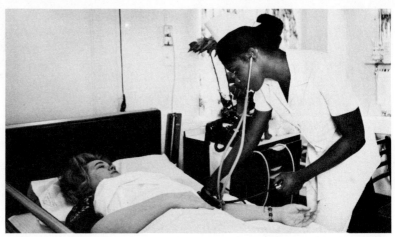

Photograph by Irene Fertik.

Stage 4: Depression   When the "but" is dropped, the response is merely "Yes me" and the patient becomes depressed. For the first time he or she begins expressing grief and sorrow. There is a mourning of the past, of matters left undone, of the total and inevitable loss of life. These patients need to be sad and withdrawn. Attempts to cheer them up interfere with the real, normal, and necessary depression which precedes acceptance.

Stage 5: Acceptance   The acceptance of death brings peace and quietness. Death is no longer frightening or enraging. Acceptance is not a position of resignation or giving up; it is a sense of victory. "My time is very close now and it's all right." At this stage the dying have finished their business and have their houses in order. They are at peace with themselves.

Kübler-Ross has been instrumental in helping us all, professionals and families alike, in accepting death as part of life. She has learned from hundreds of dying patients that they all know when they are terminally ill, whether they have been told or not. She has learned that doctors can be honest and genuine in telling patients that they are seriously ill without limiting hope or life. Giving a patient a specific time limit on life is incorrect and unnecessary. The dying need understanding and, always, a glimpse of hope in order to live until they do die. Hope and some degree of self-control, even in small matters such as the choice of a dessert at mealtimes, allow patients to die with dignity. All the dying patients Kübler-Ross interviewed wanted to talk, to share their experiences and themselves. They wanted to express how they felt about dying and what it meant to them. They needed most of all to know that the doctor would stay with them until the end. The fear of being abandoned in life seems stronger than the fear of death itself.

The families and close friends of people who are dying go through the same stages as the patients do. Usually, however, the person who is dying progresses faster than others and may reach a stage of acceptance before they do. Friends may continue their denial longer than the patient. The great need of those who are dying is to be able to express their feelings, to ask questions which may have no answers, and to continue communicating until it becomes impossible. Doctors, nurses, and families who continue to deny death create a barrier to that communication.

THE TIMING OF DEATH

There is a time to be born and a time to die, wrote the preacher in Ecclesiastes. But when? Most of us are prepared to be born by being biologically developed enough to live outside the uterus. But how many of us are prepared to die? How many of us die having accepted death and having put our houses in order? This is the time to die, peacefully, quietly, at the end of a long and full life. But death is not always on time. It comes before birth, during childhood, at the peak of life, and it sometimes is delayed beyond the loss of useful, productive potential.

One of our major concerns with death and dying is that we cannot always predict it. Death is often sudden, coming with little or no warning, as with heart attacks and automobile accidents; these give victims no time to feel angry, depressed, or accepting. The impact on survivors is staggering, and leaves wounds that do not easily heal. If death comes early in life, even when there is some time to prepare, we are flooded with grief and rage at the loss of not only what was but what might have been. There seems so little sense or reason in the death of the young, of those who have not had a chance to fulfill their promise in life.

Another concern is our conflict over whether or not we should be allowed to control life by terminating it. There is a time to kill and a time to heal, but how is that time to be determined? How much burden for setting the time can and should people assume? Religious and legal answers to this question were first given when there were relatively few medical means to reverse the course of death and when the quantity of life was of more concern than the quality. The answers were grounded in the belief that God gives life, it belongs to Him, and only He can take it away. Death by war, capital punishment, euthanasia, abortion, and suicide make us ask whether the commandment "Thou shalt not kill" is a sufficient guide to life, given the changes in medical technology, population, and morality. The commandment has been conveniently waived for war, the slaughter of animals, and executions. Often we fail to recognize that these deaths are killing: "We have almost grown accustomed to it; war is a cause of death like cancer and tuberculosis, like influenza and dysentery. The deaths are merely more frequent, more varied and terri-

U.S. Army Photograph.

ble." So speaks the German soldier in *All Quiet on the Western Front* of
the war that was to end all wars, World War I.

Should we be, on the other hand, so concerned with promoting life
that we prolong it past any hope of more than a vegetable existence?
This is the question posed by euthanasia. Euthanasia comes from two
Greek words, *eu* meaning "well" and *thanatos*, meaning death. It thus
means a good or happy death, a death with dignity. It is less than dignity
to die in prolonged agony or in total unconsciousness, being kept alive
only by a life-support machine. Euthanasia is not "mercy killing," an act
of *commission* such as injecting air into a patient's bloodstream. Euthanasia is accomplished by an act of *omission,* one which permits death.
One method is to withhold life-support systems (not plugging them in)
and another is to halt life-support treatments (pulling the plug).

Religious views on euthanasia are divided. Many theologians feel
that it is not right to use extraordinary means to prevent a person who is
nearly dead from dying in peace. Others feel that "It is impossible to
support the claim of the right of 'death with dignity.' A right to death
does not exist. . . ." (Father Gino Concetti, *Time,* Nov. 3, 1975) The medical profession is generally in favor of euthanasia; in one survey of doctors, eighty percent said they had practiced it (Hendin, 1973, p. 78). Ultimately, it is the physician who controls, by his or her medical
decisions, whether or not a patient will be allowed to die with dignity.

Should we attempt to support a new life which is deformed, unwanted, the result of rape or incest, which is a risk to the mother's life? This
is one form of the question of abortion. Can we force a woman to use her
body for gestation or to risk a dangerous, illegal abortion if legal abor-
tions are not available? As with euthanasia, this question is fundamental:
is every life, no matter what its quality, worth prolonging? A pregnant
woman has the responsibility for answering this question and for living
with the consequences of her decision.

Does an individual have the right to end his or her own life? We all have the potential to commit suicide, to make the decision that death is preferable to life and to act on that decision. The American view of suicide, in contrast to some other cultural views, is strongly negative. There is no honor in taking your own life in this country. We are encouraged to believe that life always serves more purposes than does death. However, suicide is the only sure way of controlling the time, place, and manner of death. It is the way to conquer the uncertainties, to make death definite. A. Alvarez, author of *The Savage God: A Study of Suicide,* and a man whose suicide was not successful, says, "I assume now that death, when it finally comes, will probably be nastier than suicide, and certainly a great deal less convenient." (1972, p. 284)

Very few who attempt to commit suicide are actually determined to end their lives. It is estimated that two-thirds of all suicide attempts are really attempts to get help for problems which seem unbearable. Another thirty percent are ambivalent about dying. They may see death as a relief from suffering or problems but they also have impulses to continue living. Only about three to five percent who attempt self-destruction are intent on succeeding (Coleman and Hammen, 1974).

The majority of people who attempt suicide give some clues to their intentions before they act. They are depressed, agitated, or withdrawn and may even say, "I wish I were dead." Some will talk of their plans. Often these, and other clues, aren't taken seriously; they may go unnoticed until after the attempt. True indications of suicide are difficult to differentiate from disturbed, worried, or depressed behaviors which do not lead to a suicide attempt. This is one reason we do not always take suicide threats seriously. Those who are seriously suicidal often make all their preparations for death, settle their financial matters, and carefully plan their deaths by highly lethal methods. And they may give no indication to anyone.

Melancholia (*From* A Psychiatrist's Anthology *by Louis J. Karnosh, The Occupational Therapy Press*).

The family and friends of a suicide victim experience grief at their loss and they often feel guilt and anger too. Wasn't there something we could have done to prevent death? Why did I let the pleas for help go unheeded? What right did she have to upset my life in this way? Am I my brother's keeper?

ACCEPTING DEATH

What can it mean to know that death is on its way and to be aware of the inevitability of nonlife? It can mean that we live a fuller and richer life. Preparing this chapter has given me the opportunity to have death on my mind for some time. Behind the lines I have written are many personal thoughts of death. I have recalled times of grief brought by death, the pain I felt because I did not tell my father how much I loved him before he died, and I have been reminded of how precious life really is. Each thought of death has brought a thought of life, of today, and of caring in the present. It is important to know that we will die and that those we love will die. Then we know that we do not have time to be casual, thoughtless, or selfish in our relationships. We do not have time to waste with bitterness, regret, or guilt. We only have time to live.

What is important is to realize that whether we understand fully why we are here or what will happen when we die, it is our purpose as human beings to grow — to look within ourselves to find and build upon that souce of peace and understanding and strength which is our inner selves, and to reach out to others with love, acceptance, patient guidance, and hope for what we all may become together.

In order to be at peace, it is necessary to feel a sense of history — that you are both part of what has come before and part of what is yet to come. Being thus surrounded, you are not alone; and the sense of urgency that pervades the present is put in perspective: Do not frivolously use the time that is yours to spend. Cherish it, that each day may bring new growth, insight, and awareness. Use this growth not selfishly, but rather in service of what may be, in the future tide of time. Never allow a day to pass that did not add to what was understood before. Let each day be a stone in the path of growth. Do not rest until what was intended has been done. But remember — go as slowly as is necessary in order to sustain a steady pace; do not expend energy in waste. Finally, do not allow the illusory urgencies of the immediate to distract you from your vision of the eternal . . . (Kübler-Ross, 1975, pp. 166–167).

EXPLORATION 14.3

Write Your Obituary

Date:

Place:

_____ died yesterday at _____

from _____ .

(S)he is survived by _____ .

At the time of his (her) death he (she) was working on becoming _____ .

His (Her) major contributions were _____ .

(S)he will be remembered for _____ .

(S)he will be mourned by _____ because _____ .

The last thing (s)he said was _____ .

The body will be _____ .

Flowers may be sent _____ .

In lieu of flowers _____ .

Share your obituary with those in your class.

(This exploration is adapted from *Values Clarification: A Practical Strategies for Teachers and Students* by Sidney B. Simon, Leland W. Howe, and Howard Kirschenbaum, copyright 1972 Hart Publishing Company, Inc.)

Find a quiet place where you will not be interrupted. Take a fantasy trip, imagining that you are dying. You are reviewing your life. What do you remember best in your life? What memories bring you pleasure and which bring you the most pain?

What experiences and accomplishments have given meaning to your life? Do you wish you had done anything differently in your life? Do you have any regrets? Were there choices you weren't aware of? Ones you were afraid of? Do you wish you had spent more or less time with anyone in particular? Is there anything you wish you had said or done that you didn't?

Think about what you valued in life. What was important to you?

Now you have only one hour to live. Whom do you want to spend your last hour with? How and where do you want to spend this time?

Think about your fantasy now, aware that you are alive and living. Did you discover something that you can do differently? Can you think of choices you would like to make, people you would like to be with, things you need to say? Are your values what you want them to be? Does the person(s) you wanted to spend your last hour with know how you feel? Have you discovered something you wanted to change?

(This exploration is adapted from James and Jongeward, *Born to Win*, 1971, Addison-Wesley, Reading, Mass., p. 241.)

MAXIMIZING THE PROCESS OF DYING

Death has been taboo in America. We are seen by some to be a death-denying society. Arnold Toynbee observed that death is Un-American, an affront to our inalienable rights to life, liberty, and the pursuit of happiness. But within the last few years there have been changes in our attitudes towards death and dying. We have increased our interest in mortality and in the quality of dying. It is estimated that two or three books are published each week on death (Robert Heinhold, *New York Times*, Aug., 1974). College curricula are including courses in thanatology (the study of death).

The interest in dying has not been a fad of the general public. The medical profession has begun approaching death in positive ways, rather than brushing it aside as an indication of their failure. Medical and nursing schools are using the work of Elisabeth Kübler-Ross and others to train health-care specialists to be death-care specialists also. These people are encouraged to examine their own attitudes towards death and their own fears, for often these are communicated to dying patients.

Another approach to dying is aimed at reducing the number of

Photograph courtesy of National Save-A-Life League, New York City.

suicidal deaths. There are over 200 Suicide Prevention Centers in the
United States. Their purpose is to provide help to the large number of
people who are ambivalent about living and dying. Suicide Prevention
Centers have 24-hour-a-day telephones manned by trained workers.
These workers help identify a caller's problems, evaluate the likelihood
of an immediate suicide attempt, help the caller assess resources for support, and, if necessary, see to it that the caller gets to an appropriate
resource. Often the most valuable service of Suicide Prevention is in
providing someone who will listen and clarify callers' problems.

The United States is beginning to import a special institution for the
dying, an alternative to costly hospital confinement and nursing homes.
This is the *Hospice,* a "place where travelers are given rest and hospital-
ity and where a home is made for those who are in need or sickness."
(Hendin, 1973, p. 95) Hospices have existed in England for more than
seventy years. They serve as homes for those with terminal illness, those
who are frail, lingering in life with a prognosis of little time, and others
who have nowhere else to go. They are not equipped with life-support
systems nor do they attempt to cure their residents. The atmosphere is
one of relaxation and warmth. Guests are encouraged to do as much for
themselves as possible and to be in charge of their own needs. Visitors
are welcome at all times, including children and pets. Medical attention
is for the relief of suffering and pain.

Other approaches to maximizing the experience of dying are experimental uses of nontraditional pain reduction. Hypnosis and acupuncture
are two, LSD is another. Dr. Stanislav Grof, at the Maryland Psychiatric
Research Center, has found that for some, LSD can bring peace, beauty,
and a serene approach to impending death as well as relief from pain.
Some of his patients have experienced a death and rebirth with LSD.

They seem to be able to face their fears and work through them to a final acceptance of death in a way that few dying people are able to do.

Another way of maximizing life through death is donating one's body for medical research or one's organs for transplant. By these gifts medical knowledge is increased and others are allowed to continue their lives without the impairment of faulty kidneys, livers, lungs, corneas, or hearts. As the technology of tranplantation is improved, more and more of the living will find prolonged life through donors' generosity. Donation may be made by a signed statement from the donor (with two witnesses) or by survivors; laws vary from state to state.

Thousands of Americans have settled the question of euthanasia for themselves and have signed "living wills" (see Box 14.1) asking that they be allowed to die with dignity. This document is not yet legally binding; however, it is being honored by many doctors.

BOX 14.1

A LIVING WILL

To My Family, My Physician, My Clergyman, My Lawyer:

If the time comes when I can no longer take part in decisions for my own future, let this statement stand as the testament of my wishes:

If there is no reasonable expectation of my recovery from physical or mental disability, I, _____ , request that I be allowed to die and not be kept alive by artificial means or heroic measures. Death is as much a reality as birth, growth, maturity, and old age—it is the one certainty. I do not fear death as much as I fear the indignity of deterioration, dependence, and hopeless pain. I ask that medication be mercifully administered to me for terminal suffering even if it hastens the moment of death.

This request is made after careful consideration. Although this document is not legally binding, you who care for me will, I hope, feel morally bound to follow its mandate. I recognize that it places a heavy burden of responsibility on you, and it is with the intention of sharing that responsibility and of mitigating any feelings of guilt that this statement is made.

Signed _____

Date _____

Witnesses _____

Prepared by The Euthanasia Educational Council
250 West 57 Street
New York, N.Y. 10019

SUMMARY
1. Death is a process; it is the final stage of the life cycle. There are medical, biological, psychological, and social criteria by which the time of death is established.
2. One of our concerns with death is its finality. The question of life after death is answered negatively by some and affirmatively by others. We do know that some of our genetic material may remain, memories of us remain, and a few dollars worth of chemicals remain after death.
3. We experience the concept of death in childhood according to our level of mental development, although the reality of death is often denied us. Death is denied with the use of euphemisms and when it is removed from the routine of everyday life. It is denied when it is presented repeatedly and is devoid of emotional significance.
4. We experience death in our fantasies and dreams, for various reasons. We often experience death with fear. We experience death as the loss of those close to us; death brings grief.
5. The experience of death for the dying has been described by Dr. Kübler-Ross in five stages: denial, anger, bargaining, depression, and acceptance. Hope and assurances that they won't be abandoned are the strongest needs of the dying.
6. Death is not always predictable. In situations where we do have control over the timing of death, we find some conflicting moral, ethical, and legal issues. Euthanasia (death with dignity), abortion, and suicide involve questions of the quality of life and human responsibility.
7. The awareness and acceptance of death can bring a greater value and meaning to life.
8. The process of death is maximized by the acceptance of death as an aspect of life. Other aids are suicide prevention centers, the Hospice, the use of LSD with the dying, body and organ donation, and Living Wills.

Suggested Readings

Becker, Ernest. *The denial of death.* New York: Free Press, 1973. A Pulitzer Prize winning work synthesizing theological and psychological views of man's nature and our efforts to escape the burdens of life and death.

Hendin, David. *Death as a fact of life.* New York: Warner, 1973. A realistic look at the legal, medical, and emotional aspects of death.

Keleman, Stanley. *Living your dying.* New York: Random House; Berkeley, Ca.: The Bookworks, 1974. Through working with images and becoming aware of our feelings about death we can beneficially experience dying before our death.

Kübler-Ross, Elisabeth. *Death: The final stage of growth.* Englewood Cliffs, N. J.: Prentice-Hall, 1975. A renowned authority on death presents her views and selections by others—ministers, rabbis, doctors, nurses, personal accounts by those near death, and their survivors.

Mitford, Jessica. *The American way of death.* Greenwich, Ct: Fawcett World, 1967. A harsh view of the death business in America and the ways we deny death in our funeral practices.

Rosenthal, Ted. *How could I not be among you?* New York: Avon Books, 1975. At the age of thirty, Ted Rosenthal was told he had acute leukemia. This is his story, written in the last months of his life, expressing his rage, terror, and the freedom he discovered.

Michael Weisbrot

ULTIMATELY

. . . life must be understood backwards.
But . . . it must be lived forwards.

Soren Kierkegaard
(*Journals of Kierkegaard: 1834–1854*)

I am a member of my species and of my culture. Both have had a part in determining my potentials. I am a unique manifestation of interactions, developing in my own way in my own time. No one else is or ever will be this singular combination: me.

My life, from birth to death, is a search; it is a quest for finding and knowing my potentials, and for making them actual. Only I can discover my self by repeated experiences of myself in living.

The older I get the more discoveries I make; every day provides me with experiences in choosing to develop in one way rather than another. At any point in my life, I am the sum of the choices I have made, the experiences I have had.

My choices are forks in the road; they come one junction at a time. Every time I choose the North fork, I am unable to follow the path to the South or the West or the East.

Every choice I make is limited by the perspective I have at the moment I choose. What I believe to be determines what is for me. Many times I cannot change events; I can only change my viewpoint. I can only strive to be aware.

Choice is not easy. The more aware I am, the more difficult it can seem. But the more I know what I want, the less my anxiety. The more aware I am of my real self, the truer to myself I can be, and the more I can grow.

I grow when I connect with others. When I fear closeness or a commitment to intimacy I limit my potentials for humanness. If I live with the intent to be as truly honest and disclosing with another as I can be, and to trust his or her intent to be concerned for me, then I can maximize my chance for intimacy.

I am true to myself when I understand my sexual potentials and when I choose my sexual expression. When I know I am responsible for my sexual feelings and can be responsible for my own sexuality, I am maximizing my humanness.

I am true to myself when I am not playing a stereotyped role. I am true to myself and to others when I perceive all human beings as individuals and do not judge them with narrow and limiting preconceptions of sex roles.

The best times in my life are those in which I know I am playing games worth playing — games worthy of me, of my effort and mastery.

I need not be bound by ordinary consciousness if I seek to actualize my own inner potentials and to utilize my brain's capacity for intuition, dreams, and other altered states. I can best increase my consciousness with intention and self-control.

As long as I am alive I want to choose. I want to live until I die; I want to *grow* older as I live. I want to know and be able to respect myself. I want to see my past as the series of choices which brought me here to my present. I need to see the effects of my choices; I do not need to hold onto the past with regret.

I am not always aware of an experience as a choice. But as I look back I am sure that all experiences, good or bad, were just the right ones to bring me to this moment.

I can and will choose again, not making the same choices as before, but the next choices.

My life is a quest in which I discover my potentials, actualize some, and ignore others. My quests end when I die. I need to remember, every day I live, that death will come—and that life is now. My quests are ultimately fulfilled in the living of my life.

GLOSSARY

Active listening   A communication technique which avoids the interference of a listener's judgements.

Age norms   Standards of correct or appropriate behavior according to age, as implied in the admonition "Act your age."

Agism   Discriminatory or otherwise negative attitudes toward old people, often based on the assumption that they are no longer of value to society.

Androgyny   The state of being both male and female in one.

Anima   *See* Shadow

Animus   *See* Shadow

Approach-approach conflict   *See* Conflict

Approach-avoidance conflict   *See* Conflict

Avoidance-avoidance conflict   *See* Conflict

B-cognition and D-cognition   *Being* cognition and *Deficiency* cognition are terms coined by Abraham Maslow to describe two types of thinking or knowing. The first refers to thinking devoid of immediate needs, roles, and projects; the second is goal oriented, directed toward making sense of the world.

Behaviorism   A psychological viewpoint that focuses on observable behavior and stresses the importance of environment in learning.

Behavior modification   The use of experimentally established learning principles to change human behavior.

Biofeedback   Methods of teaching a person to control biological functions such as brain waves or muscle tension, using machines to report and amplify normally undetectable physical processes.

B-love and D-love   *Being* love and *Deficiency* love, terms coined by Abraham Maslow to refer, respectively, to love characterized by an active concern for the well-being of another, and love characterized by seeking in another to meet one's own deficiences.

Classical conditioning   A form of learning in which an automatic or innate response is transferred to a situation where it does not ordinarily occur.

Cognitive dissonance A state of tension that arises when a person holds two thoughts, attitudes, or beliefs that are logically inconsistent.

Contact comfort The reassurance that comes from physical contact with familiar and pleasing people and things.

Corpus callosum The "hard body" of fibers that connect the left and right hemispheres of the brain and carry information between them.

Cortex The outer layer of the brain; it is deeply folded in humans and is the "higher" brain that characterizes our species; short for cerebral cortex.

Data reduction Screening out that information which comes to us through our senses in greater amounts or intensity than we can use in making sense of the environment.

D-cognition *See* B-cognition and D-cognition

Denial A defense mechanism for avoiding a threatening thought, person, or object by acting as though it does not exist.

Depressant Also known as sedative-hypnotics (alcohol, opiates, barbiturates, and tranquilizers), these drugs induce drowsiness and some loss of inhibition as they slow the activity of the brain.

Discriminate The process of distinguishing between closely related or highly similar items.

Disembodiment According to Ronald Laing, the loss of contact with one's experience such that a sense of separation occurs between one's self and one's body.

Displacing A defense mechanism by which an emotion felt for a particular person, object, or situation is transferred to something or someone else.

D-love *See* B-love and D-love

Ego In Freudian theory, the ego is that component of the personality which mediates between the id and the superego, as well as responding to the environment.

Ego boundary The outer limits of what is familiar to us; it expands as we grow and gain experience.

Ego defense The ego uses various unconscious mechanisms (repression, denial, etc.) to protect itself from anxiety and conflict. These mechanisms are known collectively as ego defenses.

Extraverted *See* Introverted-extraverted

Feedback Information from some outside source that lets us know what and how we are doing.

Free association A Freudian technique of therapy in which a patient is encouraged to say whatever comes to mind.

Gender identity Sense of being and belonging to one sex and not to the other; most strongly influenced by how one is treated, i.e., as a male or a female.

Generalize To respond similarly to stimuli that resemble one another.

Genetic Refers to those characteristics of an individual which are transmitted to him or her biologically, rather than those learned after birth; *genes*, the units of heredity, provide the basic genetic material in the substance DNA (deoxyribonucleic acid).

Habituation Gradual adaptation to constant stimuli until they become unnoticed.

Holistic Refers to the basic assumption that the whole is greater than the sum of its parts; in psychology, implies that the whole of one's experience, both in one's consciousness and in reality, has properties that are not simply the result of combining its parts.

Humanism A psychological viewpoint that stresses the individuality and worth of each person; every person is free to choose his or her path to enrichment and the development of unrealized potentials.

Human sexual response cycle The four phases of sexual response (excitement, plateau, orgasmic, and resolution) that follow from erotic stimulation.

Hypochondriac One who shows excessive concern with and complains about one's physical state.

Id According to Freud, the id is the most primitive part of the personality and is made up of unconscious impulses.

Identification The unconscious act of assuming qualities or traits that one sees in someone else in order to be more like that other person.

Imprinting The forming of long-lasting social attachments to another; these attachments are learned very quickly during a critical period of development. (An imprint is a lasting impression.)

Instincts Complex behavior patterns that are innate, or built in, and do not require learning or practice.

Introverted-extraverted Carl Jung's terms for basic personality types; the introvert is motivated by and interested in the inner or personal world, while the extravert is oriented primarily toward the outside environment.

Learn To more or less permanently change one's behavior as the result of experience.

Libido A Freudian term that refers to the energy which maintains all life processes. This instinctual force is sexual, although it serves other drives.

Loneliness anxiety The fear that one may be left alone or left out and thus have to spend one's life in solitude.

Long-term memory A term referring to those things we remember permanently.

Menopause That point in the life of human females when menstruation ceases, occurring usually between the ages of 45 and 55.

Negative feedback Signals in the form of failure, punishment, or disapproval that discourage a person from continuing a behavior. (*See also* Feedback)

Neurons Nerve cells; the basic elements of the nervous system which receive and transmit physiological and psychological information.

Neurotic A term used to characterize behavior which is rigid and ineffective in its goal of avoiding anxiety.

Nymphomania Refers to a woman with a lusty sexual appetite or who is sexually active. A term of no scientific value, yet still popular in common language.

Operant conditioning A form of learning in which persistence of a response depends on the effect it has on the environment.

Oedipus complex In Freud's theory, the period from 3 to 6 years, during which a male child falls in love with and sexually desires his mother and wishes his father dead. A female child, similarly, sexually desires her father and hates her mother.

Personal constructs The ways in which humans construe, interpret, or attach meaning to experience.

Prejudice A belief characterized by the oversimplification, overgeneralization, and distortion of some small element of truth.

Projection Attributing to others one's own desires, attitudes, and motives; seeing these feelings as coming from sources outside oneself.

Psychedelics This group of drugs includes Mescalin, psilocybin, LSD, and marijuana. These "mind-expanding" substances affect the nervous system in ways not yet clearly understood.

Psychic contactlessness   According to Wilhelm Reich, that state of detachment which comes about when we avoid relating emotionally to others.

Psychoanalysis   A psychological viewpoint, developed by Freud, that stresses intrapsychic conflict as a cause of human problems and sets to treat these problems by helping the patient gain insight into the unconscious.

Psychosocial crisis   According to Erik Erikson, a stage in the developmental process at which an important problem must be solved (even temporarily) in order for an individual to continue growing into the next stage.

Psychosomatic   A term consisting of the root words *psycho* (mind) and *soma* (body). It is used to refer to the wide variety of bodily responses, healthy and unhealthy, that are thought to be related to psychological processes.

Public self   The personality which is presented to others, sometimes in order to mask the real self.

Random schedule   (*See* Schedule of Reinforcement)

Rationalization   A mechanism for defending oneself against unwanted attitudes or behavior by making excuses or giving reasons.

Reaction formation   Masking an undesirable trait or attitude by presenting the opposite trait or attitude.

Real self   The true or authentic core of one's personality.

Refractory period   That period following orgasm when a man is incapable of having another orgasm.

Regression   Reverting to behavior of an earlier stage of one's development in response to stress in the present.

Reinforcement   A stimulus that increases (positive reinforcement) or decreases (negative reinforcement) the probability of a particular response being given.

Repression   A common ego defense that pushes painful or disturbing thoughts or feelings out of one's consciousness.

Schedule of reinforcement   The "timetable" by which reinforcements occur in operant conditioning. With a random schedule of reinforcements, rewards or punishments are distributed every so often rather than regularly.

Schizophrenia   A persisting state of disembodiment, in which one loses contact with the real world of people and events.

Security operations   According to Harry Stack Sullivan, behavior which we produce in order to remain "safe" in the opinions of others.

Self-concept   Those judgements one makes about one's worth or value.

Self-fulfilling prophecy   A presumption or expectation that influences behavior in a way that meets the expectation itself.

Self-ideal   The person that one would like to be or that one feels one should be.

Self-image   A picture or private representation one has of oneself.

Serial monogamy   The practice of limiting one's serious relationships (such as marriage) to *one partner at a time,* in contrast to staying with one partner forever.

Shadow, Anima, Animus   Defined by C. G. Jung, hidden personality components which are often projected onto others; *shadow* is our unconscious aspect, *anima* our feminine aspect, and *animus* our masculine aspect.

Socialization   The process by which an individual learns to behave in a manner approved by his or her society.

Stereotype   An object (or person) to which are attributed characteristics of the class to which it belongs, regardless of the individuality of that object (or person).

Stimulant   A group of drugs, including amphetamines and cocaine, which elevate mood, increase alertness, and reduce fatigue by increasing the activity of the central nervous system.

Stimulus-response   The basic mechanism from which patterns of behavior (habits) are built when individuals respond in the same way to repetitions of the same stimulus.

Stranger anxiety   The fear of unfamiliar people.

Superego   This component of the personality, according to Freud, is responsible for one's standards of conduct and morality. It is the source of self-approval and guilt.

Symbiotic   Refers to the relationships of close association, especially when these are advantageous to all involved.

Unconscious   According to Freud, those innate impulses, as well as wishes and repressed memories, of which we are unaware.

Withdrawal   Physically or psychologically removing oneself from a frustrating, anxious situation.

REFERENCES

Adler, A. *What life should mean to you.* New York: Putnam, 1959.

Adler, R., & Towne, N. *Looking out/looking in.*, San Francisco: Rinehart Press, 1975.

Alberti, R. E., & Emmons, M. *Your perfect right.* (2nd ed.) San Luis Obispo, Ca.: IMPACT, 1974.

Allport, G. W. (Ed.) *Letters from Jenny.* New York: Harcourt, 1965.

Alvarez, A. *The savage god: A study of suicide.* New York: Random House, 1972.

Andelin, A. P. *Man of steel and velvet.* Santa Barbara, Ca.: Pacific Santa Barbara, 1975.

Andelin, H. *Fascinating woman.* New York: Bantam, 1974.

Andersen, M. S., & Savary, L. M. *Passages: A guide for pilgrims of the mind.* New York: Harper & Row, 1973.

Anderson, R. I never sang for my father. In O. L. Guernsey, Jr. (Ed.), *The best plays of 1967–1968.* New York: Dodd, Mead, 1968, 277–298.

Ardrey, R. *The territorial imperative.* New York: Atheneum, 1966.

Assagioli, R. *Psychosynthesis.* New York: Viking, 1965.

Avila, D. L., Combs, A. W., & Purkey, W. W. *The helping relationship sourcebook.* Boston: Allyn and Bacon, 1971.

Baba Ram Dass (Richard Alpert), & the Lama Foundation. *Be here now.* New York: Crown, 1971.

Bach, G. R., & Deutsch, R. M. *Pairing.* New York: Avon, 1970.

Balint, A. *The early years of life: A psychoanalytic study.* New York: Basic Books, 1954.

Bandura, A. *Principles of behavior modification.* New York: Holt, Rinehart and Winston, 1969.

Barbach, L. G. *For yourself: The fulfillment of female sexuality.* Garden City, N.Y.: Doubleday, 1975.

Bardwick, J. M. *Psychology of women: A study of bio-cultural conflicts.* New York: Harper & Row, 1971.

Barnard, J. *The future of marriage.* New York: Bantam, 1972.

Bateson, G. *Steps to an ecology of mind.* New York: Ballantine, 1972.

Becker, E. *The denial of death.* New York: Free Press, 1973.

Bem, S. L. Androgyny vs. the tight little lives of fluffy women and chesty men. *Psychology Today,* September 1975, 58–62.

Benston, M. The political economy of women's liberation. In E. H. Altbach (Ed.), *From feminism to liberation.* Cambridge, Mass.: Schenkman, 1971, 199–210.

Bergson, H. *Time and free will: An essay on the immediate data of consciousness.* (Trans. by F. L. Pogson) New York: Macmillan, 1959.

Berne, E. *Games people play.* New York: Grove, 1964.

Berrill, N. J. *Man's emerging mind.* New York: Dodd, Mead, 1955.

Birth control handbook. Montreal: Montreal Health Press, 1973.

Boston Women's Health Collective. *Our bodies our selves, a book by and for women.* New York: Simon & Schuster, 1973.

Bowlby, J. *Maternal care and mental health.* Geneva: World Health Organization, 1952.

Brecher, E. M. *The sex researchers.* New York: New American Library, 1971.

Brecher, R., & Brecher, E. M. (Eds.) *An analysis of human sexual response.* New York: New American Library, 1966.

Bronowski, J. *The ascent of man.* Boston: Little, Brown, 1973.

Broverman, I. K., Broverman, D. M., Clarkson, F. E., Rosenkrantz, P. S., & Vogel, S. R. Sex-role stereotypes and clinical judgments of mental health. In J. M. Bardwick (Ed.), *Readings on the psychology of women.* New York: Harper & Row, 1972, 320–324.

Brown, B. *New mind, new body — biofeedback: New directions for the mind.* New York: Harper & Row, 1975.

Brown, L. A. *The story of maps.* New York: Bonanza Books, 1949.

Cabot, N. H. *You can't count on dying.* Boston: Houghton Mifflin, 1961.

Calder, N. *The mind of man.* New York: Viking, 1970.

Campbell, J. (Ed.) *The portable Jung.* New York: Viking, 1971.

Carroll, L. *The annotated Alice: Alice's adventures in wonderland & through the looking glass* (with notes by M. Gardner). New York: New American Library, 1960.

Castaneda, C. *Journey to Ixtlan.* New York: Simon & Schuster, 1962.

————. *Teachings of Don Juan: A Yaqui way of knowledge.* New York: Ballantine, 1968.

————. *A separate reality: Further conversations with Don Juan.* New York: Simon & Schuster, 1971.

————. *Tales of power.* New York: Simon & Schuster, 1974.

Chafetz, J. S. *Masculine/feminine or human? An overview of the sociology of sex roles.* Itasca, Ill.: Peacock, 1974.

Chesler, P. *Women and madness.* Garden City, N.Y.: Doubleday, 1972.

Chesser, E. *Salvation through sex: The life and work of Wilhelm Reich.* New York: Morrow, 1973.

Chiappa, J. A., & Forish, J. J. *The VD book: For people who care about themselves and others.* New York: Holt, Rinehart and Winston, 1976.

Christian, J. L. *Philosophy.* San Francisco: Rinehart Press, 1973.

Coleman, J. C., & Hammen, C. L. *Contemporary psychology and effective behavior.* Glenview, Ill: Scott, Foresman, 1974.

Comfort, A. (Ed.) *The joy of sex.* New York: Crown, 1972.

————. *More joy of sex: A lovemaking companion to the joy of sex.* New York: Simon & Schuster, 1974.

Coopersmith, S. *The antecedents of self-esteem.* San Francisco: Freeman, 1967.

Coutts, R. L. *Love and intimacy: A psychological approach.* San Ramon, Ca.: Consensus, 1973.

Cowgill, D. O., & Holmes, L. D. (Eds.) *Aging and modernization.* New York: Appleton, 1972.

Deacon, J. J. *Joey.* New York: Scribner, 1974.

De Beauvoir, S. *The coming of age.* (Trans. by P. O'Brian) New York: Putnam, 1972.

Deckard, B. S. *The women's movement: Political, socio-economic, and psychological issues.* New York: Harper & Row, 1975.

Dector, M. *The new chastity and other arguments against women's liberation.* New York: Coward, McCann, 1972.

de Ropp, R. S. *The master game.* New York: Dell, 1968.

De Rougemont, D. The crisis of the modern couple. In R. N. Anshen (Ed.), *The family: Its function and destiny.* New York: Harper & Row, 1949.

Donne, J. Devotions XVII. In H. Gardner & T. Healy (Eds.), *Selected prose.* London: Oxford, 1967, 100–101.

Downing, G. *The massage book.* New York: Random House and Berkeley, Ca.: The Bookworks, 1972.

Duberman, L. *Gender and sex in society.* New York: Praeger, 1975.

Durrell, L. *Justine.* New York: Pocket Books, 1957.

Eliot, T. S. Four quartets. In *Collected poems 1909–1962.* New York: Harcourt, 1952, 200–209.

Ellis, A. *Reason and emotion in psychotherapy.* New York: Lyle Stuart, 1962.

————. *Sex without guilt.* New York: Grove, 1965.

Erikson, E. *Childhood and society.* (2nd ed.) New York: Norton, 1963.

————. *Identity: Youth and crisis.* New York: Norton, 1968.

Fabun, D. *Three roads to awareness.* Beverly Hills, Ca.: Glencoe Press, 1970.

Falk, R. *Women loving: A journey toward becoming an independent woman.* New York: Random House and Berkeley, Ca.: The Bookworks, 1975.

Faraday, A. *Dream power.* New York: Coward, McCann, 1972.

Farrell, W. T. Guidelines for consciousness raising. *Ms.,* February 1973, p. 15.

————. Beyond masculinity: Liberating men and their relationships with women. In L. Duberman, *Gender and sex in society.* New York: Praeger, 1975a, 216–247.

————. *The liberated man.* New York: Bantam, 1975b.

Farson, R. *Birthrights: A bill of rights for children.* New York: Macmillan, 1974.

Felstein, I. *Sex in later life.* Baltimore: Penguin, 1970.

Festinger, L. *A theory of cognitive dissonance.* Stanford: Stanford University Press, 1957.

Firestone, S. *The dialectic of sex: The case for feminist revolution.* New York: Bantam, 1970.

Forster, E. M. *Howard's end.* New York: Vintage, 1954.

Fort, J. *The pleasure seekers: The drug crisis, youth and society.* New York: Grove, 1969.

Fraiberg, S. H. *The magic years.* New York: Scribner, 1959.

Frankl, V. *Man's search for meaning.* New York: Simon & Schuster, 1970.

Freedman, M. *Homosexuality and psychological functioning.* Belmont, Ca.: Brooks/Cole, 1971.

Freud, S. *The basic writings of Sigmund Freud.* New York: Modern Library, 1938.

Friedan, B. *The feminine mystique.* New York: Dell, 1963.

Friedenberg, E. Z. *The vanishing adolescent.* Boston: Beacon Press, 1959.

Fromm, E. *The art of loving: An enquiry into the nature of love.* New York: Harper & Row, 1956.

Frost, R. The road not taken. In E. C. Lathem (Ed.), *The poetry of Robert Frost.* New York: Holt, Rinehart and Winston, 1969, 51.

Gager, N. (Ed.) *Women's rights almanac 1974.* Bethesda, Md.: Elizabeth Cady Stanton Publishing, 1974.

Gagnon, J. H., & Simon, W. *Sexual conduct: The sources of human sexuality.* Chicago: Aldine, 1973.

Gardiner, W. L. *Psychology: A story of a search.* Belmont, Ca.: Brooks/Cole, 1970.

Gibran, K. *The prophet.* New York: Knopf, 1963.

Ginott, H. G. *Between parent & child.* New York: Avon, 1965.

Glasser, W. *Reality therapy.* New York: Harper & Row, 1970.

Goodman, P. *Growing up absurd.* New York: Vintage, 1960.

Gordon, T. *Parent effectiveness training.* New York: Wyden, 1970.

Gornick, V. Woman as outsider. In V. Gornick & B. K. Moran (Eds.), *Woman in sexist society.* New York: Basic Books, 1971, 70–84.

Green, B. R., & Irish, D. P. *Death education: Preparation for living.* Cambridge: Schenkman, 1971.

Green, H. *I never promised you a rose garden.* New York: New American Library, 1964.

Gregory, R. L. *Eye and brain: the psychology of seeing.* New York: McGraw-Hill, 1966.

Gunther, B. *Sense relaxation.* New York: Macmillan, 1968.

———. *What to do till the messiah comes.* New York: Macmillan, 1971.

Hacker, H. M. Class and race differences in gender roles. In L. Duberman, *Gender and sex in society.* New York: Praeger, 1975, 134–184.

Hall, C. S., & Nordby, V. J. *A primer of Jungian psychology.* New York: New American Library, 1973.

Hall, M. H. A conversation with Masters & Johnson. *Psychology Today,* July 1969, 50–60.

Hampden-Turner, C. *Sane asylum: The dramas of Delancey Street.* San Francisco: San Francisco Book Co., 1976.

Harding, E. M. *The "I" and the "Not-I": A study in the development of consciousness.* Princeton, N. J.: Princeton University Press, 1965.

Harlow, H. F., & Zimmermann, R. P. Affectional responses in the infant monkey. *Science,* 1959, **130**(3373), 421–432.

Harlow, H. F., & Harlow, M. H. Learning to love. *American Scientist,* 1966, **54**(3), 244–272.

Harris, T. A. *I'm OK—You're OK.* New York: Harper & Row, 1969.

Hartley, R. E. Sex-role pressures and the socialization of the male child. *Psychological Reports,* 1959, **5**, 457–68.

Hendin, D. *Death as a fact of life*. New York: Warner, 1973.

Henry, M. (with Renaud, H.) Examined and unexamined lives. *Research Reporter*, 1972, 7(1), 5–8.

Hertzberg, H., & McClelland, D. C. K. Paranoia. *Harper's Magazine*, April 1974.

Hettlinger, R. F. *Human sexuality: A psychosocial perspective*. Belmont, Ca.: Wadsworth, 1975.

Hittleman, R. *Introduction to yoga*. New York: Bantam, 1969.

Holmes, T. H., & Masuda, M. Psychosomatic syndrome. *Psychology Today*, April 1972, 71–72, 106.

Horner, M. S. Fail: Bright women. *Psychology Today*, November 1969, 32–38, 62.

Horney, K. *Our inner conflicts*. New York: Norton, 1945.

Howard, J. *Please touch: A guided tour of the human potential movement*. New York: Dell, 1970.

Hunt, M. *The natural history of love*. New York: Knopf, 1959.

———. *Sexual behavior in the 1970s*. Chicago: Playboy Press, 1974.

Huxley, A. Human potentialities. In R. E. Farson (Ed.), *Science and human affairs*. Palo Alto, Ca.: Science and Behavior Books, 1965, 32–44.

Huxley, L. A. *You are not the target*. North Hollywood, Ca.: Wilshire, 1974.

Huyck, M. H. *Growing older*. Englewood Cliffs, N.J.: Prentice-Hall, 1974.

If death shall be no more. *Time*, Nov. 3, 1975, 58.

Imara, M. Dying as the last stage of growth. In E. Kübler-Ross, *Death: The final stage of growth*. Englewood Cliffs, N.J.: Prentice-Hall, 1975, 145–163.

James, M., & Jongeward, D. *Born to win: Transactional analysis with gestalt experiments*. Reading, Mass.: Addison-Wesley, 1971.

James, M., & Savary, L. M. *The heart of friendship*. New York: Harper & Row, 1976.

James, W. *Principles of psychology* (1890), Vol. 1. New York: Dover, 1950.

Janeway, E. *Man's world, woman's place: A study in social mythology*. New York: Dell, 1971.

Janov, A. *The primal scream: A revolutionary cure for neurosis*. New York: Putnam, 1970.

Jourard, S. M. *The transparent self*. (2nd ed.) New York: Van Nostrand, 1971.

———. *Healthy personality: An approach from the viewpoint of humanistic psychology*. New York: Macmillan, 1974.

Kagan, J. *Understanding children: Behavior, motives, and thought*. New York: Harcourt, 1971.

Kaplan, A. G., & Bean, J. P. *Beyond sex-role stereotypes: Readings toward a psychology of androgyny*. Boston: Little, Brown, 1976.

Kaplan, H. S. *The new sex therapy: Active treatment of sexual dysfunctions*. New York: Brunner/Mazel, 1975.

Katchadourian, H. A. & Lunde, D. T. *Fundamentals of human sexuality*. (2nd ed.) New York: Holt, Rinehart and Winston, 1975.

Keleman, S. *Living your dying*. New York: Random House and Berkeley, Ca.: The Bookworks, 1974.

Kelly, G. A. *The psychology of personal constructs*, Vols. 1 & 2. New York: Norton, 1955.

Kierkegaard, S. *In fear and trembling/The sickness unto death*. (Trans. by W. Lowrie) Garden City, N.Y.: Doubleday, 1954.

————. *Journals of Kierkegaard: 1834–1854.* (Ed. and trans. by A. Dru.) London: Collins Press, 1969.

Kinget, G. M. *On being human: A systematic view.* New York: Harcourt, 1975.

Kinsbourne, M., & Cook, J. Generalized and lateralized effects of concurrent verbalization on a unilateral skill. *Quarterly Journal of Experimental Psychology,* 1971, **23**, 341–345.

Kinsey, A. C., Pomeroy, W. B., & Martin, C. E. *Sexual behavior in the human male.* Philadelphia: Saunders, 1948.

Kinsey, A. C., Pomeroy, W. B., Martin, C. E., & Gebhard, P. H. *Sexual behavior in the human female.* Philadelphia: Saunders, 1953.

Koch, J., & Koch, L. *The marriage savers.* New York: Coward, McCann, 1976.

Kohlberg, L. Stage and sequence: The cognitive-developmental approach to socialization. In D. A. Goslin (Ed.), *Handbook of socialization theory and research.* Chicago: Rand McNally, 1969, 347–480.

Korner, A. F. Individual differences at birth: Implications for early experience and later development. *American Journal of Orthopsychiatry,* 1961, **41**, 608–619.

Krantzler, M. *Creative divorce.* New York: M. Evans, 1974.

Kübler-Ross, E. *On death and dying.* New York: Macmillan, 1969.

————. *Death: The final stage of growth.* Englewood Cliffs, N.J.: Prentice-Hall, 1975.

Laing, R. D. *The divided self.* Baltimore: Penguin, 1965.

————. *The politics of experience.* New York: Ballantine, 1967.

Langer, E. J., & Dweck, C. S. *Personal politics: The psychology of making it.* Englewood Cliffs, N.J.: Prentice-Hall, 1973.

Leonard, G. *The ultimate athlete.* New York: Viking, 1975.

Lessing, D. *The four gated city.* New York: Bantam, 1969.

Levitin, T., Quinn, R. P., & Staines, G. L. A woman is 58% of a man. . . . *Psychology Today,* March 1973, 89–91.

Lilly, J. C. *The center of the cyclone: An autobiography of inner space.* New York: Julian Press, 1972.

Luce, G. G. *Body time.* New York: Bantam, 1973.

Ludwig, A. M. Altered states of consciousness. In C. T. Tart (Ed.), *Altered states of consciousness.* Garden City, N.Y.: Doubleday, 1969, 11–24.

Luft, J. *Of human interaction.* Palo Alto, Ca.: National Press Books, 1969.

Luthman, S. G. *Intimacy: The essence of male and female.* Los Angeles: Nash, 1972.

McBride, W., & Fleischhauer-Hardt, H. *Show me! A picture book of sex for children and parents.* (Trans. by H. Davies) New York: St. Martin's, 1975.

McCarthy, B. W., Ryan, M., & Johnson, F. A. *Sexual awareness: A practical approach.* San Francisco: Boyd & Fraser, 1975.

McCary, J. L. *Sexual myths and fallacies.* New York: Van Nostrand, 1971.

Maccoby, E. E., & Jacklin, C. N. *The psychology of sex differences.* Stanford: Stanford University Press, 1974a.

————. What we know and don't know about sex differences. *Psychology Today,* December 1974b, 109–112.

MacKellar, J. *Rape: The bait & the trap.* New York: Crown, 1975.

Marshall, B. (Ed.) *Experiences in being.* Belmont, Ca.: Brooks/Cole, 1971.

Maslow, A. H. *Toward a psychology of being.* (Rev. ed.) New York: Van Nostrand, 1968.

_____. *Motivation and personality.* (2nd ed.) New York: Harper & Row, 1970.

_____. *The further reaches of human nature.* New York: Viking, 1971.

Masters, R., & Houston, J. *Mind games: The guide to inner space.* New York: Dell, 1972.

Masters, W. H., & Johnson, V. E. *Human sexual response.* Boston: Little, Brown, 1966.

_____. *Human sexual inadequacy.* Boston: Little, Brown, 1970.

Masters, W. H., & Johnson, V. E., with R. J. Levin. *The pleasure bond.* New York: Bantam, 1975.

May, R. (Ed.) *Existential psychology.* (2nd ed.) New York: Random House, 1969.

Mead, M. *Male and female.* New York: Morrow, 1949.

Michner, J. A. *The fires of spring.* New York: Random House, 1949.

Mitford, J. *The American way of death.* Greenwich, Ct: Fawcett World, 1967.

Money, J., & Ehrhardt, A. *Man and woman: Boy and girl.* Baltimore: The Johns Hopkins Press, 1972.

Montagu, A. *Touching: The human significance of the skin.* New York: Columbia University Press, 1971.

_____. *Man and aggression.* (2nd ed.) New York: Oxford, 1973.

Moreno, J. L. *The first psychodramatic family.* Boston: Beacon Press, 1964.

Morris, J. *Conundrum.* New York: Harcourt, 1974.

Morrison, E. S., & Underhill, P. M. *Values in sexuality: A new approach to sex education.* New York: Hart, 1974.

Moustakas, C. E. *Loneliness.* Englewood Cliffs, N.J.: Prentice-Hall, 1961.

Murphy, G. *Human Potentialities.* New York: Basic Books, 1958.

Murry, P. The liberation of black women. In J. Freeman (Ed.), *Women: A feminist perspective.* Palo Alto, Ca.: Mayfield, 1975, 351–363.

Mussen, P. H., Conger, J. J., & Kagan, J. *Child development and personality.* New York: Harper & Row, 1974.

Naranjo, C., & Ornstein, R. *On the psychology of meditation.* New York: Viking, 1971.

Needleman, J. *The new religions.* New York: Doubleday, 1970.

Neugarten, B. L. *Middle age and aging: A reader in social psychology.* Chicago: University of Chicago Press, 1968.

Neugarten, B. L. Personality change in late life: A developmental perspective. In C. Eisdorfer & M. P. Lawton (Eds.), *The psychology of adult development and aging.* Washington, D. C.: The American Psychological Association, 1973, 311–335.

New outlook for the aged. *Time,* June 2, 1975, 44–51.

Nowlis, H. H. Perspectives on drug use. *Journal of Social Issues,* 1971, **27**(3), 7–22.

O'Neill, N., & O'Neill, G. *Open marriage: A new life style for couples.* New York: M. Evans, 1972.

Ornstein, R. E. *The psychology of consciousness.* San Francisco: Freeman, 1972.

Pearce, J. C. *The crack in the cosmic egg: Challenging constructs of mind and reality.* New York: Pocket Books, 1973.

Perls, F. S. *Gestalt therapy verbatim.* Lafayette, Ca.: Real People Press, 1969.

Peter, L. J., & Hull, R. *The Peter principle.* New York: Morrow, 1969.

Petras, J. W. (Ed.) *Sex: Male/Gender: Masculine: Selected readings in male sexuality.* Port Washington, N.Y.: Alfred, 1975.

Piaget, J. *The origins of intelligence in children.* New York: International Universities Press, 1952.

Pierson, E. C., & D'Antonio, W. V. *Female and male.* Philadelphia: Lippincott, 1974.

Pleck,·J. H., & Sawyer, J. (Eds.) *Men and masculinity.* Englewood Cliffs, N.J.: Prentice-Hall, 1974.

Poland, R. G. *Human experience: A psychology of growth.* St. Louis, Mo.: Mosby, 1974.

Polk, B. B., & Stein, R. B. Is the grass greener on the other side? In C. Safilios-Rothschild (Ed.), *Toward a sociology of women.* Lexington, Mass.: Xerox College Publishing, 1972, 14–23.

Prather, H. *Notes to myself.* Lafayette, Ca.: Real People Press, 1970.

Provence, S., & Lipton, R. C. *Infants in institutions.* New York: International Universities Press, 1962.

Ralston, N. C., & Thomas, G. P. *The adolescent: Case studies for analysis.* San Francisco: Chandler Publishing Company, 1974.

Ramey, E. R. Boredom: The most prevalent American disease. *Harper's Magazine,* November 1974, 12–22.

Ramey, J. W. Intimate networks. *The Futurist,* August 1975, 175–181.

Ramey, J. W. *Intimate friendships.* Englewood Cliffs, N.J.: Prentice-Hall, 1976.

Reinhold, R. Changing winds of death. *New York Times.* August 18, 1974.

Reisman, D. *The lonely crowd.* New Haven: Yale University Press, 1950.

Remarque, E. *All quiet on the western front.* New York: Heritage, 1929.

Richards, M. C. *Centering in pottery, poetry, and the person.* Middletown, Ct.: Wesleyan University Press, 1964.

Richards, W., Grof, S., Goodman, L., & Kurland, A. LSD-assisted psychotherapy and the human encounter with death. *Journal of Transpersonal Psychology.* 1972, 4(2), 121–150.

Roache, J. Confessions of a househusband. *Ms.,* November 1972, 25–27.

Rogers, C. R. *Client-centered therapy; its current practice, implications, and theory.* Boston: Houghton Mifflin, 1951.

———. A theory of therapy, personality, and interpersonal relationships, as developed in the client-centered framework. In S. Koch (Ed.), *Psychology: A study of a science,* Vol. 3. New York: McGraw-Hill, 1959, 184–256.

———. *On becoming a person.* Boston: Houghton Mifflin, 1961.

———. *Carl Rogers on encounter groups.* New York: Harper & Row, 1970.

———. *Becoming partners: marriage and its alternatives.* New York: Dell, 1972.

Rogers, C. R., & Stevens, B. *Person to person: the problem of being human.* New York: Pocket Books, 1971.

Rokeach, M. Faith, hope, bigotry. *Psychology Today,* April 1970, 33–37.

Rosenfeld, E. *The book of highs: 250 methods for altering your consciousness without drugs.* New York: Quadrangle Books, 1973.

Rosenthal, T. *How could I not be among you?* New York: Avon, 1975.

Roszak, B. & Roszak, T. (Eds.) *Masculine/feminine: Readings in sexual mythology and the liberation of women.* New York: Harper & Row, 1969.

Rothchild, E. Emotional aspects of sexual development. In A. M. Juhasz (Ed.), *Sexual development and behavior.* Homewood, Ill.: Dorsey Press, 1973, 5–19.

Rubin, Z. *Liking and loving: An invitation to social psychology.* New York: Holt, Rinehart and Winston, 1973.

Rush, A. K. *Getting clear: Body work for women.* New York: Random House/Berkeley: The Bookworks, 1973.

Samuels, M., & Bennett, H. *The well body book.* New York: Random House/ Berkeley: The Bookworks, 1973.

Satir, V. *Conjoint family therapy.* Palo Alto, Ca.: Science and Behavior Books, 1964.

———. *Peoplemaking.* Palo Alto, Ca.: Science and Behavior Books, 1972.

Sayers, D. *Unpopular opinions.* New York: Harcourt, 1947.

Schachtel, E. G. On memory and childhood amnesia. In P. Mullahy (Ed.), *A study of interpersonal relations.* New York: Grove, 1957, 3–49.

Schiffman, M. *Self therapy.* Menlo Park, Ca.: Self Therapy Press, 1967.

———. *Gestalt self therapy.* Menlo Park, Ca.: Self Therapy Press, 1971.

Schutz, W. C. *Joy: Expanding human awareness.* New York: Grove, 1967.

Seligman, M. E. P. Submissive death: Giving up on life. *Psychology Today,* May 1974, 80–85.

Severin, F. T. *Humanistic viewpoints in psychology.* New York: McGraw-Hill, 1965.

Sexual attitude restructuring guide. San Francisco: National Sex Forum, 1975.

Sheehy, G. *Passages: The predictable crises of adult life.* New York: Dutton, 1976.

Simon, S. B. *Meeting yourself half way: 31 values clarification strategies for daily living.* Niles, Ill.: Argus Communications, 1974.

Simon, S. B., Howe, L. W., & Kirschenbaum, H. *Values clarification.* New York: Hart, 1972.

Singer, J. L. *Daydreaming.* New York: Random House, 1966.

Skinner, B. F. *Walden Two.* New York: Macmillan, 1948.

———. *Beyond freedom and dignity.* New York: Knopf, 1971.

Slater, P. *The pursuit of loneliness: American culture at the breaking point.* Boston: Beacon Press, 1970.

Sperry, R. W. Left-brain, right-brain. *Saturday Review/World,* August 1975, 33.

Stevens, J. O. *Awareness: Exploring, experimenting, experiencing.* New York: Bantam Books, 1973.

Stoll, C. S. *Female & male: Socialization, social roles, and social structure.* Dubuque, Iowa: William C. Brown Company, 1974.

Stonecypher, D. D. *Getting older and staying young.* New York: Norton, 1974.

Sullivan, H. S. *The interpersonal theory of psychiatry.* New York: Norton, 1953.

Tart, C. T. (Ed.) *Altered states of consciousness.* Garden City, N.Y.: Doubleday, 1972.

Tiger, L. *Men in groups.* New York: Random House, 1970.

Tillich, P. *The courage to be.* New Haven: Yale University Press, 1959.

Toffler, A. *Future shock.* New York: Random House, 1970.

Toman, W. Birth order rules all. *Psychology Today,* December 1970, 45–49, 68–69.

Unbecoming men. Washington, N.J.: Times Change Press, 1971.

United States Department of Labor. *Why women work.* (Rev.) Washington, D.C.: Employment Standards Administration: Women's Bureau, May 1975a.

———. *Twenty facts of women workers.* (Rev.) Washington, D. C.: Employment Standards Administration: Women's Bureau, June 1975b.

Vavra, R. *Tiger flower.* New York: Reynal, in association with William Morrow, 1968.

VD handbook. Montreal: Montreal Health Press, 1973.

Van Dusen, R. A., & Sheldon, E. B. The changing status of American women: A life cycle perspective. *American Psychologist,* 1976, **31**, 106–116.

von Franz, M., & Hillman, J. *Lectures on Jung's typology.* Zurich: Spring Publications, 1971.

Warner, S. J. *Self-realization and self-defeat.* New York: Grove, 1966.

Watts, A. *Psychotherapy East and West.* New York: Mentor, 1961.

Weil, A. The natural mind: A new way of looking at the higher consciousness. *Psychology Today,* October 1972, 51–96.

———. Forward. In E. Rosenfeld (Ed.), *The book of highs: 250 methods for altering your consciousness without drugs.* New York: Quadrangle, 1973.

Weisman, A. Psychosocial death. *Psychology Today,* November 1972, 77–86.

Wheeler, J. All the baby did was cry—and it nearly cost her life. *Arizona Daily Star,* April 22, 1973.

Wheelis, A. *How people change.* New York: Harper & Row, 1973.

White, R. W. Competence and the psychosexual stages of development. In M. R. Jones (Ed.), *Nebraska symposium on motivation, 1960.* Lincoln, Neb.: University of Nebraska Press, 1960, 97–140.

———. *Lives in progress.* (3rd ed.) New York: Holt, Rinehart and Winston, 1975.

———. *The enterprise of living: A view of personal growth.* (2nd ed.) New York: Holt, Rinehart and Winston, 1976.

Wickes, F. G. *The inner world of childhood.* (Rev. ed.) New York: New American Library, 1968.

Williams, R. L., & Long, J. D. *Toward a self-managed life style.* Boston: Houghton Mifflin, 1975.

Wilson, S. T., Roe, R. L., & Autrey, L. E. *Readings in human sexuality.* St. Paul, Minn.: West, 1975.

Wolfe, T. *Look homeward angel.* New York: Scribner, 1929.

The world almanac and book of facts: New York: Newspaper Enterprise Association, 1975.

Wrenn, R., & Mencke, R. *Being: A psychology of self.* Chicago: Science Research Associates, 1975.

Yablonsky, L. *Tunnel back: Synanon.* New York: Macmillan, 1965.

Yee, Min S. (Ed.) *The great escape: A source book of delights & pleasures for the mind & body.* New York: Bantam, 1974.

Yevtushenko, Y. A. Zima Junction. In *Selected poems,* (Trans. by R. Milner-Gulland & P. Levi), Baltimore: Penguin, 1964, 19–51.

INDEX